Lost Worlds of 1863

Lost Worlds of 1863

Relocation and Removal of American Indians in the Central Rockies and the Greater Southwest

W. Dirk Raat
Professor Emeritus, State University of New York,
Fredonia

With a Foreword by
Navajo and Laguna Pueblo Artist Steven Jon Yazzie

This edition first published 2022
© 2022 John Wiley & Sons, Inc.

The right of W. Dirk Raat to be identified as the author of this work has been asserted in accordance with law.

Registered Office
John Wiley & Sons, Inc., 111 River Street, Hoboken, NJ 07030, USA

Editorial Office
111 River Street, Hoboken, NJ 07030, USA

For details of our global editorial offices, customer services, and more information about Wiley products visit us at www.wiley.com.

Wiley also publishes its books in a variety of electronic formats and by print-on-demand. Some content that appears in standard print versions of this book may not be available in other formats.

Library of Congress Cataloging-in-Publication Data
Names: Raat, W. Dirk (William Dirk), 1939- author.
Title: Lost worlds of 1863 : relocation and removal of American Indians in the Central Rockies and the Greater Southwest / W. Dirk Raat ; with a foreword by Navajo artist Steven Jon Yazzie.
Description: Hoboken, NJ : John Wiley & Sons, Inc., 2022. | Includes bibliographical references and index. | Contents: Prologue: Indigenous peoples in a global context : myth, struggle and survival -- Slavery and removal in California and the Far West -- Lincoln, free soil and Fremont: the Emancipation Proclamation and Indian slavery -- Commentary: Lincoln and the Pueblos -- Numu (Paiute) wanderings, trails, and tears -- Commentary: The military and the boarding school -- Great Basin tribal politics-- Western Shoshones, Southern Paiutes and Colorado Utes -- The Arizona & New Mexico-Sonoran experience -- The long walk of the Navajo -- Commentary: The Hopi-Navajo land controversy -- Death of Mangas Coloradas, Chiricahua "renegades", and Apache prisoners of war -- Treasure hunters hunting deer hunters : Yavapai and Apache gold -- With friends like these : the O'odham water controversy -- Commentary: Mormons and Lamanites -- From removal ("ethnic cleansing") to genocide -- From battle to massacre on the Bear River -- Slaying the deer slayers in Mexico : the Yaqui experience -- Epilogue: After relocation, from Geronimo to Houser.
Identifiers: LCCN 2021009928 (print) | LCCN 2021009929 (ebook) | ISBN 9781119777625 (paperback) | ISBN 9781119777649 (adobe pdf) | ISBN 9781119777632 (epub) | ISBN 9781119777656 (ebook)
Subjects: LCSH: Indian Removal, 1813-1903. | Indians of North America--West (U.S.)--Treatment of. | Indians of North America--West (U.S.)--Government relations--19th century. | Whites--Relations with Indians. | West (U.S.)--Race relations--History--19th century. | Indians of North America--West (U.S.)--Crimes against. | United States--History--Civil War, 1861-1865--Influence. | Racism--West (U.S.)--History--19th century.
Classification: LCC E98.R4 R33 2022 (print) | LCC E98.R4 (ebook) | DDC 973.04/97--dc23
LC record available at https://lccn.loc.gov/2021009928
LC ebook record available at https://lccn.loc.gov/2021009929

Cover image: "Uprooting of a Dine' Family" from Navajo and Laguna Pueblo artist Steven Jon Yazzie's mural entitled *Fear of a Red Planet: Relocation and Removal* at the Heard Museum in Phoenix, Arizona (2000). Yazzie also wrote the foreword to *Lost Worlds of 1863*. It's a personal note in which he speaks of his family's trauma and survival tactics at the Boarding School, and his grandmother's contemporary experience (1980s–1990s) of forced removal in what has been called the "Second Long Walk." Yazzie also contributed several images to the book.
Cover design by Wiley

Set in 9.5/12.5 STIX Two Text by Integra Software Services, Pvt. Ltd, Pondicherry, India
SKY10031913_121321

Genocide *(jen'ə sīd'), n. the deliberate and systematic elimination of a national or racial group. The attempt to eradicate a people or a culture from antiquity to the present. Historically, genocide has taken three forms—physical, biological, or cultural—usually, with some exceptions, functioning in conjunction with one another.*

In Memoriam

This book is dedicated to the memory of indigenous peoples who did survive, as well as those who did not, the **devastation** *and* **massacres** *of the nineteenth and early twentieth centuries.*

Contents

Illustrations

x

Maps

Foreword

Remembering Relocation, Removal and Fear: The Mural and Beyond

In 1999 I received a grant through the Mid Atlantic Arts Foundation and the National Endowment for the Arts to participate in a yearlong project with the Heard Museum in Phoenix, Arizona. The project included six months of community outreach, research, and planning, and led up to a five month period of painting a site specific mural for the Heard Museum in the artist's studio (book store.) The mural was designed in a non-traditional sense; it was to be painted on canvas and adhered to the gallery walls in the newly designed Ullman Learning Center, which would also house a new family-friendly exhibit called "We Are Arizona's First People." The main focus of the new gallery and exhibit was to celebrate the 22 federally recognized Native people of Arizona in 22 different kiosks, each arranged along a meandering path throughout the gallery, where small samples of indigenous culture could be seen, heard, and understood through hands-on activities.

The theme of the mural was initially designed to act as an extension of the gallery's thematic focus of celebration and triumph. But as the design of the gallery was still being solidified, I was struggling with the potential outcomes of my own painting plans. I wanted to tell the real story of conflict and resolution, of fear and struggle, and the issues of identity, which haunted me in my personal work. With innocuous stories incased in those kiosks, I continued my research in the early stages of the project.

A large portion of my research involved travelling to each of the 22 Native Tribes and speaking with representatives of each Nation. I was continuously inspired by the compelling and unifying stories I heard travelling to these destinations on the road with the Heard Museum staff. Ongoing discussions with the Heard's education department, primarily Joe Baker and Wendy Weston, proved essential in helping me focus on the late nineteenth century era to the present day.

Joe Baker's influence on me and the mural cannot be overstated. His knowledge, guidance, and trust in me throughout the entire project were essential to the success of the piece. He helped me navigating my new museum experience at the Heard, protecting me from the politics of the institution and encouraged me to make a statement that resonated with me. I was mostly concerned with painting a truth about a history. A truth I had heard throughout my life, bequeathed to me through elders, cousins, uncles, and aunts, through the stories of our family. At the onset of painting the mural I was fully committed to telling it like it is, and like it was.

My own family's stories of boarding school trauma and survival, and a more contemporary story of my grandmother's experience (being removed permanently from her home in Cactus Valley, an area located in the central-eastern region of the Navajo Nation, on Black Mesa, Arizona), steeled my resolve. In my lifetime, that area has been contested space, reclaimed by the Hopi or lost by the Navajo. The recent relocation is known as the "Second Long Walk."

It was stories like these and many others that inspired me to focus on what I knew and what I was culturally bound to reveal. "The Navajo Long Walk" is a primary section in the mural, exploring the uprooting of the Navajo people and the rise of Colonel Kit Carson, as a complex character in the frontier west, and the positioning of power and reservation policies in the region. He was ultimately responsible for the capturing, uprooting, and the imprisonment of many Navajos to Bosque Redondo, in New Mexico. Raat expands on this story in detail, covering the events, timelines, and tense relationships in the region that led to the aftermath in *Lost Worlds of 1863: Relocation and Removal of American Indians in the Central Rockies and the Greater Southwest.*

The question I had about telling the true stories was crystallized on an early site visit in 1999 to the Ullman Learning Center. Some of the issues I was grappling with at the time were: *What rights and responsibilities do I have to paint stories that are not my own? What images and histories could best represent a reflection of the past that also distill the contemporary experience?*

As construction began in the Ullman Learning Center, I visited with a Yaqui construction worker who was installing the giant timber beams that are now located near the center of the gallery. He was from the town of Guadalupe near Tempe, Arizona. He confirmed my own misconceptions of tribal identity having mistaken him for a Latino. He jokingly said, "Everyone thinks we are Mexican, but we are Yoemen." Our brief encounter struck a chord and I recognized this moment of cultural confusion was a starting point for the mural, and a way for me to understand the struggles and histories of the Yoemen people. The Yoemen had migrated north from their homeland in Sonora to areas near

Sells, Tucson, and Guadalupe, close to Tempe, Arizona. Their story of Diaspora is one of the longest in indigenous struggle in the West, and is well documented and discussed in Raat's chapter, "Slaying the Deer Slayers in Mexico: The Yaqui Experience."

The mural I painted was more than 160′ long and was roughly 7′ 5" in height. One section also touches on a number of important issues and regional policies the US government and Mexican regimes designed and imposed on indigenous people in the Southwest. This section also explores the ecological forms of removal and the effects damming along the Colorado River had on floodplains, creating unnatural annual flows, and the introduction of invasive plant and fish species that nearly wiped out the native fish and plants along the shoreline. I also painted forms of new economies on essential waterways, like that of the Casinos along the river from Cocopah to Laughlin. The origin of the westernization of the Colorado River area and its people is discussed in depth in Chapter 6 of Professor Raat's work entitled "Treasure Hunters Hunting Deer Hunters: Yavapai and Apache Gold."

The boarding school section of the mural was informed by my elder relatives' horror stories of being forced to conform to Western Culture in Boarding Schools. Schools, where the goal was, as Captain Richard Henry Pratt is quoted in the commentary following Chapter 2 ("The Military and the Boarding School"), "Kill the Indian ... and save the man."

In the late spring of 2000, I completed the mural, "Fear of a Red Planet: Forced Removal and Relocation." "Fear of a Red Planet" was added into the title after overhearing Craig Smith, the Museum photographer, comment about how potentially challenging some of the imagery I created could be for some Heard members. I added "Fear of a Red Planet" to the title as I realized so much colonization and conflict are rooted in the fear of the unknown and the inability for dominant cultures to acknowledge its own amnesia of progress.

"Amnesia of progress" is a phrase that is stenciled in the mural. It was coined by the writer Jonathan Bond, a close friend and frequent collaborator. The phrase is well suited to the subject matter of "Fear of a Red Planet: Forced Removal and Relocation;" that of forced migration and extinction of a people for the benefit of a dominant culture, with no credence for the human cost.

"Fear of a Red Planet" is also an indirect reference to a mockumentary called "Fear of a Black Hat," a comedy about the rise and fall of the controversial musical group N.W.A. (Niggaz Wit Attitudes). "Fear of a Black Planet" is the title of N.W.A.'s most famous album; the reference in the Mural title to both "Black Hat" and "Black Planet" is about the co-mingling of parody and fear, which is how the dominant culture relates to groups in the minority.

The story of forced relocation and removal is a major theme in Raat's *Lost Worlds of 1863*. Raat has expanded on the relational aspects of numerous activities and atrocities that coincided around the 1860s, a pivotal and momentous time in our collective histories. While the mural I painted "Fear of a Red Planet: Forced Removal and Relocation" looks into this time period a great deal, it is only a piece of the greater story.

Colonization and imperialism remain a painful memory, but an essential one for us to learn from if we can. Raat's *Lost Worlds of 1863* draws us closer to what is at stake between all cultures and people on this planet. By focusing on this period his work sheds new light on the complexities at play at a pivotal time in our not too-distant past.

Steven Jon Yazzie
Phoenix, Arizona

Preface

As enemies, the Mexicans were nothing in comparison with the White Eyes who came in from the east. White Eyes is not the exact meaning of our word for them; a more exact meaning would be Pale Eyes.

Ace Dalugie, patriarch of the Mescalero Reservation,
Son of Juh, Leader of the Nednhi Apache

This is a history about the relationship between what Apache patriarch Ace Dalugie called the Pale Eyes and their opposite numbers, the "redskins" as the Pale Eyes derisively called them. Whites or Pale Eyes usually had a skin color that was not white but flesh colored or a light brownish pink color. As for the "redskins," they were seldom only red but ranged in skin color from a dull yellowish brown (khaki) or a light grayish brown (beige) to bronze and reddish-brown.

Only the caste system the whites brought with them dictated a false dichotomy between being "white" and "red," with the "redskins" being assigned the external and subordinate role that racism and casteism required. The history of the Greater Southwest is one in which "whites" maintained the illusion of their superiority by dehumanizing indigenous peoples. As social and cultural historian Gary Michael Tartakov noted, "It [they] dehumanized others to build its [their] own civilization."[1]

The relationship between "whites" and "redskins" involved a more diverse group than even Dalugie noted. Prior to and after the Civil War many blacks and ex-slaves came west as cowboys, miners, and soldiers, as did Chinese workers, as well as Mexicans, mulattos and *indios* from the southern and eastern states (including those individuals who were African-Native Americans). The diversity involved members of both sexes, including females as mothers (including single, divorced, and widowed), pioneers, farmers, cowgirls and ranchers, prostitutes, housekeepers, property owners, entrepreneurs, headwomen, scouts, homesteaders, educators, and warriors. In any case, these were the antagonists that were involved in a major drama of the nineteenth century, the relocation and removal of indigenous societies in the Greater American Southwest. The book is entitled *Lost Worlds of 1863* and the drama of relocation centers around that pivotal date in western history.

The inspiration for this work comes both from my activity as a docent at the Heard Museum in downtown Phoenix, Arizona, as well as a vacation trip I took in the summer of 2012. That summer, my wife and I, accompanied by our dog Nacho, drove through Owens Valley on our way to Lake Tahoe to visit our children and grandchild. On the way I noticed a historical marker commemorating the removal of several hundred Owens Valley Paiutes to Fort Tejon. This military reservation was located across the Sierra Nevada between the Los Angeles Basin and the Central Valley. I noted to my wife that this was the same year Kit Carson and his military allies forcibly began to remove several thousand Navajos from northeastern Arizona to central New Mexico. This coincidence led me to investigate further the significance of "1863" and this book is the result of that inquiry.

The primary theme of this work has been derived from a mural painted by the Navajo artist Steven Jon Yazzie that is in the collection of the Heard Museum in downtown Phoenix, Arizona. In the year 2000, Yazzie spent more than six months creating a mural that illustrated the diaspora experience of tribal peoples in the Greater American Southwest. These tales speak of the removal and assimilation policies of the United States government (or in the case of the Yaqui, the Mexican regime of Porfirio Díaz) vis-à-vis the southwestern indigenous populations, and the resulting uprooting of indigenous peoples from land and family. The Yazzie mural covered three walls in the Ullman gallery and focused on the nineteenth century stories of the Navajo, Yaqui, and Colorado River people, as well as the boarding school period that began in 1878. Yazzie's mural is entitled "Fear of a Red Planet: Relocation and Removal," and was the motivating force behind the current work.

There are many ways to parcel up the past. Some historians talk about historical periods, such as the Age of Reason or the Cold War era. Others speak of centuries, generations, or decades—all terms of convenience. The most daring and enjoyable histories are those that proclaim that the course of human events centered on a particular year, with 1492 an especially appealing year. According to Louis Menand, writing in *The New Yorker*, these are known as one-dot histories.[2] Those books with one-year titles are melodramatic and somewhat ahistorical. So let me assure the reader that the one-dot theory of history does not apply in the present case.

This study concentrates on the nineteenth century history of the Indians of the Greater American Southwest. The year "1863" receives special note, but only as a "hook" or focal point that allows the reader and scholar to experience and interpret the events that took place before and after that date. The events of that year are not necessarily a precursor to those that follow, or the consequence of what went before. The year "1863" is simply one window into the past where one can see several locales and tribal groups and events associated with those locales. As for the geographical area, it is called the Greater Southwest, a region that extends beyond the current boundaries of Arizona and New Mexico to include the Mexican states of Sonora and Chihuahua, and reaches as far as the northern boundaries of California, Nevada, and Utah (as well as the Great Basin area of southern Idaho). These two ideas will be further developed in the introduction.

A Brief Word about Organization and Usage

With the exception of the Prologue, the subject matter is organized around several case studies in which the narrative is developed from early historical times through the late nineteenth and early twentieth centuries. Following the Prologue, the first chapter focuses on the topic of Indian slavery and Lincoln's Emancipation Proclamation of 1863. The subject of Indian slavery is not simply a digression, but part of the argument that the so-called "Great Emancipator" paid no heed to the problem of "de facto" Indian slavery and as such one more reminder of his lack of empathy for the Indian people. This chapter introduces the reader to the general environment of the Civil War era in which Lincoln's lack of an Indian policy led to the precedents of relocating Indian people from Minnesota to the Missouri country, and depended upon the military to enforce the removal plans. Preoccupied with restoring the Union, Lincoln did little to control the western volunteers' anti-Indian zeal. His main concern was to create treaties so that land could be acquired by and for the advancing white frontier. After the Minnesota relocation the Numa or Paiutes were removed from the Owens Valley, the Navajo from Arizona, and the Mescalero relocated to Bosque Redondo. The massacres at Bear River and Sand Creek were the unintended results of a policy designed to wrestle land and resources from the Indian people.

After the Lincoln introduction, the following chapters treat of the Owens and Northern Paiute, the Great Basin Shoshones, Southern Paiutes, and Colorado Utes, the Navajo, Apache, Yavapai, and O'odham, and finally the Northwestern Shoshone and Yaqui experiences. I have included four shorter sub-chapters or mini-chapters after some of the chapters. These were originally to be called cross-bars but they went too long. Called "commentaries," all treat of a theme presented in the previous chapter, while the commentary on "Mormons and Lamanites" reflects themes found in several chapters.

These case studies and "commentaries" are not all-inclusive, and do not detail the numerous examples of indigenous groups in the Greater Southwest, such as the Cheyenne and Arapaho of Colorado, various Pueblo groups in New Mexico, the western Comanche, or a variety of California Indians, and others.

The chapter on the Bear River Massacre could easily been included in Part One since Cache Valley, Utah and Preston, Idaho would fit the geographical description of "the Far West." So too could the chapter on the Yaqui deportation be included in Part Two under "The Arizona and New Mexico–Sonoran Experience." They were placed in a separate section under Part Three because of the extent of the violence that was associated with each event. And because the Sand Creek Massacre of 1864 is generally well known to most readers, it does not receive special attention here. It was, in fact, partly the result of a precursor event less well known as the Bear River Massacre of 1863.

In the Prologue I develop an overview, including a global dimension, on the phenomenon of relocation and removal. The Epilogue not only summarizes the content, explaining the major examples of relocation and removal, but also several sub-themes as well. It also has something to say about current and future happenings, especially on the topic of survival. Since, apart from the introductory material, the subject matter is organized spatially around individual case studies, the reader is cautioned about seeking a chronological narrative. Instead, the reader is encouraged to seek out those case studies of interest and read them as separate episodes. The Prologue and Epilogue attempt to develop the interrelationships and similarities between the various chapters and provide some unity.

Another forewarning, each case study has an extensive history of the pre-contact, Spanish, and Mexican worlds that created the context for the events of 1863. My focus on ceremonial rites and Indian belief systems was developed so as to illustrate the relationship between sacred landscapes and personal identity. Relocation not only removed the people from the land, but the land from the people and by so doing robbed these people of their identity.

As for usage, the common misunderstanding of today's non-Indian community is that these indigenous peoples prefer to be called Native American rather than American Indian. In an informal 2005 survey conducted by Wendy Weston, Navajo, Director of American Indian Relations at the Heard Museum, of several indigenous peoples, when asked: "As a Native person, what term do you prefer to be identified by?," most respondents preferred to be identified as American Indian and/or their specific tribal affiliation. As the respondents said, "Native" or "Native American" is a term "which anyone born in the US has the right to be called."[3] Although, as cultural theorist Gerald Vizenor reminds us, while "Indian" is an invented name that does not come from any native language, "Native American" at least distinguishes native inhabitants in the Americas from the people of India.[4]

As for other options, "indigenous" might be confused with an indigent state of poverty. Referring to Hopi and Zuni ancestors, this writer has trouble saying "Ancient Pueblo" in lieu of Anasazi, since the word "Pueblo" is Spanish and not Indian, and it substitutes a perfectly good Navajo word for "old enemy" and replaces it with an idea of questionable ancestry. Some words, like "Tarahumara" and "Rarámuri" are derived from the same word "Talahumali," and are used interchangeably.

Because of these problems I have contented myself by using most words in place of each other. All of the words require qualifications, and no one term can be used in any and all occasions. Be prepared to read about indigenous peoples, Spanish terms like Navajo, or Navajo tribal terms like Diné, translations of terminology like "The People" or "Two Village People," Natives, North American Indians, Amerinds, First Nations, Native Americans, *indios,* and just simply Indians. No one said it was going to be easy.

As for spelling, I have preferred to spell "Shoshone" with an "e," not an "i" (Shoshoni), although several sources spell it "Shoshoni." Again, I spell "Paiute" with an "a," although some writers prefer "Piute."

The word "settler" usually refers to whites. However, it should be remembered that often times the Indian was the settler who was confronted by unsettled invaders. This was true in the early times when Hernando Cortés and his Indian allies conquered Tenochtitlán, an Aztec city of 250,000 to 300,000 urbanites, as well as in the nineteenth century when Mormons encroached upon the Northwestern Shoshone settlers of the Cache Valley of Northern Utah.

The word "slavery" can cause consternation in some quarters. Although I use the term throughout the book, it might be more accurate to speak of "de facto slavery," a form of bondage that whatever it is called is in fact "slavery." The word implies the ownership of a person or persons by another or others. That ownership comes from outright purchase or exchange of goods for a person, or acquisition of another through kidnapping or violence. Synonyms include "servitude," "bondage," and "indenture," while slaves were often called "servants" or "peons." Historian Andrés Reséndez, in his book on Indian enslavement in the Americas calls this type of "de facto slavery," which is a form of bondage and involuntary servitude, *The Other Slavery.*

Whatever the arrangement is called, "de facto slavery" was a form of coercion that was often accompanied by sexual and economic exploitation of the enslaved person. The brutal actions of enslaving were often an adjunct to violence in the form of warfare, rape, homicide, massacre, mutilation and removal or deportation.

In early colonial days Englishmen made war captives out of the Indians of the southeastern parts of the United States and forcibly sent them through the port of Charleston to slavery in the plantations of the West Indies. Between 1770 and 1810, Spanish soldiers escorted three thousand Apache "prisoners-of-war" to Mexico City. Women and children became domestics in central Mexico, while the Apache men were sent to work the fields and ports of Cuba. By the nineteenth century Mexican slave traders were busy kidnapping Navajo women and children to serve as domestics and laborers in the fields and homes of New Mexico. A similar situation occurred in California. Slavery or "servitude" was justified on the grounds that the uncivilized savages were having their souls saved by the actions of Christian overseers.

As for the use of the words "genocide" and "holocaust," because of the volatility of these words I have use them sparingly. In some instances, where extermination was not the object but land acquisition was, "ethnic cleansing" may be the preferred phrase. This study follows the definitions of genocide of the Proposed Convention on Prevention and Punishment of the Crime of Genocide (1997) intended to supersede the United Nations Convention of 1948. Genocide, by these definitions, may be threefold: Physical (deliberate and direct or indirect killing of a specific ethnic or racial group); Biological (including sterilization and psychological conditions leading to birthrate declines and increased rates of infant mortality); and Cultural (eradication of the mores, habits, traditions, and languages of a specific group).

Obviously, under these definitions genocide has a long history in Asia and America in addition to and outside of Europe and Nazi Germany. According to James W. Loewen, author of *Lies My Teacher Told Me*, "Hitler admired our concentration camps for American Indians in the west and according to John Toland, his [Hitler's] biographer, [Hitler] 'often praised to his inner circle the efficiency of American extermination—by starvation and uneven combat as the model for his extermination of Jews and Gypsies'."[5] In 1928 Hitler approvingly noted that white settlers in America had "gunned down millions of redskins" and had America in mind when he spoke of "living space" or *Lebensraum* in Eastern Europe.[6]

Genocide is a form of violence that involves killing. Battles and massacres are not necessarily genocidal events unless the battle is transformed into a massacre and the intentional killing evolves into a pattern targeting a particular ethnic, racial, or religious group. But genocide of the American Indian is part of the historical record, and as my dear friend and colleague from Fredonia State University, the late historian William T. Hagan, asserted, "*Genocide* is a term of awful significance, but one which has application to the story of California's Native Americans" (and, I may add, the indigenous population of parts of the Greater Southwest in general).[7]

In June of 2020 the "Black Lives Matter" movement included a few marchers holding "Indigenous Lives Matter" signs. The demonstrators, in support of the Black Lives protestors, reminded the nation that while Native Americans consist of only 0.8% of the population, they experience 1.9% of police killings (data from the Centers for Disease Control and Prevention between 1999 and 2011).

At the same time in St. Paul, Minnesota a statute of Christopher Columbus was brought down by protestors. Columbus, whose legacy for indigenous America was one of slavery and genocide, was removed from the public sphere. As cultural theorist Gerald Vizenor states, "Columbus and his civilization would discover no salvation in the New World. The missions, exploitations, racial vengeance, and colonization ended the praise of deliverance; the conquistadors buried the tribal healers and their stories in their blood."[8]

Brendan Lindsay has noted in his book *Murder State* that "When one considers the actions of the press, state and federal governments, and the citizenry as a whole, the result was the creation of an inescapable system of democratically imposed genocide ... devised to fulfill the demands of the newly minted citizenry of California."[9] Larissa Behrendt continued this theme by arguing that indigenous people's claims of state-sanctioned genocide are still being defeated by legal traditions that reflect a legacy of colonialism and violence.[10]

Under these definitions and usages the California massacres, the Bear River Massacre, the Sand Creek Massacre, the Yaqui deportations, and the events at Wounded Knee would be described as "genocidal," while the removal of Paiutes, Navajos, Mescaleros, Chiricahua Apaches, and Yavapai would be "ethnic cleansing." Certain writers, like David E. Stannard (see below), or some of those cited above, may not agree with this distinction. As Stannard and others have noted, most white Americans thought in terms of expulsion or extermination, and they were not necessarily mutually exclusive options. Some forced marches were literally "death marches." The early years of the Indian Boarding School experiment might be called an attempt at "cultural genocide."

As for "holocaust," the word was used generally in English to denote devastation and massacres. Since 1945 most scholars, with the exception of David E. Stannard, use it to refer specifically to the Nazi genocide of Jews and others. Stannard, in his excellent and comprehensive study of the extermination of American Indians, speaks freely of an *American Holocaust*. Stannard's holocaust included the interdependent forces of disease and genocide (including slavery and racism) that brought a deadly end to the lives of nineteen out of twenty Indians between 1492 and the end of the nineteenth century.[11]

"Holocaust" is used in "Lost Worlds" in the generic sense to refer to the massacre and devastation of American Indians by non-Indians. Whether the word(s) or phrase is "holocaust," "genocide," "war crimes," or "ethnic cleansing," all would be considered criminal actions today. These and related matters will be discussed further in the Epilogue.

As dark as these themes are, it should be remembered that the indigenous peoples survived these episodes and are active today. One aspect of that survival is the current state of Indian "fine arts," and artist Alan Houser, among others, represents that survival instinct of the Native American. The holdings of the Heard Museum in downtown Phoenix, Arizona, reflect that side of the story.

Another recent change is the confirmation of Rep. Deb Haaland (Democrat/N.M.) to become secretary of the Department of Interior by President Joe Biden on March 15, 2021. The Department of Interior includes the Bureau of Indian Affairs. Haaland is a member of the Laguna Pueblo, one of the nineteen Pueblo communities in New Mexico. She is the first Native American to hold such a position. In a country in which the median income of on- and off-reservation Indians is $40,315 (between 2013–2017), compared to $66,943 for all Americans, Haaland is in a position to restore tribal sovereignty, renew reservation economies, improve conservation, and move the country's Native Americans away from dependency to independence.[12]

This work, therefore, is a tribute to those few tribes that inhabit the Greater Southwest. In 2016 there were 566 federally recognized tribes in the United States. State recognized tribes amount to 130. California tribes or *rancherías* number 108. Arizona has 22 federally recognized Indian communities. While the total indigenous population residing on the reservations may be close to 2.9 million (with another 3 plus million off the reservation), and even though part of their land and identities has been restored, only 2% of the topography of the United States is Indian Country today. The narrative of this work is primarily focused on that time when close to 100% of the terrain of the Southwest was Indian Country (see map, Figure 0-1). The colonizer's "holocaust" changed all of this by creating the "Lost Worlds of 1863."

Surprise, Arizona

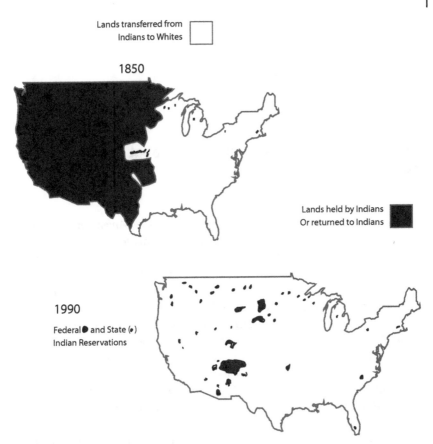

Figure 0-1 *The Progression of Land Loss.* Reconfiguration by Geraldine Raat of information found in Peter Nabokov's "The Closing In" in Part Four of *Native Americans: An Illustrated History* (Atlanta: Turner Publishing Inc., 1993), p. 369. (Central Rockies and Great Basin).

Prologue: Indigenous People in a Global Context
Myth, Struggle and Survival

Every human group has a creation myth. White Americans are no exception. Their most popular origin myth concerns the frontier: Europe was crowded; North America was not. Land in Europe was claimed, owned and utilized; land in North America was available for the taking. In a migration as elemental as a law of physics, Europeans moved from crowded space to open space, where free land restored opportunity and offered a route to independence... . Thrown on their own resources, pioneers recreated the social contract from scratch, forming simple democratic communities whose political health vitalized all of America. Indians, symbolic residents of the wilderness, resisted— in a struggle sometimes noble, but always futile. At the completion of the conquest, that chapter of history was closed. The frontier ended, but the hardiness and independence of the pioneer survived in American character.

Patricia Nelson Limerick, *The Legacy of Conquest*[1]

At first there were few white people, and they were all going west; then, as wise old Nana knew, the lure of gold, discovered far to our west, brought them in hordes. Though most of them went on, some stayed to burrow into Mother Earth for the ore sacred to Ussen. Nana was right in thinking that gold was to bring about our extermination.

Ace Dalugie, patriarch of the Mescalero Reservation
Son of Juh, Leader of the Nednhi Apache[2]

This is a study of relocation and removal of Indian groups in the Greater American Southwest centering on the events of the nineteenth century. Relocation, of course, is not only a nineteenth century phenomenon in American history. During World War II there were ten concentration camps operated by the War Relocation Authority, of which the largest was the Poston War Relocation Center in Yuma County (now La Paz County) in southwestern

Arizona. Most of the Japanese Americans living in California, 110,000 of them, were moved to Poston and other centers, including the Gila River War Relocation Center 30 miles southeast of Phoenix. Del Webb built Poston on the Colorado River Indian Reservation over the objections of the tribal council (just as the Gila River Center, located on the Gila River Indian Reservation near Sacaton, Arizona, was built over the strong objections of that reservation's American Indian government). It is a sad irony of western history that Indians, who themselves had been rounded up 80 or so years ago to be relocated and imprisoned on unfamiliar and hostile terrain, would now be forcibly hosting a new generation of Japanese American prisoners.[3]

Relocation policy was not only targeted at Japanese Americans and Indian communities, tribes, and bands, but at nuclear families and individual family heads. The Indian Relocation Act of 1956 encouraged Native Americans as individuals to leave the reservation and assimilate into the general population, i.e., urbanization of the indigenous person. The law provided for moving expenses, vocational training, four weeks of subsistence per diem, and other grants as long as the recipient went to a government designated city. By 1960 over 31,000 indigenous individuals had moved to cities. Alas, the long term effects were devastating with individuals and their families suffering from isolation, racial discrimination, and segregation. However, an unintended result was the formation of the American Indian Movement in 1968, a group that was directed by "urbanized" Indians.[4] But, of course, the removal and relocation of 1863 is the concern of this work.

Obviously, to understand that year the reader should study events that occurred both before and after 1863, and that is what this study does. But there can be no denying the importance of that year. For example, 1863 was the date of the Emancipation Proclamation; when Lincoln, attempting to foster patriotism during the Civil War, declared Thanksgiving a national holiday; the beginning of the Long Walk of the Navajo; the year of the Numa (Paiute) Path of Tears; the death of Mangas Coloradas and an acceleration of the Apache wars; the Bear River Massacre of Shoshone men, women, and children; when the Comanche leader Quanah Parker became a warrior; and when precious mineral seekers encroached upon Yavapai, Mojave, Apache, and Yaqui lands. It was also when Anglo farmers near the Gila first began to appropriate water from the O'odham communities.

That year also saw the Territory of Arizona established (divided from New Mexico Territory), and the founding of the city of Prescott (gold had been discovered at Lynx Creek outside of Prescott), and the building of Fort Whipple, near Prescott. Even before the arrival of federal officials in Arizona 20 Indians had been killed outside of Fort Whipple in spite of the peace treaty that had been signed by the federal government and the Yavapai. After 1863 Arizona's

Yavapai would lose their lives, their freedom, and their land. As an aside, I should mention that Mormon settlers and authorities were in the center of many of these events that took place in Utah, southern Idaho, Arizona, southern California, western Nevada, Sonora, and Chihuahua.

The year 1863 is a mid-century marker between the Indian Removal Act of 1830, the enforcement of which led to the removal of several Cherokee, Creek, Seminole, Chickasaw, and Choctaw from their eastern homelands to Indian Territory in eastern Oklahoma, and the Wounded Knee Massacre of December 29, 1890. The latter symbolizes the end of the Indian wars when the US Army killed as many as 150 men, women, and children at the Lakota Pine Ridge Indian Reservation in South Dakota.[5]

Finally 1863 is a time of civil war in the United States when northern Union soldiers fought their southern Confederate brothers in the bloodiest of conflicts. The inhabitants of the Southwest were not unaffected by events in the East. Many troops were reassigned to either northern or southern armies, and fighting between non-Indians and Native Americans stopped in some places, while elsewhere inter-tribal warfare ensued[6] and volunteer forces initiated the massacre of many indigenous groups.

The Civil War marked the end of that phase of Indian removal between 1830 and 1860 when land was expropriated from the native inhabitants of the lower South, stretching from South Carolina to east Texas (the "Cotton Kingdom") and the original proprietors were sent west of the Mississippi. Millions of acres of conquered land were surveyed and put up for sale by the United States, a privatization of the public domain that created one of the greatest economic booms up to that time. The expansion of cotton and the movement of slaves and slavery south and west continued the general trend of western expansion (and westernization) in general.[7] Surprisingly, the year 1834 also saw the passage by the US Congress of the Intercourse Act in which most of the land west of the Mississippi, excluding Missouri, Arkansas, and Louisiana, was declared to be Indian country.[8] The Civil War years would witness a diminishment of that promise.

With the discovery of gold in California in 1848, "argonauts" travelled across southern Arizona through the Yuma crossing at the Colorado River headed for the gold fields of California. They soon backtracked through Nevada and Arizona, and by 1863 were encroaching on the lands of the Paiute, Mojave, Yavapai, Apache, and O'odham nations. Lust for precious minerals, arable lands, and water would soon lead to the almost inevitable confrontations between industrialized and non-industrialized peoples.

Until the nineteenth century most of the world boundaries between states were not fixed. Most treaties were accords designed to prevent conflict or solidify alliances. Until the Treaty of Greenville (1795) in which annuities were institutionalized, treaties with the Indians of North America were primarily used to maintain a balance of power between France and England. After Greenville, the Louisiana Purchase (1803), the discovery of gold in Georgia (1828), and the initiation of Andrew Jackson's policy of forced ethnic cleansing (1829), treaties were negotiated between the US and the indigenous population in order to acquire the land of the latter. In 1871 Congress stopped negotiating treaties, and by 1924 extended citizenship to American Indians.

Throughout all of this, because the Commerce Clause (Section 8) of the US Constitution reserved to the federal government the right to regulate commercial relationships and land ownership "... with the Indian Tribes," questions and issues concerning the use and ownership of the lands of the native peoples was left up to the bureaucrats and politicians in Washington, D.C. to decide. This has been the situation from 1790 onward to today.[1]

By the nineteenth century Europeans and Americans began to arrange treaties between themselves or with local rulers, and from the early to mid-nineteenth century mapmaking and the map were essential to this process. The survey maps of the General Land Office made relevant the shape of the territory, and that shape would eventually gain tremendous political importance.

Akin to the Cotton Kingdom, the Greater Southwest was surveyed and mapped before the conquering troops arrived, only to be followed by gold seekers, farmers, entrepreneurs, Protestant missionaries, and Mormon settlers. And the US government was very busy negotiating treaties with Mexicans, Navajos, Shoshones and others. Treaty-making had taken on a new role, that of paving the way for settlement and development of indigenous lands, and the formalization of the subordination of tribal peoples. While the treaties may have failed from the indigenous perspective, these accords did meet the needs of the newcomers.[9]

The Indians, as obstacles to development, had to be removed. By mid-century the US government had already developed the concept of the reservation. Derived from English Indian policies, this treatment of segregating tribes in separate communities differed sharply from the Spanish and Mexican ideas of assimilation and incorporation of the Indian as a national citizen. In 1858, the commissioner of Indian Affairs described the reservation system this way: "concentrating the Indians on small reservations of land, and ... sustaining them there for a limited period of time, until they can be induced to make the necessary exertions to support themselves."[10]

As noted earlier, the geographical area under study is called the Greater Southwest, territory that is often referred to by geographers and ethnohistorians as the *Gran Chichimeca*. Anthropologist Charles Di Peso defined the Gran Chichimeca as comprehending all of that part of Mexico that is situated north of the Tropic of Cancer to 38 degrees north latitude, including Baja and Alta California, New Mexico, southern Utah, southern Colorado, and western Texas (see map, Figure 0.2). This writer would extend the line north to 42 degrees north latitude or the northern boundaries of California, Nevada, and Utah (including the Great Basin area) with the northern boundary extending from California to 97 degrees west longitude near Wichita, Kansas (see maps, Figures 0.3, 0.4 and 0.5).

More importantly, this is an ecological and historical zone of cultural interaction. It was here that Mesoamerican societies made commercial contact with the Indian cultures of the US Southwest. For example, in pre-contact time turquoise and buffalo hides came from Chaco Canyon to be exchanged for Macaw feathers and chocolate from Guatemala and Mesoamerica. This was where Anglos first confronted Spaniards in North America. This was the homeland of the Tejano–Mexicano conflict prior to 1845, or the area where Geronimo roamed freely between two nation states after 1850.

For the purposes of this study history does not stop at the border, even though there has been an international boundary since 1848. Not only did Geronimo and the Chiricahua Apaches fight, hunt, and raid in this region (paying no heed to the boundary), but treasure seekers, settlers, surveyors, munitions dealers, US Army Indian scouts, and others constantly travelled back and forth. O'odham traders exchanged goods and slaves between Mexico and the Gila Indians in the north. The Yaqui Indians of Sonora sought refuge in southern Arizona. Mormon pioneers and colonists went out from Zion in

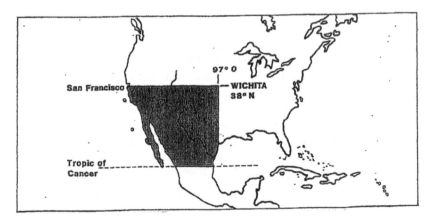

Figure 0.2 Charles Di Peso's *La Gran Chichimeca*: The Greater Southwest (including Central Rockies and Great Basin).

Figure 0.3 *Indigenous Communities of the Greater Southwest.* Abridged from Map 1-a, *Native Tribes of North America*, Map Series No. 13 (University of California Press).

the Salt Lake Valley northward to southern Idaho and southward and westward to southern Utah, Nevada, southern California, Arizona, and Chihuahua, Mexico. The history of Gran Chichimeca, named by the Aztecs for their "barbarian" neighbors who lived a nomadic life in the region, is the story of cultural, economic, and social interaction from Mesoamerican times to MexAmerica today.

Finally, it should be noted that the theme of "relocation and removal" must be expanded to include its global and contemporary dimensions. The cultural struggle between westernized and non-westernized people or between colonial and indigenous peoples is both world-wide and on-going. The ideological, spiritual, and economic imperatives of colonial expansion were not exclusively European, and the occupation of indigenous lands took place throughout India, Asia, Africa, and Latin America.

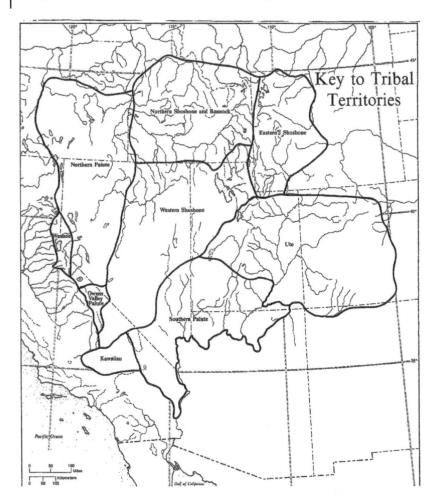

Figure 0.4 *Tribal Communities of the Northwestern and Central Parts of the Greater Southwest.* Reproduced from "Key to Tribal Territories" in *Handbook of North American Indians*, vol. 11, *Great Basin*, ed. by Warren L. D. Azevedo (Washington, D.C.: Smithsonian, 1986), p. ix.

Thus it is that immigrants from North India confronted the Veda (forest dwellers) of Sri Lanka; the Japanese government refused to recognize the Ainu who inhabited Hokkaido in the northern archipelago until the 1990s; the Bushmen or desert-based hunter-gatherers of southern Africa face extinction today because of limited resources and outsider populations; and the Yanomami and Uru Eu Wau Wau of the Amazon Basin are confronted with challenges to

Figure 0.5 *Tribal Communities of the Southern Part of the Greater Southwest (Arizona, New Mexico, and Northern Mexico).* Reproduced from "Key to Tribal Territories" in *Handbook of North American Indians*, vol. 9, *Southwest.* ed. by Alfonso Ortiz (Washington, D.C.: Smithsonian Institution, 1979).

their traditional way of life from scholars, tourists, loggers, miners and other developers.[11]

In the annals of Indian–white relations in southern South America, the Selk'nam Genocide is often recalled. When the Selk'nam was first encountered by Europeans in their homeland of Tierra del Fuego they were a hardy and vigorous people. They lived mostly undisturbed until the late 1800s, when an influx of gold prospectors and sheep ranchers who desired their land started to make intrusions. Bounties were placed on their heads. One hunter boasted that he had received a pound sterling per corpse, redeemable with a pair or two of ears. In a brief time the Selk'nam were reduced from four thousand to around three hundred, and resettled on reservations administered by missionaries. The last speaker of the Selk'nam language died 40 years ago.[12]

In North America confrontations with indigenous groups include Canadian authorities and the Inuit in the Arctic as well as the Blackfoot on the Canadian plains and the Innu of Labrador. And, of course, most individuals are familiar with the struggles between Europeans and the Maori of New Zealand, the aboriginal Tasmanians, and the Aborigines of Australia.[13]

But if the nineteenth century history of indigenous peoples was one of "struggle," the twentieth century story bears witness to the idea of "survival." Even this dichotomy is too simplistic. Not all nineteenth century Indians of the Southwest were victims of the colonizers. Human relationships are complex and some disruptions in native life were due to indigenous factors and pressures from other tribal groups. For example, several White Mountain Apaches and Chiricahuas chose to live on the reservation and adopt the white man's way of life, and held no brief for Geronimo and the other rebels. Chief Chatto, an accomplished Chiricahua raider, served as first sergeant of Apache scouts during the final campaign against Geronimo. As for the colonizers, the voices of the past are many and many soldiers, like Brigadier General George Crook, held a grudging admiration for Geronimo and his Apache followers. To only consider the indigenous peoples as victims and the colonizers as victimizers is to strip native societies of agency.

If anything, Indian people have found new ways to remain distinctive despite the power of global economies, colonial militaries, and national governments. The "vanishing American" of the late nineteenth century refused to be vanished! Reports by non-indigenous observers of cultural demise and death were wrong in the 1870s, misguided in the 1920s, and overly pessimistic today.

While many groups are losing their languages, many societies have continued to survive even stripped of their language.[14] While the boarding school experience from 1878 to 1930 discouraged the use of Indian languages by their pupils, the Navajo, Hopi, Comanche, Sac and Fox code-talkers of World War II revived their tribal tongues. Contemporary technology is being used to initiate language comeback programs, ranging from apprenticeship programs pairing fluent elders with young students to YouTube videos, or native speaker's language-learning apps for Indian students with iPads.[15] For example, the summer of 2013 saw the release of the classic George Lucas "Star Wars" movie that was dubbed by Navajo voice actors, a use of native language designed to appeal to a younger generation.[16] Evidently, while the colonial empires that first colonized indigenous societies no longer exist, the native groups have persisted.

No better example of that persistence can be found than that of the Apache painter, muralist, and sculptor Allan Houser. Born in 1914 near Fort Sill,

Oklahoma, he was the first of his Chiricahua community to be born outside of captivity. He lived 80 years dying in 1994. He is a likely candidate for the title of "best Southwestern Indian artist of the 20th century." His materials are varied and diverse—sculpting with marble, bronze, alabaster, steatite, limestone, painted steel, wire, wood; painting in oils, tempera, acrylic, casein, pastels, and watercolors—and his themes are equally varied. His six to nine foot Ga'an statutes reflect the confidence of Apache spiritualism, and his smaller works depict family and everyday life. This is the optimism of the survivalist, not the pessimism of the defeated.[17]

This then is a two-part story, of a difficult and often unsuccessful struggle to overcome powerful, outside forces, and the contemporary one of an internal and cultural determination to survive in the face of forces seeking their destruction. From the struggle with surviving have come renewal and regeneration, and this new person called the American Indian.

Part I

Slavery and Removal in California and the Far West

1

Lincoln, Free Soil and Frémont

The Emancipation Proclamation and Indian Slavery

That on the first day of January, in the year of our Lord one thousand eight hundred and sixty-three, all persons held as slaves within any State or designated part of a State, the people whereof shall then be in rebellion against the United States, shall be then, thenceforward, and forever free.
From Lincoln's Emancipation Proclamation, January 1, 1863

Free at last, Free at last, Thank God Almighty, Free at Last!
Old Negro Spiritual cited by Martin Luther King in His
"I've Got a Dream" Speech, Lincoln Square, Washington, on the
Centennial of the Emancipation Proclamation, August 28, 1963

We realize that whoever sees us, and no matter what we say to defend ourselves, the white people will think of us as dogs. We want our relatives now imprisoned at the Missouri River [Crow Creek] to remain alive. Last summer we left death behind and with no freedom to do what we wanted, we were like dead men.
Wakandhi Topa [Four Lightning] to Gen. H. H. Sibley,
Camp McClellan [Davenport, Iowa], May 18, 1863[1]

The pale-faced people [as opposed to their red brethren] are numerous and prosperous because they ... depend upon the products of the earth rather than wild game for a subsistence. This is the chief reason of the difference; but there is another. Although we are now engaged in a great war between one another, we are not, as a race, so much disposed to fight and kill one another as our red brethren.
Abraham Lincoln, Meeting with Indian Leaders, March 27, 1863[2]

Lost Worlds of 1863: Relocation and Removal of American Indians in the Central Rockies and the Greater Southwest, First Edition. W. Dirk Raat.
© 2022 John Wiley & Sons, Inc. Published 2022 by John Wiley & Sons, Inc.

On January 1, 1863, President Abraham Lincoln issued the Emancipation Proclamation. Although popular in parts of the Republican Party and in northern sections of the country where abolitionist sentiment was strong, the Proclamation was limited in scope and only one event in the long history of emancipation in the United States. For example, it did not apply to those slave states in the border area that were loyal to the Union, and did not affect those parts of the Confederacy under Union control. It did, however, transform the character of the war. One section of the Proclamation read that "I further declare ... that such persons [freed slaves] will be received into the armed service of the United States to garrison forts, positions, stations, and other places, and to man vessels of all sorts in said service."[3] The liberated would become liberators, and the enlargement of the Union Army would expand the domain of freedom.

Concerning the history of emancipation, as early as 1784 Thomas Jefferson sponsored a bill in the Continental Congress that would ban slavery from expanding into the western territories (words that were later incorporated into the Northwest Ordinance of 1787 preventing slavery north of the Ohio River). The First and Second Confiscation Acts passed by Congress in 1861 and 1862 allowed Union Armies to confiscate slaves as prizes of war and banned slavery in all places where the National Government has jurisdiction.[4]

In another example, on August 30, 1861, Major General John C. Frémont, a recent appointee as Commander of the Department of the West, in his attempt to drive the Confederate forces from Missouri, issued a proclamation indicating that the property of secessionists would be confiscated and the slaves of rebels emancipated. By November, Lincoln had revoked Frémont's Missouri Proclamation and relieved him from his command. Lincoln feared that Frémont's order would push Missouri (and other border states) to the southern cause.[5] Finally, after Lincoln's death the words of Jefferson were finally incorporated into the Thirteenth Amendment to the Constitution of the United States.

While the 1863 Emancipation Proclamation remains a significant document, the question remains, why was it so silent concerning the American Indian? And, more generally, what was the Indian policy of the Great Emancipator? Certainly, he must have known about some of the traditions of Indian slavery, and that the institution of slavery dehumanized Indians as well as Afro-Americans; and what about his contemporary, the Great Pathfinder and Republican Free-Soiler John C. Frémont? If his voice rang so loudly for curtailing the expansion of slavery into the western territories, why was it rumored that he held several de facto Indian slaves and peons at his Mariposa estate in California? These and other questions will be treated in this chapter, beginning with the history of Indian slavery in the United States.

Indian Slavery and the Slave Trade, Particularly in the Southwest Borderlands

Contrary to popular belief, American Indians were enslaved by each other and their European conquerors. In other words, the history of slavery in the United States includes slavery *by* Native Americans as well as slavery *of* Native Americans. The slavery practiced by indigenous groups prior to the European introduction of African slaves was a limited type of slavery that held people in servitude to work off a debt or serve a penal sentence. It is often called "de facto" slavery or "peonage." Sometimes, as in the case of the Aztecs, slaves were used for ritual sacrifices. Slavery was often the result of "blood" revenge practices between extended families, clans, and tribes, and most of these slaves were war captives. Kinship and community overlapped with slavery, with captives (Indian and non-Indian) often being slowly integrated into the tribe. Unlike the chattel slavery of the Europeans and Americans, slaves were not simply property (commodities, credit, or assets to secure loans, capital, and investments), and slavery usually was not accompanied by sexism (although women and children were most often the victims) and racism.

In North America, several tribes held captives as hostages for payment (pawnage) or imposed slavery on tribal members who committed crimes. The Creeks of Georgia and the Comanches of Texas were notorious "slavers" and slave traders, the Comanches often trading Sioux, Navajo, and Apache women and children to Mexicans as slave laborers and domestic servants. Fishing villages like the Yurok of northern California were acknowledged slaveholders. The Haida and Tlingit were traditionally known as fierce warriors and slave traders, and in the Pacific Northwest as many as one-fourth of the indigenous populations were slaves.[6] By the early nineteenth century Indian slavery and the slave trade extended from the Great Lakes and Canada through the Greater Southwest, including southern California.

By the beginning of the nineteenth century one of the more established slave trade routes ran from the Los Angeles area in southern California, through the Mojave district on the Colorado River, on to Zuni or Durango, to the Spanish community of Santa Fé. This had been an Indian trading trail in the pre-Spanish Southwest. At the end of the Spanish colonial era it involved Ute Indians capturing Paiutes or purchasing Paiute children from their parents, and trading them to the Mojaves for horses from California and Sonora. The Mojaves would exchange their captives at markets in northern Mexico and Alta California. Some of the horses and Paiute slaves would also be exchanged for Navajo blankets, ceramics, and buffalo skins from Santa Fé. Horses that sold for $10 each in California might fetch as much as $500 in Missouri, while young female Paiutes could bring as much as $250 in the Santa Fé market. The Utes practically depopulated Nevada and Utah of their Paiute population, with any remaining Paiutes, or "Diggers" as the locals called them, enslaved by first the Mountain Men and trappers, and later Mormon settlers. All had access to the slave trade along the Old Spanish Trail.[7]

Indian and African slavery was always a tool of European expansion. To depopulate the Carolinas and Florida of their original inhabitants in order to introduce plantation agriculture (along with the international market for commodities and labor), English and American settlers and their Indian allies captured hundreds of Indians and forced their removal from their native lands. This was accompanied by violence, rape, and warfare. From 1670 to 1720 more Indians were exported out of Charleston, South Carolina, than Africans were imported as slaves—even though Charleston was a major port city for African slaves. The Choctaws and their neighbors in the Lower Mississippi Valley, battered by raiders spent most of their lives working on plantations in the West Indies.[8]

One peculiarity of American history was the possession of African slaves by Native Americans. From the early times of colonial America Indian slaves, African slaves, and European indentured servants all lived and worked together. Over time many of the Native Americans became partially assimilated and absorbed many aspects of white European–American culture, including the "peculiar institution" of African chattel slavery.

While the practice was limited in the American Southwest,[9] the Indians of "cotton culture" country held the most enslaved blacks. This was especially true for the so-called "Five Civilized Tribes" of the Southeast, especially the Cherokees who by 1809 held 600 enslaved blacks, a number that grew to 21,000 in 1860. The Cherokee constitution, written by the Indians themselves, prohibited slaves and their descendants (including mixed-races) from owning property. When the Indian Removal Act was enforced during the 1830s, the Cherokees, Choctaws, Chickasaws, Creeks, and Seminoles took their slaves (6% of the aggregate population, or 5,000 black slaves) with them to Indian Territory (today's Oklahoma), and later supported the Confederate cause during the Civil War.[10]

By the middle of the nineteenth century Indian slavery in the Southwest was a mix of three distinct traditions. The first, of course, was the kin-ordered system of the Native Americans themselves. The second was an amalgam of Indian and Spanish practices, and was not unlike the kin-based slave societies of Africa. This borderland "slave system" paralleled the African situation in several ways, including war captives, the dominance of women and children as slaves, the absence of plantations, the practice of pawnage, the role of kinship and related customs (including, for the Spanish, *compadrazgo* sanctified by the Church, and other kinds of social interchange that extended family relations such as intermarriage, concubinage, and miscegenation), and the agency of a "conquest" state that curtailed or promoted slavery.[11]

Finally, of course, the chattel slavery that was introduced to America by Europeans and promoted in the Southwest by Anglo-Americans. Chattel slaves, unlike land or buildings, were simply movable pieces of property. This third system, while part of an international economy that did not always penetrate the borderlands, did share with the Spanish tradition the custom of discrimination (most Indians, especially the "wild" ones, were savages) and a belief in the slaveholder group of cultural and religious superiority. Racism, especially dark skin color denoting racial inferiority, and sexism were more prevalent among white Americans than Spaniards and Mexicans.

The European trade in Indian slaves was initiated by Columbus in 1493. Following the Italian mercantile tradition of the trading company (*compañía*), a small group of passive, wealthy individuals would invest in a venture in which the active partners would be shareholders. The gold seekers and/or slave traders would receive a share in the gold and/or slaves that were found or captured. Needing funds to support his New World adventures, Columbus shipped Indians to Spain where there existed a slave market that sold Africans and Muslims. The *entrada* or entry by slave raiders into the Caribbean followed this basic form. When the original inhabitants of the West Indies died out due to disease, warfare, and slavery, this mercantile tradition was carried to the Indian communities of Central America (about 650,000 Indians in coastal Central America were enslaved in the sixteenth century) and fringe regions south and north of central Mexico.[12]

As these expeditions moved from coast to mainland, the activity of slave hunting was transformed from the Italian *compañía* to the Iberian reconquest tradition of *compaña* or band of men (sometimes called "soldiers").[13] The leader(s) and ordinary men would finance the entire expedition and be whole or partial shareholders, with each man receiving a share of the booty (slaves, gold, *encomiendas*, etc.) based on the size of their share and their importance for the mission. For example, a powerful leader might receive several shares, while a horseman would only get one share and a foot soldier a half share. Many of these conquerors had personal servants, often Indians, whose skills, including slave hunting, were in high demand. These auxiliaries were known as *naborías* and were also a prelude to the history of slavery and the slave trade in Sonora and New Mexico.[14] It was a blending of these Italian and Spanish heritages that was used to conquer the Greater American Southwest.

The most common arrangement between conquered and conquerors in the sixteenth century was known as the *encomienda*. The first conquerors who received a royal grant of encomienda to the labor and tribute of the conquered Indians were known as *encomenderos*. Encomienda Indians were not technically slaves since they lived in their own villages or sedentary communities. They could not be sold as individuals or separated from their own ethnic group to live under direct European influence. Yet, in the early sixteenth century, as a group they owed the encomendero both personal service and tribute. The encomienda also furnished Spanish men with Indian concubines. Although the New Laws of 1542 tried to limit the encomienda to tribute only, outlawed Indian slavery, and guaranteed the ecomienda's existence for the life of its present holder and one successor, the encomienda (usually as a subterfuge for slavery) continued to exist well into the eighteenth century in the frontier areas of Venezuela, Chile, Paraguay, the Mexican Yucatan, and the Spanish borderlands of the Greater American Southwest. And even though the Spanish state had a stake in curtailing the owning of slaves by colonists, cannibals (such as the Caribs of the West Indies) or rebellious Indians (e.g., the Chichimeca [Apaches] of northern Mexico) could be enslaved, the latter by military personnel in the presidios.[15] The institution of the encomienda was one of the major grievances that led the Indians to rebel in the Pueblo Revolt of 1680 in New Mexico and Arizona.[16]

As the Indian population declined and the price of labor increased, the state moved to reduce the number of encomenderos and colonists who had access to Indian labor and preserve ever scarce Indian labor for state and public projects. The name for this institution was taken from the earlier period when a share was an allocation or *repartimiento*. The repartimiento was in full force in central Mexico from about 1560 to 1620, while it continued to exist in Peru (known there as the *mita*) until the end of the colonial period. Under the repartimiento Indian laborers worked in the silver mines, built forts, roads, and buildings for the army and government, and did agricultural work and construction for the Church. Again, like the encomienda, repartimiento continued to exist in frontier areas of Mexico, especially around missions and presidios in northern Mexico and the borderlands, including Florida. Although repartimiento laborers were supposed to be paid a minimal wage, and their working hours were limited, institutional means of enforcement were weak and temporary workers were often unsatisfactory laborers. Thus the colonists tended to replace them with contract workers or personal servants and/or slaves.[17]

Because the institution of Indian slavery on the frontier continued in one form or another after the New Laws of 1542, the government made a continued effort to outlaw the enslavement of Indians. This was partly simply a struggle between the royal bureaucracy and the colonists over control of Indian labor, but it was also the position of the Church based on Christian principles. In spite of a history of legislation opposing slavery, the institution persisted in the frontier zone beyond 1800 and the colonial era.

In 1769 an emancipation proclamation was issued by the Spanish Governor of Louisiana, Alejandro "Bloody" O'Reilly, stating that all Indian slaves were to be freed upon the death of their masters, and babies of slaves were to be free at birth. That next year Spanish St. Louis, according to census data, reported that 66 Indian slaves were being held in that city, mostly women and children. Obviously, the King's law stopped at the gates of the city, with all the area claimed by Spain from the Mississippi to the Rocky Mountains being untouched by the Spanish edict.[18]

On September 15, 1829, President Vicente Guerrero emancipated all slaves in Mexico. A law in April 1830, prohibited the introduction of slaves into Spanish Texas. Needless to say, Mexican frontiersmen in Coahuila, and Tejanos (Mexicans in Texas) and Anglo-Americans in Texas protested these laws and did their best to evade the law's intentions.[19] The law was not enforced in Texas. As mentioned before (see endnote 9), 25% of the population of Texas prior to 1836 consisted of African slaves.

Although slavery had been legally abolished in New Mexico while a province of Mexico, in actuality, slavery still persisted after 1850 when New Mexico acquired US territorial status. In 1858, a proslavery faction of the territory passed a slave code known as the Otero Slave Code (named for Miguel Antonio Otero, a delegate in Congress from New Mexico), and approved by Governor Abraham Rencher on February 3, 1859. This slave code was similar to those of the southern confederate states, including provisions requiring runaway servants to be arrested, fines and punishments for slaves violating curfews, and imprisonment for any person found guilty of giving a slave a sword or any firearm. This slave code specifically affirmed "that it in no way applied to peonage and that the word 'slave' designated only a member of the African race."[20]

When, in 1860, the New Mexico legislature attempted to extend the Otero Code to male and female Indians, the governor vetoed the bill. The governor explained his action by saying: "The act apparently is founded on the supposition that the Indians acquired from the savage tribes were slaves; which is not the case; neither is it in the power of the legislature to make them such .... The normal or native condition of our Indian tribes is that of freedom and by our laws they cannot be made slaves either by conquest or purchase. We may hold them as captives or peons but not as slaves."[21] The governor, like most New Mexican citizens who held peons and captives, was in denial that their form of peonage or "enforced servitude of savages" was not a form of slavery. Only African slavery deserved that epitaph.

Indian slavery in New Mexico, intertwined as it was with peonage and kinship, took several decades to die. One example of this would be the ineffectiveness of President Andrew Johnson's directive of June 1865 declaring that slavery in the territory of New Mexico was in violation of "the rights of Indians" and instructing his subordinates to participate in "an effective suppression of the practice."[22] The president's letter elicited a response from Felipe Delgado, New Mexico's Superintendent of Indian Affairs. To Commissioner of Indian Affairs, William Dole, he argued that:

> It is true that there are among the citizens of this country a large number of Indian captives ... but the object in purchasing them has not been to reduce them to slavery, but rather from a Christian piety on the part of the whites to obtain them in order to instruct and educate them in Civilization. ... This has been the practice in this country for the last century and a half and the result arising from it has been to the captives, favorable, humane, and satisfactory.[23]

Like an earlier generation of New Mexicans, the post-Civil War cohort denied that their form of servitude was slavery. It was simply a historical and customary way of extending Spain's original civilizing mission. This was the dominant "local" view until the early 1880s, and Indian slavery lasted in New Mexico well into the twentieth century.[24]

About two months after Johnson's declaration a Hopi woman staggered into Fort Wingate. She said that she and her daughter had been attacked on the road from Cubero to Fort Wingate, and that she had been beaten and battered and her daughter kidnapped. She knew that some men in Cubero held her daughter, and she requested aid from the US military in retrieving her child. The military caught up with the man who had taken her daughter, but he protested that "he had assumed a debt which the woman contracted" and had initially taken both the woman and child as security or collateral against the debt. The matter was dropped. The merger of peonage and slavery was the way the Hopi woman and child had become servile workers in the home of the man from Cubero. Involuntary servitude was the norm and American reformers could not eliminate debt bondage, let alone slavery.[25]

In the first half of the nineteenth century, from California, through New Mexico, to Texas, *gente de razón* (literally "people of reason"), that is, people of any race whose way of life was Hispanic and not Indian, maintained the Spanish practice of taking, purchasing, and ransoming Indian captives. These captives, so-called *gente sin razón* ("people without reason"), became involuntary members of Mexican households. Rarely called *esclavos* or slaves because they were legally and theoretically free, the bondage was always justified on the grounds that these pagans were baptized and received the blessings of Christianity.[26]

In 1927, Amado Chaves recalled the traditions of his family of frontiersmen by saying that:

To get Indian girls to work for you all you had to do was organize a campaign against the Navajoes or Utes or Apaches and kill all the men you could and bring captive the children. They were yours ... . Many of the rich people who did not have the nerve to go into campaigns would buy Indian girls.[27]

If the Indian servants were fortunate enough to work off their ransom or become acculturated adults, they might be released from their masters and mistresses. But as "detribalized" peoples they found themselves in between Indian and non-Indian societies, and on the bottom perch.

Obviously, many of the *gente sin razón* did not view peonage and the kidnapping of their children as a blessing of civilization. In 1852, Armijo, a Navajo headman from Chuska, voiced to the regional Indian agent the feelings of the Diné: "My people are all crying in the same way. Three of our chiefs now sitting before you mourn for their children, who have been taken from their homes by the Mexicans. More than 200 of our children have been carried off; and we know not where they are ... . My people are yet crying for the children they have lost. Is it American justice that we must give up everything and receive nothing?"[28]

Historian L. R. Bailey has coined a term for this process of assimilating alien individuals. He uses the rather formidable word *transculturalization* to describe "the process whereby individuals under a variety of circumstances are temporarily or permanently detached from one group, enter the web of social relations that constitute another society, and come under the influence of its customs, ideas, and values to a greater or lesser degree."[29] This process is a universal one, and applies equally to the white captives that become "Indianized," such as the Oatman sisters under the Mojave (see Chapter 6), non-Athapascans (white or Indian) who became members of Navajo or Apache "alien clans," or Native Americans who became acculturated peons of their Spanish and Mexican masters. It is in this context that Indian slavery, involuntary servitude, and the slave trade in the American Southwest must be understood.

The foundation for Indian slavery in the borderlands was obviously a rigorous slave trade that continued throughout the Spanish colonial era and into the nineteenth century. In the 1620s and 1630s New Mexicans looked eastward and traded iron knives, cattle, and sheep for plains products, including bison hides, robes, and Apache slaves. Backed up by a provincial government that claimed the Apaches were a menace, by the 1640s most Spanish households in New Mexico possessed Quiviran, Ute, or Apache slaves. In the early 1660s 40 colonists and 800 Pueblo Indians under the direction of the Governor of New Mexico brought over 70 captives to Santa Fé. Those who were not sold locally were sent to work the silver mines of Nueva Vizcaya (today's Chihuahua and Durango in northern Mexico).[30]

When the Plains Apache raids declined in the eighteenth century, the Comanche attacks increased. By 1750 the mounted Comanches were the most formidable military force on the southern plains, driving the Jicarilla Apaches westward to the protection of the Rocky Mountains and subduing Lipan Apaches, Mescalero Apaches, and Navajos. Chiricahuas were pushed west and south, where they roamed Arizona and New Mexico and raided the ranches of Sonora and Nueva Vizcaya. With Comanches joining up with the Utes to conduct raids, the Navajos and Paiutes almost feared their Indian brothers more than their Mexican and white neighbors.[31] These were the conditions that continued through the Mexican era and into the modern American period of Southwest history. Expanding trade meant a dynamic Indian slave trade, and this meant additional peons and slaves and involuntary laborers for the economic and social projects of the Southwest.

Before leaving the topic of Indian slavery, mention should be made of the correlations between slavery and sexism and racism. It could be argued that the southwestern traditions of involuntary servitude were accompanied by patriarchy and gender oppression. Certainly Spanish overlords, the *gente de razón* of Mexican times, and American military elites considered the non-sedentary and semi-sedentary inhabitants of the Southwest (that is, the "wild Indians") to be racially and culturally inferior to themselves. At the end of the nineteenth century most Americans considered the Indians to be "a vanishing race," and therefore the conquest of their lands was justified. As an "absent" people their Native bodies were polluted, or as white Californians described them in the 1860s, Native Americans "were the dirtiest lot of human beings on earth .... [they wear] filthy rags, with their persons unwashed, hair uncombed and swarming with vermin."[32]

> Or as a Proctor & Gamble ad for Ivory Soap
> that appeared in 1885 illustrated:
> We were once factious, fierce and wild,
> In peaceful arts unreconciled
> Our blankets smeared with grease and stains
> From buffalo meat and settlers veins.
> Through summer's dust and heat content
> From moon to moon unwashed we went,
> But IVORY SOAP came like a ray
> Of light across our darkened way ...
> And now I take, where'er we go
> This cake of IVORY SOAP to show
> What civilized my squaw and me
> And made us clean and fair to see.[33]

Because Indian bodies are dirty and impure, they are considered "rapable," since the rape of polluted bodies does not count. Or, as scholar Andrea Smith goes further to note, "For instance, prostitutes are almost never believed when they say that they have been raped because the dominant society considers the bodies of sex workers undeserving of integrity and violable at all time. Similarly, the history of mutilation of Indian bodies, both living and dead, makes it clear that Indian people are not entitled to bodily integrity."[34]

One example can be used to illustrate the aforesaid. During the second quarter of the nineteenth century a small number of trappers known as the La Bonté group were hunting and trapping southwest on the outskirts of the Great Salt Lake. The expedition of five men led by a Colorado trapper named Rube Herring soon left the safety of the lake and headed across the desert. Although Rube supposedly knew the country and was an experienced guide, his ignorance was soon apparent as the group lost their way across the waterless desert of the Great Basin desert. Late one evening several Paiutes crawled into their camp and stole two of their horses. The next day La Bonté and his men followed their tracks to the Indian village. The following morning the trappers, discharging their rifles at close quarters, killed nine Indians and captured three young girls. They also retrieved their stolen horses and acquired two more. After proceeding to scalp the dead bodies, the trappers moved on with their young "squaws" in hand. But they were still lost, and food and water was in short demand.[35]

Eventually, they were so driven to the point of hunger that one of them suggested that the alternative to starving to death would be to sacrifice one of their party so as to save the lives of the others. The idea was voted down, and La Bonté and the others, who had noticed some deer-tracks, decided to hunt for wild game. At sunset when La Bonté returned to camp he saw one of his companions named Forey broiling some meat on the embers. The young girls were gone, perhaps having escaped. In the distance he saw what he thought was the carcass of a deer. Forey shouted, "there's the meat, hos—help yourself." La Bonté drew his knife and approached the carcass, but, as his narrator George Frederick Ruxton notes, to his horror he saw "the yet quivering body of one of the Indian squaws, with a large portion of the flesh butchered from it, and part of which Forey was already greedily devouring."[36]

The La Bonté experience is an extreme example and may be a composite of fiction and reality, but it does illustrate the ideas of cannibalism and mutilation of Indian bodies. As for the eating of human flesh, even the great pathfinder and anti-slavery crusader John C. Frémont experienced cannibalism during his attempt to cross the San Juan Mountains in the winter of 1848–1849.[37]

John C. Frémont, Pathfinder and Not so Free Soiler

On January 21, 1813, John Charles Fremon was born out of wedlock in Savannah, Georgia, the child of Ann Pryor, the daughter of a socially prominent Virginia planter, and Charles Fremon, a French-Canadian refugee from Quebec who taught foreign languages, fencing, and dancing, painted frescoes, and attracted the fancy of Mrs. Pryor. A household slave called Black Hannah aided in raising young John. His father died when John was a youngster of five years of age. A truant in the private schools, he went on to college to study mathematics and the natural sciences. At age 25 he changed his surname to Frémont, adding the accent and the "t." This was to take his father's name. His father originally had been called Louis-René Frémont and had changed his name in order to avoid pursuit by British authorities in Canada. Thus John C. Frémont had now reclaimed his father's true name. Between 1838 and 1841 he served in the Corps of Topographical Engineers, assisting in mapping the country between the Mississippi and Missouri Rivers.[38]

Frémont had acquired the nickname "the great pathfinder" because of his explorations in Western America during the 1840s. His career as federal surveyor and "pathfinder" was promoted by his father-in-law, Senator Thomas Hart Benton from Missouri, and his travels were popularized by his wife and Benton's daughter, Jessie, who rewrote his journals into literary masterpieces that made him a national hero. Benton pushed appropriations through Congress that provided the financial backing for his survey expeditions of the Oregon Trail (1842), Oregon Territory (1844), the Great Basin, and the Sierra Nevada in California (1845).[39] Most of these missions fulfilled Benton's "Manifest Destiny" views of America's expansionist future, and all of them were designed to develop the national economy, from transcontinental railroads to resource development (land and precious minerals). Pushing the American Indian and his or her land to one "side" was truly the "downside" of this nationalistic worldview.

Frémont certainly earned his "pathfinder" label, even if he was often guided by more experienced mountain men like Christopher "Kit" Carson, "Uncle Dick" Wootton of Bent's Fort fame, or the eccentric "Old Bill" Williams, or a group of Delaware Indians, Sierra Natives, and Oregon Chinooks. To enlist the services of a "Kit" Carson meant Frémont improved his chances of surviving Indian attacks, thirst, hunger, and angry mules. In 1861, during the Civil War, he showed similar wisdom as Commander of the Department of the West when he recognized the military skills of Ulysses S. Grant and assisted the latter in separating the Confederacy from its terrain west of the Mississippi. His early expeditions led to the Anglo-American discovery of Lake Tahoe, proved that the Great Basin had no outlet to the sea, and described western lands and Indians along the Oregon Trail and the Sierra Mountains. His expeditionary maps were published by the US Congress and became the "Report and Map" that guided hundreds of overland immigrants to California and Oregon, and led the Mormons to the Salt Lake Valley. He was truly the "pathfinder" of the West.[40]

His good name made it possible for Frémont to purchase in 1847 the Rancho Las Mariposas land grant in the Sierra Nevada foothills outside of Yosemite, where gold discoveries enriched the young and energetic 33-year-old adventurer. He acquired large landholdings in San Francisco, including a Golden Gate mansion, and had a luxurious lifestyle in Monterey. By 1850 he was a wealthy and successful man.

Of course, what generated popularity for Frémont among the Anglo-American settlers in California from 1846 to 1850 in no way aided his legacy. Many of his actions were intemperate and ill-conceived, and reflected a mean streak not always complimentary to his character. After meeting with President James K. Polk in Washington, DC in the early months of 1845, Frémont went to St. Louis and organized a group of military volunteers who traveled with him to Sutter's Fort in California, arriving in December of that year. In May 1846 he and his volunteers, including Kit Carson, attacked and destroyed a Modoc fishing village at Lake Klamath in south-central Oregon. Although the action was supposedly in retaliation for an earlier Indian assault, the evidence suggests that the villagers were not involved in the first action. Later the blood-lust continued when Frémont and his followers without provocation wiped out a series of Maidu villages on the Sacramento River, slaughtering men, women, and children.[41]

The killing did not stop here, for in June 1846 he ordered Kit Carson to murder three Hispanics. It turned out that these men were established and respected members of California's Mexican elite, all being mayors or *Alcaldes* and governing authorities in Sonoma and Yerba Buena (later known as San Francisco).[42] Frémont then assumed leadership of the Bear Flaggers and falsely took credit for the independence of California. The revolt lasted 26 days, ending once the US Army arrived with the Bear Flag being replaced with the Stars and Stripes. Unbeknown to Frémont and his Bear Flag supporters, the US had already declared war on Mexico on May 13, 1846. Most of Alta California did not even know about the revolt, even though the rebels declared the independence of California from Mexico.[43]

In January 1847, Commodore Robert F. Stockton, commander of the Pacific Fleet headquartered in Monterey, appointed Frémont military governor of California. But when General Stephen Kearny of the US Army arrived later that year in an overland march from Santa Fé, Stockton dismissed Frémont and declared Kearny the governor. Frémont stubbornly refused to accept Stockton's decision and was extremely slow to relent. He was later convicted of mutiny and disobedience of a superior officer. While approving of the court's action, President Polk quickly commuted his dishonorable discharge sentence because of his prior service to the country.[44]

Back in St. Louis, Frémont and his father-in-law privately financed a fourth expedition in the later months of 1848 that would survey a railway line along the 38th parallel between St. Louis and San Francisco. This was the ill-fated mission that was lost in the winter snow and cold in the passes through the Sangre de Cristo Mountains. When the expedition finally made its way to Taos they were missing ten men, some, it was rumored by his political opponents, to cannibalism.[45] Still, with his triumphs and failures behind him he was sufficiently well known and close enough to power (in 1850–1851 Frémont was one of the first two senators from California to the US Senate) to receive the nomination for president of the United States by the Republican Party in 1856. This was when the nation learned of his "free soil" policies.

The Free Soil Party was founded in Buffalo, New York, and was active in the presidential elections of 1848 and 1852. It was a single-issue third-party movement that consisted of anti-slavery members of the Democratic and Whig Parties. Its banner was "Free Soil, Free Speech, Free Labor and Free Men," and its main cause was opposing the expansion of slavery into the western territories. Free soilers believed that if slavery were contained it would die out. It was not an abolitionist movement, and many abolitionists, such as William Lloyd Garrison, believed the free soil movement to be "white manism," a philosophy that would free white labor and northern businessmen from the economic competition of slavery.[46] Merging of the Free Soilers and Whigs in 1854 divided the Whig Party. In general, southern Whigs went over to the Democrats while discontented northern Whigs created the new Republican Party. The Whig and Free Soils parties disappeared from the American landscape.

As a popular military man, both Democrats and Republicans sought out Frémont as a candidate in 1856. He turned the Democrats down because he opposed their doctrine of "popular sovereignty" (that would allow the settlers to decide the issue of slavery or not in their territories), and he favored a Free Soil Kansas. He also opposed the Democratic-supported Fugitive Slave Law of 1850. So the Free Soil Democrat became a Republican and accepted their nomination. Their slogan, echoing their Free Soil Party roots, was "Free Soil, Free Men, and Frémont."[47]

A new third party joined the fray, the nativist American Party (called the "Know- Nothing Party" by its opponents, since, as a secret party, when asked about its purpose, their members would reply, "I know nothing"), which ran ex-president Millard Fillmore and gathered over 20% of the popular vote. They were basically an America-first group that opposed Catholic immigrants. While the Republicans pushed their Free Soil campaign, the Democrats warned the public that victory for the Republicans would mean civil war for the country. While the Democrats attacked Frémont's illegitimate birth, the Know-Nothings accused Frémont of being a Catholic, an absurd charge that the Republicans could not counter since they did not want to offend their German Catholic voters. When the votes were counted Frémont received 114 electoral votes while the Democratic candidate, James Buchanan from Pennsylvania, got 174. Surprisingly, Frémont lost his home state of California, with Buchanan receiving over 48% of the vote, while the Know-Nothings got 32%. Poor John could only gather in a little over 18% of the California tally.[48] Perhaps this was an omen that the future might not be as bright as the past.

The question first posed in this chapter must now be answered. If Frémont were a free soiler who opposed the expansion of slavery into the territories, and California had been a territory since 1846 and a state since 1850, how could this man, who was a friend to many anti-slavery proponents, own so many de facto Indian slaves and peons on his gold ranch in California?[49] What was his actual situation, and did his wealth come from exploiting Indian workers? Did he think Indian peonage and involuntary servitude in California was the norm, while African chattel slavery in the American West was not? And what about his wife Jessie and what was her situation? To answer these questions it is first necessary to look briefly at the traditions and customs of Indian slavery in both Spanish-Mexican California before 1850 and Anglo-American California after 1850.[50]

The system of law that the Anglo-Americans of California created after 1846 perpetuated the labor exploitation of the Spanish colonial era and the Mexican period. In the first years of military rule in California a series of martial codes restricted the freedom of the Indian, including labor contracts that bound the Indian workers to their employer, limitations on the freedom of movement of all Indians, and the development of an Indian apprenticeship that allowed whites to obtain and control Indian labor. All of these restrictions were very reminiscent of the Spanish system of encomienda and *repartimiento* of the early period, as well as the hacienda peonage of the later era—Indians were free, but not free to not work.[51]

By 1849, California had established a constitutional government. As a condition for California's entry into the Union the delegates agreed that slavery would be prohibited in that state. However, they were speaking of black slavery, not Indian slavery. As for the Indian, they were to remain what they had always been—a subservient class of workers. Accordingly, when dealing with suffrage they voted to limit it along racial and sexual lines and only allowed "white male citizens" to vote. In the final analysis, however, it was the 1850 law entitled "An Act for the Government and Protection of Indians" that defined the status and place of Indians in California society.[52]

The 1850 law stated that any able-bodied Indian who refused to work would be liable to arrest, and "vagrants" could be hired out for up to four months. Indian convicts could be bailed out by "any white person," and they would be forced to work for the person doing the bailing. Under the apprenticeship clause of the law, whites could legally obtain the services of Indian males under 18 and females under 15. A revised statute in 1860 allowed third parties to obtain Indian children without parental consent. In effect, the peonage system of the Mexican period was being extended and legalized for the post-1850 Americanized state of California.[53]

Whatever the intent of these laws, the apprenticeship clauses had the effect of encouraging kidnapping and selling of Indian children. Desperados and reckless criminals plied their trade in the frontier areas of northern counties like Humboldt, selling and ransoming their human prey to eager participants in southern California. Young Indian women and child "apprentices" were forcibly wrested from their families and communities and sold to miners, ranchers, and farmers. While most worked in mining, ranching, and agriculture, many of the female slaves became domestic servants. The state was approving a form of Indian servitude not found in the earlier Spanish and Mexican period, crossing the boundary from peonage to slavery. It has been estimated that over 4,000 children were stolen between 1852 and 1867, with the prices for Indian women and children dependent upon sex, age, physical attributes, and usefulness.[54]

A typical feature of this trade was that Indian girls as young as eight or nine were sold by their captors to other whites expressly as sexual partners. Sometimes they became concubines. Otherwise they would be used until they became useless. In December 1861, according to historian James Rawls, the *Maryland Appeal* "commented that, while kidnapped Indian children were seized as servants, the young women were made to serve both the 'purposes of labor and of lust.'" In 1862 a correspondent to the *Sacramento Union* wrote about the "baby killers" of Humboldt County who "talk of the operation of cutting to pieces an Indian squaw in their indiscriminate raids for babies as 'like slicing old cheese.' ...The baby hunters sneak up to a rancheria, kill the bucks, pick out the best looking squaws, ravish them, and make off with their young ones."[55] Boys as young as 12 were also enslaved, and given the disparity in power between master and slave, the conjecture is that pedophilia may have been a likely result.

In spite of the protestations of the Anglo-Americans of California, relations between Indians and whites in the Southwest paralleled those between blacks and whites in the Confederate South. Although California did not create slave codes like those in New Mexico, their laws and rules restricting Indian freedoms were similar to the infamous Black Codes of the South. Indian passes and the practice of limiting Indian mobility were similar to restrictions on blacks in the post-war South. Vagrancy and bail-out provisions were similar, as were instances where Indians and blacks could not testify against their white masters.[56] While the Spanish and Mexican heritage of peonage and involuntary servitude was important for slavery in California, the racism, sexism, and violence that accompanied Indian slavery after 1850 became commonplace throughout much of the Indian Southwest.

In the early period prior to 1850, California Indians provided a variety of tasks for their white overlords, from laboring as mechanics and domestics to deckhands and lumbermen. The gold-rush of the late 1840s meant that most laborers were headed for the gold fields, and therefore the scarcity of labor for the remaining jobs required the use of Indian workers. And the Argonauts needed food for them and fodder for their livestock. Beef was in great demand. The California cattle boom extended the Mexican tradition of utilizing Indian labor on the *ranchos* and haciendas. In the 1850s most of the cattle ranches in Bernardino and Los Angeles counties used Indian laborers who were permanently attached to the soil, who were, as one contemporary observed, "no better than slaves." Eventually, the "great drought" of 1862–1864 brought an end to the cattle industry, with many "useless" Indians becoming homeless vagabonds.[57]

Of course, the dominant activity in the early years after the 1848 discovery of gold was not ranching but mining. The Hispanic tradition of the *repartimiento* or allocation was transferred from the farms to the mines, with the white miner and his Indian worker having a relationship not unlike the traditional ranchero and his Indian peon. One Argonaut estimated that within months after the initial discovery of gold, four thousand Indians worked alongside two thousand whites. Just as the Indians on the ranchos were considered as stock, so too were those who worked in the mines. And those whites, like Johann Sutter in Sacramento, who already controlled a body of Indian laborers before the 1848 strike, had an advantage over the newcomers in working the placer mines. The outsiders were naturally jealous of the old-timers.[58]

After the initial discoveries Indian laborers began to disappear from the mines. This disappearance coincided with the arrival of the newcomers who had no prior experience with the Hispanic history of Indian exploitation. For them the Indian was useless since most Indians in their experience had been hostile and a threat to their security. In March 1849, three years after Frémont's volunteers had decimated the Klamath Indian village in south-central Oregon, and one and a half years after the Whitman massacre left 13 dead missionaries in Walla Walla, Washington, 7 Oregon prospectors raped several Maidu women on a *rancheria* near the American River. This led to retaliation by Indian men and an escalation of violence in which Indians from the village of Colima were killed, arrested, and executed. It was no accident that the Colima site had been the place where Sutter had positioned his mill, and Sutter, of course, had generated much of the outsider's anger and jealousy. After news of this incident spread, Indians in the mines fled from the whites fearing for the safety of themselves and their families. The jealousy of the newcomers had ignited an era of mutual fear and outrage, and a decade of Indian wars.[59]

This is the California context in which John C. Frémont's activities and ideas can be judged. First, it must be noted that in the late 1840s, prior to the discovery of gold, Frémont was essentially a tourist and newcomer. His behavior toward the Indian was not any more sophisticated than that of his fellow Oregonians who fought, killed, and raped Indians. Had he stayed only an explorer, his reputation as "the great pathfinder" would have been secure, but his decision to purchase the Mariposa estate transformed the surveyor into an unsuccessful entrepreneur.

The 43,000-acre estate, in the Sierra foothills only 40 miles southwest of Yosemite, had been the favorite hunting ground of the Cauchile Indians. Similar to other white rancheros, his land had been carved out of previous indigenous properties. Like his neighbors, he surrounded himself with de facto Indians slaves that worked his fields, and after the discovery of gold and silver on the Mariposas River, his Sonoran managers administered the Indian mineworkers. One of the prospectors was a black servant named Saunders, whose family was still in slavery, who was working the Mariposa mines for the purpose of working off his purchase price of $1,700.[60] Generally speaking, while Frémont was generally consistent in his "free soil" views and his opposition to African chattel slavery in the South, he, like many of his contemporaries in the West, had a blind eye when it came to the issue of Indian slavery.

Jessie (Benton) Frémont was equally involved with the institution of Indian slavery. Throughout the 1850s and 1860s the most constant demand for Indian labor was that of Indian servants—male or female, young and old. In her Monterey house a Mexican chef oversaw Indian men who did most of the cooking, aided by Indian boys who hunted for food and assisted in the preparation of meals. Jessie noticed a remarkable similarity between the average California household and the "life of our Southern people." In California it was typical for ladies of the house to be "surrounded by domesticated Indian girls at their sewing." At Mariposa, Mission Indians were obtained by the Frémonts and required to work at laundering and other domestic chores. Jessie bragged about "playing Missionary" to a group of local Indians, plaiting their hair, and dressing them in starched calico and clean white undergarments. She was able to civilize these dirty people and transform them into "picturesque peasants."[61]

For Jessie to play missionary was in character, as she had always wanted to experience the man's world, from her teenage days as a tomboy, through her vicarious experiences of her husband's explorations and adventures (as described in her writings of her husband's exploits), to her playing the role of Spanish missionaries domesticating and Christianizing their Indian subjects. Her maternalism was the counterpart to the paternalism that fostered Indian servitude, and she was as consistent in her "free soil" views as she was inconsistent on the subject of slavery. In this way she was her husband's wife.

It must be remembered that "abolitionism" and the "free soil" movement were not identical, and that, as aforementioned, the abolitionist William Lloyd Garrison denounced the Free Soil Party as a white man's party that was only concerned with ending slave labor's competition with free white labor. Garrison, by the way, had written an editorial as early as 1829 criticizing the forced removal of Indians from the Southeast. In the 1850s many abolitionists and crusaders, like John Beeson and Wendell Phillips, spoke against Indian slavery and in favor of reform of the Indian service of the United States government.[62] Frémont, while consistently favoring the anti-slavery point of view when talking about African chattel slavery, was ultimately a white man who ignored the rights of Indians as human beings and saw them as useful sources of labor to be exploited. His views on these matters were shared by many northerners, including the Abraham Lincoln of 1863 and after.

Lincoln and the Indians

The path to emancipation of the Afro-American slaves was a rocky one, and who better to follow that road then the "great pathfinder," John C. Frémont. But the trail was narrow with many false exits, and as luck and fate would have it, Lincoln and Frémont crossed and met on that trail several times. Most of these engagements were less than friendly, especially the emancipation edict controversy of 1861.

As already mentioned, on August 30, 1861 Frémont, as commander of the Western Department, issued a controversial proclamation putting Missouri under martial law and declaring that anyone who took up arms against the Federal government, or supported those who did so, will have their property, including slaves, confiscated. By November Lincoln had rescinded the proclamation and relieved Frémont of his command, telling Jessie Benton Frémont in person that "General Frémont should not have dragged the Negro into it." Yet, the second Confiscation Act passed by Congress and issued by Lincoln in July 1862 was very similar to Frémont's proclamation in regard to the confiscation of property of persons disloyal to the United States.[63]

Another major confrontation came in May 1864 when Radical Republicans, meeting in a separate convention one month before the Republican convention, nominated Frémont as their candidate for president. These were anti-slavery zealots who thought that Lincoln was too moderate in his plans for the reconstruction of the South. With the Civil War still raging, Lincoln was later nominated in June as the Republican candidate for president, while a pro-Union Democrat from Tennessee, Andrew Johnson, received the vice-presidency nod.[64] In the very near future Lincoln would be assassinated, and Frémont, over the next 26 years, would die a slow death after a series of scandals and financial and political failures.

Most presidents, including Lincoln, had limited experience with Indians, and even less knowledge. On those occasions in the White House when he met with Indians personally he would speak to them in Pidgin English saying to them "Where live now?" and "When go back to Iowa?" He had little doubt that they were an inferior people, and an obstacle to America's progress and development. His major concern was winning the Civil War, after that his highest priority was settling and developing the west. The Homestead Act of 1862 accelerated white settlement of lands formerly occupied by Indians, and many of the treaties he signed opened up Indian lands for the development of the transcontinental railroad. His Indian policy mainly was one of making treaties with the Indians that would remove them from the lands the settlers coveted.[65]

Lincoln's Indian policy was carried out by the Office of Indian Affairs, a bureaucratic entity that was created by the secretary of war in 1824 and moved to the Interior Department in 1849. The major and minor posts of the Indian system were filled by "spoils of office." The commissioner of Indian affairs reported to the secretary of the interior, who in turn was responsible to the president. Lincoln's appointees were William P. Dole of Pennsylvania for commissioner and Caleb Smith of Indiana for secretary of interior. Both men were politicians with no special expertise in Indian matters. A variety of Indian agents assigned to tribes and reservations reported to regional superintendents, which in turn were responsible to the commissioner. Claimants, contractors, and traders all milked the Indian system for federal monies. All of these offices together comprised the Indian patronage system of the Lincoln administration, and many people believed, as did Bishop Henry Whipple of Minnesota, "that the Indian Department was the most corrupt in our government."[66] When it came to Indian affairs, Lincoln was more the politician than the statesman.

Apart from making some limited attempts to keep the Confederacy from allying with the Native Americans of the Indian Territory (Oklahoma), the only Indian matter that drew Lincoln's attention away from the Civil War was the Minnesota rebellion of Santee Sioux (also known as the Eastern Dakotas) in the summer of 1862. The insurrection began when several starving and hungry Sioux killed several hundred white settlers ostensibly because the government had failed its treaty responsibilities to provide the Natives with annuities and rations. Corruption in the Indian system was the main reason for the Sioux's plight. Monies earmarked for Indian care had been funneled to

Minnesota from its congressmen and ended up in the pockets of Indian agents and contractors. Corruption at the higher levels of the Indian system had worked its way down throughout the entire bureaucratic network.[67]

Sioux testimony, like that of Wabasha, a Dakota leader, suggested that the war was caused by crooked traders who took advantage of his people. According to Wabasha, the traders first tricked a small faction of his people to sign an agreement in which the Sioux agreed to sell land on the north side of the Minnesota River in exchange for "horses, guns, blankets, and other articles." As Wabasha continues, "By the result of this paper signed without my consent or knowledge, the traders obtained possession of all the money coming from the sale of land ... and also half of our annuity for the year 1862." Soon after he learned that a war party had been formed by Little Six's band and fighting had commenced. "I got on my horse and rode up to the store," Wabasha said, and "I saw that the traders were already killed."[68]

The rebellion triggered a full-scale war. The uprising resulted in a terrible tragedy in which hundreds of Indians and whites lost their lives, most of whom were innocent and had not condoned the war.[69] This occurred at a precarious time for the Union as the federal forces were in disarray, with General John Pope being defeated at the Battle of Bull Run (Second Manassas) and Robert E. Lee about to attack Washington. Rumors circulated that the Minnesota rebellion was a Confederate conspiracy designed to bring the British to the southern cause. It's no wonder that Lincoln responded by ordering General Rufus Saxton to organize black soldiers, an action that was later formalized in the famous Emancipation Proclamation of 1863. The Indian rebels were defeated two months after it started. About fifteen hundred Indian women, children, and old men were among the prisoners. Many of the men were put on trial in front of a military tribunal—the result, 303 warriors were sentenced to death.[70]

Lincoln reviewed the cases of the 303 accused men. Attempting to moderate the military's decision and the demands of the Minnesota voter, Lincoln carefully walked the tightrope of public opinion. As he said, "Anxious to not act with so much clemency as to encourage another outbreak of one hand, nor with so much severity as to be real cruelty on the other, I ... [ordered] the execution of such as had been proved guilty of violating females." Since only two Indians were guilty of rape, he then decided to distinguish those who participated in "massacres" from those who fought "battles." On December 26, 38 Indians were hung at Mankato, Minnesota.[71]

The aftermath of the Minnesota rebellion shaped Lincoln's Indian policy for the west. First, the western Indians would be treated strictly as a military problem, and the military would be given carte blanche authority to deal with the "wild" Indians of Arizona and Colorado. Secondly, that policy would be one of removal and relocation. In April 1863, 270 Dakota men were moved from Mankato, Minnesota, to a prison camp in Davenport, Iowa, where they were imprisoned for three "gut-wrenching" years. In July of that year the military drove eight to ten thousand Indians out of Minnesota into Dakota Territory, including the scalping and mutilation of insurrectionist leader Little Crow (see Figure 1.1). An 1864 expedition went up the Missouri River as far as Yellowstone with the object of destroying as many Indians as possible. As a concession to the remaining condemned Sioux, instead of execution they would be removed from the state of Minnesota and resettled in the Upper Missouri.[72]

And even though most Winnebagos (Ho-Chunk) had not been involved in the 1862 rebellion, they too were forced to relocate to Crow Creek in Dakota Territory. They had to move because the settlers in Minnesota wanted their Winnebago land. Like the Sioux, the removal trip cost many lives, especially of women and children. Once they arrived at Crow Creek they found that they had been forced to trade good land for inferior, sandy soil. Finally, as usual the 1,300 Winnebagos were surrounded by 600 white profiteers and the brutality of military guards.[73]

The 1863 removal and relocation of the Mescalero Apaches and Navajos to Bosque Redondo in New Mexico took place in the shadow of the Minnesota uprising, and was the result of Lincoln's wartime militarization of the Indian problem. As the Sioux reservation was opened up to white settlers, it was closed to the Sioux and they were forgotten. Although Lincoln's humaneness was shown in his clemencies of several Santee Sioux warriors, it was still the largest mass execution in American history in which the guilt of the accused was in doubt. His Minnesota policy, shaped in part by the realities of politics and the pressures of the Civil War, became the template for Indians elsewhere, with Arizona's Navajos, Mescalero Apaches from west Texas, and Paiutes south of Lake Tahoe being relocated, and Cheyennes and Arapahos in Colorado being massacred at Sand Creek by the military. The army had proposed a

Figure 1.1 *Portrait of Sioux Chief, Little Crow (1824).* From *Native Americans: An Illustrated History* (Atlanta: Turner Publishing, Inc., 1993), p. 327.

similar removal plan for the California Indians where they would be relocated from the mainland to a concentration camp on Catalina Island. Fortunately, Commissioner Dole halted these preparations.[74] Lincoln's last proclamation was also militaristic in that he ordered the execution of any soldier found guilty of smuggling arms to the Indians.[75]

Earlier in 1858, while debating the status of slavery with Stephen Douglas in the famous Lincoln–Douglas debates for the senate in Illinois, Lincoln argued not for the equality but for the freedom of the "Negro." The words of Douglas more clearly reflected the public sentiment. He contended that he was opposed to "negro" citizenship in any form, saying that "I believe this Government was made on the white basis. I believe it was made by white men for the benefit of white men and their posterity for ever, and I am in favor of confining citizenship to white men, men of European birth and descent, instead of conferring it upon negroes, *Indians* [italics mine], and other inferior races [audience response—'Good for you; Douglas forever']."[76]

A more vengeful attitude was expressed by the citizens of Minnesota in a May 6, 1863 article of the *Saint Paul Pioneer*. The steamboat *Northerner* was sent to St. Paul to pick up refugee Dakotas, mostly women and children, who were being sent to Crow Creek in Dakota Territory. Before it could take them aboard it needed to unload a hundred or so emancipated slaves who were brought north to act as mule drivers for the army's spring expedition against Little Crow and the Dakotas still in rebellion. As the newspaper said: "The *Northerner* brought up a cargo of 125 niggers and 150 mules on Government account. We doubt very much whether we benefit by the exchange. If we had our choice we would send both niggers and Indians to Massachusetts, and keep the mules here."[77]

Lincoln shared the biases of his generation. According to Lincoln the Indians were savages, while the white man was civilized. In spite of the Civil War, Lincoln noted, white men generally shunned war and sought peace, while the "redmen" were disposed to fight and kill one another. Christianity was superior to any Indian religion. They were an inferior, vanishing people who were destined to be pushed aside by white Americans. Like the Minnesota voters who decried slavery in the southern states, he was silent about the degradation and exploitation of America's Native Americans. Like his protagonist Frémont, he closed his eyes to the plight of the Indian.[78]

Yet the memory of Lincoln was that of "the Great Emancipator." Shortly after Lincoln's death, Kirby Benedict, a federal judge in the Territory of New Mexico, wrote a eulogy to President Abraham Lincoln. It ended with these words: "The voice of the blood of Abraham Lincoln will never cry in vain to Heaven from the free ground upon which it has been shed."[79] Lincoln was the author of one of the most important documents in the history of the American Republic. His leadership during the Civil War in which he destroyed the institution of Black slavery and preserved the Union at all costs made Lincoln a great statesman. Not only did Lincoln, a grieving father, manage affairs on the domestic front, he also gave to Mexico material and manpower that enabled Benito Juárez and his Republican Army to defeat the imperial armies of France and Austria. In this latter sense Lincoln was not only a great national leader, but was an important international figure as well.[80] Yet, and unfortunately, from the point of view of many Indians "the Great White Father" was ultimately just another politician.

Commentary: Lincoln and the Pueblos

Like most presidents, Lincoln had little or no knowledge and experience with the American Indian. On a personal level he considered them inferior to the white man and dealt with them in a paternalistic way. Most of the Indian matters that confronted him in office were handled by other officials in his administration. Lincoln's Far West policy was to promote the interests of the transcontinental railroad, miners, farmers, and preachers. In other words, Lincoln personified the ideals of "Manifest Destiny," which held that the Indians were an obstacle to the expansion of western civilization and must be removed to make room for Christianity, mineral extraction, farming, and the railroad. Most of the Lincoln administration activities involved the cession of Indian lands and the removal and relocation of the Indians from their homelands. While he did get involved in the Sioux conflict in Minnesota, and was concerned with the affairs of the pro-Union Cherokee, he took no part in the events in the New Mexico territory involving Navajos and Mescalero Apaches. The Navajo Long Walk was administered solely by military personnel of the New Mexico district.

His paternalism did reveal itself in his treatment of the Pueblo Indians. Perhaps, Lincoln, like many of his compatriots, considered them to be more "civilized" than the average "savage" because the Pueblos lived in a sedentary way, dwelling in apartment compounds and practicing agriculture. Pursuing the model of the Spanish King in 1620 and the example of the Mexican government in 1821, he awarded Pueblo leaders with silver-headed ebony canes engraved with his name:

> Lincoln
> President. U.S.A.
> (Name of the pueblo)
> 1863

As scholar W. Dale Mason notes, "These canes recognized the sovereign status of the pueblos. The canes are still revered in the pueblos today and are used to symbolically legitimize the authority of the pueblo governments."[1]

2

Numu (Paiute) Wanderings, Trails, and Tears

In 1863 Company G of the 2nd California Cavalry was sent to Owens Valley to reinforce fellow troopers assisting American settlers at war with Paiute Indians. On the way, the soldiers surrounded a Tubatulabal village near Keysville and killed 35 to 40 Indian men. On the return trip, the troops marched About 1,000 Paiutes to the Tejon Reserve, bringing 300 to the fort, which had been closed in 1861 ... . Neither the Indian agent nor the military provided enough food to sustain the captives.

Office of Indian Affairs, San Francisco, July 11, 1864[1]

You would make war upon the whites [taibo's]. I ask you to pause and reflect. The white men are like the stars over your heads. You have wrongs, great wrongs, that rise up like the mountains before you; but can you, from the mountain tops reach and blot out those stars ... . What hope is there for the Pah-Ute? From where is to come your guns, your powder, your lead, your dried meat to live upon, and hay to feed your ponies while you carry on this war. Your enemies have all of these things, more than they can use. They will come like the sand in a whirlwind and drive you from your homes.

Numaga (Young Winnemucca), Pyramid Lake Paiute,
Indian Leader and Speaker, April 1860[2]

This time he [Wovoka, Mason Valley, Nevada, Paiute and Initiator of Ghost Dance movement in 1887] hadn't left his body to follow the shamans' path under the earth or into the shadowy realm of animistic powers and magic; instead, he visited a monotheistic Heaven and spoke to a very Methodist-sounding God with strong Mormon leanings.

Gunard Solberg, *Tales of Wovoka*[3]

Lost Worlds of 1863: Relocation and Removal of American Indians in the Central Rockies and the Greater Southwest, First Edition. W. Dirk Raat.
© 2022 John Wiley & Sons, Inc. Published 2022 by John Wiley & Sons, Inc.

The early 1860s was a time of turmoil and conflict for the Paiute peoples of Owens Valley east of the Sierra Nevada Mountains, as well as the Northern Paiutes of the Pyramid Lake region in what was then Utah Territory and present-day western Nevada. Even in eastern Nevada where the Overland Stage Company ran from Salt Lake City to the Schell Creek Mountains (immediately east of present-day Eli, Nevada), a distance of 225 miles, an eight-month war took place between the cousins of the Northern Paiutes, the Goshutes, and the white intruders. At least 16 whites were killed, and over 50 Goshutes died before peace was achieved in October 1863.[4]

These incidents and conflicts were followed by events that eventually led to the disintegration of the Paiute homeland and, of course, the Paiute sense of family and identity. The so-called Keyesville Massacre of 1863 resulted in the death of at least 35 Indians,[5] including many Paiutes, and that event was followed by the removal of nearly a thousand Owens Valley Paiutes to Fort Tejon and the region of southern California. There many would succumb to measles and other "European" diseases.

The Pyramid Lake War of 1860 was followed by the Mud Lake Massacre of March 1865 when old men and women, as well as children and little babies, were burnt alive, including one of Chief Winnemucca's wives, Tuboitony.[6] The disintegration of the Pyramid Lake Reservation led these Northern Paiutes to wander from federal reservation to federal reservation, from army camp to army camp—first at Camp McDermit in northern Nevada, then the Malheur Reservation in Oregon, and after the Bannock War of 1878, to the Yakama Reservation beyond the Columbia River in Washington. The latter was a forced march that became, for the Paiutes, their own "Trail of Tears."

After the Dawes Act of 1887 the Paiutes were to be given 160 acres on an individual basis for parcels of marginal land. Many received nothing, and instead they were forced to form small ghettos adjacent to white communities in hopes of doing odd and dirty jobs the white man or woman would not do. It is not surprising then that the ancient Ghost Dance Religion would be revived in hopes of restoring the traditional Paiute values of homeland, family, community, and identity—a heaven on earth that would exclude the white outsider.

Numa and Numa Folkways

Historically the Paiutes consisted of three related groups of indigenous peoples in the Great Basin: the Northern Paiutes of western Idaho, eastern Oregon, northeastern California, and most of Nevada (an area of over 70,000 square miles); the Owens Valley Paiutes in the arid basin between the eastern slopes of California's Sierra Nevada Mountains and the western faces of the Inyo and White Mountains; and the Southern Paiutes of southern Nevada and southern Utah, northern Arizona, and southeastern California. The Owens River runs approximately 180 miles north to south through the Owens Valley. The word "Paiute" has been interpreted to mean "Water Ute," but the term the people use for themselves is usually *Numa*, meaning "the people." However, some northern Paiutes, such as the Pyramid Lake Paiutes and a scattering of Owens Valley inhabitants, prefer *Numu* (also Neh-muh), while Southern Paiutes call themselves *Nuwuvi*, both terms also meaning "the people."[7]

Demographic estimates vary depending on the source, but a general approximation for the late 1850s would be about 6,000 Northern Paiutes in western Nevada and 1,000 Owens Valley Indians. By 1980 the figure would be 5,123 Northern Paiutes throughout California, Nevada, and Oregon, and about 1,900 Owens Valley Paiutes. Only about half of that latter number still live in the valley, the rest having moved to Los Angeles and elsewhere.[8]

The Paiutes linguistically belong to the Numic branch of the Uto-Aztecan family of languages. Although the language of the Northern Paiute is similar to that of the southern branch, the Southern Paiutes speak the Colorado River Numic language, which is more closely related to Numic groups other than the Northern Paiutes. The Numu of Owens Valley speaks Mono, a language closely related to that of the Northern Paiute even if many "northerners" claim that they cannot understand the speech of "southerners."[9] Many Paiutes speak dialects similar to those spoken by the Shoshone. Historically there were approximately 21 Northern Paiute bands, with two or more other enclaves in contiguous areas of California.[10] The Owens Valley group consisted of six distinctive tribal groups, while the Southern Paiute traditionally had between 16 to 31 subgroups or bands.[11]

The Northern Paiutes and the Owens Valley segment developed cultures and societies well adapted to the harsh realities of a desert environment. Generally speaking, the Owens Valley environment was favorable to that prevailing elsewhere in the Great Basin, allowing the Owens Valley Paiute to develop a semi-settled life unknown in other parts of Numu territory. Depending on the season, most northern Numic speakers occupied a specific camping place centering on either a foraging range or a lake or wetland that provided fish and/or waterfowl—although dependence on fishing and communal duck hunting was virtually unknown among the villagers of Owens Valley. Pronghorn antelope, mountain sheep, deer, and rabbits were the objects of communal hunts, while piñon nuts would be gathered in the mountains. The Paiutes traded pine nuts and salt for acorns and acorn flour from the California tribes. Grass seeds and edible roots supplied nutrients in the meadows and marshes.[12]

Owens Valley Paiute housing took a variety of forms. Most Paiutes had a "mountain house" that was a high altitude structure (above 6000 feet) used during fall and winter consisting of two upright posts with side beams sloped from the ground in the shape of a tent. The roof was made of pine boughs. The winter "valley house" was larger in diameter, 15 to 20 feet, built around a 2-foot deep pit with tules and earth covering the outside. Summer houses were simple semicircular brush windbreaks, not unlike the general Great Basin wikiup. The most durable structure was the sweathouse or communal assembly lodge, a semi-subterranean house that could be as much as 25 feet in diameter. It was used as a men's house or dormitory, a community meeting house, a sweathouse, and a ceremonial center. The erection of a sweathouse was supervised by the group's headman, who also nominally owned and maintained the structure.[13]

Like their eastern cousins, the Western Shoshone of southern Nevada—individuals, nuclear, and extended families—moved freely between communities and tribelets, which, again like the Shoshone, named their subgroups after food sources. For example, the Kuyui Pah (Pyramid Lake) Paiutes were known as *Kuyuidokado* or *Cui-Ui Ticutta* (kuyui eaters). The kuyui (or cui-ui) is a bottom feeder sucker ancient to, and found only in, Pyramid Lake and sacred to the Numu. Likewise, the Carson City Paiutes were known as "tule eaters," while the Mono Indians of California were "brine fly eaters."[14]

The Owens Valley Paiutes were unique in that from at least the beginning of the nineteenth century (and maybe dating from aboriginal times) they were practicing irrigation that was, as one source described it, "simply 'an artificial reproduction of natural conditions' existing in the swampy lowlands of Owens Valley."[15] The practice continued until the forced exodus of the Owens Valley people to Fort Tejon in 1863 and the subsequent depopulation of the area. Communal labor was utilized to construct and maintain check damns and feeder ditches that directed the spring runoff to swampy grounds where yellow nut-grass and other bulbous plants were harvested by Indian farmers using digging sticks in the fall. As anthropologists Sven Liljeblad and Catherine Fowler have noted, "At the time of European contact, artificial irrigation of wild crops in Owens Valley was an integral part of communal activity and an essential feature of traditional village organization."[16] As several scholars have observed, the Owens Valley group is the best example in North America of a group that developed its own system of "vegeculture."[17]

Politically, the Paiute subgroups and bands were led by headmen or head speakers, usually referred to by outsiders as "chiefs." Ordinarily, the main leadership positions were chosen by consensus or election by a small group of Paiute elders, and most often the speaker was a hereditary leader. Apart from the headman, other lesser but important roles included those of shaman (who could be either male or female), rabbit boss, mediator, and spokesman or spokeswoman.

One of the more important "chiefs" of the Northern Paiutes was Captain Truckee of Pyramid Lake. He was well known to emigrant parties since Truckee often served as their guide through the Sierra Mountains to California. The emigrants even named the Truckee River after him. At one time he joined John C. Fremont in the Bear Flag Revolt of 1846. When he died in the fall of 1860 his son, Winnemucca ("Old Winnemucca," not to be confused with his nephew Numaga, "Young Winnemucca"), followed his father's policy of maintaining friendship and peace with the *taibo* or white man (see Figure 2.1). Winnemucca left Pyramid Lake in 1865 after the Mud Lake massacre, traveled to the mountains in Oregon, and never returned to Pyramid Lake. He died in 1882. His daughter, Sarah Winnemucca (Thocmetony), became an important mediator and translator for the Paiute people and championed their cause throughout her life (see Figures 2.2 and 2.3).[18]

Figure 2.1 *Chief Winnemucca (or Old Winnemucca), ca. 1870.* Noe and Lee Studio, Virginia City, Nevada. Courtesy of the Nevada Historical Society.

Figure 2.2   *Sarah Winnemucca (Thocmetony)*. Numu/Northern Paiute. Courtesy of
Nevada Historical Society.

    Like the Apache and Navajo, an important ritual for the Paiute was the menarche or puberty rite. After her first menstrual period, the young girl would be isolated for four days in a special hut built by the girl's mother. During this time she would take cold baths, undergo steaming in a pit, and avoid all the taboos against drinking cold drinks, touching her hair or face, and eating animal food and eggs. Again, like the Apache Sunrise Ceremony, she could only scratch her head with a stick and not with her fingers. She would run in the direction of the sunrise in the morning and sunset in the evening. On the morning of the fifth day the ceremony would close with a cold water bath. At subsequent menses she would use the head scratcher, avoid men, and wash her entire body. Akin to puberty rites elsewhere, the ceremonies and rituals were as important for the community as for the individual.[19]

Figure 2.3 *The Winnemucca Family: Sarah Winnemucca (Thocmetony), Old Chief Winnemucca, Sarah's brother, Natches (Natchez or "boy"), Captain Jim (Pyramid Lake Chieftain), and unidentified boy.* The youngster was identified by Joe Ely, Historian of the Intertribal Council of Nevada as Ed Winnemucca, adopted by Sarah. She found him abandoned in a barn during an Indian war. Photo likely taken in Washington, D.C. in 1880. Information by Catherine Magee, Director, Nevada Historical Society.

The Paiutes had several creation stories that told about the beginning of the earth, the formation of Paiutes and mankind in general, the origin of death, and resurrection after defeat and death. The hero Wolf (known as Tap or U'nŭpi in Owens Valley, or "Isha" for the Pyramid Lake peoples) was lonely, so he made Coyote ("Itsa" for Pyramid Lake Paiutes) and they paddled around the entire flooded world. Since they had no earth to run back and forth on, Wolf took some dirt and placed it in the water, where it continued to spread and grow larger until the earth became as it is today.[20]

The origin of Paiutes and mankind occurred after Korawini, the beautiful woman who lived in Long Valley north of Owens Valley, killed all the men in the world who loved her but Coyote. She had killed them by biting them with her vagina teeth (*vagina dentata)* during intercourse. Coyote fooled her by changing his penis into a brush that was used to rip her vagina teeth out, and Korawini became pregnant. Eventually, she gave birth to all mankind's children, including the Paiute offspring of Coyote.[21] In one rendition the first children consisted of sons and a daughter. The boys as they grew up continued to fight each other so they were sent away. After the dissidents were sent off, Coyote married his daughter who then gave birth to humanity. In a later version the exiled children became the Pit Indians of Northern California, the Bannocks in Idaho, and the Owens Valley Paiutes.[22]

Concerning the birth of death, Coyote and Wolf were arguing. Wolf laid down the rule that the human being must have two deaths. Coyote said, "No, there ought to be only one death so that when a man dies he shall stay dead and, if he is your brother or cousin, you can marry his wife." This is the reason there is only one death.[23] In mourning the death of a loved one contemporary practice includes the "Cry Dance" and burning the possessions of the deceased whose name is not uttered by those who knew him or her.[24]

As for resurrection, in one story Isha the hero Wolf was killed in battle only to be brought back to life by his brother Itsa the Coyote who had retrieved his dead brother's scalp from the enemy and brought it home where Isha once again reappeared.[25] Another ceremonial dance that assures subsistence and life to the participants is the "Round Dance," a dance that was performed during fishing season, before the pine-nut harvest, and prior to the fall rabbit drives. This is the dance that Wovoka urged his "Ghost Dance" followers to perform so as to resurrect an indigenous heaven.[26]

Like their Bannock and Shoshone cousins, the aboriginal history of the Paiutes is very incomplete. Because of their linguistic affinity, they may have had a similar past, including thousands of years in the deserts of the Great Basin, or shared a history of a rapid expansion from Death Valley to the Great Plains. It is believed that Southern Paiutes moved into the southwestern region of what is now the United States around 1000 C.E. It is known that Northern Paiute speakers from eastern Oregon had contact with Numic speakers near the Snake River in the early 1700s, and it was this contact that introduced them to horse transportation.[27]

Although direct contact with Europeans was rare for the Northern Paiutes, Southern Paiutes encountered the Catholic Padres Silvestre Vélez de Escalante and Francisco Domínguez in 1776 when the fathers were seeking to find an overland route from New Mexico to California. Later the arrival of Spanish, Mexican, and American explorers facilitated the slave trade that brought new suffering to the Southern Paiutes. Navajo and Ute Indians exchanged their Paiute slaves for horses, guns, and ammunition from New Mexican and American traders.

Once they adopted horse culture, Northern Paiutes developed mounted "bands" that, in conjunction with their Northern Shoshone cousins, traveled beyond the Rocky Mountains to the Plains in search of buffalo. But even in the early nineteenth century most Paiute groups were seemingly without horses if the testimony of Meriwether Lewis and William Clark or Hudson's Bay trapper Peter Skene Ogden can be trusted. Throughout the 1830s historical documents seem to indicate that most Northern Paiutes were carrying on a traditional subsistence culture without the aid of horses or firearms.[28]

The period of expansion of the use of the horse and the rise of raiding parties in the 1850s coincided with the discovery of gold at Sutter's Fort and the establishment of the California Trail that channeled emigrants through the heartland of Nevada's Paiute population. This mass migration impacted the subsistence patterns of the natives, with seed plants, fuel sources, water holes, and large game being virtually eliminated on both sides of the trail.[29]

By 1859 gold and silver had been discovered in the Virginia Range in western Nevada. The Comstock Lode not only produced a mass of silver and gold that created millions of dollars for their San Francisco owners, but led to the founding of the twin mining towns of Virginia City and Gold Hill and the arrival of hundreds of settlers who were involved in mining and ranching.[30] At around the same time Mormons arriving from northern Utah began settling the best lands of the Southern Paiutes, founding Las Vegas in 1857 and Saint George in 1861. Meanwhile, intent on establishing an outpost of faith in the San Bernardino area, Mormon miners discovered gold and silver in the mid- and late-1850s in the Amargosa Valley and Panamint Mountains at the southern edge of Owens Valley.[31]

In 1861 cattlemen from the San Joaquin Valley and the Tejon country of southern California started driving their herds through Walker Pass and Owens Valley to the booming markets of the new mining centers in Nevada. Eventually, they established permanent ranches in Owens Valley and the grazing of their cattle destroyed the native plants that were an essential part of the Paiute diet. Rather than face starvation, the Paiutes began to prey on the ranchers' cattle, and hostilities between Indians and whites started.[32] The era of confrontation had begun.

Pathway to Oblivion

Concerning Anglo-American activity, the Owens Valley story begins (like most narratives of the mid-nineteenth century West), with the discovery of gold in northern California in 1848 and the migration of argonauts to the gold fields that next year. After California obtained statehood and territories created for Utah and New Mexico in 1850, the West was divided into five military departments with fewer than 13,000 troops to garrison a frontier of more than a million square miles. Militia and local volunteers were necessary to support the national military effort. After Fort Sumter fell in 1861, most of the public believed that federal troops should protect the Pacific coast and that the Indian conflicts of the western interior should be a secondary priority. Just as the pre-Civil War period saw gold seekers moving from California to the mining fields of the West and Southwest, so too did a California Indian policy move eastward from the Pacific coast to the interior mountains and deserts of the Greater Southwest.

During the second season of gold mining, the summer of 1849, prospectors started spreading throughout the Sierra Nevada Range. Those that went south from the Sacramento and American Rivers usually stopped off at Stockton for supplies and equipment. Before long Stockton had become an important trading center. Argonauts from Stockton might travel 110 miles to the diggings on the Stanislaus River, or travel another 50 miles to the Merced River. Another 20 miles would take them to the Mariposa stream. If the adventurer went up the Merced he could look for gold in Yosemite. After all, no less a person than John C. Fremont had found gold at his Mariposa ranch, and if placer mining could be successful at Mariposa, the "mother vein" might be in the mountains of Yosemite.

The more daring of souls could hike 366 miles all the way up the San Joaquin River to what is known today as the John Meir Wilderness Area south of Yosemite. In one year, 1849, the San Joaquin Valley increased by more than 80,000 individuals. The old 1820 *El Camino Viejo* road, that connected the Los Angeles Basin with San Francisco along the west side of the San Joaquin Valley, would be used by prospectors, merchants, and settlers alike. All of this was not good news for the indigenous population.

Generally speaking, where prospectors go ranchers and farmers will follow, along with merchants and bankers. The only real problem was that Indians always seemed to be using the best lands. Ergo, white Americans had to resolve the problem by removing the Indian, either through the actions of miners' militias, vigilante groups, citizen posses, or federal troops. Enter the protagonist of the Mariposa Indian War, 1851–1853, a wild white fellow with at least five Indian wives known, ironically enough for an Indian fighter, as James D. Savage.[33]

Although at first Savage was doing the tedious work of panning for gold on the Merced River, by 1850 he quickly abandoned that activity by setting up a trading post outside of Mariposa followed by another on the Fresno River. When an Indian raid destroyed his Fresno operation, the governor quickly authorized Savage "Major" of the "Mariposa Battalion," comprised of three companies of volunteers. A few "Yosemites" (Awanis or Ahwahnees) were killed, some were taken hostage, and Teneiya (or Tenaya), headman of the Awanis, was captured. Overall, the Mariposa Battalion had mostly succeeded in being the most likely first group of white men to camp in Yosemite.[34]

The final episode came in 1853 after two miners were killed by Indians in Yosemite. The volunteers forced Teneiya and his followers to flee Yosemite to the safety of the Mono Indians at the northern end of Owens Valley. That expedition failed too, but in pursuing the old chief the volunteers had opened up a new route to Owens Valley via Tuolumne Meadows and Mono Pass. And, more importantly, Yosemite was safe for mining.[35]

That next year, at the urging of Edward Fitzgerald Beale, Superintendent of Indian Affairs in California, the US established an outpost at Fort Tejon in California. It was located in the southwestern corner of the San Joaquin Valley in the Tejon Canyon (known as Grapevine Canyon; *La Cañada de las Uvas*) between the Tehachapi Mountains and the Los Angeles Basin to the south and the Mojave Desert to the southeast. A year earlier, in September 1853, Beale had established the Sebastian Indian Reservation 25 miles away from the Fort Tejon site, and by the time of the founding of the Fort over 2,500 Indians, mostly Chumash (the original inhabitants of Tejon Canyon), were living there. Fort Tejon itself was launched to protect travelers along *El Camino Real Viejo* as well as settlers from attack by discontented *Californios* and angry Paiutes and Mojaves. The army was also to protect reservation Indians from their white attackers.[36]

One of the first contacts between the Owens Valley and Fort Tejon came in August 1858 when a delegation of Paiutes visited the Sebastian Indian Reservation. As the Indian Agent J. R. Vineyard reported, "The people of that region [Owens Lake], so far as I can learn, number about 1500. The delegation asked assistance to put in crops next season, also someone to instruct them in agriculture, etc .... I gave them presents of clothing and useful implements, and sent them back to their people, with the promise of transmitting their request to the great chief [President Buchanan?]."[37] The promise evidently was not enough to preserve the peace as violence continued the next year, perhaps augmented in part by the participation of fugitive Indians from the Tule River who supposedly joined their Paiute cousins in the Owens Valley.

Apparently, the loss of stock in the Santa Clara and San Fernando Valleys was large enough that, for unknown reasons, it was believed that the Paiutes and California refugees at Owens Lake were responsible. In any case, the horse thieving in southern California was significant enough that Captain John "Blackjack" Davidson wrote to his commanding officer on May 1, 1859, that "... I have ascertained conclusively that these marauding Indians are from Owen's [sic] Lake, about 200 miles above here, on the eastern slope of the Sierra Nevada, and I most respectfully recommend an expedition against them into their homes." The Post Adjutant at Fort Tejon agreed with him and Davidson soon after led a punitive expedition which was sent out from Fort Tejon to Owens Valley on July 21 of that year.[38]

Davidson's troops left Fort Tejon and traveled along the south fork of the Kern River through Walker Pass to Owens Lake. From there he journeyed north along the Owens River as far as Owens Gorge. From there he backtracked to Fort Tejon. The entire trip was more than 600 miles (see Figure 2.4).

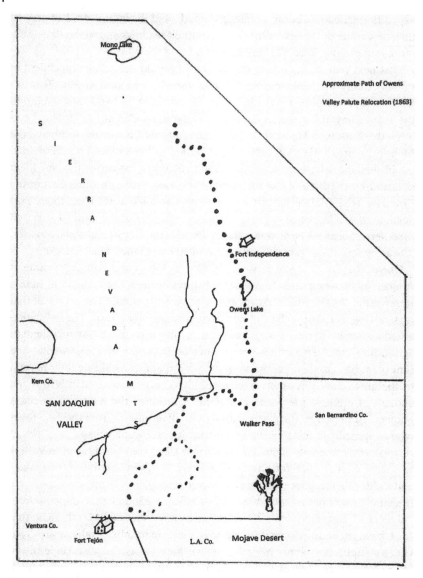

Figure 2.4 *Route of Davidson Expedition (1859) Likely Followed by Owen's Valley Paiutes in the Relocation of 1863.* Reconfigured by Geraldine Raat from information found in Philip J. Wilkie and Harry W. Lawton, eds., *The Expedition of Capt. J. W. Davidson from Fort Tejon to the Owens Valley in 1859*, published in 1926 (Socorro, N.M.: Ballena Press).

Davidson did not find any pilfered horses, so his venture was a failure in terms of recovering stolen property. Instead, he spent his time studying the land and its people. His glowing report described a peaceful people ("an inoffensive, gentle race")[39] living in a Valley characterized by mild climate, fertile soil, and abundant water. He even proposed that the government set aside a major portion of the Valley as an Indian reservation. His favorable report probably facilitated the overrunning of the Valley by miners and settlers within a few years, which, in turn, led to clashes with the native population, and then, the establishment of Camp Independence in 1862.[40]

In the same month that Davidson left for Owens Valley a Dogtown prospector discovered large quantities of gold in Mono Gulch, the same site where Jedediah Smith had found gold 30 years before. Within a few months the first township on the eastern side of the Sierra was established. By 1860 the town of Monoville, California (immediately north of Mono Lake), was the largest settlement between Salt Lake and the Sierra Nevada Mountains, peaking at about 700 residents and 22 liquor shops in that year.[41] Soon after the town of Aurora in far western Nevada was founded, with a population of 1,400 in April 1861, which would grow to over 6,000 people by 1864. With a majority of males as its base population, the most popular forms of entertainment were Chinese brothels, female prostitutes, gambling houses, badger fights, and violence.[42]

Owens Valley became the thoroughfare for travel to Aurora and other camps. As the Los Angeles *Star* noted: "Within 60 or 80 miles of Owens Lake there is an immigration of about 50 huge wagons going to Aurora, loaded with valuable goods and machinery, which can reach their destination by no other route than Owens Valley; besides which there are on the road a great many thousand head of cattle, sheep and hogs for above destination." Eventually, a new road was built that connected Aurora to San Francisco through Carson City, allowing Aurora to receive supplies from San Francisco that added to its growth. When the area was mined out the town was deserted after 1870.[43]

The winter of 1861–1862 was the spark that ignited the Owens Valley Indian War of 1862–1863. The weather was cold and wet. Sacramento reported a rainfall of over 15 inches for the month of January. Owens Valley residents said that the mountains were filled with snow, while the hills were soaked, and most of the streams became impassable. The whites could only subsist on their beef, while the extreme weather had driven off most of the game the Paiutes needed for survival. Collecting and foraging of plants became impossible.[44]

So it was that the herds of the white settlers became the only means of preventing starvation. As the native population gathered food from the ranges and ranches of the whites, violence against the Indian started. In retaliation cabins were burned and lone prospectors were killed by the Paiutes. In the spring of 1862 the settlers raided an Indian camp north of Owens Lake, resulting in 11 poorly armed Indians being killed and their dried meat destroyed. Before the war was over at least 60 whites and 250 Indians were dead. While most of the Owens Valley Paiutes sought peace in early 1861, Joaquin Jim, the leader of the southern Mono Paiutes, went on the warpath. He kept up his attacks on ranchers, miners, and the cavalry until 1864 and was never captured.[45]

Because the violence ebbed and flowed throughout 1862 and the spring of 1863, volunteer troops were sent from California to the Valley. Colonel James Henry Carleton, commander of the District of Southern California, in March 1862 ordered a calvary unit of volunteers under the command of Lt. Colonel George S. Evans to the "Owen's Lake Valley," acknowledging that the recent violence may be due to the action of the settlers and that "It is very possible ... that the whites are to blame."[46] A month later Carleton was promoted to Brigadier General of volunteers during a march to Arizona to face Confederates and Indians (see Chapter 4).

The conflict did not end until the arrival of Captain Moses McLaughlin at Camp Independence who came from Fort Tejon in April 1863. Following the trail of the Davidson expedition of 1859, the not-so-biblical Moses stopped first at an Indian camp upon the Kern River about 10 miles from Keysville.

There he lined up 35 male Indians and had them either shot or sabered. While ordinarily this kind of wholesale slaughter would not have been approved by the officers of the Department of the Army of the Pacific, as one writer has noted, "no doubt, they were tired of the continual petitions from settlers and the constant rumors of Indian outbreaks and depredations. The problems of the war between the North and the South weighed too heavily upon them to worry about the cold-blooded murder of 35 Indians."[47] With the Indian wars of the West siphoning off too many soldiers who were needed by the Union Army, perhaps the commanders believed the harsh measures were necessary.

Upon arriving at Camp Independence McLaughlin inaugurated a new policy of shooting on sight and showing no mercy. This was an innovation as the army before then had tried to protect the rights and interests of both whites and Paiutes. He also changed tactics. Instead of chasing the enemy up canyons only to be ambushed, he sent his troops up the mountains at night and at daylight would drive the Indians toward the valley where another detachment awaited. Scouts were also sent after smaller bands, searching out the tule swamps along the river and destroying everything in their way—including people. Using a scorched earth policy, which included rape and murder, the army adopted the tactic of destroying cached food supplies of the Numu. During the month of May 1863 the volunteers destroyed 300 bushels of seeds near Bishop Creek, and kept no record of the number of Indians killed or wounded. With very little food available, and their women and children starving, the Indian men soon surrendered. By June 1863, after at least 331 Indians had been killed in the previous months, over 400 of Captain George's Paiutes laid down their arms and came into Camp Independence. Throughout early July of 1863 the dejected bands of Captain Dick and Tinemaha also surrendered.[48]

With the arrival of nearly 1,000 Paiutes at Camp Independence a new set of logistical problems presented themselves. The army did not have enough rations to feed that many Indians as well as themselves. If they turned them loose the conflict between whites and Indians would be repeated. And, as for the whites of Owens Valley, they did not want the Numu in "their" valley and would certainly not leave them alone. It was obvious something had to be done as the volunteers had not planned or prepared for such a large aggregate of Indians. Finding a location outside of the Valley would not be easy as white adventurers and settlers were moving into all the good western lands. A reservation on infertile and rocky land that the whites did not want would be the usual and only solution. Fort Tejon, with its adjacent San Sebastian Reservation, would have to be reoccupied and become the target of the Owens Valley Paiute removal policy.[49]

On July 10 Captain McLaughlin had the Paiutes gather on the parade grounds of Camp Independence. With the assistance of his translator, José Chico (the same man who was personally involved in aiding the volunteers in the Keysville Massacre), McLaughlin counted the Numu and found them to number 998. Then, with the unarmed Paiutes surrounded by a volunteer force that formed a "wall of firearms," and again with Chico's assistance, the Numu were informed of the plans for their removal from the Valley. Escape was not an option as the chiefs and sub-chiefs would be the first to be shot.[50]

On the mid-morning of the next day they started their trek. The elderly, pregnant women, and children had the privilege of riding in wagons while the others, weak and dispirited, would be driven like cattle by the 70 or more cavalry soldiers plus 22 men of the Fourth California Infantry. Captain George, the headman and nominal leader of the Camp Independence Numu, rode his horse as dignified as circumstances permitted. Suffering would be great for all of them, especially the very old and very young. Many died from lack of food and water, and the trail between Owens Lake and Walker's Pass was particularly difficult. After a trip of nearly two weeks and about 225 miles, the prisoners arrived at Sebastian Reservation outside of Fort Tejon on July 22. Of the 998 captives who started the voyage, only 850 arrived—148 Paiutes had either died or escaped from the Moses of the Wilderness (see map, Figure 2.4).[51]

Again, getting the Indians to Fort Tejon and San Sebastian was more important than what should be done with them after they arrived. The army now considered them to be the problem of the Department of Indian Affairs, while the Indian Service did not have the resources to care for their charges. Starvation and hunger took many of them, while measles and other diseases took others, especially the infants. Perhaps as many as 370 Paiutes managed to escape back to Owens Valley. Captain John Schmidt reported on January 26, 1864, that a remnant of 380 Indians (two-thirds of whom were women and children) "are under no one's charge, no one to care for them, they must look out for themselves."[52] Some were transferred to the Tule River Farms when Fort Tejon was abandoned.[53] Most went into oblivion. Those that returned found the northern Owens Valley in a constant state of chaos due to the actions of Joaquin Jim's warriors.

Yet, the writing was on the wall, and the returning Paiutes soon learned that their era was over as miners and settlers arrived by the thousands with no intention of honoring the rights of Indians. Camp Independence was closed in 1863 followed by Fort Tejon in September 1864.[54]

A second "Owens Valley War" lasted from November to January 1865, and began a new wave of genocidal killing that resulted in the deaths of between 64 and 184 Owens Valley Indians.[55] Just as the Paiutes lost their lands to the incoming hordes, so too did the people of Los Angeles Basin eventually steal the water of all of the citizens of Owens Valley—Indian and non-Indian. When the 240-mile Los Angeles Aqueduct was built in 1913, it followed part of the trail taken by the marchers of 1863.[56] Later many contemporary Owens Valley Paiutes followed the aqueduct to Los Angeles. Today the remaining Numu live on three isolated reservations in the Owens Valley.

These Wandering Tartars of the DESERT[57]

In January 1844, when John C. Fremont and his group wandered from Oregon into northwestern Nevada, he came upon a body of water. He noticed a 300 foot rock or tufa formation in the lake. Since the "Pathfinder" was obviously America's Napoleon, the tufa reminded him of the Great Pyramid of Egyptian King Cheops, and therefore he named the inland sea Pyramid Lake. The 100 or so inhabitants already had a name for the lake; it was called Kuyui Pah, named after the tasty black sucker kuyui fish that lived there. The people called themselves the Kuyuidokado, or "kuyui eaters." As for the Great Pyramid rock, it was simply called "*wono*" or basket.[58]

In 1844 the lake was larger than today, measuring 40 miles long and 20 miles wide. As for depth, as writer Bernard Mergen has noted, "you could drop the island of Manhattan ... into Pyramid Lake, and all but the tallest buildings [the Empire State Building is 1,250 feet high] would be covered." Although a bottomless lake to its protectors and admirers, it is probably somewhere between

320 and 335 feet at its deepest point. The source of the lake is the Truckee River, with its headwaters at Lake Tahoe, and since Pyramid Lake has no outlet and evaporates the water is slightly saline (about 17% as salty as ocean water). This water not only supports the kuyui, which spawn in the Truckee River in the spring, but a cutthroat trout that is a species of lake salmon.[59]

Since the life of the indigenous peoples is intimately tied to the environment, it is not surprising that spawning time is fishing time and ceremonial time and prayer time. The lake was cultivated akin to the way suburbanites till their gardens, with tules, cattails, fish, and waterfowl carefully protected and utilized. Pyramid Lake was made a reservation in 1859, but not legally confirmed until 1874 (Walker River Reservation in Nevada was also proposed in 1859 and confirmed in 1874, while the Malheur Reservation in Oregon was established in 1871).[60] The history of the Pyramid Lake people since 1861 and the end of the Pyramid Lake War has been one of protecting the lake and the river that feeds it from squatters and other outside encroachments.

The decade of the 1860s witnessed the murder of close to 300 Northern Paiutes involved in interracial conflicts. Between 1860 and 1866 the Pyramid Lake population was decimated, with 850 individuals either being killed in war, dying from disease, or fleeing their homeland lake for the safety of the mountain country. A population estimated at 1,550 in 1860 was reduced to 700 by 1866. The decline continued so by 1880 they were only 396 Kuyuidokado (by 2010 the census listed 1,330 enrolled members of the Pyramid Lake Reservation).[61]

The immediate background to the Pyramid Lake War began in 1859 when war fever broke out among the white miners and settlers in Carson City and environs. This was partly the result of the starvation winter of 1859–1860 and the continuing flow of gold and silver prospectors to Paiute lands. Prior to these underlying events, however, was the immediate cause of the mysterious death of Peter Lawson in April 1859 near Pyramid Lake. Lawson, a personal friend of Old Winnemucca, was killed by a sharpshooter with a rifle. Indian Agent Frederick Dodge suspected the Mormons, but most of the residents automatically blamed the Indians for any and all violence. Dodge noted that blankets, beef, and whiskey, which Indians would usually take, were left intact at the site of the murder. While the case remained unsolved, most of the Carson City inhabitants had no doubt the murder was the result of the Pyramid Lake Indians.[62]

Another event prior to the Lawson incident (sometime between 1857 and 1859) was the murder of two pack train operators, John McMarlin and James Williams, in the high Sierra above Lake Tahoe. Arrows had been carefully placed in the bullet wounds. When the Pyramid Lake leaders were taken to task by their Comstock neighbors, they identified the arrows as Washo. The Washo chieftain was then ordered to bring in the culprits. Three Washo men were brought in to be interrogated, but on their way to prison they broke from their captors and ran. Frontier justice was immediately realized when their captors shot the three dead.[63] Later on, according to the testimony of Sarah Winnemucca, the actual culprits were two white men who were found with the money that had been stolen from McMarlin and Williams. They had planted the arrows so as to redirect the blame toward the Washo Indians.[64] In any case, it was just one more misplaced event that added to the increasing war fever of the Comstock crowd.

The final outrage of a series of transgressions by whites against Indians, including squatting on Paiute lands, stealing fish from Pyramid Lake, hunting and destroying their forests and game, and rape and murder, led to a retaliation known as the Williams Station Massacre of May 7, 1860. In this instance two brothers who ran Williams Station, a combination saloon and general store on the Carson River northeast of Carson City, kidnapped two 12-year old Paiute girls who had been out digging roots for food. They were taken back to Williams Station, held prisoner in a cellar hole, their mouths gagged with rags, and forcibly raped. Just before dark a party of nine Paiutes, including the father and brother of one of the girls, discovered the girls alive in the cellar. In their anger the Numu killed the two brothers and three other men at the station, and then burned the place down.[65] This was the Williams Station Massacre that led to the Pyramid Lake War that started on May 12 of that year.[66]

Within three days news of the "massacre" reached Carson City and Virginia City. The person who had discovered the burnt bodies, a third Williams's brother, anxiously proclaimed that at least 500 Indian warriors were on the warpath.[67] Sarcastically telling the white viewpoint, Sarah Winnemucca said, "The bloodthirsty savages had murdered two innocent, hardworking, industrious, kind-hearted settlers."[68] "Doctor" Henry DeGroot, the Comstock romantic and correspondent, reported that the Virginia City citizens were in agreement that the Paiutes should be punished. Describing the armed force that would be sent against the Indians, he noted, however, a few men "... of ruffian proclivities, who believing that an Indian war would furnish them employment at public expense, and possibly afford opportunities for securing Pah Ute ponies at a cheap rate, did all that lay in their power to promote a scrimmage of this kind."[69]

So a militia of about 750 vigilantes composed of volunteers from Virginia City, Silver City, Carson City, and Genoa was quickly formed with Carson City's most prominent citizen, Major William Ormsby, as their nominal leader, and the troops—rascals and professionals—marched toward Pyramid Lake by way of Williams Station and the Truckee River. Some of the volunteers, unorganized and poorly armed, stupidly followed a small party of Paiutes up a ravine. Once in the ravine a few hundred Paiutes appeared and, closing off any escape routes, proceeded to kill 76 of the 105 members of the vigilante army, including Major Ormsby.[70]

When the remaining volunteers returned to Virginia City from the ambush at Pyramid Lake, they barricaded their houses and gathered their women and children into places of safety. They quickly dispatched couriers to California. In the meantime, Texas Ranger "Colonel" Jack C. Hayes organized his militia. His "Washoe Regiment" consisted of 500 volunteers, and they were soon joined by a detachment of US artillery and infantry from Fort Alcatraz, California. They met up with Numaga and perhaps as many as 600 Paiutes, first south of Pyramid Lake, and later in a skirmish northeast of the lake. Many of the Paiutes scattered, either east across the Great Basin or in the rugged terrain east and north of the lake to the Black Rock and Smoke Creek deserts. Indian sources say as few as four Paiutes were killed, while other "official" military reports claim 160 Paiutes were killed, with only four regiment members killed.[71]

While the casualty numbers were probably not large, the disruption of life at Pyramid Lake was great, especially food gathering activities and fishing. Starvation was the main problem for the remaining Paiutes that had not fled, although the non-Indian position was that the influx of whites who overran the country brought clothing and food that was an improvement on their previous habits of eating mice, ants, and grasshoppers.[72]

The federal forces returned to the Carson River near the site of Williams Station and constructed what became Fort Churchill in 1861. The desert outpost was designed to curtail hostile Paiutes at the Pyramid Lake and Walker River areas, as well as protect the Pony Express and other mail routes.[73] When the "Washoe Regiment" returned to California, and the regulars withdrew to the Carson River, Old Winnemucca's people, mostly peaceful, returned to Pyramid Lake. Other returnees were not so placid and would continue depredations for the next few years. The arrival of new farmers along the Truckee River and near Pyramid Lake only aggravated their situation. Along with the squatters, vigilantes, fishermen and miners, the army at Fort Churchill would now be a permanent feature in the lives of Pyramid Lake Paiutes.

By October 1860, the month when Chief Truckee died in the Pine Nut Mountains southeast of Carson City, the Pyramid Lake War of eastern Nevada was over. But other skirmishes and battles were to continue through 1865. During May 1861 over 1,500 Paiutes assembled at the mouth of the Walker River. They were led by Wahe, who claimed to be spirit chief of all Paiutes and the brother of Old Winnemucca. A spirit chief was a leader who was believed by his followers to be immune to the white man's bullets.

Wahe and others conspired for several months. Their plan was to gain entry to Fort Churchill posing as friends of the white man, and then at a signal they would slaughter the small garrison of about forty men. The planned conspiracy was discovered by the Walker River Indian Agent, and Wahe was forced to flee to Oregon. He died upon his return to Nevada in May 1862.[74]

Other Indian troubles occurred in 1863 when E-zed-wa, chief of the Walker River Indians was killed, along with his horse, by a drunken white man outside of Fort Churchill. His body was later found in the Carson River by members of his band. Several prospectors were killed in Humboldt County in 1864 (although Indian responsibility has never been proven). Two other gold hunters were murdered by Paiutes near Walker Lake in the early months of 1865. In this instance the Indians were taking revenge on people who had recently flogged them. But the most grievous of events took place on March 14, 1865. This is known to history as the Mud Lake massacre.[75]

The killings at Walker Lake led the territorial governor, following the hysteria of Honey Lake residents who called for "exterminating the whole race," to send for the troops. Answering the call, the Fort Churchill commanders sent the young and inexperienced Captain Almond B. Wells, and a contingent of Nevada volunteers, to Mud Lake (known as Lake Winnemucca today), where it was reported that Indian cattle thieves were camped. Unaware of any danger, 30 or more Kuyuidokado were camped east of Pyramid Lake at Mud Lake.

At the site Captain Wells divided his forces into three squads and attacked the Paiute encampment. At least 29 Paiutes were killed (other sources reported 32 Indian dead). Well's report described hand-to-hand combat with no casualties among the volunteers.[76] While the annals of the Civil War called the action a "skirmish," it was reported by the leaders at Fort Churchill as an "Expedition to Pyramid Lake."[77] Only in hindsight has it been named a "massacre."

The Paiute perspective of the event, as told by Sarah Winnemucca, differs from the official explanation. Her account was later substantiated by Numaga at a peace conference at Fort Churchill. First, as Numaga reported, with the exception of three or four men in the camp, all the dead were women and children. The cattle thieves had evidently left before the arrival of Well's volunteers. Some women who tried to escape jumped into the water and were drowned, while others were shot while in the lake. The infants and babies that were still tied up in their baskets were burned alive as the camp was set on fire. At least two of Old Winnemucca's wives were killed, including Sarah Winnemucca's mother, Tuboitony.[78]

Finally, to speculate a bit, many Nevada volunteers had served time in Utah under General Connor's command and were later transferred back to Nevada.[79] It is likely that some of them knew of the Bear River Massacre of 1863 (see Chapter 8) and the follow-up campaign against Chief Pocatello, and were imbued with the kind of hatred that such actions produced. It is little wonder that the young and inexperienced officers with volunteer soldiers would take the cries for extermination literally, and while so doing make a name for themselves. As for Old Winnemucca, he would pursue his own spiritual quest in the

Steens Mountains. After the Mud Lake massacre he, and many of his followers, refused to return to Pyramid Lake.[80]

Throughout the end of the 1860s the Northern Paiutes of Pyramid Lake and western Nevada had several concerns. Violence and conflict with whites was one of them, especially in 1866 after the soldiers shot "everything that wore paint" at Rock Canyon, north of Pyramid Lake and east of the Modoc area, killing 80 Indian men and 35 women.

A more persistent problem was the activity of Indian agents on many of the "de facto" reservations, including the Pyramid Lake Reservation. They often refused to give out rations, engaged in illegal transactions then arrested and sometimes killed the Indians for engaging in illegal acts, refused to educate their children, and most of all, they would not protect the Paiutes from white encroachments. In 1868 measles killed over 100 Pyramid Lake Paiutes while the agent did nothing to aid the sick Indians (similar numbers died at Walker Lake due to typhoid fever and consumption). By mid-summer hatred of the Indian agent led many citizens of Pyramid Lake to abandon the Paiute reservation and wander to other areas, including Camp McDermit in northern Nevada immediately south of today's Oregon border. In July Old Winnenucca and 490 Paiutes came into Camp McDermit, and by the end of the year there were more than 800 Paiutes that were allocated food. There hopefully they could join the Quin River Paiutes and some Bannocks, and find a sanctuary from reservation agents at a military installation where the army would issue rations to them.[81] Yet many Paiutes, especially women, still worried about living too close to the white man.

One concern, strange to say, was cannibalism. Most whites suspected that the savages were cannibals, but in this case it was the Paiute who was concerned about the cannibalistic whites. As early as the spring of 1847 Captain Truckee and the Paiutes learned of the fate of the Donner Party in which the desperate snowbound group of whites turned to eating themselves as well as their Indian guides. The Paiutes became convinced that the whites not only killed people but ate them.[82]

As a child Sarah Winnemucca's mother, Tuboitony, told her that the whites were killing and eating people. When some whites were spotted her aunt told her mother, "Let us bury our girls [Sarah and her cousin], or we shall all be killed and eaten up."[83] As an adult Sarah remembered that her father, Old Winnemucca, had called the whites "owls," conjuring up the image of the Cannibal Owl, a Paiute boogeyman who, according to ancient tales, carried away misbehaving children and ate them.[84]

The Owens Valley Paiutes knew about Panatübiji', the Indian who experienced the cannibalistic acts of one of the first white men to enter the Valley. The stranger took Panatübij' to the body of a corpse, proceeded to cut off both legs, and returned to the camp near Soldiers' Pass where he brewed up a stew pot. At dark the white man satisfied his hunger by eating the human stew. As for his Indian hosts, they refused the stew and left the camp to hide in the caves of the mountains.[85] So, as can be seen, in the history of Indian–white relations it was not always clear who was and was not the savage cannibal!

At Camp McDermit another concern for the Paiute women was fear of rape and sexual violence by white men. Molesting Indian women was typical of life around military installations, and Camp McDermit was no exception. Sarah Winnemucca, who spent her entire life fearing rape by white men, got the military commander to declare the Indian camp off limits to both settlers and soldiers.[86]

As a youngster she and her sister were taken to a camp in San Joaquin, California. There, after Truckee had left his grandchildren to go to the mountains, hired hands working for the ferry would assault her sister. In Sarah's words, "The men whom my grandpa called his brothers would come into our camp and ask my mother to give our sister to them. They would come in at night, and we would all scream and cry; but that would not stop them."[87] Captain Truckee was unaware that in California Indian women were often seized and forced to serve as concubines.[88] Later on a major cause of the Bannock War of 1878 was the rape of a Bannock girl who had been out digging for roots (similar to the catalyst of sexual violence involving young girls prior to the Pyramid Lake War).[89]

In the late 1860s, the Paiutes at Camp McDermit were encouraged to go north to Fort Harney in south-central Oregon (McDermit would become a reservation in 1889 with some Paiutes receiving allotments a few years later). By this time the wandering Paiutes favored military posts over government reservations, so several Paiutes traveled to Fort Harney. By 1872 the Malheur Reservation, immediately east of Fort Harney, was established by executive order, and now the Paiutes were encouraged by Agent Samuel B. Parrish to settle there. Unlike many other Indian agents, Parrish, although not particularly religious, was a humane man who told the Paiutes that the reservation belonged to them and they would no longer be working for the agent. Winnemucca and his group, along with Chief Egan (Ehegante) and his followers (Egan was born a Cayuse, adopted as a Paiute, and eventually became leader of an Oregon band), went to Malheur. There by 1875 they had succeeded in digging a two-mile ten-foot-wide irrigation ditch, clearing and planting 120 acres, and building a schoolhouse.[90] It appeared that some of the wanderers had found a home.

Alas, the good life was not to last. First, the fine citizens of Canyon City, a mining town a short distance from the northwestern corner of the reservation, had petitioned the Office of Indian Affairs. Evidently, the governor of Oregon and others asserted that the Paiutes had no claim to the western side of the reservation, and that the Harney Lake basin and nearby meadows should be used by cattlemen and not Indians. Then, in 1876, Parrish was removed ostensibly because he was not a practicing Christian and religious societies, like Mormons and Methodists, were to manage the reservations for the Indian service. Enter practicing Christian William V. Rinehart, an ex-miner and Indian fighter who, unlike Parrish, could not be accused of "soft-heartedness" toward the Indians. Not humane like Parrish, he was a man of violent temper who regarded Indians as the enemy. His major goal was to push the Paiutes out of Malheur and allow the whites to encroach on what was once their newly promised land. After the harvest of 1876 when the deduction of past expenses for rations and clothing left the Numu with very little pay, Egan and the others knew that Rinehart was purposely pushing them out of the Malheur Reservation. Some went to Fort Harney, while others followed Old Winnemucca to the Steens Mountains south of Malheur Lake.[91]

Then in 1878 the Bannock War erupted, lasting from June to August 1878. A combined force of about 500 Bannock, Northern Shoshone, and Paiute warriors fought the US Army and a variety of militia and volunteer groups. The early fighting took place outside of Fort Hall, Idaho, and at Camas Prairie near the Snake River, but the later phases involved the army pursuing Egan and his warriors through the Steens Mountains and Silver Creek area south and west of the Malheur Reservation. Both the Bannock leader Buffalo Horn and the Paiute War Chief Egan were casualties of the war. When the fighting subsided most of the Bannocks returned to Fort Hall. There their connections with other tribal groups were restricted. The Paiutes at the Malheur Reservation were removed to Fort Harney, and from there 543 Bannock and Paiute prisoners of war were sent to internment at the Yakama Indian Reservation north of the Columbia River in Washington. Most of the Paiutes had not participated in the war, but their innocence was not recognized by the federal government. Because of pressure from settlers, the Malheur Reservation was "discontinued" in 1879.[92]

When the first orders were sent out, it was said that all the Paiutes on and off the Malheur Reservation were to gather at Fort Harney so that they could be provisioned and returned to the Malheur Reservation for the coming winter. This included Paiutes still remaining in Camp McDermit and environs, excluding Winnemucca's band. Although the gathering Paiutes were treated well at Fort Harney, their suspicions were heightened when they observed the settlers moving onto the reservation, constructing cabins, and preparing fences for their livestock, without the military taking any action. Then the bad news was delivered—all of the Paiutes assembled at Fort Harney were to be treated as prisoners of war and forcibly marched to the Yakima Reservation in Washington.[93]

On January 6, 1879, the journey to Yakima of 350 miles over mountains and snow began. While the agency at Yakima constructed a shed for 543 prisoners, the exact number of people who marched to Yakima cannot be known with certainty. Winter clothing was inadequate, especially for the women and children. Soldiers dragged the women and children to the wagons, while the men moved slowly through the snowdrifts shackled in chains. The casualties were remarkably light, with at least one old man, one woman who had given birth the day before, and at least four or five infants dying on the trek. They arrived on January 31 after a twenty-five-day trip on their own "Trail of Tears."[94]

As exiles the Yakima Indians would treat them as inferiors, and steal their horses and clothing.[95] In 1883 most of the Numu returned to Nevada on their own, some returning to Pyramid Lake, others to Fort McDermit, and the remainder to the Duck Valley Reservation on the border between southwestern Idaho and north-central Nevada.[96]

After 1889 those who did not receive allotments of land or were dissatisfied with the actions of the Indian agents, strove to solve their problems through other means. Most settled outside the reservations, attaching themselves to ranch families or living in colonies on the outskirts of Nevada cities. Here the women would labor as dishwashers, launderers, or housekeepers, while the men took jobs from chopping wood and doing farm chores to feeding livestock and stacking hay. Others hunted rabbits and squirrels, and took fish and game for sale.[97]

And most of them, on and off the reservation, continued their "pernicious" fandangos that irritated Agent Rinehart for so many years. But now the dance of communion, the traditional Round Dance, would usher in an Indian millennium in which all would be "peace," and "good will" would prevail between men and women of all colors.[98] The new era would be a return to the golden age of the past before their white brothers came to the Sierra. The Round Dance was known to outsiders as the Ghost Dance.

Afterthought: Desert Ghost Dancers

As has been noted, the Civil War years were a period of extreme colonialism and militarism in the history of the Greater Southwest. The Indian response, in the face of white encroachments that threatened their identity by destroying their subsistence economies, shrinking their populations because of warfare and disease, and assimilation programs that amounted to cultural genocide, was to adapt and survive by creating a kind of religious Indian nationalism. For many Indian groups the so-called Ghost Dance movement was a statement of identity and a worldview that continued from the early nineteenth century well into the twentieth century.

It was a pan-Indian, traditional religious belief system as well as a reaction to external conditions that deprived them of their distinctiveness. The Ghost Dance was in the tradition of the Round Dance, a ceremonial activity that would bring about regeneration and growth. This kind of doctrine could be used to develop a sense of Indian pride and social cohesion in the face of overwhelming white dominance, or it could become a message of defiance. In fact, it was both depending on the individual and his/her circumstance. Whether actively hostile to whites or passively accepting white dominance, the movement was a significant expression of Indian identity.[99]

Although the antecedents to the phenomenon of the Ghost Dance reach back to colonial times in US history, it is likely that the inspiration for the 1870 Ghost Dance vision of the Walker Lake Paiute Wodziwob (Grey Hair) was the Prophet Dance, the Dreamer religion of the Wanapum prophet Smohalla. The Prophet Dance movement spread from the Athapascans of British Columbia to the Paiutes in southern Oregon, and its teachings predicted that a great earthquake would eliminate the white man leaving the Indians to enjoy the fruits of the earth. Smohalla, who very likely was influenced by Mormon missionaries, traveled from Washington State to Mexico, Utah, and Nevada in the 1860s a few years before Wodziwob had his mystical trance and vision.[100]

In 1870, when Wodziwob came out of his trance he reported his trip to heaven and said that the spirits of the dead were returning to earth to usher in a "heaven on earth"—an earthly paradise. To understand Wodziwob his shamanism must be taken into account. He was a Paiute magician who could control supernatural forces, and he did this by ventriloquism, hypnosis, and sleight-of-hand tricks. He allegedly had the power to remove foreign bodies from the sick and force out the evil forces possessing a patient's body. And like the shaman-warrior Geronimo, it was claimed that arrows and later bullets would bounce off his body.[101]

There were other precedents for Wodziwob, including the activities of Wazadzzobahago in 1860, who, as head medicine chief of the Mono Lake Paiutes, supposedly was killed and burned only to be resurrected in three days when he arose from the ashes. On that third day a whirlwind came and raised the ashes in the form of a pillar. Mention has already been made of Wahe, the brother of Old Winnemucca, who professed to be a spirit chief and as such was protected from the bullets of his enemies. Wahe, it will be remembered, led the Indian conspiracy against Fort Churchill in 1861.[102] Later on, when the Paiutes were at the Malheur Reservation in 1875, Oytes, the Dreamer chief, planned to kill Agent Parrish, and told his followers that his shamanistic powers were so great that bullets could not touch him.[103]

Thus, dances, ceremonial practices, and religious beliefs similar to the Ghost Dance tradition were well established both before and after Wodziwob's 1870 trance. Wodziwob's disciples spread the doctrine beyond Walker Lake. In the Mason and Smith valleys of Nevada, areas west of Walker Lake on the Walker River, Numa-taivo, the father of Wovoka (Jack Wilson) not only taught the tricks and ideas of shamanism to his son, but carried the Ghost Dance message throughout the area. An equally enthusiastic disciple, Weneyuga, spread the religion to the Washoe people.[104] Others who were some of the first to receive the message were the Modoc people of northeastern California and the Klamath River tribes. From these regions the Ghost Dance of the 1870s went southward through the Monos, the Tule River Indians, the Panamint of Death Valley, the Chemehuevi, and Mojave. All of these were groups that had experienced dislocation and cultural decay for 20 years since California had become a state in 1850.[105]

Although the Ghost Dance has a continuous history from 1870 to 1890, a second great wave would take place after 1889 when Wovoka announced his death and resurrection, and pronounced the coming of an Indian Messiah in 1890, a pronouncement that had believers in both Indian and non-Indian communities. Wovoka told his Mason Valley people that they could chant, do the Ghost Dance, fall into a trance, and visit the land of the dead. If they did as they were instructed, Numina the Messiah, would bring the Indian dead back to life and restore the world to the way it was prior to the white man.[106]

A peculiar coincidence was the date in which Wovoka stated that the Messiah would return. Wovoka's prophecy indicated that the Messiah or Christ would return to the earth to restore America to the Indians in December 1890, the same date that the Mormon prophet Joseph Smith indicated that if he lived to be 85 he would see the face of Christ. Smith, born on December 23, 1805, although dead for many years would have been 85 on his birthday of December 23, 1890.[107] The rumor of Christ's coming was probably passed to Sioux Ghost Dance leaders by Bannock and Shoshone Mormons in Utah and Idaho. Although there is no evidence that Wovoka directly had contact with Mormon missionaries or converts, both Mormons and Paiutes shared many of the same ideals and practices.[108]

Mormons believed, as did many Paiutes, that God's curse on the American Indian was to give them a dark skin. In the Mormon Sunday School the doctrine that God's curse on the Indian (called descendants of Laman or Lamanites) took the form of an invasion by Gentiles (non-Mormons) who would conquer the Indian, but that the curse would eventually be lifted and the Lamanites would become "white and delightsome." The curse would be lifted with the second coming of Christ, and 1890 was that year for many of those "Latter Day Saints." Another notion that did not come from the Paiutes was the idea of sacred temple garments that the Saints wore that would protect them from evil influences. Although Paiute shamans like Wovoka talked about bullets bouncing off their chest, the power was a supernatural one and not a Ghost Shirt. That idea was likely developed again by Bannock Mormons who passed it on to their Sioux cousins.[109]

Just as the 1870s wave had spread the Ghost Dance ceremonies and doctrines throughout southern Oregon and California, the 1890s wave was spread eastward, first to Fort Hall in Idaho, and from there to the Great Plains, including the Dakotas and Oklahoma. The latter event was precipitated by the coming of the railroad. In 1868 the Central Pacific Railroad, following the Truckee River east from California, reached the Pyramid Lake Reservation town of Wadsworth. It eventually joined the Union Pacific near Ogden, Utah, creating a transcontinental link across the plains. By the 1890s Fort Hall was one of the crossroads of the West, a junction of the Oregon Short Line Railroads and the Utah Northern. Numerous parties of indigenous people passed through Fort Hall on their way east or west, and the Bannocks and Shoshones, who were among the first people to visit Wovoka, were anxious to spread the holy word. Ritualistic connections could now be made quickly by rail, and Fort Hall became a center of Ghost Dance activism.[110]

The tragedy of Wounded Knee took place on December 29, 1890. Although some of the warriors wore "bulletproof" shirts—Ghost Shirts—they were mostly for defensive purposes. Ghost Shirts provided some of their wearers with the idea of invulnerability. That idea of being incapable of being hurt or wounded was not new to the Paiutes and their shamans. What was new, and was not part of Wovoka's message and the Paiute way, was the Ghost Shirt.[111] After the 7th Cavalry opened fire more than 150 men, women, and children of the Lakota people lie dead on the ground. Fifty-one others were wounded. Their Lakota leader, Sitting Bull, had been killed earlier.

Wovoka's preaching included the doctrine of non-violence. He had always taught that his followers should engage in agriculture and be hired labor for the white man. After Wounded Knee he eventually silenced his other messages and sought the isolation of his Yerington Indian Colony. But Wovoka had established a religious movement that not only had continued the tradition of Indian resistance, but marked the beginning of a new fight for religious freedom that characterized the early twentieth century, from the Peyote Church to Pentecostalism.[112]

He danced his last dance in Yerington on September 20, 1932. He was 74 and had suffered from poor eyesight and hearing for some time. His wife of 50 years had died the month before. According to his son-in-law he never said that he would literally never die, only that his spirit would go on forever. He was interred in the Paiute cemetery in the town of Schurz, Nevada (see Figure 2.5). At least for this one Numu his wandering was over.

Figure 2.5   *Wovoka.* Schurz, Nevada Paiute Indian Cemetery. Photo by W. Dirk Raat, July, 2018.

Commentary: The Military and the Boarding School

The purpose now is never to relax the application of force with a people that can no more be trusted that you can trust the wolves that run through the mountains. To gather them together little by little onto a Reservation away from the haunts and hills and hiding places of their country and ... teach their children how to read and write: teach them the art of peace: teach them the truth of christianity ... the old Indians will die off and carry with them all latent longings for murdering and robbing: the young ones will take their places without these longings: and thus, little by little, they will become a happy and a contented people.

General James Carleton to General Lorenzo Thomas, Sept. 6, 1863[1]

A great general has said that the only good Indian is a dead one. In a sense, I agree with the sentiment, but only in this: that all the Indian there is in the race should be dead. Kill the Indian in him and save the man.

Captain Richard Henry Pratt (speech in 1892 at Carlisle)[2]

When one Indian boy or girl leaves this school with an education, the 'Indian Problem' will forever be solved for him and his children.
Chancellor Lipincott of University of Kansas at
Haskell Dedication (September 17, 1884)[3]

The next day the torture began. The first thing they did was cut our hair ... . While we were bathing our breechclouts were taken, and we were ordered to put on trousers. We'd lost our hair and we'd lost our clothes; with the two we'd lost our identity as Indians.
Asa Daklugie, Chiricahua Apache, 1886[4]

Your son died quietly, without suffering, like a man. We have dressed him in his good clothes and tomorrow we will bury him the way the white people do.
Captain Richard Henry Pratt, Carlisle, 1880[5]

Boarding schools for Indians have a lengthy history in the United States, dating back to colonial times when seventeenth century Jesuits established missions so as to "civilize an ignorant people and lead them to heaven." In the mid-1600s Harvard College had an Indian school on its campus as did Hanover (later known as Dartmouth College) in the eighteenth century. Prior to the founding of the Carlisle Indian Industrial School in Pennsylvania in 1879, missionaries of various faiths had established religious schools near Indian settlements and on reservations in the Greater Southwest. Most of these were known as day schools.[6]

Carlisle, established by a stern Christian, an ex-army officer and former Indian fighter named Richard Henry Pratt, was the first off-reservation boarding school. It was located in what was previously a military installation— the Carlisle Barracks that had once been a training center for the US cavalry. Carlisle became the prototype for other off-reservation schools. By 1902 the government had established 25 off-reservation boarding schools, including a dozen institutions in sites in Oregon, New Mexico, Nevada, Arizona, Colorado, California, and Montana. The Santa Fe Indian School, established in 1890, served mostly students from Southwestern tribes, as did the Phoenix, Arizona, and Riverside, California schools. By the beginning of the twentieth century nearly 18,000 students out of 21,568 were enrolled in either reservation or off-reservation boarding schools.[7]

By the early 1870s the fighting that characterized Indian–white relations had subsided, and reformers began to argue that the cost in lives and property was not worth the military effort. Grant's peace policy called for non-violent coercion by Protestant missionaries who would direct affairs on newly established reservations. These agents would both convert their charges to Christianity while teaching them the value of farming and other rural tasks. By accepting the reservation solution the federal government in effect recognized the Indians as wards of the state—the American form of colonialism.

Yet by the late 1870s the failures of reservation life, characterized by bribery and dishonesty by those who were charged with implementing the Indian policy, and by a ration system that was both inadequate and yet fostered dependency on hand-outs by an impoverished Indian people, led to new reform movement. It was in this context that the off-reservation solution was posed by Pratt and others. If overt military actions and segregation on reservations were not transforming the Indian to a civilized person, perhaps education should be tried. Education might finally detribalize Indian youths, convert them to Christianity, and provide them with the gift of the white man's civilization.[8]

Education would not only include as it aims Christianization and citizenship training, but also would incorporate the rudiments of academics such as the ability to read, write, and speak English, as well as facilitate individualization by developing a work ethic that promoted the ideal of self-reliance as well as respect for private property.[9] Education would produce assimilation, and this would result in a new American who no longer would speak his or her tribal language, avoid "pagan" thoughts and rituals, and would leave behind any notions of community and communal values. And it should be an educational process that would not be thwarted by angry parents and traditional forces on the reservation.

One solution was to distance the school children from their family and tribe. Not only did the federal officials believe that the children should be separated from their "tribal" and "savage" ways so as to become "civilized," but by separating them from their families they could be used as hostages to insure proper behavior by their parents back at the reservation. This type of education would be a different kind of relocation policy, a sort of education that would assimilate and integrate the Indian into American society. It would be a form of cultural genocide, or as one writer called it, "education for extinction."[10] And the model for organizing an off-reservation school like Carlisle would be a military one, and Richard Henry Pratt would become its first officer and teacher.

Having served in the military for the Union cause during the Civil War, Pratt, when the war was over, retired from the army to manage a hardware store in Logansport, Indiana. Pratt, finding himself temperamentally ill-suited for the hardware business, joined the regular army in 1867 and was commissioned a second lieutenant in the Tenth Cavalry, an all-"Negro" unit that had Cherokee scouts attached to it.[11] For eight years, from 1867 to 1875, Pratt spent much of his time in what would become Fort Sill in the heart of Comanche and Kiowa country fighting plains Indians. When the Red River War of 1874 was concluded, he was ordered to escort 73 prisoners of war—Cheyenne, Kiowa, Comanche, and Arapahoe—to Fort Leavenworth. On May 11, 1875 he was further ordered to transport the prisoners to the old Spanish fortress of Fort Marion in St. Augustine, Florida.[12]

It was at Fort Marion that Pratt became more of a teacher than a jailer. He decided that he would rehabilitate his prisoners and received permission to teach his captives vocational skills that would hopefully lead them to become useful citizens. He cleaned them up and gave them military uniforms to wear. The Indians were instructed on pressing their trousers and shining their boots. He instituted daily inspections in which every Indian would stand at attention at their freshly made beds. They received haircuts. For exercise they would drill in army maneuvers and participate in parade marches.[13]

They would also learn to work like white men, especially doing hard labor like stacking lumber or packing crates. Do-gooder matrons from St. Augustine served as volunteer schoolteachers, teaching English and Christian doctrine at the same time. All in all, Fort Marion was turned into a basic training camp that was part school and vocational center, with a catechism curriculum thrown in. The Fort Marion experience was later transferred to the Hampton Institute in Virginia, where 22 prisoners were sent for more schooling.[14] The Fort Marion and Hampton Institute experiences convinced Pratt that he had finally found a solution to the "Indian problem," and his program of eradicating "Indianness" could be permanently installed at Carlisle. In 1879 the secretary of the interior, Carl Schurz, gave Pratt his school. And from Carlisle Pratt's martial philosophy would diffuse outward to other reservation and off-reservation schools.

The first concern was one of physical appearance. Holding true to the gender stereotypes of the age, girls were dressed in heavy Victorian-style dresses, while the boys were issued wool military uniforms. Haircuts for the boys would follow; an activity that was especially traumatic for Apache groups. The federal government produced images of the "before and after" of the children to convince the general public of the good work being done to transform the Indian from a savage to a civilized person (see Figure 2.6). Physical bearing, a new haircut, western clothing—all meant a transformation from the brutal state of a savage to that of a civilized, American Christian. The forces of social evolution would be realized by an educational system that would produce proper-looking students who were a boon to local communities (as well as a source of cheap labor). The photo collections were not only a public relations campaign, but a successful marketing device. In selling the "before and after" images to outsiders, the school was selling itself as well.[15]

Part of the transformation included segregating the children by age and gender into companies for marching in close-order drill every morning. Music programs took the form of marching bands that accompanied the students as they drilled and marched in parades. School plays dramatized stories of the

Figure 2.6 *Before and After.* Tom Torlino (Navajo) arrived at Carlisle Indian School October 21, 1882, at the age of 22 years. After his term was disrupted in 1884, he returned to Carlisle in 1885. Credit: Cumberland County Historical Society, Carlisle, PA.

saga of Hiawatha or George Washington and the cherry tree in order to instill within them the new American mythology. Native dances were allowed, as long as they were performed on patriotic holidays or celebratory occasions—such as the Fourth of July or Thanksgiving.[16]

One poster at Carlisle encouraged male students to participate in sports, seemingly for purposes of exercise but more likely to instill military discipline. The sign urged them to "become a football player or boxer," and "learn to play a sport and become controlled and civilized." Appealing to the *machismo* of teen-agers, the poster instructed them to "develop manly aggressiveness so that you can win a trophy." Being macho meant that you can "learn to be strong and not to cry or show emotion." Finally, and this was the clincher, "learn to obey a stern fatherly authority—your coach!"[17]

All of these teaching techniques were codified in 1901 with the publication by the superintendent of Indian schools the *Uniform Course of Study for the Indian Schools of the United States*, a treatise that assumed Indian children were "too dull" to excel intellectually and could only be trained to be shoemakers or sewers of domestic clothing. The goal of the federal government was to create a docile, regimented group of Indians who would follow orders.[18]

Repression came in a variety of ways. If a student spoke his native tongue, or refused to adopt "civilized" English names, he or she would have their mouth washed out with "a bar of yellow soap" or get a "kerosene shampoo" and receive corporal punishment.[19] Homesick children would often become "runaways," either attempting to go home, or more often, finding solitude in the empty spaces that could be found within the educational compound. Some girls even held peyote meetings in their dorm rooms. Again, if discovered these students would be hand delivered to the Guardhouse for punishment, or if a boy, would have to run the "belt line." Sadistic dorm advisers would misuse their authority and inflict cruel punishment on their charges.[20]

As in many other darker phases of life in the American West, rape and sexual abuse at the off-reservation boarding school was a common event. Students were intimidated by sexual predators. One student said that "After a nine-year-old girl was raped in her dormitory bed during the night, we girls would be so scared that we would jump into each other's bed as soon as the lights went out." She continued to note that "When we were older, we girls anguished each time we entered the classroom of a certain male teacher who stalked and molested girls."[21]

When the youngsters were given work assignments outside of the campus it was very likely that they would often have to confront unwanted sexual advances and molestation.[22] While they might learn a useful vocational trade, they would also be a form of cheap labor and sexual and non-sexual entertainment for outsiders.

Another type of repression came from the missionaries and the Indian agents, as well as the teachers at the schools. This was the suppression of native religion and its replacement with Protestant, and sometimes Catholic, creeds. The reservations and schools were aided in this by the Indian Offenses Act of 1883. This bill forbade the practice of traditional rites such as praying with the pipe, as well as ceremonies such as vision quests, sweat lodge rituals, and the sun dance. Intended to civilize the Indians, the act compelled the Indians "to desist from the savage and barbarous practices that are calculated to bring them in savagery."[23] In other words, the assimilation policy of the United States as practiced in the boarding schools was to replace "paganism" with Christian civilization—the solution to the Indian problem.

But the ultimate form of repression was contagious diseases, especially tuberculosis, trachoma, measles, and influenza. The crowded conditions at the boarding schools without disinfectants and where hand towels, drinking cups, schoolbooks, and musical instrument mouthpieces passed freely among school children presented particular problems. As the Commissioner of Indian Affairs noted in 1916, after observing the brutal fact that Indian children in the boarding schools were being ravaged by disease, "We can not solve the Indian problem without Indians."[24] Cemeteries at Carlisle and elsewhere testified to the sorrowful outcomes for many at the boarding schools. As Lawrence Webster, a Suquamish student at Tulalip Indian School in Puget Sound said in 1908, "Death was the only way you could get home ... . It had to be a sickness or death before they'd let you out of there very long."[25]

In the final analysis assimilation at best was incomplete. Some scholars would prefer the word "integration" to "assimilation" in that, certain cultural traits of the majority culture, e.g., English language or the sport of football, were added to the traditional characteristics of the minority or Indian culture.[26] In seeking out their "private" spaces, many students spoke their native language and participated in tribal rituals, dances, and ceremonies. Sometimes these activities were disguised from the authorities by being performed at times that were American holidays or memorial occasions. If a student were thinking of his or her family or a traditional tribal event his or her thoughts would be formed in the native languages. Likewise, if the idea was part and parcel of the majority culture the speech would be in English.

Recent studies of the boarding school experience have demonstrated that in the early twentieth century Hopi students at the Sherman Institute in Riverside, California "turned the power" so as to create vocational and cultural opportunities for themselves from programs originally designed to destroy their identity. Through these ways the vanishing Indian refused to vanish, and by 1928 the Boarding School philosophy had changed to face the new realities of a people with a culture that would not die. Teachers such as Dorothy Dunn at the Santa Fe Indian School began to promote indigenous art, and the off-reservation Indian boarding school system eventually witnessed their students "turn the power" to make the schools work for themselves and their communities.[27]

By way of conclusion a final case study should be examined. This is the example of Sarah Winnemucca (Thocmetony) and her attempts at Indian education. After having served as a teacher at the Pyramid Lake Indian Reservation outsides of Reno, Nevada, Sarah in the spring of 1885 began to think about establishing her own Indian school. Her "model school" was initially supported with finances from Elizabeth Palmer Peabody, the Boston philanthropist who was a pioneer in the kindergarten movement. With financial help from Peabody and land available on her brother Natches's ranch in Lovelock, east of Pyramid Lake and southwest of the current city of Winnemucca, Sarah established her school for "all the Paiute children in the neighborhood." By the summer of 1886 her school, called the "Peabody Institute," was flourishing.[28]

The major difference between Sarah's school and the reservation and off-reservation schools at the time was that it was an institution established by Paiutes for Paiutes. It was not simply a passive receptor of white values and prejudices. For example, the native language was used to learn to speak English, and then the Numic speech aided in learning how to read and write English. Unlike the government schools, students were not whipped for speaking their native tongue. No effort was made to separate the children from their parents. In fact, students were urged to use their language skills, arithmetic, and industrial training to educate their parents. By 1887 over 400 children had applied to Sarah's boarding school. The school appeared to be thriving.[29]

However, by late summer 1886 the "model school" was beginning to encounter financial problems. The charitable contributions from Boston bene-factors started to dry up. Then Natches faced several monetary crises from mortgage costs to dishonest ranch hands.[30]

Before closing her door for the last time in the summer of 1889, Sarah made appeals for financial support from both her Boston friends and the US government. Although the government had created "contract" schools with missionaries on and off the reservation, it was unwilling to fund any school "for Indians run by Indians." The "model school" idea died, and Paiute children would have to wait another 38 years before they could enter the public schools.[31]

After her school closed Sarah eventually went to Henry's Lake in Idaho to live with her younger sister Elma, or as the locals called her, "Pokey." Elma was nick-named "Pokey" because she was married to John Smith, the name of the white man who befriended Pocahontas during the founding of Virginia. The nickname was for some a term of endearment, but for most Idaho whites it was a reminder for Elma of her "Indianness," that is her inferiority. In any case, Sarah, who appeared in good health, suddenly died on October 16, 1891, at the approximate age of 47. Although a common understanding is that she died of tuberculosis, it is more likely she died from stomach poisoning, either accidental or as a result of homicide. If not accidental the likely perpetrator was her sister Elma who apparently was jealous of her older sister. Elma died in 1922. The two were buried in unmarked graves; after all they were only "housekeeper" squaws unworthy of Christian burials (see Figure 2.7).[32]

Figure 2.7 *Unmarked graves of Winnemucca sisters?* No headstones; simply rocks in a circular pattern in foreground.
Photo by W. Dirk Raat, Henry's Lake gravesite, Island Park, Idaho (2019).

3

Great Basin Tribal Politics

Western Shoshones, Southern Paiutes, and Colorado Utes

> *"Let me tell you one goddamn thing. There's no way we're ever letting any of the Indians [Western Shoshones] have title to their lands. If they don't take the money, they'll get nothing."*
>
> Annonymous Interior Department Bureaucrat, 1977[1]

> *"They say they [Southern Paiutes] are afraid of the Utahs [Utes]. It is here proper to remark that the Utah have long been in the habit of stealing the women and children of these Indians and either selling them to the Spaniards or to other tribes; sometimes they were kept as servants. This practice is still continued, and hence their fear of the Utahs, and consequent refusal to settle with them at Uintah."*
>
> Thomas Sale, Indian Agent, Meadow Valley, 1865[2]

At the Treaty concluded at Ruby Valley on October 1, 1863, with the Western Shoshone or *Newe* Indians, the US government recognized the boundaries encompassing the 24.5 million acres of traditional Newe homeland.[3] This region was known as *Newe Segobia* by the Indians and included most of eastern Nevada west of the Great Salt Lake and Lake Utah, as well as parts of southern California. This area ran from Duck Valley in the north to Death Valley in the south (see map, Figure 0.4).[4]

For over 100 years the federal government and white settlers took little interest in the desolate desert lands of Newe territory. Outsiders, like Thos. I. Butler writing in 1865, described the land and the people this way: "The Indians of this section belonged to the Shoshone tribe, an inferior and propertyless people, who were so low in the scale of humanity that they never constructed a house, or wigwam, or anything that could be called by any name indicating a cover, only

Lost Worlds of 1863: Relocation and Removal of American Indians in the Central Rockies and the Greater Southwest, First Edition. W. Dirk Raat.

seeking shelter in storms—which in winter were frequent, and at times severe—behind rocks and in the lee of bushes; subsisting on pine nuts, pine burs, roots, mice, snakes, gophers, rabbits, and game of a similar character."[5] But the limited resources of this land were respected by the Shoshone people who worked hard at finding and keeping water resources, as well as natural vegetation such as badeba, doza, sagebrush, chaparral, and Indian tea. Vegetation, herbal or otherwise, could be used as food and medicine. Even the lowly lizard could heal the mentally ill and arthritis.[6] In any case, the white man did not want this land. That is until the Cold War era beginning in the 1950s brought a new interest in this desolate and unpopulated part of the globe.

Toward the end of World War II the Shoshone people, at least their representatives on the tribal council, hired the Washington-based law firm of Wilkinson, Cragen, and Barker to speak for the tribe's interest in securing title to the 1863 treaty area. When the Temoak faction of the Shoshone nation agreed to a contract approved by the Bureau of Indian Affairs, they received compensation from the Claims Commission. The contract in effect traded land for cash, and guaranteed the non-Indian's interest in Nevada as well as a generous 10% attorney's fee. The process of using the courts to steal the Indian's land had been started.[7] By 1962, the federal government (which today owns about 90% of Nevada), through the Indian Claims Commission, determined that Shoshone's title was extinguished by prior acts of white encroachment.

More importantly, federal usurpation of Newe land rights has devolved into a practice of converting "uninhabited" territory into a complex of nuclear weapons testing facilities. As recently as 1997 a nuclear device was detonated in Newe Segobia. The Pentagon has made no secret of its desire to establish an MX Missle station there, as well as establishing a nuclear waste dump in the desolated country of Yucca Mountain.[8] All of this began with the Treaty of Ruby Valley signed in 1863, a treaty that was first ignored by the government, and then overturned by that same government. Nevada's Western Shoshones has never received annuities or reservation land that was promised by the Treaty.[9] For the Indians it was simply another chapter in the long history of relocation.

Meanwhile, the first significant encounters with whites by Southern Paiutes came in 1857 when a wagon train of "gentiles" was attacked by a mixed force of a few Paiutes and many Mormon militia members at Mountain Meadows (north of present-day St. George, Utah). The Mormons tried unsuccessfully to blame the massacre that took the lives of everyone over the age of ten on the Paiutes. The Utah Paiutes, like their northern and western cousins, would find that friendship with the Mormons could be a two-edged sword.

During the 1860s Mormon settlers poured into Paiute country (see map, Figure 0.4). St. George was founded in 1861, and the best Paiute fields and water sources were quickly appropriated by Brigham Young's faithful followers. For example, fishing rights in Fish Lake were "sold" to an irrigation company for nine horses and an assortment of other items including sacks of flour and a suit of clothes. This proved to be an exception since most interlopers on Paiute land refused to pay anything for use or ownership. Mormon pioneers rapidly selected the prize tribal homelands for their own settlements. As the Paiutes lost their lands they lost their ability to feed and shelter themselves.[10]

Driven to extreme, several conflicts were initiated between Indian and settler in the 1860s, cumulating in the 1868 Circleville Massacre in which at least 16 Paiutes, including women and children, were killed and had their throats slit after they had surrendered to the Mormon militia. Although the Shivwits Reservations was ostensibly established on the Santa Clara River in 1891, the failure of the Senate to ratify the treaty meant that the Utah Paiutes were regarded as "scattered bands" not eligible for federal assistance. Unwilling to go to the Uintah Reservation where their enemy the Utes had been settled and unable to go to Shivwits, the Paiutes did not move from southern Utah. Instead they relied on Mormon welfare, odd jobs, and begging. They also continued to work in the mines owned by white interlopers, became house servants for white people, or turned into agricultural laborers.[11]

They were a source of cheap labor that aided in developing the economy of southern Utah. This was the indirect method of relocation that was adopted by whites for their Southern Paiute neighbors. As historian Andrés Reséndez notes, like the Spanish missionaries in colonial times, "... the Mormons' quest to redeem Natives by purchasing them was not too different." Both created an underclass. Both were forms of "the other slavery."[12]

As for the Utes, their history is quite unique in the annals of the West. Their traditional homeland included the mountains of western Colorado, northern New Mexico, and southern Utah (see maps, Figures 0.3 and 0.4). Their early history had been characterized by slave-raiding expeditions into Nevada and southern Utah, where Goshute and Paiute women and children would be enslaved and then traded or sold to New Mexican buyers. Their notorious slave trading had left the Southern Paiutes with a tradition of fear and enmity toward them.

Between 1855 and 1868, the major concern of the Colorado Utes was to maintain access to their mountain homelands by avoiding conflict with the whites. With the end of the Mexican War and the coming of the Americans, the Utes and leaders like Ouray were well aware of the change in the balance of power and that the guns, artillery, and soldiers of the Americans contrasted sharply with the limited military resources of the Ute communities. The Utes were more than happy to cooperate with the Anglos, especially in the context of the Civil War.[13]

Unlike their Indian enemies—the Navajos, Cheyenne, and Arapaho—the Utes received political and economic rewards by serving the Union cause. Their rivals faced removal, ethnic cleansing, internment, and dispossession. Their

Union service included fighting alongside "Kit" Carson in removing the Navajos during "The Long Walk," and again in the company of Carson, attacking Comanche, Apache, and Kiowa foes at the Battle of Adobe Walls in west Texas.[14] Both events took place in 1863 and1864. Their service to the Union forces was certain to be rewarded, and the prize appeared to come as early as 1863.

For the Utes, 1863 was a watershed. By October of that year a treaty with the United States guaranteed that the Colorado Mountains would become the reservation homeland of the Utes. Although the treaty process had been initiated by Ouray and others in 1863, the treaty was not ratified until 1868 (again with the assistance of the then-ailing Carson). The treaty of 1868 defined the Ute Reservation as embracing all of western Colorado, while the mining, ranching, and farming lands of the central and eastern portions of Colorado would be available for exploitation. The Ute nation was ecstatic (coincidently, the Navajo Treaty of 1868 that brought an end to "The Long Walk" era was ratified on the same day as the Ute treaty).[15] The Southern Utes, in particular, agreed to the treaty terms by moving to the headwaters of the San Juan and related rivers. This action averted war with the Southern Utes.[16]

Unfortunately, there would be no permanent western reservation for the Northern or White Water Utes. In spite of their service to the Union cause, the wave of dispossession started in 1873. A series of land seizures and legal abrogations diminished the once vast homeland along the western slope. In retaliation this was followed in late September and early October of 1879 with a battle near the agency at Milk River that involved Ute sharpshooters sending a volley of fire into the "buffalo soldiers" (nickname given to African American soldiers by Native Americans) and their commanders. Several federal soldiers were killed or wounded, and most of the army's mules and horses were either slaughtered or stolen.[17]

Eventually, by 1881, Northern Ute bands were paraded at gunpoint and with fixed bayonets across the Colorado and Green Rivers to the Uintah Reservation in northeastern Utah, where they joined other homeless and dejected Utes. The Indian hating that was part of the Sand Creek Massacre in the Colorado of 1864 had not dissipated by 1881.[18] Apparently, the Ute brother-in-arms was to be treated no better than any other western Indian.

The politics of the Great Basin was not too different from any other western domain. As was so often the case, US Indian policy oscillated between assimilation and segregation. Removal from traditional lands and being relocated and segregated on reservations was often rationalized by sympathetic whites as the one way the "vanishing American" could escape extermination and become assimilated into white civilization and Christianity. This was the paternalistic side of Manifest Destiny. But as historian Ronald Holt notes, "Of course one unstated goal of many in government was always the occupation and exploitation of Indian lands."[19]

Part II

The Arizona–Sonoran Experience

4

The Long Walk of the Navajos

Go ahead and kill me, and I will shed my blood on my own land. And my
people will have the land even if I die.
Manuelito (Hastiin Ch'il Hajin), 1860[1]

Try hard to get Manuelito. Have him securely ironed and carefully guarded.
General James Carleton to Major Julius C. Shaw, Cmdg. Fort Wingate,
March 23, 1865[2]

Apaches De Navajú: The Earth Surface People

The history of the Navajo is complicated and to this day incomplete. Standard interpretations of their origins are being questioned by a new generation of historians and by clan connections and oral traditions that suggest an earlier and less simplistic history. Undoubtedly, the single most important occurrence of modern Navajo history surrounds the events of the Long Walk of 1863 and its aftermath, a forced march of several thousand Navajos from northeastern Arizona to central New Mexico to Bosque Redondo beyond the Pecos River. Less well know are the lasting results of that imprisonment at Bosque Redondo, which include an ongoing land dispute between Hopis and Navajos, and the contemporary second Long Walk or relocation of Navajo peoples.

The US Census Bureau reported that as of the year 2000 the Navajo population totaled 298,200 individuals (unofficial estimates in 2005 were 325,000). Many are clustered in reservation towns like Tuba City, Kayenta, or Window Rock, while others live in rural zones such as Toyei or Rough Rock.

Lost Worlds of 1863: Relocation and Removal of American Indians in the Central Rockies and the Greater Southwest, First Edition. W. Dirk Raat.
© 2022 John Wiley & Sons, Inc. Published 2022 by John Wiley & Sons, Inc.

As many as 113,000 Navajos live outside the boundaries of the reservation proper in urban locations like Los Angeles and Phoenix, and in smaller communities like Gallup, New Mexico. The Treaty of 1868, which ended the captivity at Bosque Redondo in New Mexico, created a 3.5 million acre reservation in Northwest New Mexico and Northeastern Arizona. From 1868 to 1934, as the size of the Navajo population grew and their livestock increased, the need for more land led to a series of executive orders that augmented the size of the Navajo Reservation. By the year 2000 the Navajo Land included approximately between 16.2 and 17.3 million acres, or 25,000 square miles, that spanned the states of New Mexico, Arizona, and Utah. For the last 300 years they have been a pastoral people practicing agriculture.[3]

Like most native peoples the Navajo have been known by a variety of names. The Hopis called them *Tavusahs* (head pounders), implying they were a people who killed their enemies by crushing their heads with stones. In the 1860s the Mescalero Apache's term for Navajo was *ndaabixúnde*, literally "White Man's prisoner," referring to the Navajo captivity at Bosque Redondo. Río Grande Tewa speaking Pueblos called them *waén-sáve*, that is "Jemez Apachean" because the Navajo lived close to the Pueblo of Jemez. The first Spanish explorers called all the Southern Athapaskans *Querechos*, that is, "wandering Indians."[4]

By the early seventeenth century the Spaniards started to distinguish the Querechos by region. All of the "wanderers," which today we would call Apachean tribes, were known by the Tewa word *Apachu*, which means "strangers" or "enemies." Those Apachu that lived west of the southern Pueblos were called Apaches de Gila, the Utes in Southern Colorado were known as Apaches de Quinía, and those Querechos west of the Río Grande Pueblos, north of the Keresans and Zuni, and east of the Hopi were called Apaches de Navajó. The English word Navaho comes from the Spanish Navajó, and is derived from the Tewa *navahu*, a compound of *nava*, or field, and *hu*, or wide arroyo or valley, to form a word meaning "a large valley or arroyo in which there are cultivated fields." Those Indians who practiced horticulture south of the San Juan River and had large planted fields were known as Apaches de Navajú, or Navajos. The agrarian practices of the Navajo appeared to distinguish them from other Apache peoples.[5]

Of course the Navajos have a very simple name for themselves: Diné, or the People. When it is used to refer to people other than themselves, Diné can mean the members of a clan, or more generally, all Apacheans or even all "human beings." It is even used sometimes to refer to the gods or other supernatural beings. The present Navajo Nation is called Diné Bikéyah.[6]

The Diné, of course, are descended from the inhabitants of Dinétah, the sacred homeland that witnessed the emergence of their ancestors and the Holy People. It is the area surrounded by the four sacred mountains, with three of those mountains near northwestern New Mexico and the fourth, the San Francisco Mountains, near Flagstaff, Arizona. Dinétah also relates to another name the Navajo give themselves, that of Náhookah Diné, the "Earth Surface People" who emerged from the four underworlds to the surface of the fifth world, the Glittering World.[7]

The Glittering World

The Navajo creation story reveals the value system, world view, and the history of the People. It is also a map of the sacred landscape of Dinétah. This story places great value on peace, contentment, and harmony. The philosophy of life that most often embraces these ideas is *hózhó*, usually translated as beauty. But the term is more inclusive than that and should be thought of as a philosophical and religious goal. The meaning of life is to attain *hózhó*, perfect *hózhó*, and to regain *hózhó* when it is lost through a violation of rules or taboos. Diné author Rex Lee Jim is quoted by Navajo historian Jennifer Denetdale to show the central role of *hózhó* in Navajo life. Jim says, *"Sa'ah naagháí bik'eh hóózn nishlóo naasháa doo,"* translated as "to walk on the path of Beauty and Harmony to Old Age."[8] Navajo ceremonialism is designed to attain and retain *hózhó*–meaning balance, wholeness, togetherness, peace, beauty, health, and harmony (see Figure 4.1, Navajo Cosmogram).

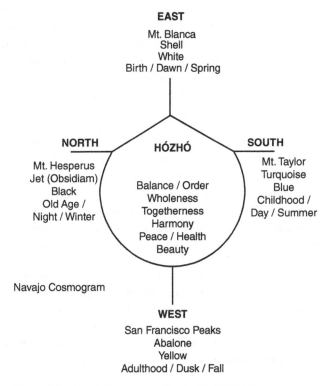

EAST
Mt. Blanca
Shell
White
Birth / Dawn / Spring

NORTH
Mt. Hesperus
Jet (Obsidiam)
Black
Old Age /
Night / Winter

HÓZHÓ
Balance / Order
Wholeness
Togetherness
Harmony
Peace / Health
Beauty

SOUTH
Mt. Taylor
Turquoise
Blue
Childhood /
Day / Summer

Navajo Cosmogram

WEST
San Francisco Peaks
Abalone
Yellow
Adulthood / Dusk / Fall

Figure 4.1 *Navajo Cosmogram.* Created by W. Dirk Raat.

In the creation story that tells how the Navajo came to be, although details may vary from clan to clan, the world was created four times before the present or fifth era. All of the pre-existing worlds were destroyed when disharmony, disorder, chaos, and ugliness (*hóchxóó*) destroyed *hózhó*. As the creatures in these four worlds evolved, from insects, animals and birds, to humans, they took the form of the *Yei*—supernatural forces or spirits. When disharmony destroyed the Fourth World, the humans emerged in the Fifth World, also called Earth Surface World or Glittering World. The journey and emergence of the ancestors of the Diné is understood as a movement from chaos to order, the obtainment of *hózhó*.[9]

The surface of the Glittering World follows the pattern of the quincunx (see Navajo Cosmogram), a design derived from the ideas of cardinality and harmony that is expressed as a five-part arrangement. For cardinality this means a circular movement through four directions to reach a fifth point that completes the rotation. When the movement around the point of axis is finished the process has completed a harmonious whole. The point of emergence (located geographically in the mesas southeast of present-day Farmington, New Mexico) is a cosmological Hogan and locus surrounded by sacred mountains on four sides in which the *Yei* as mountain spirits dwell. This quincunx pattern is a constant theme in Southwestern and Mesoamerican history.

To the East is Mt. Blanca (Dzil Hajin) at over 14,000 feet. It is located about 20 miles east of Alamosa, Colorado, in the south-central part of the state. Associated with this sacred mountain are the color White (birthplace of the sun), the precious shell, and the ideas of birth, dawn, and spring. In the South at over 11,000 feet is Mt. Taylor (Tso'dziil), 15 miles north of Grants, New Mexico (west of Albuquerque). Mt. Taylor symbolizes Blue, turquoise and childhood, daytime, and summer. In the West, near Flagstaff, lies the crater shaped San Francisco Mountains (Dook'o'oshid), where Mt. Humphreys at 12,663 feet is the highest point in Arizona. Connected with Mt. Humphreys is the color Yellow, the abalone shell which is the source for mother-of-pearl, and the notions of adulthood, dusk, and fall. Finally, to the North is Mt. Hesperus (Dibénitsah) at over 13,000 feet. This mountain is about 28 miles northwest of Durango in southwest Colorado. Mt. Hesperus symbolizes Black and the precious metal obsidian (or jet, a compact black coal) as well as ideas of old age, night-time, and winter.[10]

According to the legend, when the humans emerged into the Glittering World, they were instructed by the Holy People to found the first four Navajo clans. The spirit doing the instruction was the greatest of the Navajo *Yei*, Changing Woman, the daughter of First Man and First Woman. When Changing Woman (Asdzáá Nádleehé), who is also known as White Shell Woman,[11] reached womanhood with her first menses the Holy People consecrated her with the Blessingway Ceremony. Today, the Kinaaldá, or Blessingway Ceremony (*Hózhóji*), remains an important event for Diné girls reaching womanhood, as well as the entire community.[12]

Afterwards, Changing Woman was impregnated by the Sun as she lay upon "a flat, bare rock … face up, with her feet to the east and her legs spread comfortably apart. That way she could relax as she observed the sun make its path across the sky. That way it could shine its warmth fully upon her."[13] Her sons, the Twin Heroes (not unlike the Twin Heroes of Maya lore or Apache tales), "Slayer of Enemies" and "Born for Water," must slay the Monsters of the Fourth World in order to make the Fifth World safe for human occupancy. The destruction of the Monsters is another path from chaos to *hózhó*. Today's Enemy Way Ceremony is another ritual that celebrates the activities of the Twin Heroes, as important to men as the Blessingway is to women. More importantly, it is Changing Woman who teaches the Navajo how to avoid the disharmony that destroyed the Fourth World, and how to restore *hózhó* or harmony to the Surface World.[14]

Navajo weaving traditions express these creation story themes and the idea of *hózhó*. While various styles of tapestries and wall hangings reflect these recurring concepts, from Two Grey Hills rugs to Ganado Red and Burnham tapestries, the most obvious example would be the Storm Pattern weavings from the Shiprock area. While many contemporary weavers and collectors are skeptical of the words of trader J.B. Moore which were uttered in 1911, that the central rectangle and four zigzag arms of the Storm pattern rug represent "… one of the really legendary designs embodying a portion of the Navajo mythology,"[15] there is no doubt that the Storm Pattern rug contains motifs and symbols that represents four sacred mountain spirits, cardinal directions, a universal center (a "storm" house or hogan) and other essential aspects of *hózhó*.

So it is that the quincuncial world view of the Navajo contains a belief system in which all the sacred colors, winds, directions, precious shells and stones, life cycles, sunrise and sunset, and seasons must follow the order of the universe to assure harmony and balance. These are the concerns of Navajo ceremonialism as delivered to her people by the Changing Woman. Only *hózhó* can assure togetherness, beauty, and order. It is that middle axis or position. It is the idea of *centering*: *Hózhó* is the critical fifth point or center of the Navajo cosmos.[16]

Ancestral History to the Long Walk, 1863

Until recently it has been supposed by most non-Indian scholars that the Navajo hunters and gatherers arrived in the Southwest from British Columbia sometime prior (maybe 100 years) to the first Spanish contact in 1541,[17] borrowed farming techniques and other cultural artifacts from the Pueblos in the late seventeenth century, and because of Spanish influence were using horses and metal by the eighteenth century. All agreed that the Navajos and their Apache cousins are and were of Athapaskan linguistic stock, and that their ancestors were Athapaskan hunters and gatherers who migrated from British Columbia and the Pacific Coast.

Twenty-first-century linguistics, ethnology, and technology have modified the traditional view. The Anthapaskan ancestors of today's Navajo are descended from the Na-Dene speakers who crossed the Bering Strait between 14,000 and 12,000 years ago (the Haida and Tlingit were of the same stock). They migrated into the New World after the first Amerind group who came before 14,000 years ago and before the Aleut-Eskimo some 10,000 to 11,000 years ago. Eventually, they went both south and west to Kodiak Island and the Pacific Northwest coast. From there they eventually went into the interior and later southward to become the Apachean people.[18]

Historical linguists and climatologists argue that the first migration southward from their original location into central and southern British Columbia and the eastern Canadian Rockies came between CE 300 and 500. This movement coincided with cooler temperatures in the higher latitudes with glaciers advancing in Alaska. The Athapaskans at this time also migrated eastward as far as Hudson Bay. By CE 650 they were along the Pacific Coasts of Oregon and northern California, an area known as Cascadia. A second wave of extended families and bands broke away from the Northern Athapaskans approximately in CE 950, and eventually migrated through and around the Rocky Mountains and the Great Basin to the American Southwest. This group included Western Apaches, Mescalero Apaches, Chiricahua Apaches, and Navajos. A third wave consisted of Jicarilla and Lipan Apaches around 1300, and a fourth group, the Kiowa Apaches, departed about 1500.[19]

When the hunting–fishing–gathering Athapaskan ancestors left the north they brought with them cultural toolboxes that included the sinew-backed bow, projectile points, tailored skin clothing, coiled baskets (no pottery), dogs, and shamanistic religion.[20] Today's Navajo still practice beliefs that were characteristic of the northern Indians, including the customs of mother-in-law avoidance and fear of the dead, including the abandonment of hogans in which someone has died.[21]

They also used conical dwellings that, when in Canada, were made of birch bark, and when on the Plains, of buffalo hide. The southern Athapaskans employed the principle of the forked-pole and made their huts from mud and brush. The original Navajo forked-pole hogan, especially the male lean-to with its elongated entrance, is made very similar to the Athapaskan shelter. The female hogan, which is the center of home life, is constructed with mud, wood, or cement block and is shaped like an igloo.[22]

Using dendrochronology (tree-ring dating) archaeologists have dated hogan-type dwellings of the type used by Navajos at about C.E. 1000 in western Colorado. Proto-Athapaskans were at Promontory Caves in Utah around C.E. 1250, while Navajo home sites south of Gallup, New Mexico, have an approximate date of C.E. 1380.[23] These dates place the ancestral Navajos in the Four Corners area around the time of the Chaco florescence (C.E. 900 to C.E. 1150) and when the cliff dwellings at Mesa Verde and Kayenta were abandoned (between C.E. 1280 and C.E. 1290).

Navajo ceremonial narratives tell of ancestral Navajo hunters trading deer and antelope skins with Anasazi (Anaasází) farmers at Chaco, Aztec, and Antelope Mesa.[24] Navajo oral histories describe Diné–Anasazi relationships based on clan relationships, with perhaps as many as 25% of all Navajo clans related to Pueblos. Some of these are direct associations of Diné to Anasazi, such as the "Towering House People" clan.[25] Today, of course, Pueblos marry Navajos and their children take on matrilineal clan names. This is especially the case for Jemez, Zuni, and Zia peoples.[26]

As historian Raymond Friday Locke says, "It is not unreasonable to presume that the Navajos began arriving in the Southwest ... at least a thousand years ago ... and settled down near the Pueblos and began borrowing from their culture."[27] Therefore, it would appear that Diné culture and society today is a hybrid of northern ancestral Athapaskans, Plains Indians, and Pueblo peoples. Later history would add Spaniards, Mexicans, and Americans to the mix. And that history is a longer and more complicated one than anyone had dared thought before. And while borrowing many cultural artifacts, the People have been very creative in developing a distinctive Navajo Path.

The first historical reference to relatives of the Diné may have been by members of the Francisco Vásquez de Coronado team when they observed proto-Navajo bands on the Plains in 1541. A better description came later from the Antonio de Espejo expedition of 1582–1583 in which Espejo described a semi-sedentary people who planted maize, gathered plants, and went great distances from their *rancherías* to hunt animals. They also traded meat, hides, and salt with the Pueblos. Their extended families were organized into bands under local headmen, and they had both war chiefs and peace chiefs. The only characteristics that distinguished them from their northern cousins were agriculture and political organization. They did share some cultural traits with the Pueblos, especially ceremonial concepts that were similar to those of the Tewas.[28]

The Espejo venture was initially a friendly one between Spaniards and "Querechos," but soon fighting broke out when the Spaniards insisted on retaining Navajo captives obtained from the Hopis. The event is of interest to historians because it reveals that the Indian slave trade was a Pueblo and Hopi endeavor, and not simply characteristic of Spaniards and "wild" tribes.[29]

Slave raiding by Spaniards continued into the seventeenth and throughout the eighteenth century. In 1659 New Mexican Governor Bernardo Lopez de Mendizabal ordered troops into Navajo country in order to acquire women and children as slaves for Sonoran factories, mines, and haciendas. Between 1675 and 1678, Spanish soldiers were joined by Pueblo warriors in slave-raiding expeditions against Navajos. The use of Pueblo auxiliaries by the Spanish in their campaigns against the Navajo continued throughout the eighteenth century, although there was a period of relative peace between New Mexicans and Navajos between 1716 and 1774 when raiding by Utes was a greater problem for both Spaniards and Diné.[30]

One of the more famous campaigns occurred in 1805 when the Antonio de Narbona party (not the Navajo headman Narbona), including Mexican and Zuni scouts, entered the Navajo stronghold of Tséyi' (Canyon de Chelly) and fired hundreds of rounds into what today is known as Massacre Cave in Canyon de Muerte. The military operation resulted in the death of 115 Navajos and 33 female and child captives.[31]

Obviously, the Navajos would retaliate as Navajo counter-raiding increased dramatically between 1800 and 1820. By 1840 the Navajos were involved in constant warfare in New Mexico. A vicious cycle continued so that by 1860 it is estimated that New Mexicans may have held as many as 6,000 Navajo slaves.[32] This trade in captives (and perhaps also the association of European diseases with black magic by the friars) was the major cause of hostilities throughout this entire era.

Although the Navajos, like other Apache groups, assisted the Pueblos in their 1680 revolt against Spanish rule that led to the latter's expulsion from New Mexico, it was not until the return or *reconquista* (reconquest) of the Spaniards in 1692 that Pueblo refugees, fleeing from Spanish tyranny, joined the Navajos in Dinétah near the San Juan Valley in northwestern New Mexico. While many Río Grande Pueblos sought refuge with the Plains Apaches, and some Tewa speakers went to the Hopi mesas, perhaps as many as one-fourth of the Navajo population at the end of the seventeenth century were refugees from Pueblo Villages. Most went northwest to the San Juan Valley and its tributaries, while others, like the Christianized Hopi of Awatovi, fled to the Chinle drainage area outside of Canyon de Chelly.[33]

In any case the Puebloization of the Navajo, which had started long before the reconquest era, reached maturity during the 1692–1770 experience at Dinétah. Pueblitos, small Puebloan-style structures with defensive walls and towers, and in association with hogans, were built at this time. These buildings, useless against the Spanish, could defend their inhabitants from unfriendly Comanche or Ute raiders. Pottery, with typical black and red decoration on a red background, was probably derived from Río Grande styles.

Pictographs and petroglyphs reflected Pueblo religious motifs and beliefs, such as Katsina figures (including the Hunchback deity).[34] Apachean hunter gods were represented as masked dancers, with the Navajo *Yeis* being very similar to Hopi Katsinas.[35]

The offspring of Pueblo–Navajo reunions were integrated into the clan organization of the group, and were recognized as legitimate children of Mother Earth and part of the emergence story. More importantly, the fleeing Pueblos brought their horses, goats, cattle, and sheep (and perhaps the weaving of wool), and introduced new crops like cotton and peaches to the Diné. With the exception of cotton, these were all domesticated animals and crops that the Spaniards had brought to the Pueblos. The introduction of herd animals changed the Navajo hunter society into a pastoral one and provided the economic basis for a major cultural transformation. Navajos would no longer only be hunters and farmers, but shepherds living a transhumant life moving their flocks between winter and summer homes.[36]

The Path to the Long Walk

When Miguel Hidalgo issued his *Grito de Dolores* in 1810, he unleashed what later became known as the Mexican independence movement. This action expelled the Spanish from Mexico by 1821, including the northern frontier of New Mexico. Soon after, the Santa Fe Trail was opened and trade flowed between St. Louis, Missouri, Santa Fe, and Chihuahua City. Commerce with the Anglo-Americans meant that New Mexicans now had access to a better supply of firearms, and for the first time since the Pueblo Revolt the Navajos became a major target as captives for the slave trade. This set off a series of raids by New Mexicans on Navajos that started with the José Antonio Vizcarra campaign of 1823 and lasted until warfare ceased in the 1860s. As the number of attacks increased, the Navajos entered an era of continuous warfare with their New Mexican neighbors.[37]

The return of lost and enslaved people, more so than Navajo challenges to non-Indian claims to land, became the major issue for the Navajos at the frequent treaty negotiations that took place during this time. Hundreds, if not thousands, of Indians were held as slaves in New Mexico territory when Colonel Stephen Kearny arrived in Santa Fe in 1846 at the beginning of the Mexican–American War. After his "liberation" of New Mexico, he declared to the residents of Santa Fe that he had come as a caretaker, not a conqueror, in order "to protect the persons and property [including slaves and servants] of all quiet and peaceable inhabitants ... against their enemies ... the Navajos, and others." This, of course, was not agreeable news to the Navajos and Apaches who had earlier been fighting with their American allies against the Mexicans.

Even after the Civil War was over in 1865, of 148 captives held in Colorado counties, 112 were Navajo. The slave raiders of New Mexico were more than happy to perpetuate warfare with their Navajo neighbors in order to continue their opportunities for raiding.[38]

In addition to the slave trade, other events on the road to the Long Walk included the treachery and barbarism of US forces who murdered the Navajo headman Narbona in 1849. This was followed in 1858 by the murder of the black slave of the Fort Defiance commander, Major Thomas Harbaugh Brooks, by a discontented Navajo. This led to an ultimatum to the Navajos, and the 1860 attack on Fort Defiance by a thousand warriors under the Navajo leaders Manuelito and Barboncito (Hastiin Dagha'). The massacre of Fort Fauntleroy (Fort Wingate) the following year, where innocent Navajo women and children were shot by soldiers, only added to the tension and conflict, a situation that was not improved by the attitude of the commander of the New Mexico Volunteers, General James H. Carleton, who spoke often of his desire to remove the Navajos so their land could be opened up to gold miners and others seeking mineral wealth.[39]

Of all the occurrences mentioned above, the manner of the death of Narbona and the mutilation of his body was perhaps the most significant. In August of 1849, Colonel John Macrae Washington left Santa Fe with an army of over 360—soldiers, volunteers, New Mexican slave raiders, and Pueblo scouts. He was determined to force an end to Navajo depredations on New Mexican settlements. On August 31, Washington met in the Chuska Mountains with a group of Navajos under the leadership of Narbona. At the conclusion of the meeting one of the New Mexican volunteers said that he had spotted a horse that had been stolen from him. Washington demanded its return. The Navajos refused. Disorder and panic broke out, riflemen were ordered to fire, and when the chaos ended Narbona and six other Navajos lay dead. Then the venerated Narbona, a major headman or chief, the man who had sought peace with the Americans, was scalped by a New Mexican volunteer.[40]

Scalping was nothing new in the history of the West. Certainly Native Americans practiced it. Not as well known is the fact that the Mexican government had promoted it as a policy to rid the Southwest of Apaches and other "wild" Indians. Body mutilation was also practiced by a host of Anglo-Americans, from fur trappers to US Army soldiers. In early nineteenth-century America, Tucumseh, the chief of the Shawnee tribe, was killed and his body was flayed and cut into narrow strips. A few years later Andrew Jackson supervised the mutilation of over 800 Creek Indian corpses, cutting off their noses and slicing strips of flesh from their bodies. And, in 1863, soldiers dug up the body of the Apache chief, Mangas Coloradas, cut off his head, boiled it, and sent it to New York. As writer Andrea Smith notes, "The history of mutilation of Indian bodies, both living and dead, makes it clear that Indian people are not entitled to bodily integrity."[41]

Manuelito, who was part of the Navajo delegation and who witnessed the American brutality, was confirmed in his conviction that the Americans could not be trusted. The fact that Narbona's murder was a criminal action that did not lead to an apology or corrective action only led the Navajos to distrust the Americans. Justice was nowhere to be found. It is no wonder that the Navajos soon named the white Americans *Biláagana*, which translates as "those who love to fight."[42]

The Long Walk, 1863-1868

The Fearing Time (Nidahadzid Daa)

The Civil War in the United States brought to the New Mexican stage two characters that would be paramount in the war against the Diné, Brigadier General James Henry Carleton and Colonel Christopher "Kit" Carson. Soon Confederate troops were fighting in the Southwest. Now the federal army had to face the southern troops, and therefore, the policy of providing rations to hungry Navajos came to an end as resources were directed toward winning the war. It also meant that the old mountain man and friend and enemy of the Indians, Kit Carson, would leave his fort to join the army in its northern cause. In the spring of 1862 Carleton and his California Column of Bluecoats would clear the Confederate Graycoats from Arizona and arrive in New Mexico, where he would soon replace General Edward R. S. Canby as commander of New Mexico forces. Meanwhile, with the withdrawal of several Bluecoats (who traveled east to battle the Graycoats), Mescalero Apaches, Navajos, Comanches, Utes, and others were renewing the fight against the New Mexicans.[43]

By the summer of 1862 the Confederates had been driven from New Mexico, but the Indians where still there to fight. Carson, known as "Rope Thrower," who had enlisted to fight the "Johnny Rebs," would become, once again, an "Injun fighter." Carleton, who had known Carson earlier when they both were engaged in fighting the Jicarilla Apaches and who had the most respect for Carson as an Indian fighter, soon petitioned "Kit" to join his campaign. The Mescalero Apaches, and their traditional enemies the Navajos, would be the target.

From Fort Stanton (a hundred or so miles southwest of Fort Sumner) Carleton sent his final instructions to Kit Carson: "All Indian men of that tribe [Mescalero] are to be killed whenever and wherever you can find them. The women and children will not be harmed, but you will take them prisoners, and feed them at Fort Stanton until you receive other instruction about them."[44] Of the less than 1000 Mescaleros scattered in bands along the Sierra Blanca Mountains between the Río Grande and Pecos Rivers and into southwest Texas and northern Mexico, 500 Mescaleros were defeated by Carson's troops and forced to move to a new military post on the Pecos River known as Fort Sumner (Bosque Redondo). Local Commander, Captain John Cremony, sympathetic to the Mescaleros, attempted without success to delimit Carleton's orders.[45] Next the Navajos would get their turn to be forcibly marched to Bosque Redondo.

Although a board of officers had recommended against the site because of alkaline water, a lack of wood, the threat of floods, and fierce winter weather, Carleton's mind was made up. The prisoners would go to Bosque Redondo which would become a model reservation. His own "Fair Carletonia" would be the place where the "wild" Indians would become Christian yeoman farmers and learn to act like peace-loving Pueblos.[46]

On September 6, 1863, Carleton wrote a letter to General Lorenzo Thomas at the Adjutant General's office in Washington, DC. In that message he outlined his personal philosophy about the nature of Navajos, how they would be changed into peaceable Pueblo Indians at his model reservation, and how the old ones would die off and the young would become a new generation of Christianized Americans. In his letter Carleton said: At the Bosque Redondo there is arable land enough for all the

> Indians of this family [Navajos and Apaches] ... and I would respectfully recommend, that now the war is vigorously prosecuted against the Navajoes—that the only peace that can ever be made with them must rest on the basis that they move onto these lands, and like the Pueblos become an agricultural people, and cease to be nomads .... The purpose now is never to relax the application of force with a people that can no more be trusted that you can trust the wolves that run through the mountains. To gather them together little by little onto a Reservation away from the haunts and hills and hiding places of their country and ... teach their children how to read and write: teach them the art of peace: teach them the truths of christianity .... the old Indians will die off and carry with them all latent longings for murdering and robbing: the young ones will take their places without these longings: and thus, little by little, they will become a happy and a contented people.[47]

Carleton not only erroneously characterized a pastoral semi-sedentary people as nomadic and therefore "wild" and uncivilized, but he was mistaken about the "peaceable" qualities of the Pueblo Indians who had a long history of quarreling with each other and their neighbors.[48]

Notice too how Carleton's words speak of the Navajos as wild animals and how they would be tamed by the Bosque Redondo experiment, something akin to the principles of the Boarding School experience of 1879 and after at Carlisle, Pennsylvania and elsewhere. The model reservation, like the boarding schools of a later era, would transform these young savages into civilized young men and women; in other words, "you need to kill the Indian in order to save the Indian." Students of history call this cultural genocide.[49]

Even before his September epistle General Carleton had already rounded up several Navajos and sent them to Bosque Redondo. Having completed his Mescalero campaign, Carleton brought the attention of Carson to the "Navajo problem" and again enlisted his aid. On June 15, 1863, Carleton ordered Carson to attack the Navajo "... until it is considered at these headquarters that they have been effectually punished for their long continued atrocities."[50]

On June 23 Carleton issued a proclamation ordering the Navajos to surrender and turn themselves in by a July 20 deadline. So Kit Carson took the field against the Navajos, assisted, as usual, by Ute scouts who were anxious to be paid in Navajo slaves for their services (a practice Carleton did not approve). Carson headed out with the brutal words of General Carleton ringing in his ears: "Say to them [the Navajos]—go to the Bosque Redondo or we will pursue and destroy you. We will not make peace with you on any other terms ... . This war will be pursued against you if it takes years ... until you cease to exist or move."[51] On July 20 Carson arrived at Fort Canby (Fort Defiance) and military operations started two days later (see Figures 4.2 and 4.3).

Figure 4.2 *The Long Walk.* By artist Elizabeth Manygoats, 2006. Courtesy of Jerry Cowdrey, Sun City West, Arizona. Photo by W. Dirk Raat (2015).

Figure 4.3 *The Long Walk.* Painting (gouache on paper) by artist Narciso Platero Abeyta/Ha So Deh (1982). Courtesy of his son, Tony Abeyta (2020).

Carleton initiated a scorched-earth policy in which the troops destroyed cornfields and peach orchards, burned down hogans, poisoned water holes, and killed animals and the "animal-like" Navajos. Motivated by bounties, the soldiers also stole horses, mules, and sheep—the horses and mules were used as draft animals, while the sheep were a source of wool. Military statistics for 1863 indicate that the Navajo campaign that year resulted in 301 Indians killed, 87 wounded, and 703 captured.[52] The number of captured may be inflated since the Bosque Redondo figures show only 267 prisoners as of the end of December 1863 (or many of the captured may have escaped or died trying).[53]

On January 6, 1864, Carson left Fort Defiance with 375 troops and 14 officers for Canyon de Chelly, the last stronghold and sanctuary of the Navajo. His soldiers would enter the western mouth of the canyon near Chinle, while Captain Albert Pfeiffer would aim for the eastern end.[54] Since Carson knew of the hatred the Utes had for the Navajos, he was more than willing to enlist over a hundred of them for the cause. He was also aided by Mexican, Zuni, and Hopi scouts. Even other Navajos, the Alamo and Cañoncito Bands, called *Diné Anaái* (Enemy Navajos), assisted as informants and guides for the New Mexico Volunteer Army.[55]

Pfeiffer and his men trudged through the heavy snow and battled the cold. He came through the Canyon de Muerte and arrived at the opening a few days after Carson had entered Canyon de Chelly. He had captured a few women and children, and had discovered several frozen corpses. Meanwhile, before Carson arrived at Canyon de Chelly, over 300 Navajos had begun to stockpile food and supplies at the summit of Fortress Rock (*Tséláán*), an anvil of sandstone that measured 800 feet from top to bottom and could only be scaled by toeholds. Carson laid siege to Fortress Rock, camping below it in hopes of starving the beleaguered into submission.[56] Instead, the thirsty and hungry exiles climbed down the rock using "ropes of sash belts and yucca," as the oral histories relate, and then "filled all their water bottles with water at the water hole in the canyon [where several American guards lay sleeping] and brought them back up ... . This is how the people overcame thirst."[57] Having replenished their stores, the 300 Navajos were able to outlast the siege and escape Carson's net.

However, the scorched-earth policy eventually took its toll. Hunger was Carson's greatest ally. The empty eyes and shallow face told the story—the Navajos were literally starving to death. With little corn or meat to eat, the lucky ones had barely survived by eating berries, piñon nuts, and *tś áálbáí* (shelled, steamed corn dried, and ground to powder). The women would dry and grind it and place it in lambskin pouches along with any meat that came from hunting. Most of the Diné were not only hungry and thirsty, but suffered from the bitter cold with only sparse clothing and shelters to protect them.[58]

And the psychological and spiritual pain was too real. The women feared their children would be taken as slaves. And many Navajos did not surrender because they thought the *Bilagáanas* (white men) planned to kill them at their death camp beyond the sacred mountains. The military never told the frightened Navajos where they were going, only threatening them with guns and telling them to "go ahead—keep on going." They were certainly entering a state of *hóchxóó* or chaos, disorder, and disharmony. Historian Hampton Sides quotes one anonymous Navajo as saying: "Because of what your soldiers have done we are all starving. Many of our women and children have already died from hunger. We would have come in long ago, but we believed this was a war of extermination."[59]

Eventually, the Navajos "voluntarily surrendered," and by the end of February thousands were arriving at Fort Canby. Several hundred individuals hid out, some in the Chuska Mountains or in the North Country beyond the San Juan River, others, like Hoskinini's band, disappeared in the canyons and rock formations of Navajo Mountain. Others went to the Grand Canyon in the western Dinétah. Some avoided capture by entering the territory of the Chiricahua Apache, or by joining relatives in Pueblo villages. The remainder prepared for their Long Walk, the name the Navajos gave to this time of suffering.

The Long Walk

The Navajo were forced to march from Fort Canby in northeastern Arizona to Bosque Redondo (Round Grove) beyond the Pecos River in east-central New Mexico (see again Figures 4.2 and 4.3). Between 1863 and 1866 at least 53 walks took place as people were captured or recaptured.[60] Parties of Navajos ranged in size from under 100 to 2,500, and they walked from 375 to 498 miles depending upon which of four routes were followed. The first contingent of captives sent to Bosque Redondo in the summer of 1863 was 51 in number, 43 of whom were Enemy Navajos.

The Mountain Route, which was favored and the one used most often from 1864 to 1866, involved 424 of back-breaking miles between Fort Canby and the Bosque. Although winter weather was a problem for any route, this one left Arizona and went through Albuquerque, over the mountains to Las Vegas, and down the Pecos to Fort Sumner. It had the advantage of offering sheltering valleys and canyons in which water and wood were in good supply. Other alternate routes took the Navajo through Santa Fe or Fort Union, the latter being 498 miles. The Cañon Blanco route was the shortest, 375 miles, running east of Albuquerque and south of Las Vegas, but it was also the most desolate and roughest with little water available and only used rarely by small trains between 1865 and 1866 (see map, Figure 4.4).[61]

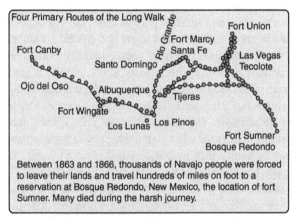

Four Primary Routes of the Long Walk

Between 1863 and 1866, thousands of Navajo people were forced to leave their lands and travel hundreds of miles on foot to a reservation at Bosque Redondo, New Mexico, the location of fort Sumner. Many died during the harsh journey.

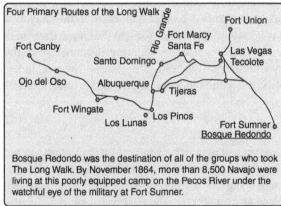

Four Primary Routes of the Long Walk

Bosque Redondo was the destination of all of the groups who took The Long Walk. By November 1864, more than 8,500 Navajo were living at this poorly equipped camp on the Pecos River under the watchful eye of the military at Fort Sumner.

Figure 4.4 *Four Primary Routes of The Long Walk.* Information and maps found in Frank McNitt, "The Long March: 1863-1867" in *Changing Ways of Southwestern Indians: A Historic Perspective,* ed. by Al Schroeder (Glorieta, N.M.: Rio Grande Press, 1973), pp. 145–169.

While a typical wagon train of military supplies moving through Navajo country would average 15 to 20 miles a day, the military escorts of Navajo prisoners headed for the Pecos averaged 12 miles a day.[62] The average trip from Fort Canby to the Bosque over the Mountain Road was about 33 or 34 days, depending on the weather and other contingencies. Obviously, travel was slower during winter months or when the Río Grande was flowing.

Between the summer of 1863 and early winter of 1866, a total of 11,468 Navajos supposedly started on their way to confinement at Bosque Redondo. How many actually reached their destination or died is not known. November of 1864 saw the highest number on the reservation: 8,570 men, women, and children. A mass desertion of about 1,300 Navajos from Bosque Redondo in June 1865 adds to the difficulty of determining how many Indians were moved to the Pecos River area at this time.[63]

One way to understand the trials and tribulations of the Diné during the Long Walk is through testimonials. One interesting interview was given to Richard Van Valkenburgh by Hastin Il'tsosigi (Very Slim Man) in 1937. Hastin Il'tsosigi died in 1939 at the age of 88, and the interview was published in the April 1946 issue of *The Desert Magazine* (pp. 23–26). When he was 12 years old in the fall of 1863, a time "When I was big enough to think about killing a Mexican, bad news came to the People. From his hogans in the Canyon de Chelly our head chief, Barboncito, sent messengers to warn all the Navajo. The Mexicans and Utes were guiding the white soldiers into Navajoland. We must break camp [Horizontal White Point, midway between Chinlé and Nazlilni] and run away to our hiding place in the Canyon de Chelly."

By dawn his family had reached their hiding place in the canyon. Noticing the damage the soldiers had already done, his father muttered "the devils burn our fields and hogans." Then there was the "crack of muskets" and "with the dying echos [sic] of the shots came the death screams of my family." Only "Very Slim Man" and his little sister survived. They decided to escape the canyon by fleeing westward across the Chinlé valley to the Black Mesa region. There they met other refugees, many of whom wanted to travel to the Grand Canyon, but most of them decided, "We'll take the chance of surrendering rather than starving to death down there half way to the Underworld!"

So "Very Slim Man" and his group went first to Wide Reeds (Ganado) where they made a rest stop. While there, a bunch of Mexicans charged at them shooting and yelling "*muerto por los Navajo coyote*" ("death to the wild Navajo"). Just then some American Bluecoats intervened and escorted the Navajos to Fort Defiance. After being harassed by Zuni and Ute Indians at Fort Defiance, they traveled eastward several days through Gallup to the site of the Old Fort Wingate near Grants, New Mexico. "Here we Navajo saw our first flour. When they gave us the bags we didn't know what it was. So we just started eating. We were an awful sight with that flour all over our hands and faces as we tried to chew up the sticky dough in our mouths."

After a good rest they went on to the Río Grande where Very Slim Man, in attempting to cross the river, was swept underwater and carried a mile or two down river where he finally emerged. Clinging to a log, he eventually was grounded on a sand bar. Fortunately, according to Very Slim Man, the prayer his mother had taught him earlier went through his mind and saved his life. On the other side, near Isleta Pueblo, "keeping clear of the *Natobo* (Enemies Near Water) [the inhabitants of Isleta Pueblo], for they were stealing Navajo children, I caught up with my people at the Place of Bells, which the Mexicans call Albuquerque."

From there the group traveled under military escort to today's Santa Rosa. As Very Slim Man, who was then 13 years old, relates: "After many suns travel eastward through mountain ranges and across great plains we came to the Pecos River. Turning south we followed its banks until we came to where there were already many Navajo living. When they saw us they cried, 'Now you have finished your Long Walk. You will never see Navajoland again!'" Although his group very likely used the Cañon Blanco road, which was the shortest route, the detour to and through Black Mesa and back to Ganado easily added 200 to 250 miles to the trip, making his travels total over 600 miles. Now he would only have to suffer the conditions at Hwéeldi,[64] as the Navajo called Fort Sumner, where Abraham Lincoln had established a reservation for the Mescalero Apache in 1864.

Another testimonial comes from Peshlakai Etsedi ("Silversmith") who was about 80 years old when he recited his account to Sallie Pierce Brewer. He was born near the Grand Canyon. His family—over 40 children, grandchildren, and great-grandchildren—lived in the Wupatki Basin along the Little Colorado River near Cameron, Arizona. His account was originally published in the *Museum Notes* of the Museum of Northern Arizona in May 1937. Etsedi was probably between six and seven years old when he participated in the Long Walk.[65]

His family was in the Grand Canyon area when they first heard that soldiers were coming from the east to take them to Hwéeldi. Their first concern was to elude the Utes. "We were afraid of the Notah [Utes]. They often came on horses to the red rock country near the Little Colorado and killed the people and took their sheep and horses, and sometimes their children." Continuing east they went past Moenkopi, across the Black Mesa, to an area near Fort Defiance by the New Mexican border. Then they headed south to the snow-clad mountains that feed the Little Colorado River, where they spent the winter. It was in this region where his father, while hunting, was killed by Mexicans. The next spring and summer they moved through Navajo Mountain to Moenkopi and the Grand Canyon. Again they heard "from the soldier leader at Huelte (Bosque

Redondo); they said that many Navajos from the eastern part of the country had gone to Huelte; that they were well taken care of at that place; that now there were not many Navajos left in the own country and the soldiers could not protect them from their enemies unless they all came to Huelte."

The People gathered in a big circle and sang a farewell song, and the religious leaders prayed for the People. The next morning they started for Hwéeldi, traveling past Sunset Creator and up the Little Colorado River to a camp near present-day Holbrook. After three days travel they came to Zuni where some Zuni men greeted their old enemies and offered them respite from their travels if the latter would accompany them back to their village. While there they lost four children, two of whom were Etsedi's sisters. Then a white man came (the first white Etsedi had ever seen), and "said the Zunis were planning not to let a Navajo man out of Zuni alive; they would keep the children and young girls but the rest of the Navajos would be killed." Etsedi's group immediately fled the Zunis who pursued them but "these men in blue clothes [US soldiers] rode all around the Zunis and pushed them back toward their homes."

The next day they came to old Fort Wingate near Grants, New Mexico. The Bluecoats "gave us flour but we didn't know how to cook it and we could not use it." A few days later, with the old women and children in wagons pulled by mules, Etsedi and some of the men walked (because the mules moved too slowly) through Cubero and Laguna to Albuquerque. Before arriving at Albuquerque his mother's uncle died and the soldiers buried him. At Albuquerque they camped inside a huge corral where other prisoners waited, and the soldiers gave them corn, bread, and meat. Those who had metates ground the bread because it was so stale and hard. Following the mountain trail they eventually arrived in Bosque Redondo. As Etsedi noted, "we got to Huelte in Gan Je En (October, or mid-season); I think we had been travelling thirty-four days from Grand Canyon to Huelte."

Another Navajo witness to the Long Walk was Indian scout John Daw. He was born about 1868 and in the 1880s was a Navajo scout for the US Army during the Apache campaigns. His testimony came from stories his parents related to him. He testified at an Indian Claims Commission hearing at Window Rock, Arizona, that took place on January 16 and 17, 1951. He was about 83 years old at the time. He spoke about military violence and indicated that the army shot many of the sick and tired. Daw, in his testimony, talked about the treatment of women: "The womenfolk on the long march were molested ... to the extent that the soldiers, after nightfall, came around and forced some of the men to go away and had sexual intercourse with these women on the long march."[66]

Collaborating Daw's testimony concerning sexism and sexual violence on the Long Walk was Jeff King. King, who was also born around 1868 south of Mount Taylor, New Mexico, testified at the same Commission hearing in 1951. He first bore witness to the death of several Navajos in the Tse Bonito area, and then went on to talk about the soldier's treatment of Navajo women: "These soldiers did not have any regard for women folks. They took unto themselves for wives somebody else's wife, and many times the Navajo man whose wife was being taken tried to ward off the soldiers, but immediately he was shot and killed and they took his wife. They did not treat the women like they should have."[67]

To conclude this section, in generalizing about the role of rape as a instrument of white patriarchal control, Andrea Smith notes that the "history of sexual violence and genocide among Native women illustrates how gender violence functions as a tool for racism and colonialism among women of color in general."[68] This was very likely the case in the nineteenth-century relocation plans of a US government that was promoting the interests of contractors, settlers, and miners, not to mention religious groups, and had to remove, from their perspective, an obstacle to progress and "Manifest Destiny."

Hwéeldi (Bosque Redondo)

By November of 1864 it was already obvious that Carleton's dream of a model reservation would not be realized. By then Bosque Redondo held 424 Mescalero Apaches as well as 8,570 Navajos. Counting the 470 soldiers and approximately 200 civilians who lived at the fort, the reservation had a population of 9,664 individuals. As Rod and Winona Passmore note, "Never in the history of New Mexico had so many people been together in one place."[69] The previous winter had been particularly severe, and US Army personnel found themselves without the necessary funds and inadequate supplies to provide for a cold, hungry people. Carleton tried to resolve the food problem by appealing to the New Mexico market with advertisements in local newspapers, and making contracts with suppliers in Missouri, Kansas, and Oklahoma—all to no avail!

A shortage of food was the most serious problem. As Robert Roessel, quoting from other sources, observes, "The Navajos had hardly anything at that time; and they ate rations but couldn't get used to them. Most of them got sick and had stomach trouble. The children also had stomach ache, and some of them died of it. Others died of starvation ... boys would wander off to where the mules and horses were corralled. There they would poke around in the manure to take undigested corn out of it. Then they would roast the corn in hot ashes to be eaten."[70] Cutworm disease killed the first two corn crops. With no corn, wheat flour and lard were used to make fry bread (a survival food eaten in the absence of traditional vegetables and nutrients).[71] Thirst, as well as hunger, became a problem because of the salty content of the Pecos River water.

Because of their unfamiliarity with the American diet, many items like coffee and wheat were often eaten unboiled or uncooked, a situation that led to diarrhea and dysentery. A lack of food forced some Diné girls as young as 12 or 13 years old to sell their bodies for as little as a pint of cornmeal. Soon venereal diseases, especially syphilis, surpassed malnutrition as the most pressing health concern on the reservation.[72]

To acquire meat the Navajos were authorized at times to hunt wild game. They also attacked freight trains and made off with the cargo, including sheep, horses, and burros. At one time Navajo warriors took 60 horses from the Mescalero herd, as well as mounts of the US cavalry. This only led to retaliation from the Apaches and the US Army, and the death of additional Navajos.[73]

Proper shelter was another concern. Carleton envisioned the Navajos living in compact pueblo-style structures like those in Taos Pueblo. This would expedite their transition from savagery to civilization. But the Navajos wanted to live in traditional, scattered hogans. Part of the concern from the Navajo point-of-view was their belief system in which they refused to live in any building where a person had died. A lack of materials eventually forced them to dig pithouses or holes in the ground that they would cover with any material they could find, from cow hides to bushes.[74] However, Navajo labor was used to shape bricks to make adobe buildings for the officers and enlisted men at the fort.

By 1864 a small hospital with nine rooms was built. But because of the Navajo views on death, and because the Diné would not enter any building where an individual had expired, the hospital remained unused for the most part. In the spring of 1864 dysentery was the main health concern. Then over the next four years a variety of diseases afflicted the Navajos including typhoid, pleurisy, and pneumonia, as well as the deadly epidemics of smallpox, cholera, and measles. Death became a daily occurrence as one disease followed another.[75] While the US government reported an official death count of 336, it was more likely a figure closer to over 2,000.

In June 1866 three women from Manuelito's band arrived at Bosque Redondo. They reported that Manuelito, who had become a symbol of Navajo resistance to the US Army and its New Mexican allies, was wounded in a fight with the Hopis. He had turned himself in earlier, but then escaped to his homeland. He now was weak and ill and wanted to fight no longer. In September he, his wife Juanita, and his band, that had dwindled in number from 500 to 23, started their own long walk from Fort Wingate to Fort Sumner.[76] Carleton probably did not know it, but the surrender of Manuelito was the beginning of the end for Fair Carletonia.

Adversaries: Whites and Navajos

After the events of Bosque Redondo, Kit Carson and Manuelito became symbolic antagonists in which White America confronted Indian America: Kit Carson—trapper, hunter, guide, scout, explorer, Indian agent, negotiator, and

Indian fighter (not to mention father and husband), and Manuelito (known by his countrymen as Hastiin Ch'ilhadjinii, or Black Weeds)—hunter, diplomat, angry warrior, expert horseman, a *rico* of good breeding, and Navajo headman (also a father and husband). Although their paths never crossed on the personal level, Carson leaving Bosque Redondo in 1864 while Manuelito did not surrender until 1866, they did represent what was right and wrong in the struggle between Americans and the indigenous peoples. Neither one was either Epic Hero or Anti-Hero, but bits of both, and whatever their differences and similarities, they were both mortal beings and members of humanity. To compare them (and their families) is not an exercise in false equivalencies.[77]

In spite of their obvious physical and cultural differences (Carson was five-foot four-inches at best while Manuelito was tall and dark whose imposing presence intimidated both whites and fellow Indians), they did share many similarities. Both, ironically, were Indian fighters. While Carson gained notoriety by slaying California Indians, Yavapais, Tonto Apaches, Mescalero Apaches, Comanches, Navajos, and Kiowas, Manuelito not only had to fight American soldiers, but ancient foes from Pueblos, Utes, Commanches, and Apaches to the Hispanics of New Mexico.[78]

If Carson could participate in the massacre of Sacramento Indians and describe the event afterwards as "a perfect butchery," as a teenager Manuelito could kill a Pueblo Indian in hand-to-hand combat, scalp his victim, and chew on the bloody skin to draw power from it and thereby become a true fighter known as the "Angry Warrior."[79] As a trapper who took Indian wives and adapted Indian ways, particularly those skills that related to survival, Carson was a white man who had become partially "Indianized." After Bosque Redondo, when fighting no longer made any sense, Manuelito, now somewhat assimilated into the white man's world, encouraged his children to go to the white man's boarding school and learn the white man's ways.

Both were illiterate, yet able to speak several languages. Carson, in addition to his home-grown Missouri twang, learned to speak French and Spanish fluently, and knew bits of Navajo, Ute, Comanche, Cheyenne, Arapaho, Crow, Blackfoot, Shoshone, and Paiute. Like Manuelito, he could also use Indian sign language. Manuelito, living in the mountain country of the Utes, was trilingual, fluent in Spanish and Ute as well as Navajo.[80]

Both had several female companions who played prominent roles in their lives. Carson had three wives. First, there was the Arapaho woman named Waa-Nibe (rendered in English as "Grass Singing") who bore Carson two daughters, including the favored first child Adeline; then "Making Out Road" (more correctly translated as "she who laid down the law," known also as "the belle of the Cheyenne" in mountain man circles); and finally, Josefa Jaramillo, the 14-year-old daughter of a prominent Taos family (who eventually produced eight children for the Carson family).[81]

Manuelito too had more than one wife. According to anthropologist Richard Van Valkenburg, Manuelito's genealogy chart shows that he had four wives and several children. Two of his wives were the daughters of important headmen, the Navajo Narbona and the Chiracahua Apache, Mangas Coloradas. A third wife was Asdzáá Tsin. And as Carson had a romantic relationship with Waa-Nibe, so too was Manuelito devoted to his faithful and constant fourth companion Juanita (Asdzáá Tl'ógi, or Lady Weaver). Juanita and Asdzáá Tsin maintained close kin relationships since both lived near the community of Tohatchi. It should be noted that Juanita (and the other wives), unlike many of their American, Mexican, and Indian enemies, were adopted by or came from a matrilineal Navajo society in which women play a dominant role and are not totally subordinate to men.[82]

In attempting to evaluate Carson's life, it is difficult to be objective. If one relies on his contemporaries, including the dime novels of the nineteenth century, Carson as frontiersman and explorer is treated as a national hero. His exploits and adventures with Indians were the source of grandiose tales in which Carson was always described as brave, patriotic, and, notwithstanding the violence, kind and tenderhearted. Since the early 1970s the pendulum has swung in the other direction, with some revisionist historians going so far as to call Carson a racist and villain who, along with George Armstrong Custer and others, perpetuated genocide against indigenous Americans. This "monster image" leaves no room for any humanitarian feelings or urges on the part of Kit Carson.[83]

There can be no doubting that Carson at times was angry and mean with other people, and that his sense of duty made him follow orders when conscience might dictate another path. The most notorious incident occurred in June 1846 when Carson was involved in the murder of three unarmed prisoners. Although accounts differ, it was likely that Carson aided, indirectly or directly, in the shooting and killing of the Californios, Juan de los Reyes Berreyesa, the respected father of the Alcalde (mayor) of Sonoma, and his two nephews, the sons of Don Francisco de Haro, who had been the Alcalde of Yerba Buena (San Francisco). Carson justified his actions by talking about wartime situations and arguing that he was only following the orders of John C. Frémont.[84] Since World War II most writers would suggest that following orders does not relieve a person of moral responsibility.

But if Carson had his harsh side, there were many times that his humanity and tenderheartedness came to the fore. Although often an absent father, he was consistent in his affection and devotion to his children. He was definitely in love with his first wife, Waa-Nibe, and stricken with grief when she died. He created a strong bond with Josefa that lasted a quarter of a century. While one overriding virtue of Carson was his sense of duty, most often in some military service, it was also displayed in his relationship with his wives.[85]

And finally, no one can deny the man's courage in the face of danger. He may not have had the political courage of the young Whig congressman from Illinois, Abraham Lincoln, who opposed the Mexican War with the "Spot Resolution" of December 22, 1847.[86] He did not display the moral outrage of a Mark Twain when the latter criticized the Spanish–Cuban–American War of 1898, or Pete Seeger whose folksongs gave courage to the opponents of the Vietnam War.

But Carson did display empathy for his enemies and had enough personal courage to not only fight them but defend them. Being a trapper had taught him the virtues of the wilderness, including the inhabitants therein. He was a good friend of the Utes, even accompanying them on a mission to Washington, DC, in 1868 in order to obtain a treaty that would guarantee them their lands. It should be mentioned that by that time he was seriously ill and on the doorstep of death. And, of course, his major concern at that time was to return to Josefa and his homeland near Taos. This is a sense of duty and a kind of personal bravery that cannot be overlooked.

In 1866, two years after the massacre of Sand Creek, Carson gave his opinion of John M. Chivington: "To think of that dog Chivington, and his hounds, up thar at Sand Creek! Whoever heerd of sich doings among Christians ... . And ye call these civilized men Christians; and the Injuns savages, du ye? I tell ye what ... Taint natural for brave men to kill women and little children, and no one but a coward or a dog would do it." At the very least, like Manuelito, Carson was not a ruthless killer and did not excuse those who were.[87]

As for Manuelito, his bravery in battle is well documented. He was a warrior, but only after the peace process broke down. His hopes as a diplomat diminished after the Treaty of Ojo del Oso (November 1846) failed to prevent the outbreak of warfare between whites and Navajos, and the aftermath in which Colonel John Macrae Washington's betrayal of Narbona resulted in the death of the Navajo headman. Narbona was widely known for his efforts to keep the peace. These events caused Manuelito to become the "angry warrior" who, along with Barboncito, led the attack on Fort Defiance on April 30, 1860. After Kit Carson started his Navajo roundup in 1863, Manuelito successfully hid out in the Chuska Mountains for three years, only surrendering himself and his family at Bosque Redondo in 1866. As one of the signatories to the Treaty of 1868, he aided his people in their return to their Navajo homeland, and accommodating himself to the new realities, promoted western education at the Carlisle Boarding School for his sons. In fact, he continued to argue that if the Navajo and their traditions were to survive they would have to be educated in the white man's ways.[88]

How to evaluate the life of Manuelito? He cannot be understood apart from the horrors his people suffered at the hands of the Americans during the "time of fear," the Long Walk, and Bosque Redondo. Carson and the US Army's use of "scorched earth" tactics and the hardships of the walk to Bosque Redondo almost destroyed the Navajo's spirit and culture. It was Manuelito, as a warrior leader, who reminded his people that the Great Spirit gave them their holy homeland surrounded by the Four Sacred Mountains and they should not leave it, and if forced to do so, they must reclaim it. Once his people returned to Diné Bikéyah they must regain Navajo sovereignty, and American education would be the "ladder" for the people to get back their pride and independence. The people must protect their resources, land, and language; in other words, promote and maintain traditional Navajo ways. In Navajo, as Gus Bighorn, a companion who rode with Manualito said, "... a warrior is the one who can use words so everyone knows they are part of the same family."[89] Manuelito was that warrior.

As for Carson's third wife, while most Americans called her Mrs. Carson, she was known in the Spanish-speaking world as Doña María Josefa Jaramillo. "Doña" was a title supposedly indicating an aristocratic heritage, while "María" both honored her deceased older sister who died in infancy and the Virgin Mary. "Josefa," the feminine form of José or Joseph, meant that in time of need she could rely upon the intercession of Joseph and Mary. Her pet name was "Chepita" (more commonly "Chipita"), a common nickname for Josefa. Carson when speaking to fellow Americans often referred to her as "Little Jo," a literal translation of Josefita or the diminutive form in Spanish. Carson's nickname for Josefa was very likely a sign of affection.[90]

Since Josefa found herself abandoned for long periods of time during her marriage to the wandering Carson, she found her identity with *la familia* or her extended family that valued her role as housekeeper, child bearer, and caregiver. Much of the time she would move her immediate household into her older sister's residence, Maria Ignacia Jaramillo, the common law wife of Charles Bent.[91]

Through the Spanish tradition of *compadrazgo* (godparenthood), Kit and Josefa became godparents of others, not always kinfolk, and assumed obligations for their welfare. These extra familial lines became so large that Carson had a hard time identifying and naming them all. According to his son Charles, the Carson extended family included three Navajos raised from childhood. His hospitality, almost legendary, was most likely due to his good temper and his wife's Mexican culture. Even though that tradition was a patriarchal one, in which authority would pass from the father to his new son-in-law, Carson's authoritarian manner was mild when compared to that of some of his Missouri compatriots or Indian male friends.[92]

Sex and gender was less a barrier to social mobility on the frontier of New Mexico than it was in central Mexico or the eastern United States. Hispanic traditions of law allowed women to maintain property separate from their husbands.[93] Many female New Mexican *ricos* received land grants from the state, or, like Josefa, were silent partners who aided in the management of ranches and farms. In addition, real estate records indicate that Josefa owned three lots in Taos. She, like her compatriots, not only maintained a household and looked after the care of her many children, but also shared with her husband the obligation of tending to the land and livestock, even when her husband was absent. And, of course, when Kit took ill she was the source of tender, loving care.[94]

The child bearing had brought the Carson household eight children, but not without costs to the personal health of Josefa. This, and her heavy responsibilities to her extended family, brought about an early death. On April 27, 1868, at 40 years of age, Josefa died from complications of child birth, or "childbed fever," the same malady that claimed the life of Kit's first wife, Waa-nibe. Nineteen years her elder, Kit succumbed to an aneurysm of the aorta one month later on May 23, 1868.[95] But the legend of Kit Carson would continue without him. As for Kit's wives, like most nineteenth-century women in western America, they continued to be invisible.

No so invisible was Juanita, the Indian companion of Manuelito. This was because influential popularizers like George Wharton James, who collected Indian artifacts and lectured his audiences concerning Native American culture, visited with Juanita and her family in 1902 and later published his portraits of Manuelito's family. Although Manualito's death in 1894 brought an end to an era, Juanita, who lived approximately from 1845 to 1910, continued to honor the tradition of her deceased war chief husband. As a matrilineal clan leader and grandmother, she became a symbol or living relic that united the traditional Diné folkways with the modern ways of twentieth-century America.[96]

During the "Navajo Wars" of the 1860s, Juanita was a constant presence alongside her husband. In 1866, she rode with him to the Bosque Redondo prison, and in 1868 she returned with him to their home in Tohatchi, New Mexico. Although it is rumored that she was once a Mexican slave held by the Navajos, she did marry Manuelito and eventually became his favorite wife. In 1894, as a widow she moved her daughters and their families closer to the village of Tohatchi, and was venerated as a mother and grandmother.[97]

In 1874, Juanita was a member of the delegation that visited President Ulysses S. Grant in Washington, DC, Manuelito was a delegate as well. The group hoped to persuade the president that the Navajos needed additional land grants in order to survive, and also wanted to eliminate the conflict between New Mexicans and their people. In the foreign environment of Washington, DC, Juanita was a comforting individual who provided familiar cuisine and social customs to her fellow delegates.[98] Photographs of her as the "weaver woman" probably stereotyped her in the Americans' mind, but for the Navajo people, weaving and Diné culture and history were "interwoven" themes.

Possibly her biographer, Jennifer Nez Denetdale, sums it up best when she says Juanita "... experienced the horrors of the Americans' war on her people and saw her children stolen by slave traders. She actively resisted American invasion of her homeland. After 1868, she experienced the effects of American civilization on herself, her family, and her Navajo people. Today she remains a grandmother still remembered by her descendants as one who was generous, beneficent, and wise."[99] Perhaps the stories of Juanita, Josefa, Waa-Nibe, and "Making Out Road" can assist in making visible the history of women in the American Southwest.

Treaty of 1868

It was obvious to government officials in Washington, D.D. that the Carleton "model reservation" experiment was a failure as early as 1865. A Joint Special Committee of both houses of Congress investigated the conditions on the reservation, meeting and listening to the complaints of the Bosque Redondo captives. On February 25, 1867, Carleton was removed from duty in New Mexico and booted upstairs to the Department of the Gulf of Texas.

In the spring of 1868 General William T. ("Tecumseh") Sherman arrived at Fort Sumner to negotiate a new treaty with the Navajo headmen. Upon arriving, the somewhat shocked Sherman wrote to Ulysses Grant what he observed: "I found the Bosque a mere spot of green grass in the midst of a wild desert, and the Navajos had sunk into a condition of absolute poverty and despair." Custody of the Navajos had already been transferred from War to Interior, meaning in effect that the Navajos were no longer considered "prisoners of war." All of this prepared the stage for the Treaty of 1868.[100]

On May 28, 1868, the negotiators met at Fort Sumner. While General Sherman was the main spokesperson for the United States, several Navajo headmen represented the People including Delgado and the two warriors from the battle at Fort Defiance, Barboncito, and Manuelito. Jesus Alviso was the Indian interpreter, while James Sutherland provided the Spanish translation.[101] Since communication had to go from English to Spanish, and Spanish to Navajo (and vice versa), it is obvious that many of the ideas and stipulations of this complicated treaty were not understood by the Indian peacemakers.

Sherman opened the session by suggesting that some of the Navajos would be sent to the Indian Territory south of Kansas. This idea was met with Barboncito's response: "I hope to God you will not ask me to go to any other country except my own. It might turn out another Bosque Redondo. They told us this was a good place when we came but it is not."[102] By June 1 a treaty was concluded which allowed the Diné to return to a portion of their homeland near the Four Corners. It was agreed to by 19 headmen and Indian leaders, including Barboncito and Manuelito.[103]

The first article stated that all warfare between the two parties would cease. Article II defined the boundaries of the new reservation: 5,200 square miles bounded on the north by the 37th degree of latitude; south by a line running east and west through Fort Defiance; the west to be a longitude of 109 degrees, 30 minutes embracing the outlet to Canyon de Chelly; and on the east a parallel of longitude that would intersect the old Fort Lyon and Bear Spring.[104]

The eastern parallel purposely did not include Navajo claims to the Chaco country or the ranching areas around today's Farmington. The settlers and ranchers of northeastern New Mexico were having their claims recognized by the government. This also meant that as the Navajo population and livestock multiplied over the years, they would be forced to look for land and resources outside the boundaries of the original treaty. This expansion, partly promoted by a series of executive decrees by the US government, would accelerate the conflict over land between Hopis and Navajos (see Commentary: 1868 & The Hopi-Navajo Land Controversy), and many Navajos would find themselves once again being relocated.

Article VI pledged the People to send their children between the ages of 6 and 16 to school. Article IX included several provisions about what the Navajos could not do, especially "make no opposition to the construction of railroads now being built or hereafter to be built, across the continent." Other provisions spoke to the needs of the People as they adopted agriculture (a tenet of civilization), and promised provisions of seed, farm tools, and livestock, including sheep.[105]

Shortly after the treaty was signed the first contingent of Navajos finally left Bosque Redondo. On the 18th of June, one hundred and seventy-six people left with an escort of soldiers. But before the Navajos could go home they had to wait five months at Fort Wingate for the reservation to be surveyed. Eventually they returned home.[106] As they passed through the sacred Mount Taylor, you could hear the words and chants of the People as they sang their traditional prayer:

> As I walk, as I walk
> The universe is walking with me
> In beauty it walks before me
> In beauty it walks behind me
> In beauty it walks below me
> In beauty it walks above me
> Beauty is on every side
> As I walk, I walk with Beauty.

Like their ancient ancestors, the People could leave the disorder of Bosque Redondo behind them, and approach a new life in which the spirit of *hózhó* would prevail.

Postscript: Centennial

In May 1968, as part of its Centennial celebration of the Treaty of 1868 and Navajo liberation, the Diné community made a concerted effort to identify any survivors of the original Long Walk. As a result, twin sisters living in Rough Rock were located and identified as survivors. The twins had been born in Bosque Redondo in 1865, and at 103 years of age they were still active in herding sheep and tending to the needs of their two families. Mrs. Crooked Neck and Old Man Mud's Wife were guests of the Navajo Nation at the Treaty Parade in Fort Defiance on June 1, 1968 (see Figure 4.5). They symbolized the fortitude and strength of a people who willed themselves to survive.[107]

Mrs. Crooked Neck and Old Man Mud's Wife

They, too, made the Long Walk—in 1868.

Figure 4.5 *Mrs. Crooked Neck and Old Man Mud's Wife: They, too, made the Long Walk— in 1868.* Permission and Photo by Martin A. Link, Gallup, N.M. (June 1, 1968, Treaty Signing Day parade, Twins as Grand Marshalls).

Commentary: The Hopi-Navajo Land Controversy

> *1st Reg't N.M. Vol's*
> *Aug. 13, 1863*
> *Col. C. Carson, Comm.*
> Inscription, Keams Canyon *(Pongsikya)*, Hopi Nation[1]

Famed anthropologist Ruth Underhill in her book *The Navajos* wrote, concerning the arrival of US troops at *Diné Bikeyah* (the Navajo homeland) with orders to remove the Navajos, "How willingly all these tribes [Utes, Hopis, Zunis] gave their aid! ... To the Hopi and Zuñis, the new protectors, supplied with guns and food, were like the realization of a dream ... . The Navajos were reaping the harvest of the years they had been Lords of the Soil."[2] The defeat of the hated *Tavasuh* (Hopi word for Navajos) and their Long Walk appeared to the Hopis a manifestation of divine righteousness. Having lost faith in the military organization of the Mexicans to protect them from their nomadic enemies, their hope was with the Americans. It also seemed to bear out a trust the Hopis had in the US government to act as their defender, a trust that was soon proven to be ill placed.[3]

From Fort Canby, New Mexico, Colonel "Kit" Carson wrote to the Adjutant General stationed in Santa Fe on December 6, 1863. In that message he noted his use of Zuñi Indians as "Spies," and his involvement of Hopis in the attack on the Navajos. Carson said that on November 21st he "... arrived at the Moqui [Hopi] village. I found on my arrival that the inhabitants of all villages except the Oribis had a misunderstanding with the Navajoes, owing to some injustice by the latter. I took advantage of this feeling, and succeeded in obtaining representatives from all the villages—Oribi excepted—to accompany me on the war path. My object in insisting upon parties of these people accompanying me was simply to involve them so far that they could not retract—to bind them to us, and place them in antagonism to the Navajoes."[4]

And although the Hopis, like the Pueblo Indians in general, are generally considered by outsiders to be a peaceful people, their history is filled with instances of militarism and violence. The tragedy of Awatovi is the foremost of these. In the year 1700 the leaders of Oraibi, Mishongnovi, Shongopavi, and Walpi gathered their followers and attacked the Christian converts of Awatovi. Trapping the Awatovi men in their kiva, the invaders shot down arrows and threw torches into the underground chamber. Those who escaped were chased down and murdered and dismembered, while the village was burned and the women captured and divided up among the conquerors. The next day the Hopis returned and crushed every remaining artifact. As author Emily Benedek notes, the village would "melt back into the earth."[5]

Frank Waters, in his controversial work entitled *Book of the Hopi*, wrote that the greatest effect of the Awatovi calamity was upon the Hopi themselves. He writes that the "destruction of one of their own villages, and their ruthless massacre of their own people for betraying a human tolerance toward a new faith, was an act of religious bigotry that equaled if it did not surpass the cruelty of the hated Christian 'slave church' itself ... . Now in one act of unrestrained hate and violence, they had committed a fratricidal crime of mass murder that nullified their own faith and stamped forever an ineradicable guilt upon the heart of every Hopi."[6] Although a harsh judgment, the Waters observation does lay to rest the stereotype of the Pueblo as a peaceful person.

According to Hopi belief, while the Navajos were confined at Bosque Redondo several Tavasuh medicine men came to Walpi to implore the Hopis to help them be released from imprisonment. The Navajos assured their Hopi hosts that when their people returned they would respect Hopi beliefs, possessions, and land. To guarantee their word they gave the Hopis two sacred bundles, both of which permitted the holder to control animal and human life. Although there is no evidence that the Hopis were influential in securing the release of the Navajos, it is likely that a meeting took place between the two peoples after the Navajos returned from Fort Sumner or Hwéeldi.[7]

The Treaty of 1868 which ended the Navajo internment and started the return to Diné Bikeyah contained within itself the seeds of the later land dispute with the Hopis. Although the treaty partitioned some of the Diné homeland as a reservation, it also gave much of the best Navajo land that was in western New Mexico to the US government. The intention was one of reserving and promoting the rights of New Mexico rancher families, including the notorious Wetherill brothers of Mesa Verde and Chaco Canyon fame, by moving the eastern boundary westward of the current town of Farmington.

Without marked boundaries, and unaware of the geography of the reservation as defined by the treaty (not to mention that during the negotiations uneducated former Navajo slaves acted as translators for the People as communication went back and forth from English to Spanish to Navajo), the returning Diné often settled outside the reservation lines. Eventually, having lost lands in New Mexico, and experiencing a population boom of people and livestock, the Navajos expanded in a westward direction where the Hopi had lived for hundreds of years. This westward push almost made it inevitable that there would be a collision between the two communities.[8]

Because the Hopi homeland was public land, having never been withdrawn from the public domain as a reservation, and the government was powerless to remove its opponents from such land, the federal government was forced to act. In this instance the undesirables were two Anglos who allied themselves with those Hopi families that were opposing the government-run boarding schools. The action came in the form of an executive order in 1882 by President Chester A. Arthur creating a Hopi reservation of nearly 2.5 million acres around the Hopi mesas "for the use and occupancy of the Moqui [Hopi] and such other Indians as the Secretary of the Interior may see fit to settle thereon." At the time there were approximately 300 Navajos and 1,800 Hopis living within the boundaries of the 1882 reservation.[9]

In response to the Diné migration pattern, and because most of the land near the Navajo reservation was of little interest to non-Indian outsiders, the 1868 boundaries were constantly being expanded between 1878 and 1934. Between those dates the Navajo reservation was increased 14 times through executive orders and congressional acts. Thus, according to the Hopi handout sheet entitled "The Meek Shall Inherit the Earth, unless they are Hopi Indians," the US government "... began a system of 'rewarding' Navajo trespass through the issuance of Executive Orders."[10] When the 1868 treaty lines were drawn the Navajo reservation was about 5,200 square miles, while in 2010 it was over 25,000 square miles.

Until the 1930s Washington was indifferent to the Hopi–Navajo land struggle. Then, in 1934, the Indian Reorganization Act became law. This so-call "New Deal for Indians" created tribal constitutions and governments, and in the case of the Hopis, accelerated the polarization between traditional and modern Indians. Traditional Hopis clung to their village councils and promoted local autonomy over allegiance to any tribal government organized from above and outside the community.

In 1936, to reduce livestock destruction of the environment by Navajo sheep, the Hopis were given exclusive use of a portion of the 1882 joint use area (JUA) for grazing that was known as District Six. This act forced the first relocation of Navajo families. Still, by 1958, 8,800 Navajos lived in the JUA zone while only 3,700 Hopis resided there. In that year the two tribes sued each other trying to determine rightful ownership of the 1882 reservation. By 1965 District Six had been expanded to over 650,000 acres and over 100 Navajo families were expelled from the District. Many of these families moved just outside the District boundaries, to be relocated again at a later date. Hopi complaints about Navajo land use led to the 1974 Navajo–Hopi Land Settlement act which authorized the equal division of the 1882 reservation between the two tribal groups. Once again 12,000 Navajos and 300 Hopis were relocated to the other side of the fence.[11]

With the discovery of precious minerals and water resources, what had been an inter-tribal conflict became a national and international one. What might be called "internal colonialism" was the result. For example, in Mexico under the Porfiriato (1876–1911) the Porfirio Díaz regime provided foreign (US and Great Britain) corporations with oil and mineral concessions and cheap labor. Domestic elites in government and business formed alliances with their foreign counterparts. Both American and Mexican elites benefited from the arrangement, much to the chagrin of the masses that made their discontent known in the uprising known as the 1910 Mexican Revolution.

Likewise, the Hopi and Navajo reservations became a kind of third-world region that attracted the attention of outside interests, especially ranchers, oil men, uranium miners, coal mining interests, and water resources people.

These outsiders would seek leases from friendly tribal governments in which Indian elites waged exclusive power. In the case of the Hopis it was the affluent and least traditional Sekaquaptewa family that in the 1970s owned the Hopi craft business, tourist shuttles, and construction outfits. They stood the most to gain from the partition of the JUA, especially if the relocation of Navajos would lead to new grazing rights by the family. Wayne Sekaquaptewa, editor of the local newspaper and head of the local Mormon Church, used his position in both places to stir animosity between the two tribes. He was aided by legal council and a Salt Lake City public relations firm with connections to the Mormon Church. Those Navajos in the JUA were no threat to the average Hopi, but were in the way of the interests of domestic elites and outsider groups. Eventually, Indian politicians in both tribal governments agreed to lease part of the Black Mesa to the Peabody Coal Company, an agreement that could sacrifice the environmental interests of both tribes.[12]

Relations between Hopis and Navajos have varied from good to bad. Obviously, many individuals from both groups have had congenial relationships based on religious concerns, commercial interests, and family or clan ties. Intermarriage has long been a common tradition among the two peoples. On the other hand, relocation has acerbated what had already been unfriendly relations between some families.

For example, Jerry Kammer in his book *The Second Long Walk* speaks about the case of the Melvina Navasie family who lived in the Jeddito Valley from the 1920s through the 1950s. The Navasies were Hopis living in a sea of an increasing population of Navajos. When Malvina was a child in the 1940s herding her family's sheep, individual Navajos on horseback would chase her away from grazing lands they wanted for their own livestock. They would use whips to attack her, and then would go further by vandalizing the Navasie home and trampling their crops. In the 1950s they went so far as to hang Malvina's father by his feet in a Navajo hogan. He died a month later. By 1978 the Navasies were eager to see the Navajos relocated, even though her own family was forced to relocate to the Hopi partition area because their own lands in Jeddito had been given to the Navajos.[13]

And then there is the case of Emma Bahe, a Navajo member of the Towering House clan. Her family, like the Navasies above, lived in Teesto near the Jeddito Valley. In Malcolm Benally's collection called *Bitter Water*, Bahe, participating in a documentary video that was filmed in the late 1990s, is quoted as follows:

"A lot of people have relocated. All of our sheep have disappeared ... it is only the sheep who give us a way to sustain our families ... . One morning all of a sudden some BIA rangers showed up. Back then, they hauled fences around to fence animals up ... They fenced the horses in ... so, we had to confront them ... I saw a man holding a rope. I took his rope from him ... [and] as they [BIA police] passed by, I was going to whip [with the rope] the driver's hands ... but I missed ... and only whipped the truck. They stopped their trailers and a woman police officer jumped out at me. I just stood there. 'Why did you whip the police car? You are breaking the law!' she said to me. 'You are also breaking the law by taking my horses!' I said to her ... . So they hauled me to jail—with the horses. I went to jail with my horses. They even brought the rope. (Smiles) They even brought the rope to jail."[14]

In November of 1992 it appeared that the land dispute might be over. Navajo and Hopi leaders, after 18 months of arduous negotiations, had signed an agreement that in principle would end the further relocation of Navajos who wanted to remain on the Hopi Partition Lands. The agreement required the Navajos to acknowledge that they had no claim to the disputed land while the 250 Navajo families (2,000–3,000 people) could stay as good neighbors under a lease agreement that required them to "become Hopi," that is, follow the rules and laws of the Hopi Tribe. To compensate the Hopis for previous losses, they would receive $15 million and 500,000 acres of land near Flagstaff, Arizona. The land would be composed of parcels. These would be roughly equal, one-third private land (to be purchased at fair market prices), one-third state land, and one-third Forest Service land.[15]

Unfortunately, before the ink was dry on the understanding, the media publically announced the agreement and anti-Indian sentiments came to the surface. Politicians, from the governor of Arizona to the mayor of Flagstaff, voiced their opposition. Callers to radio talk shows in Phoenix opposed the giveaway to "conquered peoples" who do not need "special favors." Sportsmen feared that the Forest Service land would be closed to hunting, fishing, and recreation. It was somehow very un-American to make a deal with the first Americans. As the late Senator John McCain noted, "When you winnow down the objections, it comes down to the fact that local residents don't want Indians to own land that's become their local playground." Faced with the public opposition, the Navajo families residing on the disputed lands rejected the agreement and lease proposal. Olive branches were withdrawn. The land problem continues to this day.[16]

What on the surface appears to be a battle over land rights between Navajo and Hopi, is upon deeper investigation a cultural and spiritual struggle. Navajo creation stories lay claim to land spreading from New Mexico to the Grand Canyon. Traditional narratives speak of the movement of Holy People and Diné throughout the entire area. Changing Woman, upon leaving the Diné, went west to the Pacific Ocean. In 1863, before the Long Walk, many Diné were scattered across the whole region. And, as pastoralists, they needed grazing lands to survive. As the Navajos say, "Sheep is life." Holy People created the sheep. You burn incense to them. Sheep hide is your bed. Sheep wool is your money. When there are no sheep, there is no rain. Many sheep bring lots of rain. Why would the government ask them to vacate lands that the Hopi will not live on?[17]

As for the Hopi, they are an ancient people with roots in the Four Corners area (where Utah, Arizona, Colorado, and New Mexico intersect) that predate those of the Navajo, especially if you connect them to the Anasazi and their hunting-gathering ancestors.[18] Their creation stories speak of emerging from three worlds into a fourth world. Here the people followed migration patterns forming the sign of the swastika (a migration symbol for the Hopi). From the four corners of the world the Hopi finally arrived near the Hopi mesas, the center of the world. Each kiva is a sacred underground chamber with a symbolic umbilical cord connecting the past to the present, the dead with the living, the periphery with the center. The spiritual forces, the Katsinum, emerge from the kivas to provide the living with the lessons of the departed ancestors. As the earth's caretakers, the Hopi are a ceremonial people with strong ties to the dry, wind-whipped mesas.[19]

The Hopi traditional land base is much larger than the joint use area defined by executive decree and recognized by the US Land Claims Commission. While most Hopis are reluctant to leave the spirituality associated with the mesas to venture outward, they do use the surrounding area for timber, grazing their sheep, hunting and gathering, and ceremonial purposes. The threats from the Navajo residents also discourage Hopi settlement outside the mesas, with many Hopis testifying to having their sheep camps or houses destroyed by Navajo hoodlums.[20]

Probably the most important claims to land outside the mesas lie with the need to visit the religious shrines. There are at least eight major shrines in territory outside the mesas. These shrines range as far west as the Supai Descent Trail (Co Nin Ha-hao-pi) in the Grand Canyon and in the east to Lupton (Nah Mee Tuikah) near the New Mexico–Arizona boundary south of Window Rock and Gallup. To the north Navajo Mountain (Toko Navi) in southern Utah is another shrine, while to the south is the Apache Descent Trail (Yache Ha-hao-pi) along the Mogollon Rim south of Holbrook, Arizona. Other shrines are located at Bill Williams Mountain and Bear Springs (west of Flagstaff), Woodruff Butte (immediately south of Holbrook), and Betatakin Ruin (west of Kayenta and south of Navajo Mountain).[21] And of course, the katsinum dwell in the San Francisco Mountains outside Flagstaff for six months before traveling to the Hopi mesas after the winter solstice in December of every year. In its own way this country is as vast and sacred to the Hopi as is Dinétah for the Navajo.

So the people are not going anywhere. Over 200,000 Navajos, "people of the cultivated fields," and 9,000 Hopis, "the peaceful ones," are struggling to survive in a land with too many people and too few resources. Perhaps the final resolution will come in the future. Many Hopi cattlemen are married to Navajo women, and their children will form a new generation. If together they can build, as they have, a new, modern health clinic, then perhaps the next generation can resolve the current difficulties. With the injection of a bit of humor, and humility on everybody's part (including the politicians and the non-Indian citizens of Arizona), the olive leaves can be resurrected.[22]

5

Death of Mangas Coloradas, Chiricahua "Renegades," and Apache Prisoners of War

Men, that old murderer [Mangas Coloradas] has got away from every soldier command and has left a trail of blood for 500 miles on the old stage line. I want him dead ... tomorrow morning, do you understand? I want him dead.
General Joseph Rodman West, January 18, 1863[1]

The greatest wrong ever done to the Indians.
Geronimo's description of the death of Mangas Coloradas to his interviewer, S. M. Barrett, 1906[2]

My father was a good man; he killed lots of White Eyes.
Ace Daklugie, son of Juh [pronounced Hō], Nednhi headman, to Eve Ball between 1947 and 1955[3]

Once I moved like the wind. Now I surrender to you and that is all.
Geronimo (Goyahkla), on surrendering to General George Crook, Cañon de los Embudos, March, 1886[4]

The fate of the Chiricahua Apaches was an extreme example of the terror of relocation and removal in the nineteenth century. It started with the deceitful way that Cochise was treated by Americans in the Bascom affair in 1861. Then, in January 1863, Mangas Coloradas was treacherously taken prisoner and assassinated by members of the Grand Old Army of the Republic. This accelerated a series of Apache–American wars for the next 23 years that was only concluded when Geronimo surrendered in Mexico and the entire Chiricahua

Lost Worlds of 1863: Relocation and Removal of American Indians in the Central Rockies and the Greater Southwest, First Edition. W. Dirk Raat.
© 2022 John Wiley & Sons, Inc. Published 2022 by John Wiley & Sons, Inc.

community, including non-combatants, was sent into exile in Florida and Alabama as prisoners of war. Their incarceration lasted until 1913.

Relocation, initiated in 1782, was continued in 1830 when President Andrew Jackson signed a law ordering the removal of Cherokees and others to lands west of the Mississippi River. The policy received new vigor with the Abraham Lincoln administration in which Sioux, Winnebago, Navajo, Paiute, and others were removed from their homelands. Most Native Americans believed that they had been purposefully placed in their homeland by the Great Spirit. The local landscapes were peppered with sacred spots that were mystical and unbreakable. Put them in an alien landscape, as relocation did, and their gods could no longer speak to them, and they would lose all identity. On the other hand, for the descendants of the Old Testament, their sojourn through life led through the natural world to the other-earthly heaven. They were instructed by their Heavenly Father, not the false gods of nature-worshipping tribes. These Americans had little sense of place or locale and were oblivious to the Indian's concerns. As writer Frederick Turner notes, "There can be few clearer examples of white America's lack of relationship to the natural world than this policy of removal."[5]

General Background: the Chiricahua Indé

All the Apachean tribes were known to the Spanish as Apachu (or *'a paču*), a Pueblo word meaning "enemy."[6] As related in Chapter 4, all of the "wandering Indians" in the Southwest were distinguished by region. For example, all of those Athapaskan speakers west of the southern Pueblos were known as Apaches de Gila. The Apaches themselves, like the Navajos (or Diné) and others, have another word to describe themselves. That word is Indé (with alternative spellings depending on dialect that include Ndee and Nṇēē), which means "People" or "Human Beings."[7]

If Indé means the people, then *Indeh* is the Apache word for "The Dead," as in a vision where the Indé see themselves attacked by the White Eyes and becoming the Indeh. This, by the way, was the vision that Usen,[8] the Life Giver, gave to Juh prior to his death by drowning in November of 1883. Juh was the Apache spokesman who led the southern band of Chiricahuas in northern Chihuahua in the mid-nineteenth century. Indeh was also the name the Indé gave to themselves when they became prisoners of war in Florida after 1886. Their prison guards, the White Eyes, were *Indah*, "The Living."

Linguistically the Southern Athapaskans can be organized into seven major groupings. In the mid-nineteenth century this included the Navajo in north-western New Mexico and northeastern Arizona, the Western Apache (including the San Carlos, White Mountain, Cibecue, and Dilzhe'e or Tonto Apache) in east-central and central Arizona, the Jicarilla Apache in northwest and northeast New Mexico, the Lipan Apache of southwestern Texas, the Kiowa-Apache who broke off from their cousins to live in Oklahoma and the plains country, the Mescalero east of the Pecos in New Mexico and south into Texas, and the Chiricahuas west of the Río Grande and south of the Gila in southwestern New Mexico, southeastern Arizona (as far west as the San Pedro River Valley), northeastern Sonora, and northwestern Chihuahua.

Excepting the Navajo, today's population is somewhere between 22,000 and 28,000 individuals, with the Western Apache numbering as many as 21,000 plus, while the Chiricahuas number less than 1,000 descendants of prisoners of war living either on the Mescalero reservation, or on land allotments in Fort Sill, Oklahoma. During Mangas Coloradas's lifetime the Chiricahuas probably did not exceed 3,000 and dropped to as little as 500 plus by the time of the Florida captivity.[9]

The timeline for the entry of Apacheans into the Southwest varies with the historian or anthropologist. As mentioned before (see Chapter 4), recent studies place Western Apaches, Navajos, Mescaleros, and Chiricahuas in the Southwest after AD 950, with the Lipan and Jicarilla around 1300, and the Kiowa-Apache after 1500. The latter might have broken off from the Southwestern tribes to become Plains people after 1500.

More traditional theories suggest that all the Apacheans, with the exception of the Kiowa, came into the Southwest about AD 1400. The earlier arrivals hunted at the margins of the mountains and then slowly moved westward. The Navajo and Western Apache arrived first, followed by the Lipan and Jicarilla by 1600, with the Mescalero and Chiricahua Apache moving westward in the early seventeenth century.[10] The latter were very likely being pushed out of the plains and into the mountains of the southwest by the Commanches to their east. When the Chiricahuas moved south into the Mexican plains after 1700 they pushed, in turn, the Tarahumaras into the canyons and mountains of the Sierra Madre.

Athapaskan organization is very confusing, to say the least. Each linguistic collection had its own array of political and cultural traits. For example, the Navajo, influenced by the Pueblo peoples and the Spaniards, developed into farmers and shepherds. The Western Apache superimposed a system of 60 clans based upon maternal kinship over the geographical areas associated with bands. Some scholars even divide the Western Apache into 20 sub-bands, from the Aravaipas to the Mormon Lake and Fossil Creek Indians.[11] The Western Apache also practiced agriculture more intensely and thoroughly than the hunting-gathering-raiding Mescaleros and Chiricahuas. The Jicarilla were heavily influenced by the Plains Indians to their east and the Pueblos to their west, with the result that their culture included the hunting and raiding traditions of the plains with the trading and seasonal agriculture of the Pueblos.

For lack of a better term, it can be stated that the Chiricahuas were loosely organized into bands. Although the number varies with the scholar, most historians would argue that in the nineteenth century there were four bands, each identified with a particular geographical area.[12] The Nednhi (Ndé'ndi, or "Enemy People") were called the southern Chiricahua, and they lived mostly south of the Bavispe River and in the Animas Mountains of northeastern Sonora and southwestern New Mexico, and around the Río Casas Grandes and Río Janos in northwestern Chihuahua. The Chihenne or "Red Painted People" were the easternmost group, and they roamed the region west of the Río Grande that centered on Pinos Altos and the Mimbres Mountains of New Mexico. The western Chiricahua were the Bedonkohe ("In Front of the Enemy"), and they lived in the Mogollon Mountains near the headwaters of the Gila River. Mangas Coloradas was born into this band. Finally, Cochise's assemblage was known as the Chokonen ("Mountainside People") and as the Central Chiricahuas they ranged from the San Pedro River in southern Arizona through their strongholds in the Chiricahua and Dragoon Mountains to the mountains of southwest New Mexico and northern Chihuahua.

The basic unit of Chiricahua society was the nuclear family. Because it was a matrilineal organization, upon marriage men would take up residence near their wife's family in an extended family arrangement. One or more extended family arrangements would make up a *ranchería*, and several rancherías would consist of a local group or family cluster directed by a Headman and/or a Head Woman. Three to five local groups would make a band. The *cacique, jefe*, or leader of the band would sometimes have influence over a particular band, or two or more bands and local groups depending on the situation and needs of the People.[13] In any case the allegiance of the individual Apache was to the local group, not the band.

The terms "chief" and "tribe" always have to be qualified. The Apaches did not have the political unity and organization that the words "chiefdom" and "tribe" imply, and people called "chiefs" did not always have military authority over their followers. A so-called chief was a leader who inspired others. The person who can give the most, provide food and security for the most, is the leader or "chief." He who can articulate the plight and hopes of the people is the "first speaker" or leader. He is not necessarily a warrior. He must care for people, not only kill people. Cochise led by integrity and moral example, as did Mangas Coloradas.[14] A person, like Geronimo, who was a shaman-warrior, was not a chief. He may have possessed the "Power," a gift from Usen, and led his people in warfare, but he was not a "chief." Sometimes a "chief" like Mangas Coloradas managed a portion of the people in a band, and other times he united several bands under his leadership or formed alliances with other bands. At times a headman might be chosen by his followers, and other times, as in the case of Cochise's sons Taza and Naiche, the selection was hereditary.

The Chiricahua creation story, not unlike that of the Navajo and Hopi, begins with the People emerging from the underworld. Usen is the Life Giver and Creator of the Universe, including the Cloud Land or Happy Place where the spirits of good people go. Although the White Eyes could theoretically go to the Happy Place, it is unlikely since, as Chief Juh's son Daklugie noted, "... that'll never be done now, not with Geronimo there." Daklugie further observed that, while Apaches could relate to parts of the Old Testament, "... I doubt many Apaches understand [the idea of] your queer three-headed God. And we make no pretense of loving our enemies as you say you do."[15] Dakulgie, like many contemporary Apaches, mixed his religious notions from both traditional and non-traditional sources.

Over the years, since the imprisonment of 1886, many Indé have developed a syncretic religion composed of Christian and non-Christian elements. One example would be today's Sunrise Ceremony in which at times the Virgin Mary is considered the blessed Mother of Usen, the Creator of Life.[16] The Sunrise Ceremony, which celebrates the life-giving force of White-Painted Woman, the first woman of Creation after the flood, was and is the most important ceremony of the Western Apaches and their Chiricahua cousins.

According to the oral traditions many of the people of ancient times were destroyed by the waters that covered the entire earth except the "White-Ringed Mountain" south of Deming, New Mexico. Hiding in an abalone shell, White-Painted Woman was saved from drowning. After the flood the monsters were killing the remaining human beings. These monsters took the form of a giant, an eagle, a bull buffalo, and an antelope. Then the spirit of Usen came to White-Painted Woman and instructed her to give birth. The spirit said "... lie down on your back and take your clothes off out there. You must have a child by the rain. That boy, when he is born, you must call Child-of-the-Water." The spirit said, "Let the water fall on your navel."[17] And so White-Painted Woman was with child. In some accounts she not only gave birth to a male child, but twin sons, the other boy being named Killer-of-Enemies.

Child-of-the-Water eventually slew the giant with his bow and arrow, sending four arrows in his direction with the fourth one penetrating the giant's heart and "So Child-of-the-Water had killed the giant." When White-Painted Woman saw her two sons and learned about the slaying of the giant she was very happy and sang a song for these boys. She then gave out a high, long cry that you hear today at the girl's puberty rite. Later Child-of-the-Water destroyed the eagle with his war club, and killed the Buffalo Bull and the antelope monster. Although his mother was very happy and sang songs to her twin sons, the one monster that escaped was Death, the result of Coyote throwing a rock in a river and watching it sink. As the old ones say, "Then Coyote threw the rock and it sank. After that the people began to die off."[18]

The Sunrise Ceremony today is a four-day puberty ceremony that takes place in the summer after a young girl experiences her first menses. Usually it starts on a Friday and goes the weekend through Monday morning. Close to a year may expire between the first menstruation and the ceremony. During that time a trusted "godmother" figure will train the young girl on the responsibilities of adulthood, emphasizing the four crucial life objectives that the ceremony seeks to realize. The young girl must seek to attain a healthy old age implying that she has spent her life staying on good terms with the supernatural forces. A second objective is to attain a harmonious disposition, while a third objective, symbolized by morning runs and the molding of her body by the godmother, is physical strength. Finally, prosperity and freedom from hunger are symbolized by the buckskin on which the girl dances.

The four Mountain Spirits also perform at the Sunrise Ceremony. The Mountain Spirit Dancers, or Crown Dances, represent the sacred cardinal points, winds, and colors to the Apache. They are known as *Ga'an* to the Western Apache and the Chiricahuas (while the Eastern Apache know them as *Gaa'he*). Just as Child-of-the-Water triumphed over the evils of the world, so too do the Ga'an dancers protect the People by ensuring their well-being and sheltering them from disease and enemies. It is taboo for anyone to recognize the dancers as persons they know. The impersonators are the Spirits of the Mountain.[19] They are part of shamanic curing ceremonies.

During the ceremony the Ga'an, accompanied by a fifth dancer known as the Grey One or the clown, wield their wooden swords and dance around the fire. The clown acts as a messenger for the other dancers. He carries a bullroarer that produces a distinctive resonating sound to accompany the singers and drummers. It was believed that the sound enticed the wind and rain to aid in the recovery of a sick person.[20] The ritual is not only a transformation rite for the young girl, but an important act that reasserts traditional Apache values, including the importance of place and family.

In the Sunrise Ceremony, the young girl literally is transformed into White-Painted Woman (or White Shell Woman), just as the Crown Dancers "become" the sacred mountain spirits. This is akin to the Hopi who, wearing the garb of specific katsinam, become those katsina spirits, or also like the *Yei* of the Navajo, mountain dwelling supernaturals whose cooperation is critical for the community's well being. The conclusion of the ceremony involves a community blessing bestowed upon the group by White-Painted Woman that assures harmony, cohesiveness, and regeneration (the life force) for the entire group or band.

The Mountain Spirit Dancers and the Grey One perform each evening during the four-day Sunrise Ceremony. The now-deceased Chiricahua artist Allan Houser has celebrated the Ga'an dancers in his art and sculpture (see Figure 5.1). The dancers, their bodies painted black with either zigzag designs or four-pointed stars on their chests, wear black hoods over their heads and faces (like those worn by Navajo *Yei*). The Ga'an regalia include the wearing of an elaborate wood superstructure on the top of the head not unlike the "tablitas" of Hopi katsinam.[21]

According to Philip Cassadore, an Apache authority on the Sunrise Ceremony, "the Ga'an are predictable, stable. The foundation of the world rests on them. The Grey One is unpredictable. He represents chance that

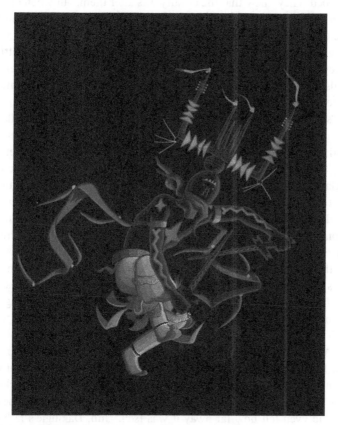

Figure 5.1   *Ghan Dancer* by Allan Houser. Gouache on paper 19.5 × 29. 1959. Courtesy of Houser Foundation and Heard Museum.

comes into a person's life. With the predictable and unpredictable together there is equilibrium, balance. One needs to have strength, balance, to face the unpredictable in life."[22] The Sunrise Ceremony as performed today is likely a product of Apache contact with their Navajo cousins and Pueblo neighbors. Because of this ceremony the four Mountain Spirit Dancers and the clown guarantee to the community the harmony and cohesiveness necessary for the community to survive.

The testimony of Daklugie speaks to the importance of the ceremony even during the Apache Wars of the nineteenth century. He noted that "... Ceremonials for the Maidens are the most sacred of all our religious rites, and in the old days they were observed individually when the girl reached maturity. No matter what the situation the rite was held ... . Once, when my people left San Carlos for their dash for Mexico, they got into the Stein's Peak range and stopped. They knew that the cavalry was after them, but when one of the mothers announced that her daughter had reached maturity, the band had to observe the puberty rite. Women were baking mescal when we were attacked from the north and west."[23] Geronimo (Goyahkla) once halted his battle with US forces long enough to conduct a puberty ceremony for his daughter.

Rituals and ceremonies in honor of the Child-of-the-Water were important for adolescent boys as well. When growing up the male children followed the warrior's path as laid out by Child-of-the Water, beginning with a cradle-board ceremony and continuing through the "Putting on the Moccasins" which celebrated the infants' release from the cradle-board. Their early years were spent running and hunting in the mountains in hopes of sharing the power and spirit of the Ga'an. As a teenager, Geronimo, as an apprenticed warrior, participated in four raids. He learned the special language of the warrior, and learned to fight and defeat the monsters. Like the young girls of the Sunrise ceremony, he drank only through the drinking straw and scratched only with the scratching stick. He learned that eating pork, bear, snakes, or fish was taboo. As Elbys Hugar, the granddaughter of Chief Naiche, noted, "We don't eat anything that breathes under water." Apaches believed that water animals possessed the spirits of bad Apaches. After the four sacred campaigns, and at the age of 17, Geronimo was admitted to the council of warriors. His was the path of warfare; the path of Child-of-the-Water.[24]

Most Apache leaders had the "Power," a spiritual force that derived from animals or birds and a gift of Usen. According to Daklugie, "Chief Chihuahua [Chokonen] had the Power over horses ... . He could heal them of sickness or wounds." Concerning Lozen, the sister of Victorio, she "... could locate the enemy and even tell how far away it was [sic]." Juh, Daklugie's father, and Geronimo could foretell the future and had the Power to handle men.[25] Geronimo allegedly could control the weather by redirecting lightning or bringing rain.[26] He could even halt the dawn until his warriors were ready for the morning ambush. He could walk across the desert without leaving footprints. And when the voice of Usen spoke to him a fourth time he was told that "No gun can ever kill you ... I will take the bullets from the guns of the Mexicans, so they will have nothing but powder. And I will guide your arrows."[27]

Although the Chiricahua lifestyle was semi-sedentary, with occasional farming of corn, beans, and squash, the bulk of their sustenance came from hunting and gathering. As in most hunting-gathering societies, the men did the hunting while the women and children did the gathering. Hunting was done most often in the spring, before the crops were ripe, or in the autumn when the meat and animal hides were at their best. During the summer and early fall the women and children would gather acorns and wild plants in the mountains, and when the cold would drive the People to lower altitudes they would collect their primary food—mescal or agave cactus that would be cooked in an underground pit. While originally the mountains provided a variety of ecological zones for food, they also provided relief from the summer heat. After the Spaniards and Mexicans arrived they could also be used to hide from their pursuers and to cache food, ammunition, and supplies.[28]

The Chiricahuas were also known for their expertise in raiding and warfare, two very different activities. Although the O'odham villagers were the object of early attacks, raiding increased with the arrival of the Spaniards in the Southwest. When the Spanish churchmen, soldiers, and colonists came, they brought with them their horses, sheep, cattle, and other livestock. Although the Spanish naturally thought of people stealing their livestock as a hostile act, it is not clear that the Indé saw it the same way. Unaccustomed to viewing livestock as private property, the Apache may have looked at Spanish livestock as a new kind of wild game. In fact, the first horses and cattle they encountered prior to the Spaniards themselves were feral, and raiding to the Apache was simply another form of hunting. And raiding was always a limited activity that did not necessarily involve violence. The raiders usually wanted horses but would often leave other livestock alone with the hope of raiding again at a later date.[29]

Yet it is true that warfare often accompanied raiding, as war parties were avenging past wrongs (blood revenge) that often included seizing captives as well as killing the enemy. These acts of war would lead to counter acts of revenge in a never-ending cycle of violence and chaos between Spaniard and Apache, Mexican and Apache, and finally, American and Apache.

The Greatest of Wrongs: Apache History to 1863

Narrator Stephen Trimble in a general history of Southwestern Indians noted that "The Apaches set the northern limits to New Spain. Confrontation began early; when Apaches raided Spanish expeditions for horses, the soldiers retaliated and by doing so brought down the brunt of Apache revenge in full-scale war expeditions."[30] In Apachería, what the Spaniards called the Apache homeland, the *españoles* not only fought and killed the Apaches, but also sold their women and children into slavery. The Chiricahuas retaliated by raiding south into northern Mexico, while the Western Apaches attacked the O'odham and Navajo peoples, and the Dilzhe'e (or Tonto Apache), along with their Yavapai neighbors, raided the Havasupais and Hualapais. After 1786, the Spaniards made peace with the Apaches, convinced them to live near the presidios, gave them rations and mescal (the latter resulting in drunken binges), and rickety rifles that might be usable for hunting but not for warfare. This purchased peace lasted until the end of the Spanish era in 1821.

While Apache fortunes declined, the Comanche and Ute situations improved. Spain's policy of divide-and-rule meant that Spaniards were often allied with Comanches and Utes against the Apache. The Comanche became a major link in the network that connected Indian slaves with the market in New Spain. Mescalero and Chiricahua Apaches were cut off from the horse trade with New Spain and the French gun merchants of the Mississippi Valley. Their indigenous enemies forced them off the plains into the range and basin country of southern Arizona and northern Mexico. Many Apaches became prisoners of war and were forced to labor in the mines, factories, and farms of northern New Spain. At the same time counter raiding against Spaniards, Pueblos, Comanches, and other Indian groups increased. The era of endemic warfare ensued and persisted throughout Mexican times.[31]

As Mexico won its independence from Spain in 1821 it entered the world of global politics a weak debtor nation, especially when its rivals included the up-and-coming Americans. It was on the periphery of the world -economy, and was dependent on agriculture and mining through highly coercive forms of labor.[32] Factious priests, discontented landlords, ambitious politicians, and a conservative hierarchy of churchmen and bureaucrats fought one another, like Hernando Cortés, for "glory, gold, and god."

With economic ruin on the horizon in the form of abandoned haciendas, flooded mines, and, after 1829, Spaniards fleeing with their talent and their capital, Mexico could not afford to administer the Southwest frontier. On the frontier the Jesuits had been expelled in 1767, and the Franciscans did not have the resources to administer in their absence. And the federal army was needed to fight disputes in Mexico City, not wild Indians on the frontier. The presidios were reduced in number, and Sonora and Chihuahua had to rely on less experienced militia soldiers for fighting. The locals were left with the obligation of pacifying the *indios*, an obligation they soon filled after 1835 by placing a bounty of $100 on every male Apache scalp. While hiring scalp hunters and paying for scalps turned out to be a rather inefficient form of genocide, it did arouse the hatred of the Chiricahuas for the Mexicans. The policy led the Apaches to cease taking prisoners of war, and instead they turned their male captives over to female relatives of slain Apache men for torture.[33] The dislike of Apaches for the Mexicans had no limits. And the most effective Apache chieftain who directed that hatred during the period between 1835 and 1863 was Mangas Coloradas.

Mangas Coloradas was the name the Mexicans gave to him. It came from his nickname Kan-da-zis Tlishishen, or "Red Sleeves." His Apache name was Dasoda-hae meaning "He Just Sits There." He was always a big man, being at least 6 feet 4 inches tall when he was in his 70s. Self-confident, he displayed generosity to his People and wisdom in addressing their problems. He was a devoted family man, and usually rode at the head of his warriors. Born a Bedonkohe, he married into the Chihennes, and in his prime attracted followers from all four of the Chiricahua bands. His favorite area was the Pinos Altos region of western New Mexico. In his later years his most important bond was with his son-in-law Cochise, the legendary leader of the Chokonen. And peculiarly enough, he was the one Chiricahua who generally trusted the Americans, and until 1860–1861 did not seek war with them.[34]

His main enemies lived in Sonora, and like Cochise and Geronimo, he came to despise those *mexicanos* who practiced the art of scalping and executed their Apache male enemies while selling the Apache women and children into slavery. The authorities and soldiers from Sonora would feign friendship, ply them with mescal, and then slaughter them indiscriminately. The Sonorans often crossed into New Mexico and Chihuahua to massacre Indians that were supposedly under the protection of the Mexican authorities. These circumstances led to a constant state of warfare so that Mangas Coloradas and his followers were involved in an unending series of clashes with their Mexican counterparts.[35]

Two major incidents soured Mangas Coloradas and the Chiricahuas on the Mexicans. The first occurred in 1837, and is known as the Johnson Massacre. John Johnson, an Anglo living in Moctezuma, Sonora left that place in early April with a small mercenary army of 22 Mexicans and "gringos" with authorization to hunt down hostile Apaches. On April 22, when the Apaches entered his camp to trade peacefully, the "white eyes" unleashed their surprise by firing a small swivel cannon "charged with metal scraps" at the Indian traders, killing at least 20 Apaches and wounding several others, including women and children. One of the dead was Juan José Campá, a leader of the Nednhi Apache.[36]

Although contemporary accounts do not mention the presence of Mangas Coloradas, it is obvious from oral history sources and other evidence that the great leader was either there or very influenced by this event. After the Johnson affair Mangas Coloradas became more aggressive and actively sought vengeance on the

Mexicans. He underwent a metamorphosis, for it was one thing to attempt to defeat the Apache in warfare, another to perform a treacherous attack without regard to age or sex. A new stone had been overturned by the Sonorans, and it was called "extermination."[37]

The second incident occurred in July 1846, several months after the beginning of the Mexican War and one month prior to the arrival of General Stephen W. Kearny, commander of the Army of the West and its 1,500 men, at Santa Fe. This was the so-called Kirker Massacre. James Kirker was an Irishman who came to New York in 1810 and migrated west to Saint Louis in 1817 before arriving in Santa Fe in 1824. Hired as a scalp hunter by the Governor of Chihuahua in the 1830s, throughout the 1830s and into the mid-1840s he led a group of mercenaries in hopes of exterminating Apaches. Near Galeana, Chihuahua, on the evening of July 6 the Indé, invited to a feast and in a festive mood (and supposedly under the protection of a treaty agreement), imbibed in mescal and whiskey and by morning were lying in a drunken stupor. In the early morning of July 7, 1846, Kirker's party slaughtered between 130 and 148 Chiricahuas in their sleep. They killed everyone they could, including pregnant women and children. After the deed they marched to Chihuahua with their scalps carried on poles and were greeted by the Governor, a group of priests, and a marching band.[38]

Mangas Coloradas was once again greatly angered and agitated. In his description of the event he said that "my people were invited to a feast; aguardiente or whiskey was there; my people drank and became intoxicated, and were lying asleep, when a party of Mexicans came in and beat out their brains with clubs."[39] Most of the victims were not "hostiles;" they belonged to the moderate and peaceful factions of the Chokonen band. After 1846, every Chiricahua band, moderates and "hostiles," went to war against Mexico. For the rest of the era Mangas Coloradas would reject all peaceful entreaties from the Mexicans. And there would be more challenges in the near future, that group of "white eyes" known as Americans.[40]

The years between 1845 and 1860 were relatively peaceful for the Americans and the Chiricahuas. The American war against Mexico began in the spring of 1846. When Kearny arrived in Santa Fe on August 18, 1846, he quickly occupied New Mexico and went about establishing a temporary government. Although the Apaches were unaware of his new-found friendship with the Hispanic population of New Mexico, and his enmity toward their enemies (i.e., Apaches and Navajos), he was well received by the indigenous population who were happy to see the Americans at war with their long time enemy, the Mexicans. A subtle shift of power was happening in the American Southwest as Sonora and Chihuahua shifted their concern away from "genocide" for the Indians to the possibility of invasion by the US Army. When Mangas Coloradas met Kearny for the first time on October 18 near the abandoned Santa Rita del Cobre outside of Pinos Altos, he and a few Chihenne warriors gave Kearny a friendly reception.[41] With the exception of a few misunderstandings, Mangas Coloradas maintained peaceful relations with the Americans, especially the US Army, until the discovery of gold at Pinos Altos in 1860 and the Bascom incident of February 1861.

Gold fever was the catalyst that would speed up the process of conflict between Mangas Coloradas and his American friends. After the Gadsen Purchase of 1853, which ceded territory south of the Gila River by Mexico to the United States, the US military was treaty bound to prevent indigenous raids into Sonora and northern Mexico from US territory. The Apache homeland now fell largely into American hands, and the Americans were no longer at war with their eternal enemy. As development occurred in the 1850s, the American Southwest and northern Mexico slowly became economically integrated into the American monolith. The Americans were now free to deal with the "Indian problem."

Just as the discovery of gold at Sutter's mill in 1848 attracted over 300,000 colonists between 1848 and 1855 who aided in the enslavement of the California Indians; or the Argonauts of 1862 and 1863 searching for the "Golden Fleece" along the Colorado and Hassayampa Rivers in Arizona displaced their Quechen, Mojave, and Yavapai hosts (see Chapter 6); or the George Armstrong Custer expedition of 1874 into the Black Hills of Dakota where gold was discovered by his men on August 2,[42] a discovery that would lead to the disaster of the Little Bighorn and the eventual demise of the Sioux Indians—so too would Hicks, Birch, and Jacob Snivley make the first strike of gold in the Pinos Altos Mountains on May 8, 1860, sending gold-crazed men from Mexico, California, Texas, and Arizona into the heartland of Chiricahua country. Within one month over 500 miners had arrived at Pinos Altos, and Mangas Coloradas no longer could tolerate the now Anglo–Mexican presence in a land that defined his place and identity.[43]

The miners were unlike the earlier intruders. The trappers passed through the country following the beaver to California. Even the employees of the Butterfield Overland Mail Company were small in number and did little harm to the hunting and gathering grounds of the natives. So too for the surveyors who traveled through Apache country trying to determine an international boundary. But the miners were different. They did not traverse through Apache country, they came to Apache country. They did not jog through and around Mother Earth. Instead they dug into the ground and defaced Mother Earth. As men without women, they became men with many women—women who were often the object of rape and mistreatment. Their presence would soon draw other Anglos to the area as ranchers, farmers, merchants, prostitutes, ministers and priests, and soldiers—and they provided beef, foodstuffs, equipment, sexual and social services, religious support, and protection for the community of miners.

And, of course, they lusted after gold, a metal that was taboo to the Apache. Chiricahua Apache Dan Nicholas told Eve Ball that "An Apache may pick up nuggets from the dry bed of a stream but he is forbidden to 'grub in Mother Earth' for it. It is the symbol of the sun and hence sacred to Ussen [sic]. I have never seen an Apache wear anything made of gold."[44] In addition, the miner population was made up of rugged individuals who themselves were often fugitives from justice. They had no sensitivity to the Native Americans, and often while intoxicated, would form miner's militias such as the Gila Rangers or the Arizona Guards to engage the Apache enemy.[45] Therefore, their presence in Pinos Altos was not only disturbing to the Apache, and a source of violence and conflict, but a dishonor of Usen.

As for the other incident, the infamous "Bascom Affair" of 1861 started with the kidnapping by a group of Apaches of a "coyote" or half-breed child of a Mexican mother and an Irish father. The boy was later known as Mickey Free. Second Lieutenant George N. Bascom left Fort Buchanan near the Sonoita Valley and traveled to Apache Pass to parley with Cochise concerning the alleged kidnapping. Cochise, his wife Dos-the-seh (daughter of Mangas Coloradas), his infant son Naiche, his brother Coyuntura, and two other male relatives came to Bascom's station. Cochise denied that any member of his band had done the kidnapping. Bascom, not understanding the nature of Chiricahua political organization, detained Cochise and his family and told him that he would be under house (tent?) arrest until the boy was returned to his parents. Cochise cut his way out of the tent and fled, leaving his relatives in Bascom's custody. Because Bascom would not negotiate with him for the freedom of his relatives, Cochise retaliated by capturing a Mexican train and torturing to death his four white prisoners. Bascom responded by hanging six Apaches, including Cochise's brother Coyuntura, and his two adult male relatives. He did release Cochise's wife and infant son.[46]

As Dakulgie noted, "From that time on Cochise (c. 1805–1874) harassed the invaders." Historian Edward Sweeney, whose account of the Bascom affair differs from that of Dakulgie, is in agreement with the later when he said that "... no reputable historian can dispute the impression that war between Cochise and Americans began after the affair." Later that year, Mangas and Cochise allied their bands and strove to drive all Americans from Apache country. In Mangas Coloradas own words spoken in September 1862, he was "... at peace with the world until the troops attacked & killed many of his people." While gold had been discovered earlier at Pinos Altos in 1860, he was now ready to declare war.[47]

In early 1861 the miners began to abandon the Pinos Altos mines. The Overland Mail Company had also withdrawn. Then the army began to evacuate the military posts in Apache country. Cochise threatened to exterminate all the white farmers and ranchers in Arizona, and without the protection of the military they too would flee for their lives. Soon the trail from Mesilla to Tucson was devoid of whites. By July 1861, the two leaders, Cochise and Mangas Coloradas, emboldened by the withdrawal of the enemy, joined forces in order to force the remaining Anglos to leave New Mexico. Little did they know that the United States was in a civil war and federal troops were being recalled east to face the threat of Confederate troops out of El Paso and elsewhere.[48]

Then in the spring of 1862 the Chiricahuas faced a new reality. Not a return from the Río Grande of the troops that went east, but the arrival of a volunteer American force from California. The California Column was under the leadership of Brigadier General James Henry Carleton and had come to repel a Confederate invasion of New Mexico. When the Confederate threat was defeated, Carleton turned his attention to the native populations, especially the Navajos, Mescaleros, and Chiricahuas.

Several skirmishes occurred between Carleton and the Apaches, the most important being the battle of Apache Pass that took place in July of that year. The Apaches had planned an ambush that would prevent the soldiers from getting to the water resources at Apache Spring. Howitzers allowed Carleton's troops to own the high ground and avoid disaster. Eventually, Mangas Coloradas would be wounded, and, after the fighting, was taken to Janos by his Apache warriors, where a Mexican doctor nursed him back to health. With the fighting over Carleton established a new post near Apache Pass called Fort Bowie.[49]

A few months later, with his wounds healed, Mangas returned to his beloved Santa Lucía Springs and the Mogollon Mountains. The Bluecoats had punished his Chiricahuas for their hostilities of the past 18 months. It was time to retire, seek peace, and live the life of a farmer. But Carleton had other ideas, and he would make Mangas Coloradas pay for his past infidelities.[50]

In September of 1862 Mangas Coloradas sued for peace, but Carleton, who at about the same time was to order the death of all adult male Mescaleros, paid no attention to Mangas's entreaties. He had seen the evidence of death and destruction in the skeletons, corpses, and depredations in the mines and ranches. He was new to the region and had not experienced the history of peaceful solicitations and unlimited parleys that the diplomat Mangas Coloradas had had with whites. He thought that by executing Mangas Coloradas he could bring an end to the conflict. Instead, of course, it would only initiate a new series of counter offenses and violence.

Carleton ordered Lieutenant Colonel Joseph Rodman West (soon to become Brigadier General of volunteers) to arrest Mangas Coloradas. West, in charge of the New Mexican troops near Pinos Altos, planned a scheme to ensnare the Chiricahua leader. He would use the services of Jack-of-all-trades-Swilling, who was serving as a scout in the anti-Apache campaign. Meanwhile, in early January 1863 Mangas Coloradas and a splinter group of his followers journeyed to New Mexico and Pinos Altos to receive rations and make peace with the Americans. They went to Pinos Altos against the earlier advice of Geronimo and the later warnings of Victorio and Nana.[51]

Outside of Pinos Altos, Swilling (perhaps in the company of pathfinder and prospector Joseph R. Walker) practiced his chicanery with the Apache leader when Mangas, thinking he was entering a peace parley, was taken ransom by Swilling and his militia. Mangas Coloradas, now a prisoner of the whites, dismissed Victorio and one of his sons with a warning to them that they "were not fooling with Mexicans now." Swilling turned Mangas Coloradas over to Colonel West and his troops, who in turn consigned him to a small adobe room at Fort McLane south of Pinos Altos.[52]

On the evening of January 18, 1863, Mangas was being watched by his sentries. New guards came on duty at midnight, and around 1:00 AM they started teasing and torturing him by heating their bayonets over a fire and then putting them to the legs and feet of Mangas. When Mangas reacted to these acts the two guards each fired shots into his head. West's earlier command to kill Mangas was fulfilled. West later reported that Mangas was killed after attempting to escape, an official lie that was later repudiated by several California volunteers who talked about the incident.

Soon after his body was dug up and uncovered by some soldiers. They then proceeded to decapitate the body of the Apache leader, boil the head, and send it east. Mangas's head was first sent to the famous phrenologist Orson Squire Fowler in New York City. From there it ended up in the Smithsonian Institution in Washington. This was just one more example of mutilation in the history of US–Indian affairs. Carleton's so-called "Black Flag" policy only served to further increase the hostilities between the two peoples. It was, as Geronimo said, the "Greatest of Wrongs."[53]

Cochise, Geronimo, and Guerrilla Warfare, 1863–1886

The death of Mangas Coloradas only exacerbated the already troubled relationship between the Americans and the Apaches. Throughout the decade of the 1860s the Apaches, especially the Chiricahuas, held the field. According to narrator Stephen Trimble, "the US Army spent $38 million from 1862 to 1871 to kill 100 Apaches (including old men, women, and children.) The Apaches themselves killed over 1,000 American troops and civilians during the same time."[54]

Kit Carson, who was busy rounding up the Navajo and sending them to Fort Sumner in 1863–1864, later fought the First Battle of Adobe Walls in November 1864 in which 400 US soldiers and Ute Indians confronted over 1,000 Comanche and Kiowa Apaches in the Texas panhandle. This was the largest Indian War battle in the nineteenth-century history of the Great Plains.[55]

But more violence took place in Arizona's Arivaipa Valley in late April of 1871. There, an alliance of several white Americans, 30 to 40 Mexicans, and almost 100 Tohono O'odham Indians (also called Papagos) had left Tucson and hiked past Camp Grant (and the federal army) to the nearby Arivaipa Apache campground in the bottom of the lower canyon. On the morning of April 30 they surrounded the Apaches and murdered nearly 150 men, women, and children in their sleep. The day before there had been between 400 to 500 Indé camping in Aravaipa. Most of those who escaped were male hunter-warriors. The protection that the US Army had assured the Aravaipa was nowhere to be found. The "Camp Grant Massacre," which is what its eastern critics called it (as well as the Marias Massacre of 1870), violated the spirit of an ongoing change in the nation's Indian policy that President Ulysses S. Grant had called since 1869 his "Peace Policy."[56]

In 1869 Grant announced his policy that the US would no longer continue to make war against the Apaches and other "wild" ones. In the context of the long history of relocation, he would make peace with the Indians and place them on reservations. His hope was one of civilizing the savages by putting them on reserves where they would have the advantages of civilization such as farming, raising stock, and acquiring an education. This of course would involve the abandonment of hunting grounds. The "Peace Policy" acknowledged the several attempts at peace that the Apaches had made in the past. Of course, those Indians that could not be civilized, or found outside the reservation, that is, the "bad ones," would have to be killed.[57]

The application of the "Peace Policy" in Arizona soon led after 1872 to the establishment of three reservations—Camp Verde for the Northern Tonto Apache and Yavapai, San Carlos for many of the White Mountain and Aravaipa Apaches, and Fort Apache for some of the other Western Apache groups. The Camp Verde Reservation was on the upper Verde River, San Carlos was east of what would in 1875 become the mining town of Globe (itself east of Phoenix), and Fort Apache was west of the White Mountains north of the San Carlos Reservation. Outside Arizona a fourth reservation was established in the Mogollon Mountains at Tularosa, New Mexico. The Chihennes under Victorio had been sent there from Ojo Caliente, the hot springs west of the Río Grande that was the traditional sacred grounds of the Chiricahua.

In 1872, to implement his "Peace Policy," President Grant relieved Major General Oliver O. Howard from his duties with the Freedmen's Bureau and dispatched him on a mission of peace to the Southwest Indians. For all of his paternalistic and ethnocentric views, Howard believed that the Indians should have deeds to their own properties and that their land should be used to cultivate "civilization." He understood that the policy of extermination was wrong, and that most conflicts developed because of the white man's greed and not the Indian's deceit.[58]

Howard traveled to Tularosa where they met Victorio and Taglito ("Red Beard"); the nickname the Chiricahuas gave to Thomas J. Jeffords, an Indian agent, scout, and friend of Cochise. Jeffords agreed to set up a meeting with Cochise who reportedly was in his stronghold in the Dragoon Mountains. Jeffords and Howard hired an Indian guide named Chie who was the nephew of Cochise. The four of them then journeyed to Ojo Caliente where Howard met another Chiricahua named Ponce who was said to be the son of Mangas Coloradas and Jun's *segundo* (the apprentice who is being trained as a successor). He agreed to be the expedition's guide and interpreter. Since Howard's agreement with Jeffords was that they not be accompanied by troops, the final group that finally caught up with Cochise consisted of Howard, his aide, Jeffords, and the guides, Ponce and Chie.[59]

Cochise greeted his friend Jeffords warmly, and was courteous to the general. He told Howard: "Nobody wants peace more than I do. I have killed ten white men for every Indian I have lost, but still the white men are no less, and my tribe keeps growing smaller and smaller, till it will disappear from the face of the earth if we do not have a good peace soon."[60] He repeated what he had told an earlier peace commissioner, "... that the great people that welcomed you with acts of kindness to this land are now but a feeble band that fly before your soldiers as the deer before the hunter."[61]

The agreement placed a large reserve of public land near Sulphur Springs and Apache Pass adjacent to Fort Bowie. Because Jeffords would have complete autonomy as the agent chosen by Cochise, General George Crook and the army at Fort Bowie would not be able to intervene in reservation matters. But the Mexicans were a separate matter, and Cochise, like Mangas Coloradas and Geronimo, had no love for the Sonorans. The Chiricahua Reservation located in southeast Arizona adjoined northern Sonora, and Howard's failure to get an agreement preventing the Chiricahuas from raiding Sonora became a major grievance for the US authorities.[62] In any case, within two months, 600 Nednhi led by Juh joined the 450 followers of Cochise.[63]

Cochise was now content—the reservation was organized, and Jeffords had brought some sympathetic stability to the life of the band. And the location of the reservation was on ancestral grounds. Hopefully, the nearby army would provide security from their Anglo and Indian enemies, and not interfere with the domestic concerns of the Chiricahuas. And, best of all, the endless cycle of violence would stop.

The only major problem was the inability of Cochise to control the various Chiricahua groups, with Apaches from Tularosa and Nednhi tribesmen from Chihuahua visiting the Chiricahua Reservation in order to get provisions and then continuing on to raid Sonora. The main route to manhood and leadership had always been raiding, and slipping away to Mexico was the easiest way to gain success with family and band. Then, unfortunately, on June 8, 1874, Cochise died of natural causes (stomach cancer?).[64]

Without the leadership of Cochise, limited as it was, the situation at the Chiricahua Reservation worsened. Soon the Chiricahuas at Tularosa and Sulphur Springs were ordered to leave their reservations and go to captivity at San Carlos. Daklugie described San Carlos as "the worst place in all the great territory stolen from the Apaches. Where there is no grass there is no game. Nearly all the vegetation was cacti. The heat was terrible. The insects were terrible. The water was terrible.... Insects and rattlesnakes seemed to thrive there; and no White Eye could possibly fear and dislike snakes [a taboo item] more than do Apaches."[65] The choices seemed to be either slavery or imprisonment at San Carlos, or death in the battle with the White Eyes.

Although by 1876 John P. Clum, the San Carlos Indian Agent, succeeded in concentrating over 5,000 Chiricahua and Western Apaches, several others followed Victorio, Juh, and Geronimo in fleeing reservation life. Chaos ensued throughout the decade of 1876 to 1886 with bands moving on and off the reservation. First, the Apaches would flee the reservation to the security of Mexico's Sierra Madre Mountains, then they would peacefully return to seek out relatives, recruits, and rations, and then they would flee again to the mountains. Each time the dissidents and renegades would be sought and fought by the Mexican *federales* (national army), *rurales* (rural militias), US Army personnel, California Volunteers, and Apache and Yavapai scouts.[66]

It was at this time that Geronimo (Goyathlay or Goyahkla, "one who yawns"; 1829–1909), who had been fighting Mexicans and New Mexicans for 25 years, came to the attention of the Americans.[67] Not because he was an Apache leader fighting for his people, but because he was a reservation Indian who refused to "stay put." Initially in 1877, because he refused to go to San Carlos, he was captured at Ojo Caliente by Clum with the assistance of over 100 White Mountain policemen. In irons he climbed aboard an army wagon, and escorted by the cavalry he arrived at San Carlos with 16 other prisoners on May 20. Once again he found himself behind bars, a situation he would have to tolerate for four months.[68] Geronimo would lead his renegades in three more breakouts from San Carlos, the first in 1878, another in 1881, and the last one in 1885.

Between Geronimo's first breakout and his second, two events of importance took place. The first occurred between September 1879 and October 1880 and is called the Victorio War. After being forced to move between his beloved Ojo Caliente homeland, San Carlos, and the Mescalero Reservation in the Sierra Blanca (north of Tularosa, east of the Rio Grande in south-central New Mexico) several times, Victorio and his three hundred plus warriors battled thousands of American and Mexican forces. By April he could no longer find sanctuary on the Mescalero Reservation, and therefore, retreated into Mexico. On October 15, at Tres Castillos, Chihuahua, surrounded by Mexican troops, he and many of his followers were annihilated.[69]

Oral history tells us that Victorio died from his own hand, and suggests that if his sister Lozen had been with him with her "Power" he would not have been defeated. As James Kaywaykla, an apprentice in Victorio's band noted: "I have always believed, along with many other Apaches, that had Lozen been with us at Tres Castillos her brother would never have ridden into the trap of the Mexican cavalry."[70]

The death of Victorio made of him a martyr to the Apache people. Geronimo and his warriors now strengthened their resolve to fight even harder against the White Eyes. Earlier, in January 1880, after three months of fighting in the Victorio War (fighting that involved a major battle in October 1879 in northern Chihuahua and a massacre at Carrizal), Geronimo and Juh and their followers had left the battlefield and returned to San Carlos.[71] There, Geronimo, while subordinate to Juh, slowly allied himself with the Chiricahua headman, Naiche, Cochise's son. They would soon become unlikely participants in what would become known as the Battle of Cibecue Creek of 1881, the second major event of the time. The White Eyes called it the "Cibecue Massacre."

The concentration and relocation policy that the US government had been pursuing since 1871 and Grant's "Peace Policy" eventually led to the discontentment and dissension of the Apache peoples. In early 1875, as part of the consolidation of Indian agencies, Camp Verde was closed and 1,476 Tonto Apaches and Yavapais were brought to San Carlos. In June, Fort Apache was closed with several White Mountain Indians going to San Carlos. In January 1876 they were joined by the Cibecue tribe, another Western Apache group. And in June of that year several hundred Chiricahuas left Fort Bowie for San Carlos. This is the policy that created the receptive audiences for the Prophet.[72]

Many Apaches, especially the Cibecue, were willing to listen to a prophet and medicine man or woman who would promise them that their old lifestyle could be resurrected and their dead chiefs return. During the summer of 1881 that prophet appeared in the form of the Coyotero Apache shaman and

medicine man Noca del Klinny (also called Nakadoklini) who performed ceremonies, prayers, and dances at Cibecue Creek. He communicated with the
spirits of dead Indians. For example, Juh and Nana (Chihenne chief), leaving
Geronimo and Lozen at their Cibecue campsite, accompanied the Prophet up
a hill and, feeling the gathering of the Power, saw in the mist three figures
forming—Mangas Coloradas, Cochise, and Victorio.[73] The dead said that there
should be peace with the White Eyes, but that they would not return until the
white people leave their country, and that "the whites will be out of the country
when the corn gets ripe."[74] Usen would resolve all difficulties. This was the
message of Noca del Klinny that aroused both whites and Apaches.

Trouble exploded in August when the military and civil authorities became
worried that the Prophet was plotting a revolt. Orders went out for the arrest of
the Prophet. On August 30 two troops of cavalry and a company of Indian
scouts, including some of Noca del Klinny's own Cibecue people, arrived from
Fort Apache at the Prophet's wikiup near Cibecue Creek. After the Prophet was
arrested and in the custody of the US military, several Apaches arrived and violence broke out. When it was over 7 soldiers had been killed and 18 Apaches lay
dead on the ground, including the Prophet, his wife and his son. Whether the
Apaches knowingly set up an ambush, or were the victims of a misconceived
interference in their religious life by the White Eyes is still being debated.[75]

Some of the Apache scouts had mutinied and joined their brethren in the
fight. The troops made a hasty retreat to Fort Apache, where two days later the
Apaches attacked in retaliation for the death of their medicine man. The military reacted with a massive offensive in the White Mountains and around San
Carlos, sending several Indians fleeing in several directions. This included
Geronimo, Naiche, and Juh and approximately 400 Chiricahua warriors,
women and children, who fled to the stronghold of Mexico's Sierra Madre.
This was Geronimo's second breakout. He would return to San Carlos in 1883
and 1884, only to have his third, and final, breakout in 1885.[76]

The last chase that led to the surrender of Geronimo and his 36 followers and
relatives started in March 1886 and was conducted by General George Crook.
At the *Cañón de los Embudos* (Funnel Canyon) in northern Chihuahua, Crook
promised Geronimo that he would only be in exile in Florida for two years,
after which he and family could retire at San Carlos. While most of Chihuahua's
followers returned with Crook to San Carlos, Geronimo, Naiche, Lozen and
their small group of dissidents once again fled back to Mexico. With Geronimo
in flight General Crook, after ordering Chihuahua's 77 people to board the
railway cars at Bowie Station to be sent East under armed guard, finally
resigned and was replaced by General Nelson Miles.[77]

This time the new commander took 5,000 troops, one-fourth of the US Army,
and, with the aid of Chiricahua Apache scouts, found and negotiated with the
37 free Apaches. Geronimo and Miles met each other at Skeleton Canyon just

north of the border. On September 4, 1886, Geronimo and his small group of followers laid down their arms and agreed to return to Fort Bowie.[78]

With Geronimo, Naiche, Lozen, and the others in his hands, Miles ordered all of the people who had been living peacefully at San Carlos and Fort Apache, including Indian scouts in the service of the US government, to departure points near the railway terminals. The Fort Apache group, after a long and difficult walk from the fort, left from Holbrook in 18 railway cars. The 383 Chiricahuas at San Carlos, including 103 children, were sent east to join their friends and relatives in exile. Geronimo soon received the same fate. Obviously, the White Eyes did not understand that sending the People into exile was a way of attempting to kill them—not their bodies, but their spirits. As western writer Steven Trimble notes, quoting Chiricahua headman Chihuahua summing up the sorrow of his people, "It would have been a good day to die."[79]

For the Americans this was the end of 44 years of Apache tactics and guerrilla warfare. Apache scout and Geronimo critic Jason Betzinez warned the White Eyes: "You white people can now go about your business without fear of attack by the Apaches. But you are still subject to being preyed upon. Beware of your own, who are seeking an easy path to wealth at your expense!"[80]

Many of these wealth seekers had been the gold hunters and their supporters that the Apache had hunted themselves. Just as hunting was related to raiding, so too was hunting the prelude for ambush and other guerrilla tactics. The Apache heritage of guerrilla warfare went back to Spanish and Mexican times, and included tactics, technology, and strategy that made them some of the most elusive and unpredictable foes the Americans had ever encountered.

Until the mid-1880s the Apaches were militarily superior to their American foes. Part of the reason for this was their knowledge and use of the local environment, as well as their cultural traditions that emphasized the training of youth and the leadership of elders. Obviously, the Chiricahua knew their homeland. It was sacred to them. This was an advantage that very few American soldiers had. Apache lands included not only barren desert with flats and canyons but also mountains covered with pine forests and water resources. As a mountain people, the Apache learned to hunt and gather in this rugged terrain. And when it came to warfare they knew how to use the mountains to flee from their pursuers, establish alternative campsites, and cache food, clothing, and ammunition. They also knew how to establish rendezvous points each day when leaving their campsites. These were used if the group had to split up after a successful raid or ambush.[81]

As for training, young Apache apprentice warriors would be required to run long distances over unfriendly terrain, running as many as 70 miles a day. Instruction in hunting developed the concealment skills that an aspiring warrior would need. They learned to move across the land with speed, and they had a stamina that went far beyond their Mexican or American soldiers chasing them. Their hunting-gathering skills meant that they were never too far from water or wild food, and they could march for days without much sleep. Leaders, like those who became shaman-warriors and chiefs, were usually selected by the community for the meritorious skills they demonstrated (although Cochise's sons were an example of hereditary succession).[82]

The Apache lifestyle was dependent upon raiding. The horses and cattle of Sonora and Chihuahua were the life blood of the Indé. Apache warriors would gather loot to consume and goods to be traded. The enemy's property would then be moved north of the border or to an adjacent Mexican state to be traded and exchanged for guns and ammunition. Raiding, of course, would provoke a reaction from the Mexicans and Americans, and to respond to these reactions the Apaches developed their strategies and tactics of guerrilla warfare.[83]

These responses included everything from evasion, a variety of ambush tactics, and direct and indirect attacks. The most obvious evasion tactic was to manifest the facade of fleeing while in reality leading their pursuers into a surprise attack. Sometimes the Apaches would wear *serapes* and sombreros to disguise themselves as Mexicans, hoping to fool both their Mexican and American opponents. Women and children were often used as decoys to trick the enemy into following them into an ambush. A common technique was to lay a trail with footprints (or horse prints) and then double back to take up a concealed position. At times they would use the *ad hoc* ambush known as the "roadside bomb" technique. These would be killing zones located, not in the mountains, but in apparently flat terrain where the pursuers thought ambush would be unlikely. But small, narrow gorges and arroyos could conceal a fighter until the enemy was on top of them. This is the type of ambush used by Cochise in 1862 at Apache Pass at a time when the Apaches were still reliant upon bows and muzzle-loading firearms with limited range that could be used in close-order fighting.[84]

Other aspects of Apache fighting were the targeting of their enemies' horses and mules so as to destroy their means of transportation. Capturing pack mules often led to the taking of provisions and ammunition that the Apache needed. Apaches quickly adapted American technology, especially firearms. The Sharps carbine, developed during the Civil War, was a breech-loading weapon that became available to the Apaches through trading and raiding. By 1880 the Apaches were using the Winchester repeating rifle for short-range shooting ("The gun that won the West"), and the Springfield and Remington single-shot rifles for longer effective ranges. Most Apaches carried a cartridge belt that supported a pistol holster and a knife. The constant fire of the repeating rifles often gave the illusion of a large band, with American ranchers often estimating an enemy force of over 200 when in reality there might only be as few as 15 warriors. And, if truth be told, the Apaches earned their reputation as terrorists who tortured their enemies (even if their foes often exaggerated the extent).[85]

All of these factors outlined above explain the Apache successes, but ultimately the Apache resistance failed. Probably the underlying cause that led to failure was attrition in numbers due to demographic decline. Two hundred years of warfare against the Spaniards, Mexicans, and Americans took its toll. So too did the introduction of European diseases. Chiricahuas, who numbered in the thousands in the days of Mangas Coloradas, were down to a few hundreds when they finally surrendered. Although they may have had temporary tactical victories, the final defeat of Geronimo came when the US government deployed 5,000 men to search for fewer than 15 warriors and 20 followers.

An American tactic that was used by several commanders, including the Spanish in the eighteenth century, but perfected by General George Crook, was to exploit inter-tribal rivalries. And the best way to do this was to hire and train Indian scouts.[86] Yavapai scouts went after fellow Yavapai, as well as Apaches. White Mountain Apaches and Navajos sought out Chiricahuas, and anti-Geronimo Chiricahuas like Chatto were used to find Geronimo in Mexico. General Cook, when speaking about his campaign against the Yavapai, said that he pitted "savage against savage" recruiting Yavapais and Apaches "fresh from the warpath."[87]

Finally, there is the issue of alcohol abuse. The general pattern began by the Spanish but well established by Mexican times, was to induce the warriors into town for an evening of social drinking. The Apaches would get drunk, and in the early morning, still in a stupor, they would be attacked by the Mexicans and killed for their scalps. Many Apache losses to Mexicans and Americans were associated with consumption of alcohol. While teswin or corn beer was most often the culprit, much stronger drink came from the agave plant from which can be produced mescal and tequila. And, of course, there were always the American merchants and traders who had guns and whiskey to trade. The problem of Indian addiction may have had a biological basis as well, as 30% of people of Asian ancestry have few or none of the genes that produce enzymes in the liver that break down alcohol. In any case, it was alcohol abuse that was Geronimo's fate that led to his death on February 17, 1909.[88] His fellow prisoners of war were not so lucky.

Prisoners of War, 1886–1913

The Apache captives left Fort Bowie and/or Fort Apache by rail to either Fort Marion in Saint Augustine, Florida, or Fort Pickens, across the bay from Pensacola, Florida. The first group that arrived on April 13, 1886, at the Castillo de San Marcos (as Fort Marion was called before the Adams-Onis Treaty of 1819–1821) was the 77 Chiricahuas who followed Chief Chihuahua. They had traveled by train from Fort Bowie to Fort Marion. Concerning that trip, Charles Fletcher Lummis, a reporter for the *Los Angeles Times*, noted that "The soldiers were necessary to protect these poor savages from the 'civilized' whites along the way ... . There are plenty of alleged white men who would jump at the chance to signalize their bravery by shooting a captive squaw through a car window, if they had received sufficient notices to brace themselves with brag and whiskey."[89] Then in September, 383 men, women, and children, all under guard, arrived at Fort Marion. This included members of the New Mexican Warm Springs band that had joined other Chiricahuas in hostile attacks.[90]

Eventually, several women and children from San Carlos came to Fort Marion. So too did Chatto, who as a scout had aided the US Army in tracking and finding Geronimo. Chatto, and another 13 men and women, had gone to Washington, DC, to meet the president to discuss removal to Indian Territory. Although they had been promised safe return to Arizona, their departing train was stopped and they were rerouted to Florida as prisoners of war. A few Indian Scouts who had served in the US Army also joined the other prisoners at Fort Marion. Evidently, being peaceful or serving as an ally of the US Army was not enough to escape imprisonment. Over time the total number of prisoners at Fort Marion varied between 447 and 500, with the number seldom exceeding 500.

On September 8, 1886, Geronimo and his small group of relatives and followers departed Bowie Station. Their train stopped at San Antonio, and the Apaches were certain that they were about to be murdered by order of the US Army. They then spent six weeks as prisoners at Fort Sam Houston, where once again they were worried about an attack from the White Eyes. On October 26 they arrived at Pensacola, where the railroad cars separated and the one with the women and children went on to Fort Marion. After October, Geronimo, Naiche, and 15 other warriors were joined in Fort Pickens by Mangas (the son of Mangas Coloradas). There would soon be additional prisoners. All of their wives and children were several hundred miles away at Fort Marion.[91]

Because of overcrowding at Fort Marion the newcomers had to live in tents. By September there were over 130 tents in the compound. The conditions were unsanitary with limited toilet facilities and very little disinfectant. The St. Augustine tourist community added to the danger of contagious disease. Tired and dirty, the September contingent succumbed rapidly to malarial fever (this was before the Spanish–American War of 1898 that led to a discovery of the causes of malaria). The children were especially subject to tuberculosis and acute bronchitis.[92] Health conditions at Fort Pickens were better, especially since most of the prisoners were healthy adults. Yet the constant coming and going of Pensacola tourists did not help matters, and yellow fever was always a concern for the commanding officer.

One official estimate indicated that between April 13 and November 17, 1886, of the 498 Apaches imprisoned in Florida, 99 had died at St. Augustine and Fort Marion, while another 30 children had succumbed to tuberculosis and other ailments at the boarding school at Carlisle, Pennsylvania (about 30% of the children died). The death rate for all Apaches (24%) was three times as great as the normal rate for non-Indian peoples. By the end of 1889, the statistics had not improved as one-fourth of the captive Apaches had died. Five years later contagious diseases had taken the lives of 40 to 50% of the Chiricahua prisoners in Florida and Alabama.[93]

Because of the activities of outside advocacy groups, the War Department in April 1887 ordered the prisoners at Fort Marion moved to the Mount Vernon Barracks 30 miles north of Mobile, Alabama (see map, Figure 5.2). Apache children were sent to the Indian School at Carlisle. Over a year later in the spring of 1888 Geronimo and the 47 prisoners at Fort Pickens joined the Alabama group. The Crook promise that they would be returned in two years was kept, except the prisoners ended up in Alabama, not Arizona.

Mount Vernon was not a paradise either. Eugene Chihuahua, the son of the chief, described the Mount Vernon incarceration site this way: "We had thought that anything would be better than Fort Marion with its rain, mosquitoes, and malaria, but we were to find out that it was good in comparison with Mt. Vernon Barracks. We didn't know what misery was till they dumped us in those swamps." Chihuahua commented further, that "It rained nearly all the time and the roofs leaked. On top of that the mosquitoes almost ate us alive.

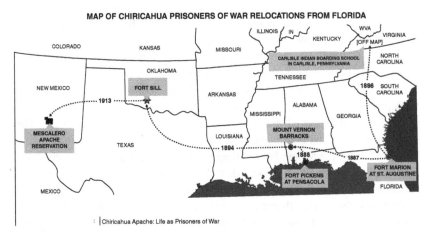

MAP OF CHIRICAHUA PRISONERS OF WAR RELOCATIONS FROM FLORIDA

Figure 5.2 *Map of Chiricahua Prisoners of War Relocations From Florida.*
Map reproduced from Janet Cantley, *Beyond Geronimo* (Phoenix: Heard Museum, 2012), p. 33.

Babies died from their bites. It was hot and steamy ... . It was worse than St. Augustine; it was terrible. Everything moulded [*sic*] —food, clothes, moccasins, everything."[94]

Although anything made by Geronimo was in demand by the tourists, most of the Chiricahuas suffered the indignities of the place, from "consumption" and the "coughing sickness" to boredom and homesickness. Once again, white friends of the Indians pressured the administration to move the Apaches. Finally, on August 6, 1894, Congress enacted legislation that allowed the remaining 407 Chiricahuas to be removed to Fort Sill, Oklahoma where buildings, tools, and livestock would be provided "for their support and civilization."[95]

The Comanches and Kiowas greeted their Indian cousins when they left the train near Fort Sill. Although they were still prisoners of war, the place was an obvious improvement over Fort Marion and Fort Pickens. Again Eugene Chihuahua can be quoted, saying: "We could see the mountains ... . There were mesquite beans, and we began gathering and shelling them. We hadn't seen one since we were taken to Florida. We gathered several hundred bags of them. And there were deer—not so many as at Turkey Creek, but a good many ... . The best of all was to hear the coyotes sing, and the cry of the quail too."[96]

The first winter they lived in wickiups, but they soon built small two-room dwellings connected by breezeways. The men started preparing the land for cattle by digging postholes, cutting fenceposts, and stretching wire. Some of the children began returning from Carlisle. Many babies were born. Yet the artificial conditions of internment, especially a diet high in carbohydrates and sugars, caused many digestive disorders and brought about the death of a large number of infants during the hot summers. As scholar Henrietta Stockel notes, "The Apaches continued to cough, spit, sneeze, sweat, and shake at Fort Sill, still suffering with the diseases acquired in Alabama" (almost 300 died at Fort Sill).[97] Eventually, the missionaries were allowed to join the soldiers, and many of the younger adults who had recently returned from Carlisle joined the Dutch Reform Church (the Dutch branch of the Presbyterian Church).[98]

Even Geronimo said that "the Jesus road is good" and was baptized a Christian, his piety is a bit questionable since he also professed a belief in Usen. Yet problems of liquor still plagued the Chiricahuas during their stay at Fort Sill, in spite of the earnest attempts by the soldiers and missionaries to stomp out alcohol abuse and the violence associated with it. As mentioned before, Geronimo, on February 17, 1909, having gotten drunk on whiskey and sleeping overnight without cover in the cold and wet weather contracted pneumonia and died.[99]

With the death of the great Apache warrior-shaman, whose skills as a brave and courageous fighting man were admired by friend and foe alike, the US government no longer had any justification for keeping his Indé People imprisoned. In 1913, the federal government granted them freedom, with some

Chiricahuas choosing to join their Mescalero cousins in New Mexico while the others stayed at Fort Sill. Raymond Loco, grandson of Chief Loco, said that "The day of separation was a great day of sorrow. There was weeping and wailing, in part due to separation [from kinfolk and friends] ... Freedom as defined by the whites is hard for the Indian to give expression to. He knew only freedom when the buffalo roamed the plains, when the rivers ran clean, and when the grass was green and abundant."[100]

Between 176 and 187 Chiricahuas chose to move to the Mescalero Reservation in New Mexico, while 84 to 88 of the more acculturated Fort Sill Apaches settled on land purchased from the Comanches and Kiowas. These 260 plus people were all that remained of the 519 captives. The exile had finally come to an end.[101]

As noted, for over half of the original community the end had come a lot earlier. Usen's children—Mangas Coloradas, Cochise, Victorio, Juh, Lozen, Geronimo, and the others—were in the Happy Place, that final resting spot of trees, grass, and game; the Cloud Land, where hunting, gambling, and polygamy took place. And with Geronimo there, no White Eyes need apply.

Aftermath

Not all the Chiricahuas went east as prisoners of war. A small number of Juh's followers escaped the roundup of the 1880s and fled to the Sierra Madre Mountains of Mexico. In the 1890s another group of Western Apaches from San Carlos may have joined them in the Sierra Madre. Ranging through mountains 200 miles in length, the Apaches would descend to steal livestock in Sonora, Chihuahua, Arizona, and New Mexico. Within twenty years of Geronimo's surrender settlers started to populate the Sierra Madre, and confrontation with the Apaches ensued.[102]

As tensions increased the situation came to a head in 1927 with the murder and kidnapping of members of a Mexican family near the village of Nacori Chico, 75 miles south of Agua Prieta, Sonora. The last raiding incident was recorded in 1929 when Apache Juan's band crossed the continental divide from Sonora to steal horses and cattle at a "cow camp" near the Gavilán River in Chihuahua.[103]

These incidents led to an extermination campaign by the Mexicans that concluded in 1937 when most Apaches had been eliminated. In 1937, the Norwegian explorer, Helge Ingstad, hired two Mescalero Indians to act as guides to help him search for the lost Apaches of the Sierra Madre. Although finding fresh signs of Indians, he never encountered any Chiricahuas or Western Apaches. When the contemporary journalist Richard Grant joined the hunt belatedly in the early 1990s he came across Geronimo's stronghold which he described as "the perfect location for a marijuana camp."[104] This time Geronimo was thwarted—the White Eyes could gain entry into the Happy Place.

6

Treasure Hunters Hunting Deer Hunters: Yavapai and Apache Gold

> *When the White people come, lots of Yavapai get killed. This here is our home. But when the White people come, they take it away from us. White people come here and they get gold. If the White people would not kill the Indians, it would be all right. But they kill them, kill them, and I don't know why they do that.[1]*
>
> John Williams, Yavapai (approximate date 1974)

> *The sentiment here is in favor of an utter extermination of the ruthless savages who have so long prevented the settlement and the development of the territory.[2]*
>
> Letter from Office of the Secretary of the Territory of Arizona, Fort Whipple, March 5, 1864

The Yavapai: the [Four] Peoples of the Sun

The ancestral territory of the Yavapai amounted to over 20,000 square miles, or over one-sixth of the present state of Arizona. If one were to draw a triangle over that part of present day Arizona that was the traditional homeland of the Yavapai, one would place the apex around the cool elevations of the San Francisco Mountains near Flagstaff. From this tip, one line would go in a southwestern direction toward the Castle Dome Mountains that lie near the confluence of the Gila River with the Colorado River in the low lying barren plains of the Sonoran desert, the other line would extend from the San Francisco Mountains southeast to the summit ridges of the Mazatzal and Pinal

Lost Worlds of 1863: Relocation and Removal of American Indians in the Central Rockies and the Greater Southwest, First Edition. W. Dirk Raat.
© 2022 John Wiley & Sons, Inc. Published 2022 by John Wiley & Sons, Inc.

Mountains, following the Verde valley through the basin and range country of Arizona. Just as the Colorado River formed the western boundary of the Yavapai country, the Verde River and the Gila River defined the eastern and southern edges respectively. This was the native land or *Shi Keeyaa* of the Yavapai. Needless to say, the area of the few Yavapai reservations that exist today amount to only a small percentage of the original homeland.[3]

Within this territory the Yavapai peoples lived in extended family groups, camps, or *rancherías* and survived in a hostile environment by hunting everything from deer and pronghorn antelope to rabbits and squirrels, and gathering wild plants and nuts. Some limited horticulture was practiced as well, especially by the northeastern Yavapai. They spoke a Yuman or Hokan dialect (as did the Colorado River Indians and the Hualapai and Havasupai of the Grand Canyon) and tattooed their faces like their Colorado River neighbors. Their traditional allies included the Mojaves and Quechans of the lower Colorado River.

By the nineteenth century the Yavapai were essentially four peoples: Tolkepayas in the west; Yavapés (or Yavepe) in the central area around the Prescott–Jerome Mountains; the southeastern Yavapai or Kwevképayas (also Kewevkepaya) in the Tonto Basin and the Pinal and Superstition Mountains; and the northeastern Wipukepas (or Wipukpa) around Sedona and the middle Verde valley (see map, Figure 6.1). Although some anthropologists refer to these four as *subtribes*, they are best understood as four separate peoples. They did not have a single political leader or tribal chieftain. Each group was comprised of extended families or *rancherías* with individuals who would intermarry and cooperate for purposes of war or trade. All four peoples lived in their own distinct geographic area and seldom relocated. Their membership in the group came from their birth in that particular geographical zone.[4]

Their life styles, while generally similar, differed because of land forms, natural resources, and elevation and temperature. The western Yavapai, living in a low lying desert area where temperatures were hot and rainfall rare would gather cacti, agave, mescal, and creosote brush while hunting mountain sheep in the Castle Dome and Kofa Mountains. Unlike the other groups, they formed agreements with the Quechans so as to practice floodplain agriculture, gather mesquite pods, and collect salt and shells. On the other hand, the Wipukepas, Yavapés and Kwevképayas, having access to higher elevations, more adequate rainfall patterns, and a variety of vegetation, were able to gather everything from saguaro fruit and Palo Verde beans to acorns and piñon nuts, while hunting deer in the Bradshaws and rabbits on the Agua Fria and Hassayampa Rivers. Of course, they were all inhabitants of a desert country.

The indigenous peoples to the east, called Tonto Apaches by the Europeans, were known by their Navajo and Western Apache neighbors as the "Dilzhe'e

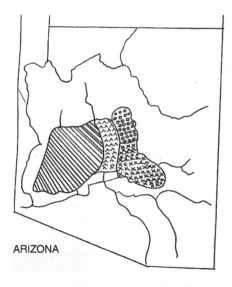

◎ WESTERN YAVAPAI (*TOLKEPAYAS*)

◎ CENTRAL YAVAPAI (*YAVAPÉS*)

◎ NORTHEASTERN YAVAPAI (*WIPUKEPAS*)

◎ SOUTHEASTERN YAVAPAI (*KWEVKÉPAYAS*)

Figure 6.1 *Yavapai Territory, ca. mid-nineteenth century.* Reconfiguration by Geraldine Raat of information found in Timothy Braatz, *Surviving Conquest: A History of the Yavapai Peoples* (Lincoln and London: University of Nebraska Press, 2003).

diné," meaning "people with high pitched voices." Both Europeans and Navajos referred to the Yavapai and some of the Western Apache as Tonto Apaches. The Spanish called them "Tonto" from the Apache word "koun'nde," meaning "wild rough people." "Tonto" in Spanish can mean "loose," "foolish," or "stupid." Their territory overlapped with that of the Yavapai to the west, stretching from the San Francisco Mountains and Oak Creek Canyon, then following the Verde River to the Salt River, and ending at the Tonto Basin. They were concentrated in what today is the area around the city of Payson. Generally speaking the Yavapai were west of the Verde, while the Tonto were to the east. Although smaller in stature than the Yavapai, and speaking an Athapaskan tongue like all Apaches, they did form mixed bands with the Yavapai and joined in a common effort to fight both the Navajos and the Pimas (Akimal O'odham).[5]

As already noted, the Yavapai have been known by a variety of names. The historical literature designated the Yavapai as Apaches, Yuma Apaches, and Mojave Apaches. This is partly understandable due to the overlapping of Yavapai and Apache territory along the Verde valley, as well as the Yavapai's temporary residence along side other Apaches at the San Carlos Indian Reservation following their military defeat by General George Crook in 1875. The reference to Yuma Apaches and Mojave Apaches may reflect the close ties that the western Yavapai had with their Colorado River neighbors.[6] It also reflects a general ignorance on the part of Americans who thought all mountain peoples in Arizona constituted a single, monolithic "Apache tribe" that needed to be exterminated.[7]

When the Spaniards made contact with the Yavapai in the late sixteenth and early seventeenth centuries they called them "cruzados," a reference to the crosses on their foreheads and/or the Hopi "tablitas" on top of their heads.[8] The latter were cross-shaped ornaments akin to the headdress of Yavapai and Apache crown dancers (also typical of Hopi katsinas). Tolkepayas (southwestern Yavapai), who lived between the Harquahala and Harcuvar mountains, called themselves "People of the Two Mountains." Northeastern Yavapai referred to themselves as the "people of the red rocks," a reference, perhaps, to the reddish colors of the Sedona countryside. The *Handbook of American Indians* (Hodge, 1907, 1910) said that the Yavapai were known as "enyaeva pai," "enyaeva" meaning "sun" and "pai" translated as "people." Some scholars interpreted this as "crooked-mouth people" or "sulky" people, while others said it could mean "sun worshipers." The consensus view seems to be "People of the Sun."[9]

Ancestral Yavapai (to 1863)

"We come out at Sedona, the middle of the world. This is our home ... . Across the river at Camp Verde, maybe four, five miles north from there is Montezuma Well. We call it *Ahagaskiaywa*. This lake has no bottom and underneath the water spreads out wide. That's where people came out first." When the hole flooded with water all people were killed except for Kamalapukwia, "Old Lady White Stone," who survived by hiding in a hollow log. "She is the first woman, and we came from her, she came out of Sedona, and that's where all the Indians come from." A second creation occurred when Kamalaplukwia "... went to that cave where the water drips down all the time. She lay down there and the water came down and hit her. Made her a baby. A little girl." A third creation happened when the daughter was impregnated in a similar fashion. "She got pregnant, and when she got the little baby, it was a boy: *Sakarakaamche.*" After his mother was killed by an eagle, the Boy Hero "... kills everything that is mean, and cuts it up." One must remember that "... In those days all kinds of animals eat people. Bear, owl, bull, eagle. They were bad ones at that time." Sakarakaamche killed these bad animals, cut them up, and scattered them all around the mountains. Now the monster animals are not angry, for example, the "... Bulls are no longer mean. Don't eat people now." When the third creation was destroyed by fire, a new people arrived to begin the present, or fourth, era. So say the northeastern and central Yavapai about their beginnings.[10]

A couple of observations can be made concerning the Yavapai origin story. First, and not surprising, is the similarity of this tale to those of other North American Indian groups. The Navajo counterpart to *Old Lady White Stone* (or her daughter) is *Changing Woman* and *White Painted Woman* for the Chiracahua Apache. They are all forms of the Earth Mother. Just as *Water* or *Rain* impregnated the Yavapai grandmother and her daughter, so too was White Painted Woman made pregnant by *Waterfall* or *Rain (*or thunder and lightning). The boys who were born to Changing Woman were named *Born-for-Water* and *Monster Slayer*, and the twin children of White Painted Woman were called *Child of Waters* and *Slayer of Enemies*. All of these Twin Heroes, like *Hunahpu* and *Xbalanque* of Maya lore who had to slay the Lords of Xibalba, and akin to Sakarakaamche, had to kill the monsters of the Fourth World to make the Fifth World safe for human occupancy (in the Yavapai case it was the Third or Fourth World). The similarities between the Mesoamerican creation mythology and those of North American Indians may be due to cultural diffusion between Mexico and the Southwest, or simply the common views of the practitioners of naturalistic religion.[11]

The other observation that can be made is that unlike displaced nineteenth-century Anglo-American settlers who were recent arrivals in the West, and like most Native Americans, the Yavapai Hero story tells us that the Yavapai had a sense of place and centrality. Individuals were not only born in this area, but all of humanity came out of Montezuma Well, the Middle of the World. This geocentric view will be shattered when the White Man tears them from their homeland and their families.

Just as Yavapai storytellers vary in their accounts of the beginning, so too is the view of archaeology somewhat confused. Most scholars agree with anthropologist E. W. Gifford, who published major studies on the Yavapai between 1932 and 1936, that the three ethnic groups—the Hualapai west of the Grand Canyon, the Havasupai in and along the southern edge of the Grand Canyon, and the Yavapai—branched from a common stock in recent history.[12] Linguists assert that they all speak a language of the Hokan group. As ethnographer Stephen Hirst notes, "... the Hokan mother tongue may have been the language spoken by the first humans in the Americas as much as 20,000 years ago."[13]

Displaced Hokan peoples traveled south and west leaving linguistic traces in California, Arizona, and northern Mexico. In southern California the Hokan dispersal created the Chumash and Diegueño groups, while other migrants went into Baja California. Some of these people traveled into the Gila River Valley two or three thousand years ago to form the Yuman branch of the Hokan. A ceramic making Hokan speaking Patayan culture, that practiced floodplain agriculture after 700 C.E., successfully increased its numbers. The surplus population left the Colorado River after 1300 C.E. and went east to the Arizona highlands to become the Upland Yumans. As historian Timothy Braatz has argued, after the disturbances of the fourteenth century, the historic Yavapai included descendants of both pueblo dwellers and river cultivators.[14]

Because Yavapai creation stories and origin myths do not mention migration patterns and displacement of previous inhabitants in their territory, it is difficult to rely on oral history sources to reconstruct the aboriginal past of these people prior to European contact. The Yavapai practice, similar to that of lower Colorado River Yumans, was to erase the memory of the dead through cremation of corpses, burning of dwellings and possessions of the dead, and not mentioning the names of those no longer living.[15] Pai separation and creation stories do suggest that a children's quarrel led to hostilities that resulted in the Yavapai breaking away from the Havasupai.[16] In any case, the archaeological, ethnological and anthropological record, while limited and partial, can give us a general overview of their "prehistory" history.

Prior to their contact with Europeans the Yavapai were generally similar to the Hualapai in patterns of religion, social organization, material culture, and subsistence. Shamanism and curing rituals dominated their religious life, with sacred areas centering in Sedona and the Verde Valley. *Rancherías* usually consisted of nuclear or extended family units, including up to ten households that hunted and gathered in the spring and summer. These summer camps, based on ties of kinship and economic needs, were the basis of social cohesion. These seasonal camps would come together in larger groups during the winter season, usually under the leadership of an advisory headman. They lived in rock shelters, caves, abandoned cliff dwellings, and domed thatch huts (*uwas*) that were open ramadas in the summer and closed shelters in the winter. Before the arrival of smallpox, carried by European soldiers, churchmen, colonists and their Indian allies, their population has been estimated to be around 3,000 inhabitants. By 1863 their numbers had been reduced to between 2,000 and 2,500.[17]

As mentioned before, the vast range of Yavapai territory covered a variety of environmental and ecological zones, and because of this there were regional variations in subsistence patterns. Like most indigenous groups, hunting, a high-risk, low yield activity, was done by the men, while gathering, a low-risk, high yield pursuit, was the work of women and children. Deer and pronghorn antelope hunters from the Sedona area were especially expert in the use of fire in hunting drives. Yavapai also hunted bighorn sheep, rabbits, rodents, raccoons, bobcats, tortoises, birds, and lizards. Fish, frogs, and waterfowl were usually avoided.[18]

Agave (mescal) was a year-round staple food. In the spring women harvested squawberries, agave hearts, and leafy greens. Summers meant moving to a lower elevation and gathering mesquite beans and palo verde seedpods and saguaro cactus fruit. Autumn offered acorns, walnuts, piñon nuts, yucca, prickly pear, and assorted berries. Tubers and agave were exploited in the winter. Hundreds of different plants were used, not only for food, but for medicine, tools, and clothing. Cultivated corn, beans, squash, and melons supplemented the Yavapai diet; especially in areas were horticulture was possible such as along the edge of the Colorado River, the Verde Valley, and Castle Hot Springs east of Wickenburg.[19]

Intertribal alignments were developed in the ancestral era that was retained after the Europeans arrived in the late sixteenth and early seventeenth century. These were both trading networks and military alliances. The Mojave, acting as middlemen, traded goods from the coastal region of California that the Chamush occupied through the Serrano territory in the California uplands to the Colorado River Valley. From there goods were exchanged with Pai and Yavapai peoples who transmitted items from Zuni in New Mexico. This long-distance trade network moved marine goods and corn, beans, mesquite, and pumpkins in exchange for Pueblo and Navajo woven goods and pottery, as well as deer, antelope, rabbit meat, animal skins, and mineral pigments from the Pai country.[20]

There were also two extensive tribal alliances that historian Timothy Braatz calls "amity–enmity alignments." These were social networks that promoted cooperation in food sharing, intermarriage, and warfare. The two alliances linked groups in western and southern Arizona with their counterparts in southern California and Baja California. The strongest core of one alignment consisted of Yavapais, Apaches, Mojaves, and Quechans and extended into California to include the Chemehuevi, Northern Serranos, and Chumash. The other alliance included the Cocopas and Maricopas of the lower Colorado Valley, the Pai of the Grand Canyon area, and the Pimas (Akimal O'odham) of the Colorado-Gila region, as well as the Diegueño (today known as the Kumeyaay)[21] of southern California and the Paipai of Baja California. While the western Yavapais joined raiding parties with the Mojave and Quechan Indians, the eastern and Verde Valley Yavapais assaulted Pimas and Maricopas in the company of Western Apaches. These were not prolonged battles, but quick actions that led to attack and swift retreat. As time went on through the

Spanish–Mexican era and the Anglo-American period, slave raiding increased with the Yavapai the object of Maricopa–Pima slave raiders. These raids, of course, often led to counter raiding on the part of the Yavapai. Finally, individual bands or camps of Hualapais and Yavapais would confront each other in local skirmishes.[22] All of these intertribal alliances and struggles continued throughout the Spanish–Mexican epoch (1583–1848) and after.

One of the earlier contacts that Spain had with the Yavapai came in 1583 when Antonio de Espejo was led to the Jerome Mountains by Hopi guides.[23] His companions were disappointed to only find more copper than silver along the tributaries of the Hassayampi. Hopi leaders in 1598 also guided Marcos Farfán de los Godos to some mines located in the land of the "Cruzados." Between 1604 and 1605 Juan de Oñate, seeking a route to the sea, traveled down the Bill Williams and Colorado Rivers to the Gulf of California. The Spaniards probably traded a few glass beads that the Yavapapi could substitute for red seeds on their necklaces. No doubt the steel swords, firearms, and livestock (especially horses) left a major impression on the Indians and explain their timidity toward the outsiders then and later. Obviously Christianity, at least the symbol of the cross, affected them.[24]

Yet after these initial encounters there were no European contacts with the Yavapai for the next two centuries. The influence of the Jesuit fathers, like Father Eusebio Kino in the late seventeenth and early eighteenth century, or a Franciscan padre such as Francisco Garcés in the 1770s, only extended to the Pima country south of the Gila in the case of Kino, or to the Yuma area where Garcés met his death in 1781, when he was killed, along with 90 other Spaniards, by Quechan warriors (and, some allege, Yavapai fighters). This event marked the beginning of the end for Spanish exploration in the borderlands.

While the Yavapai had few direct contacts with Spanish outsiders, they did experience Spanish culture indirectly through their tribal networks. For example, they could trade food items with the Pueblos in exchange for woolen goods and European commodities. As late as the mid-nineteenth century the Hualapai used their trade links to exchange Pueblo goods to the Mojave for horses, and in turn the horses were traded with the southern Paiutes for guns that the Paiutes had acquired in trade with the Mormons of Utah and Arizona.[25]

When Kino introduced domestic animals to northern Sonora, livestock raiding increased. To acquire livestock Yavapai and their Apache allies would make raids against Pima and Maricopa Indians, as well as Spanish ranchos in northern Mexico. The growth of Spanish communities necessitated additional labor, much of which was forced and physical. Therefore, slave raiding increased in order to supply these communities with enslaved workers. Pima and Maricopa raiders would capture Yavapai women and children that were traded with the Spaniards, and eventually toward the end of the eighteenth century Yavapai raiders were acquiring Pima captives that could be traded for horses from the Spaniards.

One unwanted gift of the Spaniards was European disease, especially smallpox. Here again trade routes were important. Those natives that lived in compact villages or towns and had regular contact with the Europeans endured the most agony. Scattered communities in mountainous regions suffered less than those in humid, lowland areas. Throughout the Americas more than 90% of Amerindians were killed by foreign infections, including measles and influenza as well as smallpox.[26] The American Indian had no medical history of these diseases, and with no immunity they succumbed rapidly.

The Yavapai, like the Mojave, had fewer contacts with Europeans and lived in relatively isolated zones in scattered rancherías. While the Quechans may have experienced a decline of 25% in the nineteenth century, the Yavapai suffered at most a 15 to 20% decline when its population dropped from 3,000 before European and Anglo-American diseases struck to 2,500 after 1863.[27]

The Mexican period in the Southwest lasted from 1821, when the Spanish were ousted from Mexico, to 1848 when Mexico lost half of its national territory at the conclusion of the Mexican–American War. The domain the US won included the entire American Southwest. When Mexico inherited the northern frontier from the Spanish, it did not have the military, political, or religious resources to govern the region adequately. The military and political concerns centered on Mexico City and its provinces, and the religious missions once started by the Jesuits and continued by the Franciscans faltered. As the missions were phased-out many mission Indians, especially in California, were forced to flee into towns and cities and were usually debased as homeless and unskilled underlings. Mexican law dictated the closing of communal lands and the assimilation of all "indigenes." This exercise in early nineteenth century liberal capitalism was opposed by most Indian groups, from the Mayas and Zapotecs in the Yucatán and Tehuantepec to the northeastern Huaxtecs and the Yaquis and Apaches of Sonora. Again, remoteness was the gift that kept giving as the Yavapai lived in splendid isolation from Mexico and the Mexicans.[28]

While the Mexicans were busy with civil affairs and pacifying various parts of their nation, the Mexican governor of Santa Fé did grant permission to several trapping parties to work the Gila, Salt, and Colorado Rivers. American and French mountain men, the better known being Ewing Young, Kit Carson, and Antoine Leroux, hunted deer and trapped beaver along the Salt, up the Verde, and along the Bill Williams River. The Yavapais, while avoiding major skirmishes, did make quick raids on these groups and others hoping to steal a horse here and a mule there. By the end of the 1840s the trapping era was over, but the American invasion had only started.[29]

Between 1848 and 1863, the Yavapai country was slowly being edged in by American soldiers, colonists, and miners. By 1863 only the isolated Yavapai and Apache uplands and the rugged Navajo plateau homeland remained free of American expansion. The 1850s saw the establishment of Fort Yuma in the river bottoms below the mouth of the Gila near the Colorado River, and the construction of Fort Mojave in the spring of 1859. These frontier posts pacified the Indian peoples of the lower Colorado River, and provided protection and provisions for emigrants on the Gila Trail traveling from Tucson to San Diego.[30]

A few skirmishes did occur, such as the combined Quechan–Mojave–Yavapai assault on Fort Yuma in 1852, or the June 1, 1857 battle at a Maricopa settlement near Pima Butte (near Maricopa Wells in the Sierra Estrella, a series of watering holes used by travelers on the Gila Trail, eight miles north of present day Maricopa, Arizona) in which a coalition of over 100 Quechans, Mojaves, and Yavapais engaged in a surprise attack on their Indian enemies. With the battle supposedly over the Yavapais withdrew. At that moment a group of mounted and armed Pimas arrived and killed most of the badly outnumbered Quechans and Mojaves. By 1863, aided by the US Army, the Pima, along with a group of ruffians known as the Gila Rangers, would now dominate southern Arizona. The American occupation had overwhelmed the Colorado River Indians, and now it would be the Yavapais who would receive a similar fate.[31]

Perhaps the most significant event at this time was the so-called Oatman massacre that occurred in February of 1851, and had a lasting influence that set the stage for the American invasion of 1863. Royce Oatman, and his wife Mary Ann, Brewsterites or members of a Mormon splinter group that followed the prophet James Colin Brewster, were determined to travel to the "land of Bashan," an earthy, tropical paradise that existed somewhere around the mouth of the Colorado River. He, like everyone else, was also motivated by tales of "gold in them there hills." They and their seven children (by the time they reached the Gila there might have also been a newborn baby) left their Illinois farm in May of 1850, joined several other families in Missouri in July, and by February found themselves (having abandoned their traveling companions in Tucson and Maricopa Wells) floundering along the Gila River several miles beyond Gila Bend and approximately eighty-plus miles from Fort Yuma (near today's Painted Rock Petroglyph Site). When a procession of Indians arrived (the 14 year old Olive Oatman counted 19 "Touto [sic] Apaches"), Royce, lacking nutrients and supplies for his family, refused to give them the requested food and within mere minutes most of the family was bludgeoned to death with knives and war clubs.

Only 14 year old Olive, 7 year old Mary Ann, and 15 year old Lorenzo, survived. Royce, his wife Mary Ann, Lucy, the eldest daughter at 17, Royce Jr., age 11, the 5 year old Charity Ann and 3 year old toddler Roland (and the newborn baby) lay dead, their faces buried in the hot quicksand of the Gila. Lorenzo's half dead body was thrown over the mesa, and the two girls were taken as captives, driven down and through the hills, barefoot on a four day journey over 40 miles to the "Tonto Apache" camp. Lorenzo, faint and injured but still alive, crawled back toward Maricopa Wells, and unable to go much further, two Pima on horseback discovered him and escorted him back to Maricopa Wells where he joined the other families.

The Oatman girls walked for four days and nights and 60 miles to the encampment of their abductors. Initially they had no idea about the motivations of these mountain Indians, only that they might be used for ransom, revenge, or cannibalism. Fortunately they soon found out that they were to be slaves to some of the women and their children. They eventually learned to speak some of the indigenous language, and their captors started treating them with curiosity and respect. In the spring of 1852, five Mojave men accompanied by a youthful female arrived at their campsite seeking a transaction in which the girls would be traded for a few horses, blankets, and beads. The deal was made and the girls were now forcibly marched for 10 days to the Mojave villages on the Colorado River. The early years from 1852 to 1855 went relatively well because the Mojave had plenty of food which they shared with their captives and the two girls were adopted by a Mojave family and the tribe. The blue tattoos they put on the chins of Olive and Mary Ann (done with cactus needles and the powder of a blue stone) were signs of acceptance into the group, and assured the Oatman girls that they, like the Mojave, would not get lost in the afterlife. Unfortunately, Mary Ann died in 1855, a year when food was scarce and the harvest poor. In February 1856, Olive was ransomed again, this time to a Quechan Indian for two horses, blankets, and beads, and the Quechan then turned her over to the military commander at Fort Yuma. On her trip to Fort Yuma Olive was accompanied by a Mojave guide named Tokwaoa ("Musk Melon"). After a short stay in Yuma, Olive reentered white society, eventually becoming a wealthy banker's wife in Texas. Her homecoming occurred five years to the month after her disappearance.[32]

The identity of the tribal group that participated in the massacre is less than certain. Olive said her captors were Tonto Apaches, a term so generic in the nineteenth century that it could include any Native Americans that could be found along the Colorado, Gila, or Verde Rivers. Margot Mifflin, the biographer of Olive Oatman, makes a reasonable case for (or against) the Yavapai based on the Oatman girl's description of food gathering and hunting methods, as well as the Yavapai traditions of clothing making, face painting, and their alliance with the Mojave.[33] While Mifflin suggests the group was likely the western Yavapai (Tolkepayas), they could just as easily been the southeastern Yavapai or a combination of Yavapai and Apache. If the Yavapai were the culprits, then this act of indiscriminate killing of whites was an uncommon event brought about most likely by the extreme conditions caused by drought and malnutrition. Other possibilities include the mountain Quechan, the Mojave, and even the Maricopa (Pee Posh), or a splinter group of Pima Indians. Historian Timothy Braatz has posed this question: "Is it possible that Quechans or Mojaves, who by then had a bloody record of conflict with US citizens, killed the Oatmans and blamed Tolkapayas, who at that time tended to avoid non-Indians or accommodate their demands?"[34]

The post-massacre Yavapai point of view is worthy of note. Hoomothya, or Mike Burns as his army captors called him, was orphaned in 1872 as a young lad of seven or eight when the US Army killed his extended family. He lived for many years with various officers and enlisted men as a ward, servant, and Indian scout. Hoomothya said that:

> The Oatman family was destroyed by Mojave Indians [as] they came across the Mojave Desert near the Maricopa settlements. [The Indians] saw the camp and [decided] that they [could] easily do them in without much notice. So they did it, and took two or three children. They tattooed the face of one girl and also dyed her hair with mud and mesquite tree pitch ... He [Natah-dav-vah, the Mojave chief] was getting shaky, and the country was overflowed with the white people, so he thought he would [fool] the whites by giving the girl to some white family, saying that he had bought the girl from the Yavapais ... So from that time the Yumas and Mojaves ... protected themselves from any blame for the murderous deed they had done. [He] said the mountain Indians had done it, [but in truth] none of the mountain Indians [Yavapais] ever saw a white man or had the chance to molest any white man.[35]

And the testimony of Hoomothya is reinforced by the views of other Yavapai informants, including that of Kehedwa (John Williams, 1904–1983) of the Fort McDowell Reservation in Arizona.

Around the year 1974, Kehedwa gave his testimony to anthropologist Sigrid Khera concerning the Oatman Massacre. In this interview he said that Pakoteh, the "Big Man," went over to Washington, D.C. and returned with his medal. Then, he said:

> ... When he comes back the Mohave tell the White people the Yavapai kill White people all the time. They bring a little White girl to the Army camp. They had put blue marks all over her face and under her eyes, and they say the Yavapai have done that. They say, they fight to get the little girl back from the Yavapai. But they lie. We don't put blue marks

under the eyes. The Mohave, the Quechan do that. Not us. Anyways, the White people think we took that little girl. They take the Yavapai to some scout camp down near Yuma somewhere and kill lots of us ... The Mohave did that to the little girl, and they said the Yavapai did that. That's why the White people are mad with us, my uncle said.[36]

So concludes the Kehedwa testimonial.

After Olive left Fort Yuma she soon became a media sensation, especially news stories that focused on the ceremonial tattoo as a sign of torture, not the esteem the Mojave intended. Between 1857 and 1858 three editions of *Captivity of the Oatman Girls* by the Reverend Royal Byron Stratton were published. Joining a long list of captivity tales in American history, the book came out a time when these narratives were very popular among middle class women. As Mifflin has noted, "the captivity story presented a tantalizing alternative to enforced domesticity."[37] Stratton filled his stories with descriptions of indolent brutes, "hideous man-animals," with "treacherous hearts" and no ambition except war and conquest. The Yavapai and their cousins were depraved redskins who engaged in unthinkable torture of their captives. Stratton's book raised a public outcry against the "savages" along the Gila River, and after 1860 it provoked an increased US military presence along the lower Colorado River and the Gila River Basin.[38]

At the same time that Stratton's propaganda was being dispensed on the east and west coasts of the United States, a Mojave shaman predicted disaster if the tribe allowed white people to settle in its ancestral homelands along the Colorado River. Today that area from Bullhead City to Parker is infested with more than 120,000 white, "illegal" immigrants,[39] and the Yavapai area from Flagstaff to the Gila River has millions of white and Hispanic invaders. And, like some contemporary Latino immigrants, yesterday's "illegals" failed to learn the native language or assimilate to Yavapai culture. Such is the inheritance of 1863.

The American Invasion, 1863–1875

The decade of violence and Yavapai battles that characterized the American expansionist phase after 1863 was called, in the words of Camp Verde chairperson Ted Smith, "a ten year Vietnam War,"[40] and it all started with the hunt for Yavapai–Apache gold in 1863. After American settlers, pioneers, and miners discovered gold in California in 1848, it was only a matter of time before they expanded into Yavapai and Tonto Apache territory. Some could not make it to California, and decided to seek their luck in Arizona. From Arizona the backtracking treasure hunters would eventually enter the Black Hills of the Dakotas where General George Armstrong Custer would discover gold in 1873, a few years before his infamous Last Stand of 1876.

There were several routes to the Arizona treasure fields. The most popular was the route to California from New Orleans. Instead of traveling the trans-Panama Railroad through the isthmus or around Cape Horn to get to the west coast,[41] these prospective prospectors sailed to Matamoros and hiked through northern Sonora up to Tucson and along the Santa Cruz River to the Gila River Trail. As noted above, many of them quit before getting to California, either at Fort Yuma or earlier on the Gila pathways and tributaries. Two ancient trails from Mexico to California, the Devils Highway (*El Camino del Diablo*) from Caborca along the Río Sonoyta to Yuma, and the Old Spanish Trail from Santa Fé, either went south or north of the Arizona fields.

Another route would be to follow the tracks of the Oatman party and leave Missouri along the established Santa Fé Trail and then south and north to the Gila Road. And finally, another path was scouted in 1853 by a military expedition under the command of Lieutenant Amiel W. Whipple. This trail went from Albuquerque, New Mexico to the San Francisco Mountains and from there to the Colorado River. That part of Whipple's survey that went from the Zuni pueblos in western New Mexico to Sunset Crossing (Winslow, Az. today) followed the 35th meridian and became the Beale wagon trail (later part of the famous Route 66, and today's Interstate 40).

In late April of 1863, a small group of prospectors, who had learned of gold discovered the previous year along the Colorado River, accompanied by their Mojave guides, continued up the Hassayampa River bottom (a tributary of the Gila) into Yavapai lands. Pauline Weaver, a US Army guide, led a group of men organized by Abraham Harlow Peeples, from Yuma to what later became known as the Weaver Mountains in central Arizona. There they camped below a small hill, where, during the evening, several horses broke away. The next morning while looking for the lost livestock, a Mexican in the employ of the notorious Indian fighter Jack Swilling, came across their horses and beneath their hooves he found "... hundreds of gold nuggets the size of potatoes." This event was later labeled the "discovery of Rich Hill," or "Potato Patch," an area nine miles east of today's Congress, Arizona. Peeples eventually established a ranch up the road from the towns of Congress and Yarnell (gold discovered in Yarnell in 1865) and that area is known as Peeples Valley.[42] A short time later Henry Wickenburg, a prospector from the California gold rush, discovered a quartz deposit near the southern end of the Hassayampa. He later named his find the Vulture Mine. He also set up a small town known as Vulture City. This site is near today's town of Wickenburg.[43]

1863 was also a busy year for pathfinder–trapper–prospector Joseph Reddeford Walker, Kit Carson's companion and John C. Fremont's guide. He had recently led a group of gold seekers from California across "Walker Pass" and the Colorado River near Fort Mojave, to the San Francisco Mountains, but found no gold. He continued on to Albuquerque and Denver. In the spring of 1862 his party of prospectors, accompanied by 60 mules, traveled via Santa Fé and Albuquerque down the Río Grande to Fort Craig and Ford West looking for gold in the headwaters of the Gila, including the San Francisco River. In January 1863, Mangas Coloradas (Red Sleeves), the respected Chiricahua Apache leader, was lured by members of the Walker party and/or the US Army to Pinos Altos for a supposed peace parley. The meeting was to work out an agreement concerning the relocation of the Apaches to the Pinos Altos area. Instead, in an act of treachery the US Army murdered Mangas Coloradas, severed his head with a Bowie knife, and sent their trophy east in an act of triumph. Unfortunately, the murder accelerated a series of Apache wars with the US Army and their scouts. Not to be delayed, the party continued to prospect the Gila and then went south to Tucson and the Pima villages. Traveling across the Gila, and now led by Swilling, they traveled up the Hassayampa where placer gold was discovered on the upper reaches on May 10, 1863.[44]

Then in June of 1863, Sam Miller and four others of the Joseph R. Walker party wondered about five miles south of today's Prescott. Miller and his companions traveled up Lynx Creek, a tributary of the Agua Fria. There they struck it rich. The trapping for pelts had been most successful, and the panning of dirt had yielded flakes of gold. The discovery was the beginning of the end for traditional Yavapai culture. It did not take long for the word to spread, and the American Argonauts were soon racing to the Yavapai lands.[45]

In February of 1863 the territory of Arizona was established having been separated from New Mexico and signed into law by President Abraham Lincoln. Shortly after the Arizona gold discoveries the town of Prescott sprung up and nearby Fort Whipple was under construction. By May of 1863 Fort Mojave was reoccupied by California volunteers. The post along the Colorado River was supposedly to keep peace between the American miners and their Mojave, Hualapai, and Chemehuevi neighbors. On October 23, 1863 General James R. Carleton issued General Order #27 from his Santa Fe headquarters establishing the Fort Whipple post and ordering "that a small military force should be sent to these new gold fields to preserve order and give security to life and property" for the mines and the farms that supply the mines. He, of course, arranged for his troops to look for gold.[46]

With an influx of hundreds of invaders swarming about the northern Yavapai country, Prescott successfully outbid Tucson to become the first territorial capital of the territory. In January 1864 the first territorial governor arrived with his entourage. Governor John N. Goodwin, who preferred the location of Prescott with its gold finds and delightful climate over the "secessionist" sympathies and Mexican influence of Tucson, greeted his new citizens by promising that his purpose in governing was that of "redeeming the territory from savage dominion."[47]

Not that civilization had arrived with the governor. Several instances of bigotry and racism occurred. "Senorians (i.e., Mexicans) and Asiatics" were forbidden by ordinance to file mining claims in the district, and black soldiers at Fort Whipple were discriminated against when they came to town. One incident at a local Prescott salon resulted in a "Nigger" who did not take off his hat as a sign of respect to white people being shot and killed by Tat the prospector. *The Arizona Miner*, a weekly citizen-miner newspaper that was established in Prescott in 1864, argued in its editorial that: "We see no other remedy—than to exterminate nearly if not the whole race of savages on the Pacific coast, and the sooner this is accomplished the better for the whole country." The bellicose *Miner* prided itself on being the "Only white man's town in Arizona."[48]

Even before the governor had arrived conflict had ensued. In December 1863 twenty "Injuns" were killed near Fort Whipple at Del Rio Springs (about 20 miles north of Prescott) where the post was originally established. The original stockade was moved to Granite Creek, about a mile north of Prescott, on May 18, 1864.[49] On January 24, 1864 the so-called battle of Bloody Tanks (also known as Pinole Treaty) involved 19 to 36 Indian deaths, depending on your source of information. Captain King S. Woolsey was the head of the Territorial Militia, a group of citizen volunteers and ruffians. Woolsey, who had gained fame by hanging Yavapai bodies from the trees of his Agua Fria ranch, and his associates, representing themselves as peace emissaries, ambushed several headmen and their followers in a small ravine that later became known as the Bloody Tanks. At least 24 of the "savages" died when they consumed the gift of flour that had been laced with strychnine.[50] Later, in August of 1866, 33 to 40 Yavapai were killed at Skull Valley west of Prescott. As Yavapai informant John Williams said, the Indians went to parley on peaceful terms but the white man "don't give them blankets. They shoot them down. Kill them."[51]

The worse massacre that occurred was the December 1872 slaughter at Skeleton Cave in the Salt River Canyon. There, inside the cave, the Yavapai had their encampment. Meanwhile 120 US soldiers and over 100 Pima and Maricopa scouts descended the steep walls of the canyon. Fighting broke out. Some American soldiers poured bullets into the mouth of the cave, while others rolled stones and boulders down the cliff into the cave entry. When the firing was over the Pima and Maricopa auxiliaries rushed in to smash the skulls of the dying. Only the acts of a few Apaches saved the lonely survivors from the Pima fury. When it was over 76 Kewevkepayas (south-eastern Yavapais), men, women, and children, lie dead.[52]

The raids, battles, and massacres led to counter-raids, counter-battles, and counter massacres. A vicious cycle had been started. General George Crook, who gave up the idea of accommodation in early 1871, presented a "recapitulation" of the depredations of this era as a justification for moving against the Indians. For the period his report listed one officer and two enlisted men killed; 41 citizens killed and 16 wounded; and 489 head of citizen's cattle stolen.[53] Yavapai informant John Williams did admit to killing Indian scouts, "but we don't kill White soldiers. White people bother us all the time, but we don't kill them."[54] Certainly the use of Pima and Maricopa scouts by the US Army were a thorn in the side of the Yavapais, but it is equally certain that many whites were killed in the violence that ensued. Yet in the final analysis the Yavapais were unable to confront the Americans and sought accommodation at a time when the US Army was abandoning it.

By 1871 most Yavapai had accommodated themselves to the idea of survival by reservation. They knew that they were badly outnumbered, lacking food and martial resources, and would be eventually destroyed by the invasion of miners and their US armies. The example of the Colorado River Indian Reservation appeared to offer a solution in which US military personnel protected the Quechan from their Cocopa enemies, and acted as a buffer between Mexican and American colonists and the original inhabitants. If the Yavapais could convince the US authorities to create reservations in Yavapai territory, hopefully with wild resources and sufficient water for horticulture, and if they were distant from their Pima and Maricopa enemies, then accommodation seemed the best policy. By living on the reservations and cooperating with the Americans, they could pacify their enemies and become part of a cash economy that could bring the Yavapai foodstuffs, cloth, and tools. Although some accommodation occurred at Camp Date Creek (renamed in 1867 as Camp McPherson, south of Skull Valley; 10 miles due west of Peeples Valley), insufficient food and enemy raiders prevented any successful attempts at Río Verde, Fort McDowell, and Camp Grant.[55]

The tragedy at Camp Grant in the late winter of 1871 showed the futility of the policy of accommodation. This military post, originally established in 1860, was located on the confluence of Aravaipa Creek and the San Pedro River. It was located some 60 miles northeast of Tucson. The Aravaipa Apaches had grown tired of living in fear of the US Army and never having enough food to eat. They agreed to settle near the post and in return for receiving the protection of the US Army, they would provide the soldiers with barley and hay. This arrangement did not please many of the residents of Tucson, and on the morning of April 30, 30 or more *vecinos* (Mexicans from Tucson; *Tucsonenses*), eighteen Tucson *gringos*, and 82 Tohono O'odham (Papago) Indians attacked the unarmed Aravaipa camp and killed between 144 and 150 Aravaipa, almost all of them sleeping women and children, and seized 29 Apache captives. Accommodation did not seem to be working![56]

The so-called "Stagecoach War" of November 5, 1871, brought an end to any hope of accommodation on the part of General Crook. On that day a raiding party ambushed a westward bound stagecoach near Wickenburg, leaving the driver and five passengers dead. Arizona citizens were quick to blame the Camp Date Creek Yavapai for the atrocity, and called for military reprisals against them. The national press picked up the story, and soon, like the Oatman massacre, the American expansionists were crying for the heads of the Indian culprits. Although a later investigation noted that the attackers took cash but left horses and leather goods behind (items valued by both Apaches and Yavapai), and soon placed the blame on a gang of Wickenburg Mexicans, the inflammatory denunciations of the Arizona and eastern newspapers had served their purpose and General Crook was free to interpret Grant's Peace Plan as any action from warfare to establishing diminished reservations.[57]

In October 1871, the Río Verde Indian Reservation came into being. It lasted until April 23, 1875. It consisted of nearly 800 square miles of the upper Verde River Valley, beginning with the northwest boundary of the Camp Verde military reserve and going north and west to include what is today Drake and Paulden in the Chino Valley and the Verde Valley towns of Jerome, Clarkdale, Cornville, and Cottonwood. Initially most of the inhabitants west of the Verde River were Yavapai, while those on the east side were Tonto Apache (i.e., Dilzhe'e). For example, Deadhorse Point near Cottonwood and on the east side of the Verde River was occupied by Tontos.[58] Many Dilzhe'e had been forced to leave the Tonto Basin and Superstition Mountains and surrender at Río Verde because of the ruthlessness of Crook's winter campaigns.

By late 1872 most of the "temporary asylums" for the various Yavapai bands had been closed, and General Crook was driving all Yavapais and Tontos to Río Verde. By late spring in 1873 all the Date Creek Yavapais were forced to leave the Skull Valley area and settle at Río Verde. All the Yavapai west of the Mingus Mountains were brought over the mountain and dumped on the Río Verde Reservation. Many of the Tolkepayas and Wipukepas were called Apache Yumas or Mojave-Apaches. Small groups of Mojaves, Paiutes, Chemehuevis, and Hualapais were also brought to Río Verde. By summer more than two thousand Yavapais and Tontos were congregated on the reservation. All Río Verde residents were prisoners of war. Any Yavapais and/or Tontos outside the reserve could be shot on sight. Although forced relocation was not pleasant, at least the upper Verde Valley was part of the original Yavapai homeland and an area of dependable water supply, agreeable climate, wild plants and animals, and well suited for agriculture.[59]

The first two years were times of desperation for the Río Verde residents. The white man's germs were more deadly than his bullets. The congestion caused by forcing too many people into a small space combined with a poor diet caused a variety of diseases, from influenza and whooping cough to malarial fever, epizootic and scurvy. To survive they had to rely upon US rations of beef, wheat flour, sugar, beans, and coffee. Like their Navajo counterparts at Bosque Redondo who were also without corn, they combined flour and lard to make fry bread. Not knowing how to make coffee, they ate the raw beans and immediately suffered dysentery, diarrhea, and stomach ailments. In any case the unfamiliar diet, so different from agave, mesquite bean flour, and cactus fruits created havoc on their already weakened digestive systems. The overall situation, including the years of violence and warfare, meant that of the 2,000 or so Yavapai in 1863, only about half that number survived by the end of 1873.[60]

To capture and arrest those Yavapais and Tontos that resisted relocation to Río Verde, General Crook enlisted "friendly" Yavapais as scouts to complete the conquest of the native people. Beginning in 1873 a company of around 40 Río Verde scouts assisted the US Army in tracking down and rounding up the "renegades," and maintaining order on the reservation. As Crook noted, he pitted "savage against savage," recruiting Yavapais and Apaches "fresh from the warpath."

This was not a new strategy. For example, the defeat of the Hualapai by the US Army in 1868 at the Battle of Cherum Peak (a few miles east of today's Chloride, Arizona) was achieved with the assistance of over 100 Mojave scouts and warriors. And when Crook left Arizona to take up the command of troops fighting the Lakota Sioux and Cheyenne at the Battle of the Little Bighorn, it was Crow and Shoshone scouts that outshone the US cavalry at the Battle of Rosebud. Again, in the 1880s when Crook was chasing Geronimo around southern Arizona and northern Mexico, he had no difficulty in recruiting Yavapai scouts from San Carlos.

As Yavapai informant John Williams said: "And when Geronimo got out of San Carlos, the White Army headman told the Yavapai, 'If you follow Geronimo and get him, you can go back to your country.' So that's how they got started as Army scouts... All the old-timers became scouts. I think they never said 'no' to the Army people because they thought they might get punished."[61]

Because Yavapais were sent after other Yavapais, it might appear at first sight that they were being traitors. However, it must be remembered that most Yavapai loyalties were to immediate and extended family, and that there were at least four separate peoples with a long history of inner-Yavapai rivalry. Family ties were more important than tribal loyalty. Serving as a scout was also a way of acquiring remuneration so that cash or ration tokens could be exchanged for goods and food that kin-folk could use for survival. Scouting was also a way of reliving the traditional martial experience of the group, where men were warriors and hunters while women and children were gatherers. And, at least after the period of exile in San Carlos, scouts, as mentioned above, were promised that if they served in the US Army they would be allowed to return to the Upper Verde Valley. Finally, scouting provided adventure and a chance to escape the boredom of everyday reservation life.[62]

To San Carlos in Tears: Exodus and Exile, 1875–1900

In spite of their many problems, the residents of Río Verde did succeed in achieving self-sufficiency, and lived up to Crook's promise that if they produced surplus goods there would be a market in the towns, mining centers, and military reservations.

With Yavapais and Tontos producing the labor, they constructed dams, built a waterwheel, and dug irrigation ditches, some over two miles long. By 1875 they had become successful farmers, combining the traditional crops of corn, beans, squash and melons with white settler potatoes (originally an ancient Peruvian food that went to Europe and came back to the United States). The crop was so successful that it brought into the Río Verde Reservation enough outside cash to replace the reliance on rations. They were even able to supply the cavalry with hay and the soldiers with vegetables, and plant a few small gardens for themselves.[63]

But, unfortunately, Yavapai and Apache success only increased the jealousy of outsiders—white farmers and ranchers who coveted their land and Tucson contractors (known as the "Tucson Ring") who were seeing their profits decline as the Indians started supplying the military with hay and food. Feeling the pressure from American settlers who wanted land and water for their livestock, and Southern Arizona businessmen who lobbied the government, President Ulysses S. Grant rescinded the Río Verde Reservation by Executive Order in April 1875, one month after February 27, 1875, when 1,476 Yavapais and Tontos grudgingly started their sorrowful 180-mile journey southward to the San Carlos Apache territory, across what contemporary Yavapai call "the Exodus Trail." The march took them through miles of cold and rugged mountainous country.[64]

Crook, who was sympathetic to the Indians and disdainful of the corruption of the contractors, was nevertheless ordered to enforce their removal and to cooperate with special commissioner L. E. Dudley from the Indian Office. Dudley was in charge of the exodus to San Carlos. Crook, for his part, promised his Yavapai and Tonto charges that if they assimilated into the white man's culture at San Carlos, that they would eventually return to the Verde Valley from that hellish, dry region of Arizona. This was a promise the Yavapai would not forget.[65]

The journey, called the "March of Tears," involved much suffering. An early problem was the rivalry between two factions, with the Tolkepayas and their Yavapai allies on one side, and Tonto Apaches and their partner Kwevkepaya and Wipukepa on the other. Squabbling over meat, whether cattle or deer, and games that turned into shouting matches, soon led, since both groups had guns, to shootouts that only the cavalrymen could stop. Many Tolkepayas left the trail and went in the direction of Yuma. Many succumbed to hunger and exposure. Many died while fording icy and flooded streams. Newborns who did not survive were buried in the mountains.[66]

As the group medic, Dr. William Henry Corbusier, noted:

> That band was composed of all ages, from babes in arms to old men; the sick and the lame, and pregnant women; all with burdens, on foot and discouraged; slow, stubborn cattle to be driven over rough mountain trails. All of these with inadequate clothing—worn out shoes or moccasins, or none at all—and snow at every turn. It was a cruel, cruel undertaking, and the marvel of it is that any of them reached their destination.[67]

Of the original number, 140 did not complete the trip, an attrition rate, as historian Timothy Braatz points out, of around 10%. By March, John Clum, the agent at San Carlos, estimated that there were approximately 1,000 Yavapais in exile at San Carlos.[68] As mentioned before, in 1863, before the violence, dislocation, and disease the population exceeded 2,000.

Initially life was hard. So hard that many Yavapais left their personal properties behind and traveled back to the Verde Valley. Many Tolkepayas soon fled to Wickenburg, Skull Valley, and points west. Some simply stagnated as prisoners of war while the federal government doled out their homelands to the new settlers. A diet of coffee, white flour, and sugar replaced the traditional one and the people were put on the road to diabetes. Christianity replaced traditional religion, and old names were Americanized and placed on the census rolls. So befuddled by Apache names the Anglo officers started calling their charges "Smith" or "Joe Tonto."[69]

Yet, throughout it all, the people survived. And more surprising, the culture did too. Crook's promise of returning home if they were acculturated motivated many of them to use new "white man" technologies and become modern farmers. They also became wage workers and broke into the cash economy. And even though their army supervisors could not speak Apache or Yavapai, many Indians were multilingual and could speak Yuman, Piman, Athapaskan, Spanish, and yes, English. While some exchanged their traditional clothing for modern shirts, pants, and skirts, most retained their "immodest" ways of wearing skimpy outfits. Although they raised sheep like the white man, and unlike the Navajo, they did not practice spinning or weaving of textiles. Even at San Carlos they continued to live in their traditional uwas. When they finally went home they went as Yavapais and Tontos, not as white men and women. Most significant, they refused to accept San Carlos as their permanent home.[70]

After 1890, with funding drying up in the Indian Service and US Army, established Reserves quit operating and the "captives" were allowed to leave. By the early 1900s the Apache Wars were over and the federal government no longer wanted to fund the concentration of American Indians. When Indian peoples found out they could leave, individuals began their long walks back to their home areas—the regions that gave them a sense of place, spiritual and personal security, and family. Many Tontos returned to Payson, while the Yavapais went to Camp Verde and the Red Rock Country, from Prescott down to old Camp Date Creek or Wickenburg and west to Bagdad (Arizona), or the Castle Dome Mountains on the lower Gila River. Like the first generation of exiles, they too left their chickens, turkeys, and cattle and went home.[71]

As John Williams testified, when he asked his father why he was leaving all his cattle in San Carlos and going home, "Oh," my father said:

> ... If we stay here, they move us away, maybe across the ocean some place. Move us over that way. We don't want to go over there, that's why we come back. We don't want to lose our land.

As Williams said, referring to the removal of the Chiracahua Apaches to Alabama and Florida after 1886, "The White people sent Geronimo over there some place, so we are afraid they send us there, too."[72]

Aftermath: Montezuma's Revenge

After 1900 a mass exodus began, and by 1902 most Yavapais who wanted to leave San Carlos had. Many took their time getting home, some as long as two years. Along the way they would take temporary jobs cutting wood, hauling water, shoveling dirt, and building roads, ditches and dams. Perhaps a new baby was born, or older people got sick, but in any case most were in no hurry to get home. And again, they were learning the ways of a cash economy and becoming more acculturated in the process. Yet when they arrived in the homeland they were in for a schock. During the 25 year exile the old places were taken over by settlers, rancher-farmers, merchants, teachers and government workers. The entire best well watered lands had been taken by the white man, and the Yavapai and Tonto were pushed to the margins as second-class citizens. But at least they were home, even if they were squatters and strangers in their own land.[73]

On September 15, 1903, President Theodore Roosevelt signed an executive order creating the Fort McDowell Indian Reservation in the lower Verde Valley where the Verde River greets the Salt River. By 1910 the federal government established a 40-acre Camp Verde Reservation. By 1916, 248 acres of farmland with water rights was established six miles up the Verde River from Camp Verde and the Middle Verde Indian Reservation came into existence. Much later, in 1935 and 1956, a total of 1,395 acres of the Fort Whipple Military Reservation were set aside for the Yavapai of the Prescott area.[74] The Dilzhe'e of Payson did not have a reservation until 1972.

In the Phoenix area and other new communities in the Salt River region, water rights became a major bone of contention between the majority culture and the Indian people. By 1910 outsiders were threatening to relocate the residents of the Fort McDowell Indian Reservation so that the waters of the Verde could be redirected to white farmers. It was this situation which eventually led to a Yavapai victory. Montezuma's revenge would take place this time not with American tourists in Mexico, but with the white community that had to face the wrath of the Yavapai physician and journalist, Carlos Montezuma (who's Yavapai name was Wassaja).

The story begins in 1871 when the Pimas captured a young Kwevkepaya (southeastern Yavapai) boy named Wassaja along with his two sisters. The sisters were sold to Mexicans, while the boy was purchased by an Italian immigrant named Carlos Gentile for $30. Gentile took the boy to Chicago where Wassaja was baptized Carlos Montezuma, grew up under Baptist influence, and eventually graduated from the University of Illinois and the Chicago Medical School. After graduation he worked as a doctor for the US Indian Office, a talented acculturated physician who could work across two cultures.[75]

In 1903 Montezuma visited his Yavapai relatives in Arizona, and by 1910 he was well aware of the movement by non-Indians to relocate the McDowell Yavapais through an allotment scheme. In 1911 he arranged for a lawyer to argue the Yavapai case and aided a delegation in testifying before the US Congress. His efforts were rewarded as the Yavapais were allowed to stay at Fort McDowell. He led a similar charge in 1920, and again was successful in his defense of his Yavapai cousins. In late December 1922, with his health declining, he left Chicago for Fort McDowell. He died on January 31, 1923, in a brush shelter on the edge of the Reservation.[76] His life cycle was complete, dying where he was born, in that place called the Yavapai homeland. Like his cousins, he was able to go home again (see Figure 6.2).

Figure 6.2 *Memorial to Skeleton Cave victims and Carlos Montezuma.* Mass burial of 76 Yavapai victims, who were killed by a combined force of the US Army and Pima and Maricopa allies at Skeleton Cave in the Salt River Canyon, is commemorated by a circle of rock adjacent to the fenced grave site of Wassaja—the Yavapai who was popularly known as Carlos Montezuma. The head stone and rock formation for the Skeleton Cave martyrs was dedicated in a ceremony in 1985.
Photo by W. Dirk Raat, October 2020.

7

With Friends Like These: The O'odham Water Controversy

He [Charles D. Poston] warned that if the non-Indian population in the area should increase without a corresponding increase in the water supply, Indians [the Tohono O'odham] would die.

Paraphrasing of Charles D. Poston's Report,
Superintendent of Indian Affairs for the Territory of Arizona, 1863[1]

Sprinkle water in the burden basket and you will smell the place of its origin.

Ofelia Zepeda, O'odham Poet and Linguistics Expert[2]

Ant o i-wanno k o i-hudin g cewagi. With my harvesting stick I will pull down the clouds.

Ofelia Zepeda, O'odham Poet[3]

The World would Burn without Rain.

I'itoi, Elder Brother[4]

The green of those Pima [Akimel O'odham] fields spread along the river for many miles in the old days when there was plenty of water. Now the river is an empty bed full of sand.

George Webb, *A Pima Remembers*, 1959[5]

Lost Worlds of 1863: Relocation and Removal of American Indians in the Central Rockies and the Greater Southwest, First Edition. W. Dirk Raat.
© 2022 John Wiley & Sons, Inc. Published 2022 by John Wiley & Sons, Inc.

In 1863, when new settlers continued to divert water from the Gila River, the Akimel O'odham (meaning "River People" and popularly called Pimas), began to protest. Farmers above the Pima villages in Safford and Florence appropriated the water of the Gila. Making conditions more unpleasant their actions coincided with the worst drought of the century. By the mid-1870s, hoping to improve their conditions, a group of Pimas and Maricopas moved to the Salt River above Phoenix where they soon were fighting over water rights with Mormon settlers. By the end of the nineteenth century surface flows had stopped and Pima farms returned to the desert.[6]

Around the same time, in the late 1880s, the O'odham southwest of Tucson (known then as Papagos; today Tohono O'odham or "Desert People"), were forced by cattlemen (whites) to leave desert areas were springs or wells in the foothills had traditionally been used as sources of water for horticulture, so that the *Milga:n* (white men's) livestock would have grazing land.[7] Non-Indian farmers on the Santa Cruz River, like their Native counterparts, diverted water by digging trenches from the river to irrigate their farms. By the early twentieth century this had resulted in the creation of a huge arroyo in which summer rains roared along the ditch instead of flooding the plain. The result was severe erosion and a lowering of the water table around San Xavier del Bac, a major center of Papago activity.[8] With water rights remaining unprotected, no water was reaching Pima and Papago fields. The O'odham were forced to shift from farming to a wage economy and from cooperatives to private farms. The first 10 years of the twentieth century were called "the black decade" by calendar-stick keepers.[9]

The Winters Doctrine, judicially crafted in 1908 and derived from Spanish law, stated that Indians on reservations were entitled to sufficient water to cultivate their lands. While often cited it was rarely enforced until 1992, its enforcement then and now dependent on the climate of political opinion. Until then, treaty rights were ignored and, as Trappist monk and Catholic mystic Thomas Merton noted, "The time will come when they [whites] will sell you even your own rain."[10] With no water the O'odham could grow no cotton for clothing; with no water they could grow no food. Eventually, being restricted to the reservations, and dependent on the US government for rations of white flour, lard, and sugar, nutrition-related diseases, including diabetes, would affect a large proportion of the adult population. Self-sufficient communities had been turned into dependencies.

Genesis: O'odham and the Sonoran Desert

In 1939 the US government created the Cabeza Prieta National Wildlife Refuge. It is located along the US–Mexican border in southwestern Arizona, between the Organ Pipe National Monument to the east (established in 1937) and the Luke Air Force Range to the west (founded in 1941 and known as the Barry M. Goldwater bombing range today). The refuge, gunnery range, and monument were positioned on land that formerly belonged to the O'odham people. It was among the granite peaks and volcanic hills of the Cabeza Prieta, a wilderness region that was a small part of the larger Sonoran Desert, that in March of 1989 a few friends and in-laws buried Edward Paul Abbey— anarchist, environmentalist, and writer.[11]

Before his death, Abbey had worked for the National Park Service, first in 1956–1957 at Arches Monument near Moab, Utah, and later in the 1960s at the Organ Pipe National Monument. His work in southeastern Utah inspired him to write his first work of non-fiction known as *Desert Solitaire*. In that book he describes the "whole nasty routine" to which most dying men are condemned, consisting of hospital oxygen tents, rubber tubes stuck up the nose, bedpans, and bedsores.[12] Better to have a clean ending in the outdoors then suffer the humiliation of an institutionalized death.

So in March of 1989, after surgery and being readmitted to the Tucson hospital a second time, and suffering from internal bleeding, he pushed his doctor aside and pulled the tubes out of his body and traveled home to die, which happened a few days later. True to their prior agreement, his limited number of friends and relatives put Ed in a sleeping bag filled with ice and drove their two trucks loaded with tools, baling wire, jerky, beer, whiskey, and Ed to the desert. That night the coyotes came and sang a song of farewell to Abbey. The next day, near the flat of a mesa, Abbey was buried. The secret location, known only to a few friends and family, contains a small marker bearing the words: "Edward Paul Abbey, 1927–1989, No Comment."

After they buried him, his two friends looked up and saw several buzzards or turkey vultures circling the grave. Abbey always said that if you are dying in the desert, "Comfort yourself with the reflection that within a few hours, if all goes as planned, your human flesh will be working its way through the gizzard of a buzzard, your essence transfigured into the fierce greedy eyes and unimaginable consciousness of a turkey vulture."[13] To become part of a turkey buzzard was Ed Abbey's idea of reincarnation. He had found a proper resting place where the buzzards fly and the coyotes sing.

One of the ironies of the Abbey burial is that since ancient times the O'odham, both Papago and Pima branches, belonged to two moieties or halves. One group is called buzzard, the other coyote. Each moiety has two clans, the four clans representing the cardinal directions in ceremonies.[14] Abbey's burial was a most appropriate way to greet the O'odham desert, that place where, in Abbey's words, "the tangible and the mythical become the same," that place where vultures soar and coyotes wail.

This Sonoran Desert was and is the spiritual and physical homeland of the O'odham. It is one of four North American deserts. The others are the Great Basin Desert, the extremely arid Mojave Desert, and along the Río Grande the Chihuahuan Desert (see Figure 10.1). Folklorist Jim Griffith, when speaking about the parched and waterless desert, said that "It gets so dry here sometimes that the trees follow the dogs" while "the west wind blows so hard in the summertime that the sun sets three hours late."[15] In northern Mexico and southern Arizona the O'odham do not call this place of bare cliffs, badlands, saguaros and chollas a desert. They speak of it as their "house of the sun." It is their home.[16]

In 1687 the Jesuit missionary Eusebio Francisco Kino initiated his *entrada* into the O'odham country of northern New Spain. He called the area, which would become northern Sonora and southern Arizona the Pimería Alta, the region of the upper Pimas. This was in contrast with the lower Pima country in southern Sonora, home of Indian tribes linguistically similar to the O'odham. The Pimería Alta encircled the northern portion of the Sonoran Desert. Its northern edge was the Gila River while its southern boundary was the Río Concepción–Altar–Magdalena network of today's northern Mexico. It was bounded on the east by the San Pedro River, and on the west by the southern Colorado River and the northern edge of the Gulf of California. This western rim also contained the Pinacate lava field and the sand dunes of the Gran Desierto. This then was the Pimería Alta, the O'odham homeland and the home of Kino's religious zeal (see map, Figure 7.1).

The landscape of the Pimería Alta can be generally described as one of wide river valleys surrounded by bare mountains with the higher elevations found in the eastern section. Precipitation amounts vary from an average of 4 to 8 inches in the western coastal regions to 10 to 16 inches in the east. Winter showers, the "female rains," come from the California coast and are usually widespread and gentle. The summer precipitation, the "male rains," starts with the July monsoon season and brings localized, flash floods, often accompanied by sandstorms. The arid western region is a desert of bursage and creosote bush, and running through it from Yuma, Arizona to Sonoyta, Mexico is a notorious trail: *El Camino del Diablo* ("the Devil's highway"), a place "hot as hell" that took the lives of conquistadores, missionaries, prospectors, and others, including more than 2,000 fatalities in the final half of the nineteenth century alone.[17]

The higher mountains in the rest of the Primería Alta support paloverde, cholla, prickly pear, barrel cactus, and the giant saguaro, as well as ironwood and mesquite trees. There is organ pipe in southern Arizona, and the huge cardón can be found near Caborca in northern Sonora.[18]

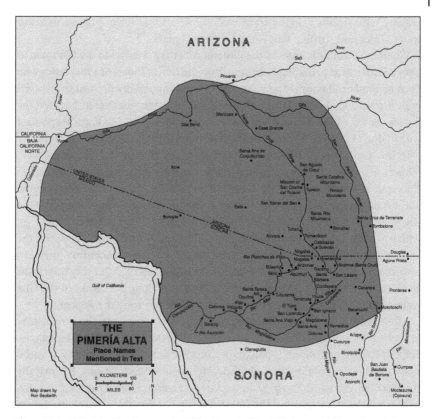

Figure 7.1 *Pimería Alta.* From p. 6 of *The Pimería Alta: Missions and More.* Copyright © by the Southwestern Mission Research Center (SMRC), Tucson, 1996. Reprinted with Permission. All Rights Reserved.

In the semi-desert grasslands above the desert floor are found various succulents, including agave, sotol, and yucca. Over 4,000 feet oak, pinyon trees, and juniper can be found, while in the higher mountains of southern Arizona, like the Santa Catalinas or Baboquivari Peak at 7,730 feet, there are forests of ponderosa and Douglas fir. Vultures share the sky with owls, eagles, wrens, quail and hummingbirds. In some of the driest desert areas small animals include kangaroo rats, while cottontails and jackrabbits, along with squirrels, skunks, raccoons, gophers, coyotes, and coatimundi inhabit the rest of the desert. Large mammals include the bobcat, bighorn sheep, mountain lions, and pronghorn antelopes. For the most part beaver, parrots, grizzly bears, and wolves belong to another era. Since 1700 the natural landscape has been changed by Europeans and Anglo-Americans who introduced water pumps and livestock grazing with results ranging from eroded ditches and fewer grasses to lower water tables and shrubs. This is the O'odham habitat.[19]

When the Spaniards entered the Pimería Alta they referred to the O'odham as Upper Pimas so as to distinguish them from the Lower Pimas or Pima Bajos who lived in southern Sonora. The word "Pima" was supposedly derived from *pi nyi maach* meaning "I don't know" in the O'odham language. Evidently when the Spaniards asked the Indians what they were called, the O'odham responded with "I don't know," a word or phrase that sounded to the Spaniards as "Pima."[20]

In any case, the Spaniards also used a variety of regional names as well: Hímeri for the O'odham along the Dolores and Magdalena, Soba for the Río Concepción area, Sobaipuri for the O'odham farmers of the wet and cool region of the San Pedro and Santa Cruz Valleys, Gileños for the people along the Gila River, and Papago (derived from *bá-bawi ootam* or "Tepary Bean People" in which Papago is a corruption of *bá-bawi*) for the desert dwellers between the Santa Cruz and Colorado Rivers. The Papago homeland, including northern Mexico and southern Arizona, was called the Papaguería.[21] After the Americans came in the mid-nineteenth century the O'odham along the banks of the Gila were called Pimas while their cousins west of Tucson were the Papagos.

All of these people were linguistically related, belonging to the Piman sub-branch of the Sonoran branch of the southern Uto-Aztecan family of languages. Today's Papago or Tohono O'odham person speaks at least 11 dialects or variations, while the Pima or Akimel O'odham, has a separate idiom. Historically the Hia C'ed, or "Sand Papagos" in the far west country, spoke at least two dialects, a northern one around the Colorado River region and a southern dialect spoken east of the Gulf of California in northwestern Sonora. Other variations were used in the Magdalena and Altar River Valleys of northern Mexico.[22]

The O'odham had at least three modes of subsistence, depending on the environment. The Hia C'ed had to adapt to the arid conditions of the western Papaguería by engaging in constant mobilization in search of wild plants, small animals, and water. These were the nomadic No Village people whose settlements were temporary camping sites, including lava-tube caves and *tinajas* (water tanks), whose population remained necessarily small (no more than three or four hundred) because of limited resources.[23]

A second mode of Piman survival could be found among the O'odham inhabitants of the central and eastern Papaguería. Here the annual precipitation of 5 to 10 inches allowed plants such as the paloverde and the saguaro to grow, and was enough water to make summer flash-flood agriculture (known as *ak chin)* a practical pursuit. After planting and harvesting their summer crops, the Papago or Desert People would temporarily abandon their field villages and travel to their winter homes located next to springs or wells in the foothills. Here the men would engage in hunting while the women collected plants. Their summer homes included a small house of ocotillo stalks alongside a ramada for sleeping and an outside cooking area. Because they had a "Field Village" as well as a "Wells Village," they were known as the Two Village people.

The Desert People relied upon animal products and wild plants for 75% of their food intake in the pre-contact period, while the remaining diet came from the traditional maize, bean, and squash agriculture of the region. Animal products ranged from deer and mountain sheep to lizards and grasshoppers. The wild crops included cacti seeds, agave, buds, onions, amaranth, as well as mesquite beans, berries, acorns, roots and bulbs of the wild potato, and the fruit of the yucca. Some of their domestic crops came from trading wild plants and salt for the cultivated plants of the Gila River area.[24]

In times of extreme need the semi-nomadic Papagos would abandon their desert villages and go to a refuge area. These areas were located on all four sides of the Papaguería and were inhabited by aggressive warlike people who practiced horticulture. To the south were the Altar Valley inhabitants. In the north and northwest were the Gila River Pimas and the Maricopa (Pee Posh) of the Gila Bend region. The refuge area in the east consisted of the Sobaípuri of the San Pedro and Santa Cruz Valleys. Finally, to the southwest were the populations around the Sonoita River (later to become a Mexican ranchería). The Papagos would maintain friendly relations with their hosts, planting temporary fields and exchanging labor for corn and beans. These were the subsistence strategies of the traditional Tohono O'odham.[25]

A final mode of survival was that of The One Village people or River People, which included the Sobaípuri of the San Pedro and Santa Cruz Valleys and the Gileños or Akimel O'odham of the Gila River area. The Sobaípuri, who were forced out of their river valleys by the Apache raids in the eighteenth century, moved to the mission area of San Xavier del Bac outside of Tucson and were eventually amalgamated with the Papagos. Their riverine settlements of this upland vegetation zone contained animals and wild plants in great abundance. The alluvial floodwaters were well suited for horticulture. With the arrival of the Europeans, the Sobaípuri improved their horticultural techniques (which included pre-Hispanic irrigation ditches) by adding enhanced Spanish methods of irrigation farming. Finally, the rivers supplied the Sobaípuri with fish.[26]

As for the One Village people along the Gila, although the people were well aware of irrigation techniques, they did not need ditches and canals to grow cotton and the Indian trinity of maize, beans, and squash. With rainfall above normal in the seventeenth century, they did not have to practice irrigation. The Gila was a slow-moving river that created swamps and runoff. The existence of islands in the middle of the Gila River were especially suitable for farming without ditches as bed rock channeled underground flows to the surface. Later, after the Europeans arrived, and akin to their pre-Hispanic ancestors, the Pima used canals and feeder ditches to distribute the water to their wheat and corn fields. Like their Papago cousins, they selected drought resistant maize for their main crop.[27] And like the Sobaípuri, they did not have to move their settlements of mud, brush and stick houses because of a plentiful supply of water.

The O'odham's basic unit of society was and is the patrilineal extended family. Married sons and their wives lived with their parents.[28] These extended familes lived in rancherías that were scattered one from the other, sometimes a quarter to a half mile apart. At times ranchería members would shift from one location to another. Where the water supply was abundant, as it was for the Pimas, their settlements would appear town-like, even though they could not be called town dwellers. Clan affiliation descended through the male line. Political authority was exercised by the village headman, along with a council of elders and certain specialists in charge of ceremonies, festivals, and warfare. Their spiritual and medical lives were dominated by shamans, not priests. On a non-sedentary to sedentary continuum the Pimas would have more compact settlement patterns than the Tarahumaras of southwestern Chihuahua and be less concentrated than the Mayos and Yaquis of southern Sonora.[29]

The current and past population figures for the O'odham are less than exact. Because of the impact of European diseases, in particular smallpox, measles, chicken pox, and new strains of flu, the O'odham population of the eighteenth century had declined considerably from pre-contact times. In 1703, Father Kino estimated the Indian population of the Primería Alta to be around 16,000 people, with about 7,000 of that number being Sobaípuris. The Gila River Pimas or Gileños were estimated to be between 2,230 and 3,050 individuals. By 1762, when the Sobaípuris had finally abandoned the San Pedro Valley because of Apache raids, the Indian population of the Pimería Alta, according to missionary sources, had decreased by half to around 8,000 people. Apache raids, intermarriage, and disease had reduced the numbers.[30]

As of the year 2014, Bernard Siquieros, curator at the Tohono O'odham Cultural Center and Museum in Topowa, Arizona, estimates that the Papago population is around 33,000, with 14,000 of that number living on the three reservations. This would be an increase of 17,000 people over the census of 1981. Another 2,000 live on nine Mexican *ejidos* or communal land holdings in Sonora. Royce Manual of the Salt River Pima-Maricopa Community indicates that the Akimel O'odham population is close to 10,000, while Kelly Washington, the director of the cultural resources center of Salt River Pima-Maricopa Indian Community (as of 2019) estimates a Pima and Maricopa population of 10,700 tribal members with 6,000 residing locally.[31]

As for the pre-contact population, the history of the O'odham before the Spanish arrival at Pimería Alta is shrouded in mystery, although most scholars believe in some variant of the Hohokam–Pima continuum. When Kino arrived his people discovered the ruins at Casa Grande and also noticed the Pima using a red-on-buff pottery. They assumed that the O'odham were somehow related to an earlier, "higher" Indian civilization. This civilization, as archaeologists know today, is called the Hohokam (or *Huhugam* from the O'odham *huhug*, meaning "to perish, disappear"), which took off around CE 700 and began to decline after 1150. The Hohokam core was in the Phoenix basin and their influence spread from the junction of the Salt and Gilas Rivers southeastward to Casa Grande along the Upper Gila, eastward to the Salado country, and northward along the Río Verde tributary. At their apogee around CE 1150 they had Big Houses, ball courts, urbanization, and a sophisticated canal system that collectively ran for hundreds of miles. Prior to their decline they have numbered as many as 50,000.

Ultimate demise came to this hydraulic society after CE 1430 when the 1385 flood on the Salt River was followed by the Gila River floods of the 1430s. Other factors may have included drought, a polluted water supply (increased salinity due to lower water levels incapable of absorbing minerals; that is why the Spaniards named it Río Salado, or Salt River), undesirable immigrants (Salados from the east?), class revolts and civil war, and warfare with outside intruders.

It is known that Piman speakers linguistically related to the populations of southern Sonora migrated north into the San Pedro and Santa Cruz Valleys, entering the Hohokam territory from the southeast in pre-contact times. The Sobaípuris occupied these valleys in the 1400s at a time that overlaps with the last phase of Hohokam history. This chronology has been verified by luminescence dates on O'odham pottery, as well as chronometric dates from multiple San Pedro and Santa Cruz sites.[32] It is likely that these O'odham either witnessed or participated in the fall of the Hohokam society. Could they have been the outside intruders? Or were they indistinguishable from the Hohokam elites and one of the people involved in a Hohokam revolt?[33]

A clue to the unsolved problems of the continuum debate may be found in the oral history traditions of the Tohono O'odham, especially the story of their culture hero *I'itoi* (pronounced Ee-toy), their creator and Elder Brother who led the O'odham people out of the underworld. Among the Akimel O'odham I'itoi is known as *Se'e'e* or *Se-eheh*, and while the name is different most of their stories about him are essentially the same as the Desert O'odham.[34]

I'itoi's sacred home (*I'itoi Ki:)* is in a cave hidden at the base of a canyon at Baboquivari Peak, the most revered of O'odham sites. The Papago basket design "Man in the Maze" reflects the I'itoi Ki:, an allegory reflecting the deeper meaning of life—the Himdag, the O'odham path or way of living. Today the O'odham visit the cave where on the ceiling and walls can be found rosary beads, chains with rings on them, medallions, bullets, and cigarettes. At the base there is even a green frog figurine—an effigy from the Hohokam era.[35]

An abbreviated story of the beginnings of the O'odham world would be as follows: In the beginning Earthmaker made the world from which I'itoi sprang. The two of them, along with Coyote, made the first people. They were not the right kind of people so Earthmaker and I'itoi destroyed them with a flood. When the waters receded I'itoi, who had gained the title of Elder Brother, created a second people out of clay. These people eventually quarreled with Elder Brother and they killed him. The people who killed Elder Brother were not the Papago and Pima, but the builders of Casa Grande (Hohokam). Resurrected, the angry I'itoi went through the underworld looking for his friends. Here he found the Papago and Pima, and so I'itoi led them to the surface world and together they drove out those people of Casa Grande. They settled down, and then I'itoi showed them the feast they must hold in order to bring the clouds down and keep the world in harmony. "Wind" and "Rain" were invited back to the community. This is the reason for the rainmaking ceremony.[36]

This ceremony is a four day event, perhaps symbolizing the role of clouds as directional makers and the four cardinal points—white clouds for east, black for west, green for south, and red for north. These sacred colors and symbols were also used for the wind sickness cure.[37] Rainmaking begins in late May and early June when the women of the community, carrying long poles made of saguaro skeleton, go out to the desert and hook with their poles the ripe fruit at the top of the saguaro cactus. It is immediately cooked over a fire and the liquid residue is strained through a woven basket. The juice is then taken to the headman of the village, and he mixes it with water and places the mixture in the council house for two or three days allowing it to ferment. Meanwhile the people outside the council house sing the rain songs.[38]

When the saguaro wine is ready, the people will continue to sing as well as dance, recite poetry, and drink wine. Over the four day ceremony the dark red juice will be consumed. Because the wine is of a low alcoholic content, much must be consumed before feeling its effects. This leads to bloated feelings and an inebriated condition that can only be relieved through regurgitation. This act itself gives the drinker a new sense of life, and the juice in somewhat altered form will be returned to the earth whence it came. After the rain ceremony the fields would be planted, the new calendar would begin, and hopefully the July monsoons would bring the clouds down. Today's wine ceremony, although important to the traditionalists, sometimes consists more of commercial beer and debauchery than ceremony (although, to be fair, this was also an opinion of the earlier Jesuits and Franciscans).

The sacred stories of I'itoi and the winemaking ceremony, essential aspects of the O'odham Himdag, may contain historical content. Archaeologist Stephen Lekson interprets these stories as a class revolt in which the oppressed O'odham raised up against the Hohokam ruler-priests who lived in Great Houses on platform mounds. He even suggests that the rebellion started at

Casa Grande and ended at Pueblo Grande on the Salt River. Although the floods mentioned in the story may have been an underlying cause, the O'odham revolt was the immediate political event that brought the Hohokam down. After the rebellion, the O'odham returned to the south to become the Pima of Kino's day and the Akimel O'odham of today.[39]

Historian Bernard Fontana and ethnobiologist Amadeo Rea go further to argue that the emergence myth suggests the Pimas, known as the *vupushkam*, "the ones who came up," were fighters who pushed the *vipishad*, "builders of the ruins," out of the Phoenix basin, sending them fleeing down the Gila River to the Colorado River, whence they followed the Colorado upriver to become a part of the Hopi people.[40] The Hohokam may also have traveled up the Verde River to Montezuma Well, and then followed the *Palatkwapi* Trail. This was an old Indian road that became a wagon trail in the nineteenth century that connected settlers in Camp Verde to the Hopi village of Walpi, a distance of around 145 miles. Hopi traditions do speak of the migration of the *Patki ngum* (Water Clan) from *Palatkwapi* (The Red City), a homeland that could be the Sedona area, the Verde Valley, or the Phoenix Basin.[41]

Another important ceremony of the O'odham, reflecting their pre-contact roots, is the deer dance. This was a cleansing ceremony that took place in the early autumn just before the people moved to their "Wells Village" in the foothills. Its purpose was to create magic over the crops that had been gathered and the deer that would be hunted so that the food would be safe to eat. In this ceremony representatives from the two moieties would participate, with the Buzzard man carrying the meat while the Coyote person held the deer tail, the latter considered to have magic properties.[42]

The O'odham deer dance ceremony is from the same Sonoran tradition as the Yaqui killing-the-deer ceremony, a drama of death and renewal, or the Huichol "magical deer" ceremony in which the deer represents the power of maize to sustain the body and peyote to feed the spirit. The Huichol residents of Jalisco and Nayarit, like most of their neighbors in the northern Sierra Madre Occidental, participated in a version of the deer dance ceremony. These then were the ceremonies, belief systems, folkways, and customs of the O'odham people the Spaniards encountered in 1687 went they pushed into the northern frontier of New Spain.

Pathway to Mesilla: Spanish and Mexican Periods

When Padre Kino and the other Jesuit missionaries came to the Pimería Alta in the late 1600s they found evidence that Spanish influences had preceded them. The O'odham population was undoubtedly smaller than that of pre-contact days, with maladies like malaria, dysentery, smallpox, and others killing perhaps as many as 50 to 75% of the people. The northern and north-western part of the Papaguería, with its scattered populations and relative iso-lation, would have fared better. The indigenous trade networks that facilitated the movement of diseases, also brought other European goods and wares, including a people already cultivating flax, watermelons, and wheat—all Old World crops.[43]

Kino and a handful of Jesuit missionaries founded mission churches in the permanent villages of the O'odham people. They acted as spiritual leaders and agents of the Spanish crown. In all, Kino founded eight mission districts (*par-tidos*) with satellite stations (*visitas*) stretching from Dolores on the San Miguel River in the south to the Gila River on the north, and from the San Pedro River on the east to the Colorado in the west. Some of the churches included, in addition to Dolores, the central valley villages of Magdalena, San Ignacio, and Cocóspera, the Río Altar-Concepción mission towns of Sáric, Tubutama, Pitiquito, and Caborca (including the far western *visita* of San Marcelo de Sonoyta), and the northern mission complex in Arizona of Guevavi, Tumacácori, and San Xavier del Bac. Kino died in 1711 in Magdalena and was initially buried under the church there (known today as Magdalena de Kino).[44] By 1767, when the Jesuits were expelled from New Spain by edict of the King of Spain, they had founded more than two dozen missions and *visitas* (see Figure 7.2).

The Jesuits reintroduced European livestock, foodstuffs, and wares to the Indians. The missionaries introduced livestock, particularly cattle, horses, mules, donkeys, goats, sheep, ducks, and chickens, as well as farm equipment like metal axes, shovels, and wooden plows. New irrigation techniques improved the traditional reliance on floodplain agriculture, and meant that the Akimel O'odham would become even more successful desert farmers.

With no Spanish institutions in Arizona north of Tucson and no direct con-tacts with Spaniards, the Gila River Indians traveled to Hispanic commu-nities to engage in exchange. They also made contact with acculturated Sonoran Pimas who visited the Gila River country. Of the foodstuffs brought by the missionaries, winter wheat was especially important for it meant that the O'odham could now harvest year round—corn in the summer and wheat in the late winter. Furthermore, since wheat suited European tastes more than corn did, the increasing number of Spanish settlements of Sonora provided a growing market for it. This, in turn, led to a marketplace for other Pima goods such as blankets and captives, and to the idea of monetary commercial exchanges in lieu of gift exchanges and bartering.[45] Wheat continued to be important throughout the history of Sonora, so much so that today while southern Mexicans eat corn tortillas, the Sonorans prefer their tortillas of wheat and lard.

Figure 7.2 Bronze statute by Julián Martínez of *Father Eusebio Francisco Kino, S.J.* in Tucson. Photo by Charles W. Polzer, S.J., courtesy of the Office of Ethnohistorical Research, Arizona State Museum.

After the Jesuit expulsion of 1767 their missions were taken over by members of the Franciscan Order, but even though they built some impressive churches and maintained some mission centers, they were on the whole unsuccessful in creating new converts and establishing new missions. They lacked sufficient financial backing from the crown, and the O'odham had lost the zeal of earlier generations.[46] At the same time a new wave of settler farmers and miners made encroachments on the more fertile mission lands, making the missionary effort more difficult.

Generally speaking, primarily because of the Apache threat to both Spaniard and O'odham, the latter were usually friendly and helpful to their Hispanic allies. But there were a few instances of conflict in Kino's day and after. In

1695, for example, after an Opata Indian, who had been hired by the Jesuit missionaries to act as an overseer to the O'odham people living in the Tubutama mission (and were obliged to work under his command), exceeded his authority by beating one of the mission Indians, the O'odham rebelled against the Opata overseer. The O'odham, true to their ancient rivalries with the Opata nation, killed the foreman, two of his Opata assistants, set fire to the mission church, and destroyed a herd of cattle. The rebels then went on to kill Father Francisco Xavier Saeta and his assistants at Caborca, and after slaughtering the mission cattle, returned home. The conflict continued to escalate and before it was over the Spanish soldiers and their Tepoca Indian auxiliaries had killed 48 O'odham in an incident known to Mexican history as *La Matanza*, The Slaughter.[47]

The next major confrontation took place during the winter of 1751-1752. Luis Oacpicagigua, leader of the O'odham warriors, led a generalized attack on the Spaniards in the Pimería Alta. Luis and his 3,000 armed soldiers attacked missionaries, Spanish settlers and their employees, soldiers, and Christianized Indians. Warfare spread from Saric, on the Altar River as far west as Sonoita, and south to Caborca. On January 5, two thousand warriors under Luis' command, mostly from the camp in Baboquívari, engaged in warfare with the Spanish army. The O'odham lost 46 men, while the Spaniards only had two soldiers wounded. By March the Spanish army was at San Xavier del Bac and Luis was forced to surrender. As for the conditions leading to the rebellion, Luis blamed the Jesuits, insisting that they unjustly punished their charges and used lands that were supposedly set aside for O'odham use. The 1751-1752 revolt occasioned the construction of two presidios, one at Altar in Sonora, the other in Tubac in Arizona.[48]

But the major military threat for both Spaniard and O'odham was the Apache, a group the O'odham called 'O:b, or "Enemy."[49] In addition, the Gila River "One Village" people feared intrusions by allies of the Apache, especially the Yavapai north of them and the Quechan Indians (referred to as "Yumas" in the early literature) around the Lower Colorado River. For these reasons they maintained friendly relations with the Cocopa and other Colorado Indians who were enemies of the Mojave and Quechan. By the mid-1850s these "friendlies," consisting of an amalgam of Lower Colorado River Indians, formed an alliance with the Pima and had resettled around the Gila Bend area of the Gila River. These collections of Colorado River Indians were known as Maricopas (Pee Posh), but historically they were usually called Cocomaricopas.

As time went on the Apache threat became greater. It is difficult to ascertain the nature of the relationship between the O'odham and Apache in pre-contact days, but Apache raiding certainly increased in intensity and frequency after the Spaniards arrived in the Pimería Alta. As has been noted, the missionaries introduced horses and wheat to Sonora, and developed mission towns that attracted other settlers. New crops created new forms of wealth, and wealthy farmers and ranchers brought in more livestock. The Apaches came to prize as food these vast herds of cattle. In the meantime the horse meant that the Apache could widen their range. As Herbert Eugene Bolton, the famed Spanish Borderlands historian noted in his classic *Rim of Christendom*, "In other words, the Spaniards raised stock and at the same time gave the Apaches the means of stealing it."[50]

By 1779 the Spaniards had withdrawn all but token forces from the frontier. With a weakening of the presidios the Apache raids were extended as far south as Durango, and west beyond Ajo in the Sand Papago country. The Gila River Pimas responded by increasing the sentinel duties of their people. A kind of universal military service was instituted that required all adult males to participate in arms drill, and to shift from vengeance raids to punitive campaigns akin to the Spanish army. The O'odham became known as valiant soldiers, and because of this reputation they were often recruited by Spanish military officials. As the Apache threat continued, the Tubac garrison was ordered to move to Tucson and along the Santa Cruz River.[51]

In 1787 Tubac was restored by a company of O'odham soldiers who had been stationed at San Ignacio. However, by this time the Spanish government had developed a new policy for pacifying Apaches by getting them to agree to live in temporary camps next to Spanish towns and by providing them with rations and outdated arms. The new policy worked for a couple of decades, and meant that the O'odham mostly prepared for battle rather than participate in Indian warfare during the end of the Spanish era.[52] By the beginning of the Mexican period after 1821, the O'odham were becoming an "economic" and "military" force in Sonora and along the Gila River.

Independence for Mexico did not translate into improved conditions on the frontier. Mexico City politicians were too busy with intrigues and rivalry to pay much attention to the North. The Mexican government lacked the resources to administer the frontier and from 1821 to the Mexican–American War of 1845 the borderlands lacked for financial, religious, and military support.

The Franciscan missions suffered from financial instability, no longer able to receive funds from either the Spanish government or their wealthy benefactors in Spain. Church lands, including O'odham fields near or on the missions, were also being seized by incoming colonists. With this occurrence the anti-clerics in government began to favor private property groups (Spanish famers, ranchers, and miners) over corporate (Church) or cooperative lands (O'odham). Much of the church property in Mexico was nationalized by an 1833 law, and the Franciscan mission system was dead by 1842.[53] The O'odham would fend for themselves. And so they did, by creating their own indigenous version of Christianity in the form of Sonoran Catholicism.

Meanwhile, with the missions declining the arrival of a new generation of Mexican farmers and gold seekers provided a revived target for Apache raiders. The Apaches, restless in the 1820s, conducted full-scale raids in the 1830s striking missions and towns in southern Sonora. Many O'odham people abandoned their traditional rancherías for the safety of numbers that could be found in defensive villages.

On October 1, 1832, two members of the town council of Guadalupe del Altar sent a letter to the Vice Governor of Sonora located at Arizpe. They reported on intelligence they had received from Gileños (Gila Pimas) that a large group of Apaches and Yumas had attacked and captured several families of Cocomaricopas, killing two of the women. The councilors went on to say that "One Cocomaricopa managed to escape and bear the news to the Gileños. These gathered together, leaving, [and] fell upon the Apaches and Yumas who were careless, and according to the marks sent me on a stick, of three trails they were able to follow, counting the dead these amounted to 138 Apaches dead and among them some Yumas; and they took from them 23 animals and the families they had captured." The report continues, "Being thirsty, they could not count the dead along the fourth trail. They assure me was plenty." The letter signed off saying that "I had no doubt of the truth of this happy fact ... . It has seemed well to communicate this good news to Your Governorship."[54]

In the 1840s Apache raids forced the inhabitants, including O'odham, out of the Santa Cruz Valley. The old mission site of Tumacacori, as well as the Tubac presidio, was abandoned in 1848. O'odham who had gone to Sonora to harvest beans were forced to battle Apaches instead. At the same time gold seekers from Sonora and the eastern United States rushed westward across O'odham territory, pushing the O'odham into the desert as Anglo-Mexican settlers fought them for water rights to the land. Those who did not move westward either settled in San Xavier del Bac or joined the mixed cultures making new homes in the town of Tucson.[55]

When the Mexican War was over in 1848, it was followed by a new boundary agreement in 1853. This was the Treaty of Mesilla, known to US historians as the Gadsden Purchase. Negotiated in 1853, it was ratified by the US Senate in 1854. In effect the agreement compensated Mexico $10 million for its loss of land, and moved the international boundary south of the Gila so as to have territory for a transcontinental railroad. President Santa Anna got the money, and Sonora lost its lands along and south of the Gila River.

The new boundary line split the Papaguería, two-thirds of which was on the US side of the border. It would take many years before the border would be enforced, and many O'odham in the western sections near and above Ajo still thought they were Mexicans as late as World War II. Most of the Sonoran O'odham moved to the area around Caborca, settled in smaller villages near the boundary, or were assimilated into Mexican villages or Arizona towns.

After the Gadsden Purchase prospectors opened up mines in the Tubac area.[56] In an unwritten agreement US authorities allowed the Apaches to raid into Mexico if they agreed not to raid citizens in the United States. After Geronimo was captured in 1886, the Apache threat was soon diminished. Now the only '*O:b* in sight would be their new friends, the Americans.

With Friends Like These: the American Amigos

Between the Gadsden Purchase of 1854 and the beginning of the American Civil War in 1861, the O'odham continued to live their usual lives behaving as if the new boundary line did not exist. Papagos continued to pass back and forth over the artificial border, going into Mexico to escape American authority and into the United States to flee from Mexican justice. This was especially the case for those Papagos, Sonoran or otherwise, who were stealing horses in Mexico, trading them to Arizona Papagos, who in turn exchanged them with their Gila cousins.[57] This trade, along with kidnapped Apache women and children, continued to flourish and was one reason the Apache–O'odham enmity persisted. Throughout the 1860s it was common practice for the O'odham to bring Apache body parts or captured Apache children to American settlements.[58]

For a decade and a half after the Gadsden Purchase the Pimas and Papagos, along with their Maricopa (or Piipaash) allies, enjoyed a kind of "favored nation" position with the US government and had friendly relations with many American settlers. Lacking enough troops to deal with the Apache threat, the American army had to rely upon the traditional indigenous enemies of the Apache to control their raiding activities. As early as 1856 the Pima were involved in a joint military operation with the United States. In that year, Juan Thomas, a Pima from Blackwater, Arizona, recorded that "The Pimas and Maricopas joined the white soldiers in a campaign against the Apaches under White Hat."[59] Although, generally peaceful with outsiders, as has been related before, the O'odham were efficient fighters who were willing to ally their forces with others, whether Spanish or American, in order to deal with the marauding activities of "Yumas," Yavapais, or Apaches.

Initially the desert country did not attract many settlers, so the US Army had to rely on the farming skills of the O'odham for provisions. The O'odham in the riverine valleys, with their "improved" irrigation techniques and wheat growing activity had become relatively prosperous farmers. By 1857 the Pimas were supplying foodstuffs to the builders of the wagon road linking El Paso, Texas to Fort Yuma, Arizona. They also provided food, animals, and shelter for the San Antonio-San Diego stage line operation. They also replaced supplies for several trading posts.[60]

The O'odham provided Forty-Niners and other weary travelers, coming or going through O'odham country, with foodstuff, livestock, and resting places. Even before the Gadsden Purchase the O'odham had come to the rescue of westward travelers, as when they came to the aid of one of the survivors of the Oatman Massacre of 1851.

As peaceful allies of the United States, the government did not have to send troops against the O'odham. Its interests and those of the settlers were being protected. And because of this special relationship, the US government recognized the O'odham people as an independent tribe, even though they were not initially provided a reservation. Because they were industrious and peaceful they could be ignored.[61]

And when the government ignored them, those white rascals who wanted to farm and ranch their lands would be free to let their cattle roam their sacred country, mine their sacred mountains, and either drive them away from their water sources, or redirect their water to themselves. And so the friendly Americans turned on their indigenous benefactors.

Most members of the US Army went east after the Civil War started. In their absence Apache raiding increased. With the war's cessation, non-Indians from both the California goldfields and from the eastern states began to filter into O'odham country. The re-entry of American dragoons to the presidios abandoned by the Mexicans attracted more farmers and ranchers to the area, all of whom began to make claims on Indian lands. Because one of the "villages" of the "Two Village" people was seasonal and temporary, the unoccupied village lands would be claimed by the intruders.[62] This was the beginning of a century-long conflict over water rights between the O'odham and *Milga:n*.

Tohono O'odham

The O'odham traditions of alliance with outsiders against their Apache foes came to a head on April 30, 1871 when a Tucson posse consisting of 6 Americans, 48 Mexicans, and 94 O'odham attacked the Aravaipa Apache in a canyon east of Camp Grant. The Aravaipa Canyon lies approximately 60 miles northeast of Tucson near the San Pedro River. At daybreak the O'odham warriors, armed with their wooden clubs, entered the canyon and caught the sleeping residents by surprise. The attack lasted less than 30 minutes. When it was over perhaps as many as 144 Apache were dead, mostly women and children. Twenty-nine Apaches were taken captive, the children among them later sold in Mexico as slaves.[63]

According to the O'odham view, the incident that led up to what was later called the "Camp Grant Massacre" started with an Apache foray into San Xavier del Bac where several cattle and horses were smuggled away from their

Papago and Mexican owners. The Aravaipa Apache supposedly had promised the US government that they would give up raiding and stealing if the troops at Camp Grant would grant rations and protection.[64] The innocence or guilt of the Aravaipa is difficult to ascertain, but in the minds of the attackers that issue had been long settled before they left Tucson. It was not until Geronimo was captured in 1886 that the Apaches ceased to be a threat to the O'odham, and by then the people had other concerns.

As early as 1862 the United States opened up the public lands of southern Arizona Territory to homesteaders. The US Congress later extended the law to cover any and all claims to mineral rights in the Papaguería. In 1863, the territory's first Superintendent of Indian Affairs, Charles D. Poston, estimated the Papago population at 6,800 and prophesized that if the non-Indians continued to increase in number without an increase in the water supply, the Indians would die. By the mid-1860s and continuing in the post-Civil War era the O'odham near Tucson were feeling the pressures of white encroachment.[65]

The Papagos pled with their American amigos to create a reservation with government dug wells that would provide a permanent home for the O'odham. In 1874 an executive order created an O'odham district at San Xavier setting aside 69,200 acres for O'odham use. The Mexicans living on the land continued using the O'odham water, grazing their cattle and farming the land. Another small O'odham district was created around the Gila Bend area in 1884. This reservation was reduced in size after non-Indian settlers in the area complained that the Indians were given too much land and water.[66]

Over time stock raising was becoming big business in the land of the O'odham. Anglo-American ranchers from Texas brought large herds into the Santa Cruz Valley south of San Xavier. The Mexicans brought in their smaller herds from Mexico. Stock raising was even borrowed by the O'odham from the intruders, especially around the Baboquívari range.[67] By the late 1880s the Papagos were losing out in the competition with outsiders for grazing lands and water rights. Even if an Indian had dug the well himself, he was soon forced off of it by ambitious whites.[68]

The O'odham were too scattered over the landscape for the Indian agent to protect them against these wrongs. Those O'odham raising cattle for the marketplace were losing their traditional values. Instead of redistributing wealth, they were learning from non-Indians to acquire individual wealth. In the meantime the cattle range was being damaged by overgrazing with mesquite trees hindering the growth of grass, and with fewer grazing areas, erosion increased.[69] Eventually many of the people gave up their traditional lives and entered the cash economy of Tucson as day laborers, railroad workers, or house keepers.

In the nineteenth century the Santa Cruz River was an intermediate stream, except in times of flooding. In places geographic formations would force the underground aquifer to the surface creating spring fed streams. One of the better flowing springs was Punta de Agua near San Xavier, a traditional source of water going back to Hohokam days. During the late 1800s, however, non-Indian farmers tried to improve and expand their agricultural fields along the Santa Cruz River by digging huge ditches that would intercept the main stream and divert the water to their farms. Other ditches were dug south of Tucson.[70]

Unfortunately, when monsoon floods hit the area the ditches were turned into huge arroyos resulting in runoff that carried away prime O'odham farmland. By 1912 the Punta de Agua ditch had turned into a massive arroyo, two miles long, twenty feet deep, and one hundred feet wide. The runoff also lowered the water table, leaving San Xavier high and dry. Another ditch below Tucson was so eroded that it became an 18-mile-long arroyo.[71]

This was the death of O'odham agriculture, even though the federal government made a meager effort to keep the corpse alive by creating a large reservation in 1916 of over 2.7 million acres west of the Santa Cruz River. The Sells Reservation, one of the largest in the nation, was now, however, a land of arroyos, not rivers. As large as the area was, it did not include the homeland of the Sand People who lost all rights to their traditional domain. Today this is the home of the Barry Goldwater Air Force Range, as well as the Organ Pipe Cactus National Monument and the Cabeza Prieta Game Range.[72] As for the future of the Papago water rights, it would be nothing but a series of negotiations with Indian agents, lawyers, bureaucrats, and, generally speaking, the national government. Some laws were passed, few were implemented. Some victories, some defeats, but the battle was never ending.

Ak-Chin Farmers

For at least 2,000 years the O'odham and their ancestors farmed the floodwaters of this area south of today's Maricopa, Arizona, near where the Santa Cruz tributary once entered the Gila River. "Ak-Chin" agriculture can be translated as floodwater farming. With a decline in Apache raiding and the arrival of the Southern Pacific Railroad in the 1870s, the Tohono O'odham converted this summer camp site into a permanent village. Many of the Ak-Chin colonists exchanged goods and labor with the Pimas along the Gila. With the decline of agriculture along the Gila and the 1918 influenza epidemic, many Pima Indians migrated to Ak-Chin. They were also joined by Piipaash or Maricopa Indians. Today the Ak-Chin speak a distinct dialect and consider themselves to be Ak-Chin O'odham, neither Tohono nor Akimel.[73]

In 1912 the Maricopa-Ak-Chin Reservation was created. In the earlier days the Ak-Chin could reach the water table and drinking water by digging shallow 10 foot wells. Only two years after the reservation was established the water table had dropped 30 feet, and by 1970 it had dropped more than 300 feet. Subsistence farming disappeared between the two world wars as most Ak-Chin Indians became wage laborers in the cotton fields of Arizona. Mechanization brought that activity to an end by the 1960s. With the water table dropping 20 feet a year the Ak-Chin were becoming desperate. Today a negotiated settlement with the Central Arizona Project brings irrigation water to the Ak-Chin farms where cotton, wheat, and potatoes are grown. The farmers are fairly efficient, and as for those potatoes, they are part of America's potato chip industry.[74]

Akimel O'odham

A few years after the Mexican-American war and the Gadsden Purchase, the wagon trail from Tucson to the California gold fields along the Santa Cruz and Gila Rivers was well traversed. Several Forty-Niners sought their fortunes by traveling this road. It was called the "Southern Overland Route" and by 1857 it had become established as the San Antonio and San Diego Mail Line. Near the junction of the Gila and Santa Cruz Rivers there were at least 12 Indian communities, the upriver or easternmost 10 being Pima, the other 2 on the west belonging to the Maricopa or Piipaash (also spelled Pee Posh) people. The history of rival warfare between the Quechan and Mojave on the Colorado River (as well as Yavapai and Apache groups), and the Cocopa–Maricopa–Pima alliance, was about to be repeated. The battle would take place at Maricopa Wells, a watering hole for mail carriers and "Argonauts," located near the two Maricopa villages.[75]

On September 1, 1857, non-Indian eyewitnesses reported a Maricopa village on fire. The event was described by Isaiah Woods, a very literate man who worked for the mail line. He said that "While camping at the wells I was witness to the largest Indian battle of the times. The Yuma [Quechan] Indians, aided by the Mojaves and Tonta [sic] Apaches [Yavapai?] as their allies, attacked the Maricopas just before daylight this morning." After the attack a Piipaash messenger went to the Pimas for help. The Pimas decided to gather a force of about 1,000 Pima warriors aided by perhaps as many as 200 Piipaash men capable of bearing arms. After the Yavapai and Apache left the field, there remained about 104 Quechans and Mojaves to face the Maricopa–Pima alliance.[76]

The Pima–Maricopa council of war determined that the enemy should be cut off from the river and their source of drinking water. By mid-day the Quechans were exhausted from thirst. As one unnamed eyewitness declared, "At that moment the Pimas and Maricopas who were on horseback rushed in upon the enemy and rode them down. After a hand-to-hand combat the Yumas were all killed except one, who was stunned by the blow of a club and lay unconscious under a heap of dead. During the night he recovered his senses and escaped. This was the bloodiest fight known, and the Yumas [Quechan] came here to fight no more."[77] It took less than a half hour for the Pimas to annihilate their enemy, with around 103 of them lanced, shot with arrows, or simply clubbed to death.[78] These Pima warriors were the proud allies of the US Army, serving in the Arizona Volunteers during the Civil War.

And it was the US Army fighting in the Mexican–American war that became the first customer for O'odham foodstuffs, especially wheat. Later, in 1862, while war was raging in the east, the US Army purchased over two million pounds of surplus Pima wheat, as well as pinole, chickens, corn, pumpkins, and melons. The Pima–Maricopa military confederation protected Anglo-Americans settlers from the Apache by the request of the army, and rescued weary travelers from hunger and thirst. The arrival of the stagecoach in the late 1850s only expanded the market for Pima goods and services. By 1870, Arizona's first agricultural entrepreneurs were selling several million pounds of wheat a year. The Pima fields were the breadbasket of the west. As Gila River medicine man Emmett White declared: "Without the Pimas being here with their wheat and horses and water, they [westward-bound immigrants] would never have made it to California." In recognition of their importance the federal government created the first Indian reservation in Arizona in 1859. Eventually increasing in size to over 370,000 acres, this home of the Pima and Maricopa became known as the Gila River Indian Community.[79]

Yet as early as 1867 the first wave of post-Civil War immigrants were starting the long tragedy of water diversion from the Gila. Farmers in the vicinity of Safford and Florence, upriver from the Gila Indian communities, began to divert water by digging canals. O'odham crops and fruits withered and died. Even the mesquite failed to grow. The people protested to Washington, D.C. but to no avail. The government told them they could move to Oklahoma. The people refused, but over 1,200 of them did travel to the Salt River in hopes of finding irrigation water.[80] Pima calendar sticks called this period the "years of famine," as drought accompanied the diversions.

The calendar stick for 1872–1873 spoke of the Salt River migration: "For several years the Pimas had had little water to irrigate their fields and were beginning to suffer from actual want when the settlers on the Salt River invited them to come to that valley. During the year a large party of Rso'tûk Pimas accepted the invitation ... . The motive of the Mormons on the Salt was not wholly disinterested, as they desired the Pimas to act as a buffer against the assaults of the Apache."[81]

By 1879 the Salt River Indian Reservation was created for these migrants, an activity that was greeted with hostility by the settlers there. As the Arizona *Daily Star* editorialized: "An Outrage to Settlers. The new Indian Reservation on Salt River ... exceeds any act of Governmental stupidity, if nothing worse, ever done in this territory before ... . With the settlers in the Salt Valley 'corralled' into an Indian Reservation, and all land entry stopped, and every landowner under Spanish or Mexican title in the southern part of the territory deprived of possession by squatters, makes this a rather interesting country for emigrants. There is scarcely a quarter section of land, with water, in the territory subject to entry."[82] Evidently their outsider voices were heard as the government reduced the original reserve from 680,000 acres to 46,627 acres.[83]

Finally in 1887 a large canal near Florence was constructed. Now no waters reached the Pima fields. By 1895 the government had to issue rations to the Gila Pimas. The calendar sticks proclaimed "no crops" or "no water" for this year. In the course of a single generation the People had been transformed from prosperous farmers to impoverished wards of the state. Without water there would be no cotton clothing. Without water there would be no food. The Akimel O'odham were forced to shift to a wage economy where others would pay them to pick cotton or collect mesquite for firewood.[84]

Throughout the first half of the twentieth century conditions worsened. The San Carlos Project of 1924 built a huge dam on the Gila River that was intended to create a reservoir of water that could be shared by Indian and non-Indian alike. The reservoir was not full until 1941. In the meantime, a dam that never impounded water did control floods, and without floods the aquifer dried out, springs dried up, trees died, and a variety of species of birds disappeared. The Coolidge Dam killed the last vestiges of life on the middle Gila River. As George Webb, a Pima author wrote: "The dead trees stand there like white bones. The red-wing blackbirds have gone somewhere else. Mesquite and brush and tumbleweed have begun to turn those Pima fields back into desert." For the most part farming is nothing more than a collective memory of a time when the river flowed freely. The new way to acquire water would take new skills and massive investments, something only their American Amigos possessed.[85]

Burying the Border

For many years after the Mesilla Treaty of 1854 the Papagos on both sides of the international border continued to live as if the boundary did not exist. Horse stealing and dealing, exchanging goods, and visiting families still occurred in a world where the borderline was more a reality to Anglos and *Mexicanos* than *Indios*. Until the 1890s and Porfirio Díaz, president of Mexico, the Sonoran Papagos continued to live on their lands and make small adjustments to the Mexican economy, intermarrying with Mexican partners, and learning some Spanish.

After 1890 large numbers of Mexican cowboys, ranchers, miners, and farmers began to encroach on their lands. In 1898 small scale warfare erupted at a mining town called El Plomo between Papagos and miners who were accused by the Indians of stealing their cattle. The incident led to some O'odham deaths and the next year Mexican soldiers disposed Papagos of their farmlands in Caborca and Pitiquito. The El Plomo incident led many O'odham to leave Sonora to both flee Mexican oppression as well as to find better wage work in Arizona then could be found in Mexico.[86]

Díaz land laws of the late nineteenth century allowed "vacant" lands to be auctioned off to the highest bidder. Many villagers lost their lands to Porfirian elites as a result of the legislation. To extend the power of the nation-state, Díaz ruthlessly pursued a policy of *mestizaje* designed to assimilate the Indians into the majority (Mexican) culture. If the O'odham refused to adopt the "civilized" norms of the Mexican people and be assimilated into mainstream culture, by either opening up their ancestral lands to "civilized" outsiders, or by integrating themselves into Mexican towns, they could be exterminated (the same fate that awaited Yaqui and Seri rebels).[87]

Many O'odham took advantage of family connections between Sonora and Arizona to flee from Porfirian tyranny and move to the United States (not unlike their Yaqui cousins). In one way they were simply using the contacts they made through their two-village lifestyle to migrate to the United States or Mexican cities. Those who did not go into exile either moved to rural towns in Sonora, married into Mexican families, or congregated near Caborca, Sonoyta, and Puerto Peñasco, with smaller populations in Pitiquito (see Figure 7.3, O'odham woman from Pitiquito) and elsewhere. A few went to the border community of Pozo Verde, across from the Baboquivari Valley on the Sells Reservation. While the Sonoran O'odham population of the nineteenth century has been estimated between 3,000 to 4,000 individuals, by the year 2002 there were only at most 2,000 Papagos in Mexico (and perhaps as few as 363), representing at least a 50 to 70% drop in population.[88]

One tie that has not been broken between the Sonoran Papago and their northern relatives is the Fiesta de Saint Francisco Xavier held on October 4 in Magdalena del Kino. Pilgrims from Arizona and Mexico may walk as many as 100 miles to attend the religious festival. The religious fiesta is held on the feast day of Saint Francis of Assisi, patron of the Franciscan order. But also honored at Magdalena is Saint Francis of Xavier, the great Jesuit saint, and his celebration is in December. A statute of Saint Francisco Xavier is found inside the Magdalena church. This is a replacement of the statute that was kidnapped during the anti-clerical hysteria of the 1920s and 1930s in Mexico. Next to the church is the tomb of another famous Francisco, Eusebio Francisco Kino, whose bones lie at the bottom of a crypt in the Church Square. Thus a fusion of

Figure 7.3 *O'odham woman making flour tortillas, Pitiquito, 1894* (Wm. Dinwiddie). From p. 18 of *The Pimería Alta: Missions and More*. Copyright © by the Southwestern Mission Research Center (SMRC), Tucson, 1996. Reprinted with Permission. All Rights Reserved.

the three famous Franciscos has created a binational festival that includes Papagos from both sides of the border.[89]

When World War II came to the reservation, the saga of Pia Machita began. In 1940 the elderly head man was around 75 years old. His winter home was the village of Stoa Pitk (sometime spelled Toapit) located in the Hickiwan district east of Ajo in the remote northwestern section of the reservation. Being a "Two Village" person, his spring and summer home was in Pozo Colorado. From his father he had learned of a Mexican punitive force that had entered southern Arizona in 1842. This memory convinced him that he was a Mexican. He flew the Mexican flag in front of his house, only allowed Mexican priests to perform services for his people, and took tribesmen to Altar in Sonora for baptism. He had never heard of the Gadsden Purchase.[90]

He was known inside and outside the reservation as an eccentric. He refused to cooperate with census takers and livestock inspectors. In 1940 he refused to cooperate with federal officials seeking to register people for the draft. Instead he encouraged all the young men to refuse to be registered. He had never heard of the "Germans and Japs," and it would be absurd to fight a war against unknown enemies. The US government had a different view and feared that Pia was an ally of the Japanese, and as rumor had it, the Japanese were preparing to attack the United States from a southern base across the Gulf of California into southern Arizona.[91]

When local authorities were unable to deliver a warrant in October of 1940, the F.B.I. got involved. Pia and several companions were arrested in May of 1941 and sent to the Pima County Jail in Tucson. While in jail he first learned to his amazement that there were more whites in the world than Papagos. Found guilty of a variety of allegations, Pia and two of his followers were sent first to the Los Angeles County Jail, whence they were taken to the federal prison at Terminal Island. He was later transferred to Missouri when the army took over Terminal Island.[92]

After serving 18 months he came back to Sells and got out of the car that was transporting him wearing a blue serge suit, store bought teeth, and a watch. He even spoke a few words of English, akin to a polite Englishman. Arizona's last great Indian war was over, as was the saga of Pia Machita.[93] If he was not an American hero like the Pima Marine Ira Hayes, one of the men photographed raising the American flag at Iwo Jima, he was a hero to those O'odham who remember when they were one people with "Two Villages" not, to borrow a title from Andrae Marak's and Laura Tuennerman's book, *At the Border of Empires*.[94]

Postscript: the Organ Pipe Oasis and Future Water Wars

At the Organ Pipe Cactus National Monument there is a place called Quitobaquito by the Park Service, but known as 'A'al Waipia (or 'A'al Vaipai, meaning "Little Spring" or "Little Water") to the O'odham. This was once a desert oasis, its waters saving literally thousands of lives over the centuries. Unfortunately, A'al Waipa is a mere shadow of its former self. These days the true desert oasis lies thirty miles to the south in old Mexico known as Ki:towak *(Quitovac,* "House of Water"*)*. In the 1980s trees rimmed the Quitovac oasis, everything from elderberry and dates to salt cedar and California palm. Nearby were fig and pomegranate trees. Back at *A'al Waipia* the trees were dying, the fruit trees putting out a few leaves but no fruit inside of an overgrown forest of mesquite. Until 1957 *A'al Waipia* had been a populated oasis not unlike the *Ki:towak* of the 1980s. By 1962, the National Park Service bulldozed 61 structures, wiping out most of the signs of human history.

This destruction was supposed to create a bird sanctuary. They did this without approval of, or consultation with, the O'odham. Without riparian trees, the birds soon left. Although not the situation today, in the 1980s there were over 65 species of birds at *Ki:towak*.[95]

Birds or not, the worm has turned in the last twenty years. Negotiations with the federal government has resulted in so-called "water settlements" approved by the US Congress and the Maricopa County Superior Court. This attempt by the *Milga:n* to address past wrongs might be simply setting the stage for a future clash over water rights.

Today, the reservations, with 2.6 percent of Arizona's population, receive 38 gallons of water per person compared to 1-gallon-per person for those living off the reservations. Even so, plumbing and water facilities on the reservations are hardly adequate, while poverty is widespread.[96] In any case, Colorado River water is likely to face shortages in the near future. Thirty million water users take an unhealthy levy on this river. Yet Indian communities are guaranteed 50% of Colorado water based on prior use. Indian-leased water rights might not be renewed in the future. With the state's population growing, climate change, and more industrial uses of water, it is not clear where Arizona is headed. By 2021 Arizona had undergone a 20 year old drought. As Earl Zarbin, a retired editor of the Arizona *Republic* notes, "it is not unreasonable to expect a reservation/non-reservation clash over the apportionment [of Colorado River water]."[97] For the historian it all sounds too familiar.

Commentary: Mormons and Lamanites

> *One long-standing popular belief among Franciscans in New Spain was that Indians were descendants of one of the ten lost tribes of Israel.*[1]
>
> [It was] *manifestly more economical, and less expensive to feed and clothe, than to fight them* [the Shoshone in particular, Indians in general].
> Brigham Young, May 30, 1852[2]

In 1863, the same year that the Mormons or Latter Day Saints were confronting the Shoshone at the Bear River in southern Idaho and the Kaibab Paiutes in southern Utah and northern Arizona, "prophet, seer, and revelator," and First President of the LDS Church, Brigham Young, received a writ from a federal judge for violating the Suppression of Polygamy Act or the "Morrill Anti-Bigamy Act" (July 8, 1862). The writ alleged that Young had disregarded at least one of the "twin sins of barbarism in the territories—slavery and polygamy," and that sin, of course was polygamy (more correctly, polygyny; known by the Mormons as "plural marriage").[3] Arrested by the US Marshal,

Young posted a bail bond while waiting for a Mormon grand jury to act. The grand jury refused an indictment.

As for the other sin of "slavery," Young knew that the intent of the law was to abolish African slavery, not Indian slavery. Young and his followers were ambivalent in their attitude and treatment of the Indians, but by 1852 Young allowed Mormons to purchase Indian minors and keep them "indentured" for up to 20 years. He instructed his brethren to "Buy up the Lamanite [Indian] children ... so that many generations would not pass ere they should become a white and delightsome people."[4]

In 1863 the Saints, who usually distrusted the federal army, did view with favor the Bear River massacre of Shoshone Indians by Colonel Patrick Edward Connor's California Volunteers "as an intervention of the Almighty" (see Chapter 8). Yet earlier, Brigham Young, who had led his expedition of followers over the Mormon trail to the Great Basin in 1846–1847, did not hesitate to speak out against the mistreatment of the Indians.

He admonished his followers to treat American Indians fairly with the purpose of converting them when possible. Some of his fellow Mormons even encouraged intermarriage with Native Americans so that the two groups might "unite" against a common enemy, the US government for instance. Young's instructions to Mormon men to marry "the Indian maidens" led several Mormons to wed Indian women in addition to their non-Indian wives.[5]

In 1857, when the Utah War with the federal government was brewing, the Mormons formed an alliance with the Utes and Paiutes, and many of the latter were converted to Mormonism. Young also encouraged southern Paiutes to seize "all the cattle" of emigrants that traveled the "south route" (through southern Utah) to California, an event that unfortunately eventually led to the Mountain Meadows Massacre where several Missouri men, women, and children were killed.[6]

Yet the ideas of friendship and conciliation with Native Americans that developed over the trail, and were revived in times of outside threats to Zion (that place in the Great Basin were the Saints were gathered), were gradually dropped as the Mormons began to compete with their lost Indian brothers and sisters for the limited resources of the high desert country. From the Bear River in Idaho to southern Arizona and from Moab, Utah to the Mormon Station in western Nevada, the Mormons first settled the Great Basin and then spread out to establish colonies in their separate state of "Deseret." In every instance they encroached upon the indigenous population.

Mormon pioneers and farmers soon appropriated water from rivers, streams, and springs, and took over infertile lands that at least produced pine nut bearing trees. The Indians who resisted these Mormon incursions were simply, from the Saints point-of-view, rejecting Christ's message and retribution was justified. From most Indian perspectives (the exception being Indian converts), the Saints were no different than the Gentiles, those non-Mormon Whites who were moving into the homeland.[7]

From and to these colonies missionaries were sent to convert the Indians and pave the way for colonization. The Indians in eastern Nevada, in particular the Western Shoshone, the Northern Paiute, and Washoe, because of their apparent poverty and lack of military knowledge, were quite passive and for these reasons there were few Mormon settlements and no significant Indian resistance. The prospects for conversion were best among the seemingly peaceful and "more civilized" Hopi, Zuni, and Pima-Papago of Arizona. Those groups that were more organized and reacted in a hostile manner were usually the horse-riding societies of the Eastern Shoshoni, Eastern Ute, Navajo, and Apache of the Southwest.

Conversion of the Indian was facilitated by the message of the LDS holy text, the *Book of Mormon*, a work that purports to be a history of the early inhabitants of this American continent and is treated, along with the Bible, as the word of God. Many Mormons speculated that the ancestors of the American Indian were members of one of the Lost Hebrew Tribes of Israel.[8]

As the story continues, the prophet Lehi led his followers from Jerusalem across the Pacific to the New World. In the Americas, Lehi's sons, Laman and Nephi, broke with each other and Laman's followers, the Lamanites, went to war against the other brother's group, the Nephites. Eventually the Lamanites destroyed the Nephites in a great conflagration that took place near the Hill of Cumorah in upstate New York. The Lamanites, who survived the wars between the two groups, became the American Indian. Because of these actions, and for rejecting Christ's teachings when He appeared on this continent after the insurrection, God cursed the Lamanites with a dark skin. For their transgressions "God did cause a skin of blackness to come upon them" (2 Nephi 5:21). Thus the Lamanites were punished for their sins by being turned "dark and loathsome." However, "in the last days" the Indians will be converted to the true church by Mormon emissaries and eventually become a "white and delightsome people" (2 Nephi 30:5–6).[9]

As a smitten people the Natives would have their lands taken from them by the Gentiles. Yet, if they converted to Mormonism and accepted Christ's teachings, they would regain their fair skin and a civilized way of life. In the last days, the converted would occupy a special place in God's plan and would become the builders of the temple of the New Jerusalem, a holy city of God that would be resurrected in the Zion of the Americas! In this respect, the *Book of Mormon* story reflected the long-standing popular belief that the American Indian was a descendent of one of the 10 lost tribes of Israel. Like the Franciscans of colonial Latin America who believed that "perfidious Jews" would be converted at the end of the world, the Mormons knew that they too were doing missionary work that was in fact apocalyptic.[10]

This too was the special message that the Mormons brought to their Indian brothers and sisters. With a limited resource base in the Great Basin, the notion of a Zion in the Wilderness was expanded to include vast areas north and south of the Great Basin. The Gathering to Zion would become a major colonization program in which Mormons and their message would extend through the Indian country from the Bannocks to the north to the Tarahumaras in the south. Once the Utes were defeated and restricted to the Unita Basin reservation, and the Shoshone had been pushed into Idaho and Nevada, the Saints could afford to initiate a more benevolent policy.[11]

Once again Brigham Young taught that it was better to deliver rations rather than death to the Indians. Jacob Hamblin, the so-called "apostle to the Lamanites," was one of the first to pick up the call for action. He carried the missionary program southward into the lands of the Paiutes, Navajos, and Hopis. Although the Navajos proved to be particularly aggressive and resistive, the Saints did succeed in converting Chief Tuba (Woo Pah) of the Hopis and his wife in 1871. Chief Tuba's baptism meant that the first Hopi convert to the true word of God had occurred.[12]

In 1873 Brigham Young called 250 Mormons to establish missions and colonies in the Little Colorado River Valley in north-central Arizona south of the Hopi mesas. The trail had already been established through the region by Lieutenant Amiel W. Whipple in 1853 when his military expedition, looking for a potential east–west railway route, recommended that a wagon road be built along the Little Colorado River area.[13] His activity led to the establishment of the Edward F. Beale Wagon Road that went from Zuni Pueblo to Sunset Crossing (Winslow, Arizona). In 1876 the Mormon Wagon trail (also known as the Mormon Honeymoon trail), went from Salt Lake City, through Lee's Ferrry, to Sunset Crossing, and was followed by 200 men, women, and children who established Brigham City (one mile north of today's Winslow). Here they were literally in the midst of the Lamanites.

Four settlements were established but by 1886 they had all failed as agricultural communities. Their communal form of social organization, known as the United Order, also collapsed. Their efforts at making Mormons out of Lamanites also failed, with many baptisms but very few active members.[14]

Further upstream the Mormon colonies were more successful, not as mission centers but as farms and ranches. On Silver Creek, a tributary of the Little Colorado River, William Flake and Apostle Erastus Snow founded the community of Snowflake in 1878. The Silver Creek towns of Show Low and Taylor soon followed. About the same time other colonies were established up the Little Colorado including Alpine, Nutrioso, Eager, and Greer.[15]

In 1877 the Saints streamed into the eastern Salt River Valley, removing the mesquite and digging irrigation ditches. The new site was called Camp Utah (Lehi). There missionary Daniel Jones joined the group and, believing he had a special mission to work among Native Americans, he attempted to enlist the aid of several Akimel O'odham, Tohono O'odham, and Pee Posh (Maricopa) in building Camp Utah. Many of the Saints were offended by Jones and his "dirty Indians" and so they left for the San Pedro River where they founded the community of St. David. Evidently missionary zeal could not overcome racial prejudice on the frontier.[16]

Meanwhile, many of the Saints pushed further down the Salt River, establishing Tempe and creating the Papago Ward north of town that contained several hundred O'odham converts. The largest Arizona community was Mesa, established by a group of Saints from Idaho and Utah in 1878. They cleaned out an old Hohokam canal and planted their crops. Mesa was incorporated in 1883.[17]

Around the same time, between 1875 and 1876, Brigham Young sponsored an exploratory and proselytizing journey to Mexico. Their mission was to look for places to colonize and to teach the gospel to the Indians. A small group of Mormons traveled on horseback through Tucson and El Paso del Norte to Chihuahua City. They were not well received in either El Paso or Chihuahua. Unhappy with their lack of success in the cities, they turned west and traveled to the rural community of Guerrero in the Sierra Madre foothills. It was here, on the edge of the Sierra Tarahumara, that the group met with its first success. There was no clerical opposition, the people were not devout Catholics, and the municipal authorities granted them permission to preach.[18]

From Guerrero they took their message to the Tarahumaras (Rarámuri), first in Arisiachi and later in Temósachi in the Papigochi Valley. These Tarahumaras were very friendly to the missionaries and were impressed by the Mormon promise that the Rarámuri, as Lamanites, would have a special role to perform at the end of the millennial era as builders of the temple at New Jerusalem. When the Mormons left the Sierra Tarahumara, the Rarámuri provided them with so much corn and beans that their pack animals were overloaded. Leaving the Tarahumara country behind, the party traveled north along the Casas Grandes River and eventually returned to the United States. Their explorations in Mexico soon led to the establishment of several Mormon colonies in the Casas Grandes area, including Colonia Juárez (1887) and Colonia Dublán (1888).[19]

By the end of the century, facing competition by other faiths on the reservation and a ruling by the Bureau of Indian Affairs that only one denomination could serve on the reservation (and usually that religious group was not the Latter Day Saints), the Mormon Indian missionary program was mostly terminated. Very few Indians were converted during the first four decades of the twentieth century. The Mormons did develop a strong adoption program in which Indian children would live with Mormon families so that they could be, first "civilized," and second, "converted."[20]

The heritage of a half century of contact had reduced the Indians in number. When the Mormons first entered what became the territory of Utah in 1847 the estimated number of Native Americans was around 20,000. By 1900 the number had plunged to 2,623, or about a decline of 86% from the Natives of a half century earlier. Most of the decline was due to disease, mistreatment, and slavery.[21]

Today Brigham Young University in Provo, Utah has the largest enrollment of Indians in any American university, and many western reservations have established a Mormon Indian ward (akin to a parish). Nearly 100 Indians were sent out on missions by the Church in the late 1980s.[22] As in the past, while many of the Mormon brethren have no more love for their Indian kindred than that of the average "Gentile" (non-Mormon), the religious message of a special role to play in the last days is an attractive one to many Lamanites.

Part III

From Removal (Ethnic Cleansing) to Genocide

8

From Battle to Massacre on the Bear River

Men, who took part in that battle, boast today of taking little infants by the heels and beating their brains out on any hard substance they could find.... I can't help but reflect how some men can make distinction between a battle royal and a massacre. I've heard a Mr. Dyer who took part in this battle, make the statement that that [Bear River] was a royal battle, but the battle of General Custer was a horrible massacre.... But it [the Bear River event] will always stand as a memory to me; the many little innocent children that suffered death because they could not help themselves.

Red Clay Frank Timbimboo Warner (Shoshone survivor of Bear River Massacre of 1863; son of Chief Sagwitch), in Preston *Citizen*, February 7, 1918[1]

The Indians were being slaughtered like wild rabbits. Indian men, women, children and babies were being slaughtered left and right. No butcher could have murdered any better than Colonel Connor and his California volunteers.

Mae T. Parry, 1976 (granddaughter of Chief Sagwitch)[2]

I should mention here that in my march from this post no assistance was rendered by the Mormons....Of the good conduct and bravery of both officers and men California has reason to be proud. We found 224 bodies on the field.... How many more were killed than stated I am unable to say.... I captured 175 horses, some arms, destroyed over seventy lodges, a large quantity of wheat and other provisions, which had been furnished them by the Mormons.

Colonel P. E. Connor, Official Report, Camp Douglas, Utah Territory, February 6, 1863[3]

Lost Worlds of 1863: Relocation and Removal of American Indians in the Central Rockies and the Greater Southwest, First Edition. W. Dirk Raat.

Much credit is due to General Connor and the forces under his command,
for their prompt and efficient services in chastising these Indians for their
outrages and depredations upon the whites, and in compelling them to sue
for peace.

John P. Wentworth, Commissioner of Indian Affairs, 1864[4]

The affair at the Bear River in southern Idaho took place on January 29, 1863.
For over a century laymen and scholars alike referred to it as a "battle." Only
since the late 1970s have locals as well as state and national governmental officials revised their earlier views to describe the deaths of at least 250 Shoshone
men, women, and children a "massacre." Although not as well known as other
Indian massacres of the nineteenth century, professional historians and other
academics began to pay attention to the event with the publication of Brigham
Madsen's *The Shoshoni Frontier and the Bear River Massacre* in 1985.[5]

Contrary to the opinions of most learned individuals, including Madsen, the
Bear River bloodletting is not only important because of the scale of the violence, but for several other reasons as well. The horrible slaughter of at least 240
"Digger" Indians on February 25 and 26 of 1860, mostly women and children,
near Fort Humboldt, California (south of today's Eureka), was easily as gruesome as the Bear River event. The difference is that the Humboldt Bay Massacre
was initiated and carried out by farmers along the Eel River,[6] while the Bear
River Massacre was planned and executed by members of the US Army and
"volunteers" from the California militia. In other words, by 1863, and in part
because of the environment of destruction that the Civil War perpetuated, the
Indian policy of the United States was becoming militarized and was no longer
only in the hands of Indian agents and government negotiators.

In lieu of rations, relocated lands, reserves, trade goods, and negotiated
agreements, the Northwestern Shoshone would suffer the ultimate removal—
sexual exploitation, mutilation, infanticide, kidnapping, death, and extermination—at the hands of the military. No longer the protector and ally of the Indian
(with the exception of the Utes, Pimas, and a few others), the US Army and the
American Civil War unleashed a brief era of violence against indigenous peoples on an unprecedented scale. The Civil War accelerated the conquest of the
West. Almost all Regulars in the Pacific Department had departed for the eastern fronts, and the western volunteer armies were more threatening to the
tribes than the pre-War Regulars had been. As historian Alvin Josephy noted,
"during the four years of the Civil War, more Indian tribes were destroyed by
the whites and more land seized from them than in almost any comparable
period ... in American history."[7]

After Bear River, Utah's military personnel communicated with their
Colorado counterparts concerning tactics and strategy, and the notorious

Sand Creek Massacre of November 29, 1864 was the result. There Colonel John M. Chivington and his volunteers killed 130 Cheyenne and Arapaho natives in spite of Chief Black Kettle showing the white flag of surrender. Howitzers and bloodthirsty soldiers had replaced military discipline and order (that same year, as has been noted earlier [see Chapter 4], Kit Carson initiated his scorched-earth campaign at Canyon de Chelly). Later, in 1868, Black Kettle's Cheyennes suffered another defeat when General George Custer initiated the Washita Massacre that resulted in over 100 dead Indians. In January of 1870, Colonel Eugene Baker massacred 173 Piegans (Blackfeet) at the Marias River in Montana. Indians were being exterminated and the military was being honored by settlers and emigrants who had despised the army a few years earlier (the most notorious of all Indian massacres was, of course, Wounded Knee, the 1890 incident in which 146 Indians were killed).[8]

After 1866 the Yavapai suffered a series of bloodlettings, the most infamous being the Skeleton Cave Massacre of December 1872 along the Salt River in Arizona when 120 US soldiers and their 100 Pima allies killed 76 southeastern Yavapai men, women, and children (see Chapter 6). After the Marias River Massacre of 1870 and the Camp Grant Massacre of 1871, in which a group of Americans, Mexicans, and Tohono O'odhams murdered over 150 Aravaipa Apache men, women, and children in their sleep (individuals who were under the protection of the soldiers at Camp Grant), the Ulysses S. Grant administration accelerated the movement to substitute negotiation and reservations in lieu of the violence of vicious killing. He knew that you could steal their lands and souls without insulting their bodies. Thus, the Bear River episode was important not only because of the scale of the killings, but as an indicator and initiator of a somewhat new militarized Indian policy in the American Southwest.

Shoshone Ways

The eastern Great Basin region and the Snake River country is the modern homeland of the Shoshone (also spelled "Shoshoni") people. The Shoshone are the northernmost group of the Uto-Aztecan family of languages, a grouping of over 30 languages spoken by indigenous peoples in the Western United States and Central and Northern Mexico. While Uto-Aztecan is spoken by Shoshones as far north as Salmon, Idaho, the southernmost extension includes the Pipil language of El Salvador. Uto-Aztecan is usually divided into two branches: a northern branch that includes the Numic languages of the West and Southwest such as Shoshone, Bannock, Goshute, Northern and Southern Paiute, Ute, Chemehuevi and the Comanche of the southern plains, as well as the non-Numic O'odham

(Pima-Papago) and the isolate Hopi; and the southern Mexican branch that includes Tepehuan, Tarahumaran, Yaqui, Mayo, Caro, Huichol, Pipil, and the Mexica's Nahuatl. The linguistic differences between Northern Paiutes, Bannocks, and Shoshones were practically non-existent, and bilingualism was the rule. The original homeland of the Uto-Aztecan languages was probably the American Southwest and Northern Mexico. Many Uto-Aztecan languages are believed to have gone extinct before recently being documented.[9]

The Shoshone people can be organized into several regional groupings, with different bands and factions moving in and out of each area. The Eastern Shoshone under the famous chief, Washakie, numbered between 2,000 and 3,000 in the mid-1850s. They ranged across southwestern Wyoming, between South Pass, Fort Bridger, and the Wind River Mountains of the Rockies to the Bear River country of the Wasatch Front in eastern Idaho. They were equestrians who had a plains culture based on the pursuit of the buffalo, but they also sought out roots, berries, and small game in the Wind and Big Horn River areas. They usually wintered along the Green River. Linguistically they were related to the 9,000 Western Shoshones who lived in the desolate salt deserts of northern Nevada and who lived by exploiting the meager food resources found in small oases and moisture-collecting mountains. They were joined in their pursuits by over 900 Goshutes known disparagingly as "Diggers" by the white emigrants who came through their country following the California trail to Carson City and Sacramento. During the early contact years most whites lumped all of the Shoshone around the Snake River as "Snakes" and those in the south "Diggers."[10]

In between these two groups were the 5,000 Northern Shoshone of central and southern Idaho and northern Utah. These included the Fort Hall Shoshone on the east Snake River plain, the Lemhi Valley Shoshone, the Boise and Bruneau Shoshone of the Boise and Bruneau Valleys, and the Mountain Shoshone of central Idaho. These groups had names that designated the food they ate—for example, the Boise River Indians were called "Groundhog Eaters," while those of the Snake River were "Salmon Eaters." Of special interest to the topic of the Bear River Massacre were the 10 bands of 1,500 Northwestern Shoshone who lived in and around the fertile Cache Valley of northern Utah and southeastern Idaho. They called themselves the *Newe*—people, Shoshone persons. According to Shoshone historian Mae Timbimboo Parry, their homeland of Cache Valley was known as *Mo Sa ad Kunie*, but other sources say Cache Valley was *Seuhubeogoi*, that is "willow river" valley.[11]

As a semi-nomadic people, the Newe followed annual cycles that brought them to prime places for gathering, fishing, and hunting. While their horse herds were not as large as their eastern neighbors, they still traveled to Wyoming to hunt buffalo. They also spent part of each year digging roots, gathering seeds, fishing for salmon and trout, and hunting small game. The Wasatch Basins provided several summer zones, while the rivers flowing into the Great Salt Lake furnished them with banks and hills that would protect them from the winter winds. Hot springs in southern Idaho were also a winter attraction. And, in particular, Cache Valley, filled with rich grasses, thick timber, and fertile soil provided an abundant menu of greens, roots, nuts, seeds, and wild berries. The mountains surrounding the Valley were filled with streams of salmon and trout, as well as plentiful game to hunt—elk, deer, rabbits, squirrels, and a variety of waterfowl. *Mo Sa ad Kunie,* or *Seuhubeogoi,* was a natural wonderland.[12]

The Newe, like other Shoshone peoples, had very little political organization. The basic residential component was the extended family or lodge, while the largest social unit was the winter camp. Membership varied within and between individuals, and bands were usually temporary arrangements to meet the needs of warfare, buffalo hunting, salmon fishing, or other social needs. One of the more important bands was organized and led by Pocatello (Tonaioza), a Bannock Creek Shoshone. Chief Pocatello and his followers were actively hostile in the region between the Snake River and the Great Salt Lake between 1860 and 1863, an area crowded with emigrants that came together where the California Trail and Salt Lake Road merged. Another chieftain was Bear Hunter. He was a contemporary of Pocatello and leader of the Shoshone who lived along the Logan River and Bear River in Cache Valley. Chieftainship, like that of Pocatello's or Bear Hunter's, shifted from person to person and was usually not hereditary.[13]

The Northern Shoshone shared many religious and ceremonial characteristics with the Plains Indians, including the vision quest, counting coup, the scalp dance, and the Sun Dance. Much of their mythology and ceremonial practices came from the Great Basin or California, including the Great Basin Round Dances that were celebrated in early spring to insure the return of the salmon. Although they expressed a belief in a creator god, known as *appi* (father), the principal mythological figures were Wolf (*pia isan*) and Coyote (*isapaippeh*). Wolf, sincere and benevolent, was the creator of mankind and the world. Wolf brought order into the universe. His opposite, Coyote, was a divine trickster who was the source of all disorder in the world. Given the egalitarian nature of their society, all men, from time to time, could be "shamans" who utilized medicinal herbs, amulets, and charms to cure illness or bring harm to their enemies.[14]

Knowledge of Shoshone history is relatively incomplete prior to the arrival of Europeans from New Spain in the late 1600s. There is archaeological evidence from Idaho and Utah that ancestors of the modern Shoshone lived in the deserts of the Great Basin for thousands of years, with cultural change occurring in the last 12,000 years due to a gradual impoverishment of flora and fauna. The horse probably reached the Shoshone in the late seventeenth century by way of the western flank of the Rocky Mountains from the Spanish Southwest. By that time the Shoshone had spread throughout the Great Basin into the fringes of the plateau country, and with their new mode of horse transportation they could venture beyond the Rockies into Montana and Canada in search of buffalo. Yet their Blackfeet enemies, armed with French guns and Spanish horses, pushed them back from the Plains by the mid-eighteenth century to the homeland they would occupy at the time of contact with nineteenth century British and American traders and trappers (it was also in the 1750s when a Shoshone group split off and migrated southward to become the Comanche).[15]

The arrival of the horse altered the life of semi-nomadic Indians. The Eastern Shoshone, like their Apache Plains counterparts, found the horse, because of its speed and power, to be essential for survival. The buffalo hunt became more important as bison products were traded for corn, tobacco, and more horses. Raiding and trading of horses also led to the taking of human captives, so that the equestrian Shoshones became a part of the slave trade industry.[16] Horse trading was also useful for making alliances with other bands such as the Nez Perce and Cayuse in northern Idaho with whom the Shoshone formed mixed villages, winter camps, and annual trading markets.[17] As indicated before, while the Northwestern Shoshone were not in general a horse people like their eastern and northern counterparts, the few horses they did have meant that their annual harvesting and hunting cycles would include brief trips to the buffalo country of Wyoming.

The introduction of the horse and firearms, combined with the western push of white settlers, caused turmoil that included mounted Indian warriors fighting each other for hunting territories, bison, elk, and deer products, captives, and trading partners. But the collision of Indian groups paled before the onslaught of American emigration.

By 1810 Andrew Henry and the North West Company had established a fur trapping post in the heart of Shoshone country at Henry's Fork of the upper Snake River. By the late 1820s Peter Skene Ogden of the Hudson's Bay Company had explored and exploited beaver throughout the Snake River drainage area, as well as the Weber and Ogden Rivers of northern Utah. At about the same time the Rocky Mountain Fur Company started operations throughout southern Idaho and northern Utah. By 1840 the buffalo, having been hunted out by Indian and white hunters, was gone from the Snake River region, and the fur trade had collapsed as well. And while the 1840s brought an end to the beaver trapping era, it did not signal a new period of quietude for the inhabitants west of the Continental Divide—it was the beginning of white emigration to Idaho, Utah, Oregon and California.[18]

The Invasion of Shoshone Country

On July 24, 1847 a religious group, that would have a greater impact on the Shoshone tribe than all of the fur trappers from Britain or the United States, arrived in the Salt Lake Valley. Members of the Church of Jesus Christ of Latter Day Saints, better known as Mormons, were fleeing the persecution and mob violence of non-Mormons in Missouri and Illinois who could not tolerate the Mormon's strange and unorthodox ways—including the practice of polygamy. Although they hoped to establish a colony in Mexican territory outside of American jurisdiction, the end of the Mexican–American war and the cession of 1848 meant that they would remain under US control and subject to federal intervention.

By 1850 Brigham Young, the man who had led his people to Utah, became the territorial governor of Utah, administrating an area that stretched from Fort Bridger in western Wyoming to Carson City in western Nevada. The Shoshone in the immediate area of settlement soon demanded payment for the lands the Mormons had settled, but second in command Heber C. Kimball reminded his followers that the land belonged to "our Father in Heaven and we expect to plow and plant it." Although the Mormons would not compensate the Indians for their land, Young did argue that it was "manifestly more economical, and less expensive to feed and clothe, than to fight them."[19] This was the Mormon version of the frontiersmen ethic, a kind of "soft Manifest Destiny." This was the doctrine the Mormon settlers would bring to Cache Valley in 1855 when the Elkhorn Ranch became the first settlement in that northern valley, followed shortly thereafter by Wellsville in 1856.

In 1857–1858 the so-called Utah War occurred. Fearful of Mormon disloyalty, President James Buchanan ordered a military force under the command of Colonel Albert Johnston to march from Fort Bridger to the Salt Lake Valley. Negotiations preceded any military action and the US Army was allowed to march around Salt Lake City into Camp Floyd south of Salt Lake and west of Utah Lake. Before the issue had been resolved several Mormon settlements were abandoned and ordered back to Salt Lake City, including the Saints in Cache Valley.

After an end to hostilities, Bishop Peter Maughan, the original founder of Wellsville, led his followers back to their uninhabited cabins in Cache Valley in early 1859. From Wellsville colonies were established that summer at Mendon, Providence, Logan, Richmond, and Smithfield. To assist in defending these communities, several "Minute Men" groups were organized.[20]

The Saints, in spite of their paternalistic attitudes toward the Shoshones, brought with them their livestock and their ranching and farming ways that competed with the Indians for natural resources. Mormon hunters enjoyed the meat and flesh of deer, fish, and birds as much as the Shoshone did. Grass fields could be grazed by cattle or cut for hay and plowed under before natural bulbs and roots could grow. Both Mormon and Shoshone were not happy to see their returning foes. Tensions were likely to rise. As storyteller Rod Miller notes, "With little regard for Indian patterns of travel, villages, or hunting grounds, the Mormon pioneers began spreading on to new land."[21]

By 1861, many Shoshone groups that had once thrived in and around the Cache Valley were now poverty-stricken. On the verge of starvation they swallowed their native pride and began to beg for food and clothing. As food and patience grew short for the Cache Valley Mormons, the starving Shoshones, denied the right to hunt for food, gave up begging and began stealing and raiding. By mid-July of that year the gathering at Blacksmith Fork in Cache Valley of as many as 1,500 Shoshones was viewed with alarm by the Mormon settlers. The year 1862 began with an outbreak of raids on the cattle herds in Cache Valley.[22] By March of that year, James D. Doty, the superintendent of Indian Affairs, visited the Valley and noted that "The scarcity of game in these Territories, and the occupation of the most fertile portions thereof by our settlements, have reduced these Indians to a state of extreme destitution."[23]

Meanwhile, since 1849 a development, more important than the Mormon settlement of Cache Valley to both Mormons and Shoshones alike, was the flood of thousands of gold-seekers headed for California. Soon the '59ers would join the '49ers looking for gold and silver at Comstock Lode, Gold Hill, and Virginia City. These argonauts caused Salt Lake City to undergo a sudden increase as a trading center for the emigrants passing through, while the Northwestern Shoshone and their Paiute allies were overwhelmed by the hordes of whites moving across their country.[24]

The 25,000 emigrants that traveled the California Trail doubled that next year, rising to 60,000 in 1852 with close to 80% choosing to go to California rather than Oregon. After 1849, 10,000 to 15,000 individuals trekked annually along the Salt Lake Cutoff to the City of Rocks in southern Idaho where the Salt Lake Road merged with the California Trail.[25] Gold hunters not only went west to Comstock, Humboldt City, and Boise, but traveled north along the Montana Trail from Salt Lake City through Logan and Soda Springs in Cache Valley to the mining center of Deer Lodge, Montana (founded in 1862; a few miles west of what would become Helena) and Grasshopper Creek.[26]

After the Civil War started, the national demand for gold boomed as war-related spending led the price of gold, relative to paper money, to accelerate upwards. As historian Dean May affirmed, the "pull of gold" and "push of war" drove the migratory process with emigrants heading west meeting treasure seekers going east from California. Silver and gold mining, hence town founding, meant that the era of the Civil War would also be the era of colonization and urbanization of the Intermountain West and the vanquishing of Indian nations. As new towns were founded and Indian lands pacified, the territory-making process proceeded in Montana, Idaho, Colorado, and Arizona.[27]

The major overland trail was the California Trail which veered off the Oregon Trail where the Raft River flows into the Snake River. The Oregon Trail started near the junction of the Kansas and Missouri Rivers close to present day Kansas City, and went west along the Platte River in Nebraska to Fort Laramie and South Pass in Wyoming. From there it continued through the Sublette Cutoff to the Bear River and Soda Springs on the edge of Cache Valley. From here the road forked, one going northwest to Fort Hall, the other, known as the Hudspeth Cutoff to the Raft River. Pioneer Margaret A. Fink noted in her diary on July 15, 1850 that " ... in eight miles [we] came to Raft River, a small stream that flowed from the mountains on our left. Here the roads fork again, the right-handed one turning off northwesterly toward Oregon, while we took the left hand one, going southwesterly toward California, leaving Snake River, and traveling up Raft River."[28]

Traveling south through the granite pass known as the City of Rocks, the Trail is joined by the Salt Lake Cutoff five miles to the south. After entering Nevada the California Trail follows the Humboldt River to the Humboldt Sink. From here the emigrants traveled either along the Truckee Route to today's Reno or the Carson Route to Carson City. After ascending and descending the Sierra Nevada Mountains, often with the assistance of Paiute Indians like Captain Truckee, the weary travelers finally arrived at Sutter's Fort or some other California mining town.[29]

By 1858 it was common to find wagon parties made up of mostly of women and children. By then the Trail emigrants had good reason to fear the Indians. Wagon traffic had ruined traditional Indian trails. Thousands of sheep, oxen, horses, and cattle had overgrazed a large zone along their trails leading to Indian resentment and resistance. Many emigrants had shot Indians for sport, an activity that transformed "good sports" into bitter rivals.

The entire area from Fort Hall through the City of Rocks to the upper Humboldt deserts of Nevada, including the northern and northeastern edges of the Great Salt Lake (a region that embraced the Oregon and California Trails as well as the Salt Lake Road), was the homeland of Chief Pocatello's Shoshone band. Near the City of Rocks and the lava outcropping known as Massacre Rocks, west of American Falls, Pocatello and his followers trapped several emigrant parties. On August 9, 1862 Pocatello's people attacked a Methodist wagon train at the City of Rocks. The following day mule and ox trains of several wagons were ambushed in a deep gully in the lava outcropping of what later became known as "Massacre Rocks." At least 14 or 15 emigrants were killed, a similar number wounded, cash stolen, and property damage of over $30,000 occurred at these two sites.[30] The whites called it a "massacre;" the Indians called it "retaliation" for the killing of Shoshones, and "resistance" to American intrusions.

Even if the emigrants made no contact with Indians, they still had many situations to fear. Their wagons, winding their ways through Idaho along the Oregon and California Trails, had to maneuver across and around sage and wormwood. The suffocating dust burned their eyes and throats. The days were hot and the nights were cold. Mosquitoes were, as one traveler complained, as "thick as flakes in a snowstorm." Margaret Fink in an entry dated July 11, 1850 protested that the "poor horses whinnied all night, from their bites, and in the morning the blood was streaming down their sides."[31] Life was not easy on the California Trail.

The decade of the 1850s also brought another threat to the Shoshone lifestyle in the form of the central Overland Mail stage and Pony Express route. Treasure hunters in California, after pausing from their work mining the earth, found that they needed paper and writing utensils, banking services that buyers could use to purchase their gold, financiers who could sell them paper drafts, and delivery services for everything from baggage to precious metals. After 1852 Henry Wells and William Fargo (later joined by John Butterfield), to meet the banking and express needs of Californians, created joint-stock companies like the Wells-Fargo Corporation and the American Express Company. These, in turn, would lead to the formation by other investors of the Central Overland California and Pike's Peak Express, a title that would attract the attention of needy westerners.[32]

The Pony Express, inaugurated on April 3, 1860, and the Overland Mail stage service ran through the heartland of Eastern, Northwestern, Western Shoshone, and Paiute country. The Pony Express route went from St. Joseph, Missouri to Sacramento, California with stations every 10 to 15 miles at various locations along the route including Fort Bridger, Bear River, Echo Canyon (Weber Station), Salt Lake House, Ruby Valley (halfway between Salt Lake and Sacramento), Fort Churchill, and finally Carson City Station. The entire trip, with horses changed every 12 miles and riders every 45 miles, took 10 days to move the mail from Missouri to San Francisco, a voyage of 240 hours and 1,966 miles. When the transcontinental telegraph line was completed in late 1861, there was no more use for the Pony Express and the service was dissolved.[33]

On June 16, 1860, acting on the economic pressure brought by lobbyists for the Union Pacific Railroad, Western Union, and a host of other railroad and telegraph interests in the east, the US Congress passed the Pacific Telegraph Act that provided a 10-year subsidy for construction of a line from the Missouri River to Carson City. On October 1, 1861, the magnetic wire reached Salt Lake City from the east. A week later the wire from Sacramento arrived in Salt Lake

City. The Mormons were ecstatic. This technological achievement mystified the Indians, with the native population referring to it as the "humming wire," the "talking wire," or the "singing wire." Very soon the indigenous peoples learned to their dismay that the "singing wire" provided their white opponents with immense advantages on the battlefield, and just as quickly the Plains Indians and their Shoshone and Goshute cousins began to attack the telegraph with a vengeance.[34] The isolation of the Shoshone homeland would now be a relic of the past.

From the early 1850s to the Bear River tragedy of 1863 tensions between Shoshone and white continued to increase. The transportation and communications network of the Americans was impinging on Shoshone ways. Emigration, mining camps, farms, ranches, town buildings, mail stations, and telegraph lines almost inevitably brought conflict and misunderstandings.

Not all the conflicts were initiated by the Indians. Many of these incidents occurred along the road between the Goose Creek Mountains of northwestern Utah (southwest of City of Rocks) and the Carson Valley—a distance of 500 miles. Another critical section was the stretch between the Bear River and the Humboldt where most emigrant trains had hundreds of head of cattle and dozens of horses and mules either stolen or killed.

Traveling through the desolate Humboldt desert, many whites had the habit of shooting Indians for sport, even if the natives had not molested them. In addition, many of the Gold Rush dregs who failed at mining would camouflage themselves as Indians and attack the emigrant trains from the protection of the trading forts. As Indian agent Jacob Holeman noted in a letter written to the Indian Office on May 8, 1852, "The *white* Indians, I apprehend, are much more dangerous than the *red*. The renegades, deserters, and thieves, who have had to fly from justice in California, have taken refuge in the Mountains—and having associated themselves with the Indians, are more savage than the Indians themselves—by the cruelty to the whites they have stimulated the Indians to acts of barbarity, which they never known to be guilty of before."[35]

The trading posts along the California Trail were filled with swindlers who traded whiskey and guns to the Indians, and overcharged their emigrant customers. Sometimes they even encouraged the Indians to steal the stock of the emigrants, exchange their livestock with the traders, and then the traders would sell the animals to the captains of emigrant trains. Depredations and continuing raids along the Humboldt were so bad that by 1857 Brigham Young called for the abandonment of the Carson Valley settlements. Four years later Chief Pocatello would become infamous for his Goose Valley raids and "massacres" in the City of Rocks area.[36]

Outside the California Trail, 25 miles east of Fort Boise along the Oregon Trail, what many white observers consider to be the most atrocious massacre took place. The event is known in the history books as the Ward Massacre and it happened during August in 1854. There Alexander Ward's emigrant party of 5 wagons was attacked by about 30 Indians (most likely Boise Shoshone, but called "snakes" by the whites, a term that also applied to Pocatello's Northwestern band). They were very likely assisted by two "white Indians" dressed and painted as Shoshones. The group was almost annihilated. Eighteen emigrants, including women and children, were killed while the Shoshone took the 5 wagons and 41 head of cattle, and stole several horses, cash, guns and pistols. Evidence later proved that the Shoshone women had mutilated their victims. Ward's teenage daughter had a hot piece of iron "thrust into her private parts," while many children were burned alive.[37] From 1854 on the Shoshone Indians, especially Pocatello's band, would be considered the enemy that must be eradicated. The era of military expeditions and Indian-hunting expeditions by militia volunteers and angry vigilantes was about to begin. The reign of terror had started.

The summer and fall of 1860 witnessed mail stations being repeatedly attacked by Ute, Bannock, and Shoshone Indians. Food was taken, horses were stolen, station personnel were killed, and buildings, coaches, and mailbags were destroyed. Other stations were abandoned for fear of being attacked. In the spring of 1862 every stage station on the Overland Trail between the Platte River and the Bear River was attacked as Shoshone warriors went on the warpath.[38]

Earlier, in 1861, communal cattle herds in Cache Valley were being run off with a large number of animals shot dead. Several hundred Shoshone Indians gathered in Cache Valley, and the Mormon residents were nervous about their presence even if many of them pledged peace with the white man. Although the summer of 1861 passed relatively peaceful, the next year began with a flurry of raids on Mormon cattle herds. The destitute Indians could no longer be controlled by bribes of food and clothing. Western newspapers reported all the gruesome details of "massacres" and scalpings with colorful language such as "Rivers of blood and mountains of Indians" and "the end of the world is at hand" as they demanded protection for the victimized settlers. Newspaper pleas and Mormon prayers were answered when word was received in Utah that Colonel Patrick Edward Connor and his California Volunteers were on their way, ready and eager to deal with the hostile Indians.[39]

The Tragedy at Beaver Creek

During September of 1861 Connor was appointed by California governor John G. Downey to recruit a regiment that would lead an expedition into Utah Territory. Ten companies, of which only seven traveled to Utah (the other three served along the Humboldt), were trained and garrisoned near Stockton, California. Although the volunteers were ostensibly to provide protection to the citizens of Utah and Nevada, security for the mail line, and safety for emigrant trains, it was obvious to Abraham Lincoln and other Union leaders that California had to maintain its ties to the North and that mail and telegraph lines must be maintained between the Pacific Coast and the eastern United States. And, of course, Connor and his boys would also be able to keep one collective eye on the Mormons and their questionable patriotism (see Figure 8.1).[40]

In hindsight it becomes obvious that several events occurred on the passage to Utah that would prove to be a warning or omen of things to come—things like the Bear River Massacre. The first observation relates to the motivations and ambitions of the Irish immigrant Patrick Connor (born, coincidentally, on St. Patrick's Day in County Kelly, Ireland in 1820). After serving as an officer of volunteers in the Mexican War, Connor moved to California where he pursued

Figure 8.1 *Col. Patrick E. Connor.* The Shoshone Community, in conjunction with the Idaho Transportation Department, established interpretive signs entitled "the largest Indian massacre in the West" in 2006 at Bear River Massacre site, near Preston, Idaho. Photo by W. Dirk Raat (2014).

his career goals of politico and entrepreneur. In Stockton he held a number of minor governmental posts as well as being a general contractor and an owner of the Stockton waterworks.[41]

After receiving the command of California Volunteers he showed ruthlessness toward Indians, allowing his men great leeway in their treatment of the native population. On one occasion he ordered his cavalry commander, Major Edward McGarry to "destroy every male Indian whom you may encounter" in the vicinity of Gravelly Ford on the Humboldt River. After the affair at Bear River, during the 1865 Powder River Expedition through Montana and Wyoming, echoing the earlier Gravelly Ford command he ordered his troops to "kill every male Indian over twelve years of age."[42]

He later led an anti-Mormon Liberal Party, actively recruited Gentiles (non-Mormons) to Utah, invested in mines, smelters, and railroads, and lobbied for every political position from US Marshal to County Recorder. To speculate, he may have even sought the governorship of Utah or the presidency of the United States. This latter ambition may have been above his pay level, but he would not have been the first military man in US history to cash in on his popularity as an Indian fighter to aspire to that high office—just ask Andrew Jackson, William Henry Harrison, or John C. Fremont.

The composition of Connor's army was another concern. The 850 or so volunteers, with their 50 wagons and several hundred head of cattle, started their march to Salt Lake City in July 1862. A few of the volunteers were reputable Stockton citizens, such as the surgeon and chaplain. Many were of Irish stock.[43] Unfortunately, too many of the volunteers were lawless freebooters and plunderers. Many were fugitives from justice or individuals who had failed at mining. Their loyalty was questionable. Wholesale desertion was a serious threat throughout the Civil War years. And, of course, they were assertive and aggressive when it came to their Indian foes, willing to kill all Indian males and rape or molest their women.[44]

Concerning the latter, the letter of April 4, 1856 of General John E. Wool, commander of the Department of the Pacific, to John S. Cunningham, Esq., is instructive. Referring to conditions in the Northwest, he noted "But for the Governors of Oregon and of Washington Territory ... I would soon put an end to the Indian War. This practice of the Volunteers of killing friends as well as enemies has greatly increased the ranks of the hostiles. As in the case of Major [?] and his party in October last killed 25 friendly Indians, 18 of whom were women and children going to the military reservation for protection; and as in the case of two Volunteer Companies on the 23rd and 24th of December last under the guise of friendship killed about 10 friendly Indians in two camps, burnt their bodies, and turned their women and children out, who in their endeavor to get to Fort Lane, 15 miles, froze their hands and feet."[45]

Wool went on to complain about those citizens who attacked his command of soldiers who were escorting several hundred Indians to the Coast reserves, and talked about citizen soldiers scalping the enemy, cutting off ears and hands and sending them to their friends as trophies. He concluded his epistle by saying "It is these shocking barbarities that gives us more trouble than all else and is constantly increasing the ranks of the hostiles."[46]

A patriotic gesture by the volunteers was also illustrative. By September 1862 Connor's men had arrived at Fort Ruby in eastern Nevada west of Utah Lake. Connor then decided to leave his men behind and travel to Salt Lake City where he found "a community of traitors, murderers, fanatics, and whores." On rejoining his men at Fort Ruby he was confronted by a scheme concocted by his California Volunteers that would bring to an end the mission of protecting the Overland Mail route. His men had requested that their $30,000 in wages due them be used to transport Connor's army to Virginia where they could "serve their country by shooting traitors" instead of freezing to death in the desert huddled around sage brush fires. Oddly enough, Connor approved of the gesture which was immediately denied by Washington authorities. The denial only served to motivate the men to seek out and kill any Indians they could find.[47] If they would not be allowed to murder "Johnny Reb," they could as least try to kill Weber Jim, Little Soldier, Bear Hunter or any other "Snakes" and "Diggers."

The frustrations of the soldiers were released when it was reported to Conner that 23 emigrants had been killed near Gravelly Ford on the Humboldt River. The colonel dispatched his favorite Irishman, Major McGarry, with the following orders: "Destroy every male Indian ... and immediately hang them, and leave their bodies exposed as an example of what evil-doers may expect while I command this district." When McGarry returned from his mission he was pleased to report that a total of 24 Indians had been killed, although he was uncertain as to whether or not they had been involved in the Gravelly Ford massacre. He would note that several were killed while trying to escape and many had been hostages that were executed.[48] As historian Brigham Madsen observed, "McGarry's brutal, and indiscriminate killing was an ominous portent for the California Volunteers."[49]

In early October, Conner departed Fort Ruby, leaving behind approximately 100 men to garrison that fort, and arrived in Salt Lake City by mid-October. Aware that Brigham Young was unfriendly to federal officials, he decided to establish a new post at Camp Douglas three miles east of the city in the foothills overlooking the Salt Lake Valley. From this vantage point Connor could observe his Mormon foes as well as protect the Overland Trail. Worried that Brigham Young's militia could attack his volunteers at any time, he installed cannon that aimed directly at the city. The cold war with Mormon authorities had started.[50]

Meanwhile, in spite of his disputes with the Mormons, Connor's major concern was with Indian depredations and raids. Conflicts continued throughout November and December. Reports reached Connor in November that a white captive who had survived the September 1860, Otter Massacre on the Snake River in Idaho, a massacre in which the boy's father, mother, brother, and three sisters had either been initially killed or later died of starvation, was being held in Cache Valley by Chief Bear Hunter's band of Shoshones. McGarry was sent once again to chastise the Indians. His volunteers skirmished with Bear Hunter's followers near Providence, Utah—the result being the death of three Shoshones and the return of the boy hostage (who was not the Otter River child but the son of a Frenchman and the sister of Washakie, chief of the Eastern Shoshone).[51]

McGarry led a second incursion into Cache Valley in December which resulted in the deaths of four Shoshone hostages. These invasions and murders and confrontations with Bear Hunter led to the typical responses by the Northwestern Shoshone as they intensified their raids on Mormon farms in the Valley, threatening to kill every settler in the area. The threats were carried out in early January 1863 when as many as 11 prospectors were killed on the Montana Trail heading south to Salt Lake City.[52] These murders only added an incentive for the volunteers to "make clean work of the savages."[53]

The Adjutant General's Office related the official version of the events that led up to the Bear River mission. In this report it was stated that "The circumstance which gave rise to the expedition against the Indians are numerous and diversified. The conception of the expedition is due to Colonel P. Edward Connor, and the brilliant execution of his plans and their glorious results are exclusively the well-earned honors of his brave officers and his no less brave men ... . Colonel Connor—from the first reports of the murder of immigrants on the Humboldt and various other localities along the northern route to California last summer— determined in cutting off the savages ... . Since that time the Indian attacks upon the whites, traveling to and from the Dakota mines, have only added determination to determination to rid the country of this terrible scourge—this perpetual reign of terror; and wherever there was the slightest hope of reaching the savages, the gallant Major [McGarry] was ordered in pursuit."[54]

It is obvious that this pattern of Indian hostility and military retaliation, with seemingly Mormon bystanders who favored feeding the Indians but were silently relieved when the Shoshone threat was forcibly removed, were the underlying causes of the Bear River Massacre. But the tone of the Adjutant General's report also reflects racist attitudes among the military brass and a disinclination to look at the militarization of the Indian problem and the overt aggressiveness of the volunteer forces. These latter concerns were the more probable causes of the battle that turned into a massacre along the Bear River.[55]

On January 22, 1863, a California Infantry Regiment, with 69 volunteers, 15 baggage wagons, and 2 twelve-pounder mountain howitzers, marched out of Camp Douglas "in a heavy snowstorm."[56] Ostensibly they were on an undertaking to protect wagon trains hauling grain through Cache Valley, but they were actually a decoy intended to deceive the Shoshone into thinking that they were on another of the white man's never ending escort missions. Three days later, after sundown, Connor, with arrest warrants in hand for Chiefs Bear Hunter, Sanpitch, and Sagwitch of the Northwestern Bands, set off with his 225 men, comprising 4 cavalry companies, 68 miles in a "fearful night march" to Brigham City (on the southwestern edge of Cache Valley). It was a covert operation designed to surprise the Indians in their winter lodges and to catch the Shoshone warriors encumbered with wives and children.[57] Before this time most incidents between the military and the Indians involved encounters between combatants when it was not midwinter with below zero temperatures, a time when both parties could move about freely. This winter campaign would be very different. Ice, snow, and cold temperatures would be Connor's allies; uncertain partners who could hurt as well as help your cause (see map, Figure 8.2).

The infantry reached Franklin (a few miles north of the current boundary in southern Idaho) in the early evening of January 28. They were now only 12 miles from the Shoshone camp on the Bear River. Chief Bear Hunter had recently visited Franklin and most likely knew about the arrival of the infantry, although he was unaware that the cavalry would arrive in Franklin at midnight.[58]

Connor immediately ordered the infantry to start for the battlefield at 1:00 A.M. They were delayed a few hours until they could find local citizens who would volunteer to scout for the army and lead them to the Indian lodges. Marching through snow that was four feet deep, the infantry was forced to abandon the two howitzers about six miles from what would become the scene of battle.[59]

While two brothers from Franklin guided the infantry, Connor himself finally persuaded the Mormon frontiersman and reputed murderer and assassin, Orin Porter Rockwell, to act as a scout for the cavalry that now numbered less than 200 officers and men because at least 75 volunteers were lost to the command because of frozen limbs. Connor, with Rockwell's assistance, left Franklin around 4:00 A.M, meeting up with the infantry and passing them around four miles from the war site.[60]

So Connor, the man who after the event would say that the Mormons were of no help to the army, and, as scholar Rod Miller noted, "distrustful of all Mormons, was forced by circumstance to trust the most notorious Mormon of them all." With the aid of Rockwell and the other Mormon scouts, the California Volunteers finally arrived at dawn on a bluff overlooking the Shoshone winter

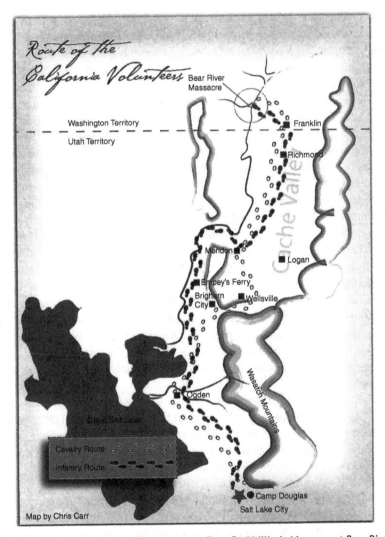

Figure 8.2 *Route of the California Volunteers. From* Rod Miller's *Massacre at Bear River: First, Worst, Forgotten* (Caldwell, Idaho: Caxton Press, 2008), p. 84. Courtesy of Rod Miller and Scott Gibson, Caxton Press. Map by Chris Carr.

camp on the *Boa Ogoi* (Bear River) the morning of January 29, 1863. From the southern bluff they could see the northern ravine where the 75 lodges were located in which approximately 450 Shoshone Indians resided. In the early dawn, the troops saw smoke rising from the morning fires that lit up the Indian camp on the other side of the stream. It was time to attack before the prey escaped.[61] The die was cast.

Contemporary visitors to the site, a few miles northwest of today's Preston, Idaho, can obtain a proximate view of the area that was the conflict zone. The Bear River, usually running north to south, takes a sharp right turn and heads west through a valley defined by slopes on both the northwest side and the southeast one. The slopes on the north are known as Cedar Bluffs. Between Cedar Bluffs and the southern bluffs lies flat grassland through which the Bear River flows. It is very likely that the early fighting took place on this flatland north of the river and east of the village lodges. Cedar Bluffs extends about 1.4 miles above the flat, a change of about 150 feet in altitude. A narrow ravine was cut through the bluffs by the erosion activity of the historic Beaver Creek (known after the massacre as Battle Creek). This was where the lodges were located. There are steep cliffs along the ancient creek bed of 6 to 12 feet in height in the area of the ravine. The ravine once was wooded, with stunted cedar trees on the nearby hills and willows camouflaging the creek area.[62] As Newell Hart said in 1932, "Now the plain was empty, the sage and the cedar were lonely, the Indians had scattered with the cavalry and the committeemen had gone home to milk the cows" (see map, Figure 8.3).[63]

From the top of Cedar Bluffs, across the flat grasslands, to the top of the southern bluffs where Connor first saw the Indian lodges, is approximately 4.5 miles. While the altitude here is around 5,000 feet, the bottom of the bluffs is approximately 4,500 feet. One can see the West Cache Canal dug in the 1890s; a canal that likely altered the flow of Beaver Creek. Today there is a discolored area on the field between the river and the ravine that indicates the historic position of the creek. Although US Highway 91 runs through the flat and up Cedar Bluffs today, in the nineteenth century the Montana Road went through the grassland immediately south of the ravine where the Indian tepees or wigwams were located. This then is the current view of the battlefield.[64]

A basic belief of the Northwestern Shoshone is that the Great Spirit resided in Cache Valley, a place where many religious and spiritual ceremonies took place. Cache Valley was known as "The House of the Great Spirit," a place of geothermal hot springs which were a source of warmth and healing. South of the Shoshone winter camp was a hot spring (known as Wayland Hot Springs today), one that attracted the attention of many Indian bands. Winters were usually mild. The forests had deer and elk to hunt, the river was full of trout, and the sage brush sheltered the hares and the quail—all objects of the hunt. Here the tribes rested, played, hunted, and held ceremonial rites.[65]

The Northwestern Shoshone defined themselves in terms of their "native land" or *debia*. Their identity came not from their relationship with others, but the relationship of others to the land.[66] The Mormon expansion and the march of volunteer armies not only meant a loss of food sources, but identity as well.

At *Boa Ogoi* the tepees were warm and the people were content. In the winter the children would use dried deer hides for sleighs. They also played in make-believe fox holes along the creek. It was a land of frolic and security. But most of all it was a spiritual place where individuals would leave their sick beds, and if they could not walk they would be pulled by riding on a deer hide, to be healed. A few weeks before January 29, several Shoshone bands gathered at Bear River for a Warm Dance Ceremony. If Connor had attacked then he would have killed thousands of Indians instead of hundreds. Pocatello and his followers were lucky enough to leave *Bao Ogoi* the day before Connor's troops arrived. Pocatello took many of the warriors with him, leaving mostly women (see Figure 8.3), children, the elderly, and the impaired behind.[67]

Band chieftains were usually selected on a seasonal basis, with changes made from one winter camp to another. Chief Bear Hunter was the leader or spokesman for this camp, while Lehi and Sagwitch Timbimboo were more than likely subchiefs. Sagwitch was usually the head of the Tongicavo winter camp west of the Promotory Mountains near Mount Tarpey on the northeastern edge of the Great Salt Lake, an area known for its mild winter weather.[68] Bear Hunter and Lehi would be killed in the slaughter, while Sagwitch would escape and become a famous survivor. His great granddaughter, Mae Timbimboo Parry, was the unofficial spokesperson for the Shoshone and would be known for incorporating the oral traditions of her people and putting in writing the first Shoshone view of the Bear River Massacre.[69]

At around 6:00 A.M. the fighting began (see map, Figure 8.4). Connor, in no mood to negotiate and before his entire infantry had arrived, ordered Major McGarry and his cavalry to ford the river and amount a frontal assault on the Indians. With some difficulty the soldiers crossed the icy river on foot and mounted the attack. As the dismounted cavalry advanced, the defenders sent out a deadly fire which, as the Adjutant General later said, "sent down the men like the leaves of autumn."[70] Of the 22 enlisted men who were killed in the battle, at least 14 died during this first hour of fighting. The warriors fought bravely until their few rifles run out of ammunition. Then arrows, lances, knives, tomahawks, rocks, and sticks were used. After the first hour the warriors and their women would be no match for the volunteers with their carbines, pistols, bayonets, and 16,000 rounds of ammunition.[71]

With the arrival of the infantry Connor ordered first a strategic retreat so that the men could cover themselves and save their ammunition. Then he ordered a combined group of infantry and cavalrymen under Major McGarry to maneuver to the northern bluffs, move down the ravine to the west side, and outflank them from the rear. While the frontal assault continued, other volunteers were ordered across Beaver Creek (perhaps crossing the Montana Road Bridge) to the west side so as to encircle the enemy and prevent any warriors from escaping the battlefield. One by one many of the warriors were dislodged from the protection of the willows of the ravine, while others were shot while

Figure 8.3   *Shoshone Women at Bear River.* The Shoshone Community, in conjunction with the Idaho Transportation Department, established several interpretative signs entitled "the largest Indian massacre in the West" in 2006 at Bear River Massacre site, near Preston, Idaho. Photo by W. Dirk Raat (2014).

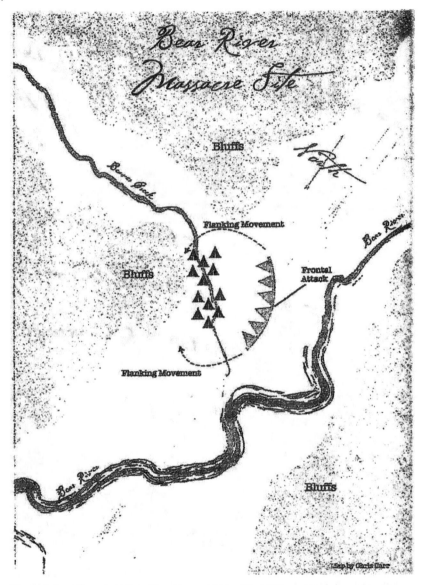

Figure 8.4 *Massacre at Bear River.* From p. 118 of Rod Miller's *Massacre at Bear River: First, Worst, Forgotten* (Caldwell, Idaho: Caxton Press, 2008). Courtesy of Rod Miller and Scott Gibson, Caxton Press. Map by Chris Carr.

trying to escape into the river. Now, after two or three hours of fighting, the volunteers rushed down the steep banks into the midst of the Indian fighters. Hand to hand fighting took place, and the volunteer's pistols and rifle bayonets proved to be most useful to Connor's cause. The Indians cried for quarters, but there were to be no quarters given that day. No distinction was made between officers and privates. Each fought on their own as needed. One lowly cavalry sergeant said "It was a free fight every man on his own hook."[72] Another volunteer, Sergeant W. L. Beach, noted, "the fight lasted four hours and appeared more like a frolic than a fight."[73] The last hour was when the battle became a massacre, a time when the volunteers could live up to their earlier reputation as "squaw killers." As the volunteers raged out of control, it was obvious that the command structure either deteriorated or was purposely ignored by both officers and enlisted men.

The close-quarters fighting soon led to, what Shoshone historian Mae Parry described as "The very cruelest and meanest killing ... of Chief Bear Hunter." Knowing him to be one of the leaders, the volunteers were eager to get to him. Suffering from a bullet wound, Bear Hunter was then captured and tortured. The soldiers became angry when the chief would not utter a word, not crying or even begging for his life. Mae Parry told of his death this way: "One of the military men took his rifle, stepped to a burning campfire and heated the bayonet until it was glowing red. He then ran the burning hot metal through the chief's ears." Another unlucky victim was Subchief Lehi who also lost his life. Of the three camp leaders, only Subchief Sagwitch survived by escaping into the river and floating under the cover of brush. After dark he and some fellow warriors fled on horseback with Sagwitch only suffering a wound in his hand. Yeager, Sagwitch's 12-year-old son, survived by playing dead on the freezing battleground.[74]

As the Shoshone tell their story, "The Indians were being slaughtered like wild rabbits." Old men, the infirm, old ladies, middle aged women, young girls, children, and infants were killed. Wounded and incapacitated Indians were killed by being struck on the head with axes. Trying to escape the ravine, many of the women with babies jumped into the river with their tots on their backs. One mother was forced to throw her small baby in the river only to see the child drown and float away, joining other dead bodies on the blood red ice.[75] Little Red Clay, the younger brother of Yeager and Sagwitch's son, and a survivor of the massacre, told the editor of the Franklin County *Citizen* (Preston, Idaho) on July 11, 1918, that he had received seven wounds at the tender age of two that he carried "... today as a souvenir of that merciless battle, when women and sucking babes met their death at the hands of civilization." He continued to complain that some of the white male veterans of that event still boast "... of taking little infants by the heels and beating their brains out on any hard substance they could find."[76]

Elva Schramm, whose great grandmother was one of the survivors, was interviewed by Aaron Crawford in Logan, Utah in April, 2006. She testified that her great grandmother had said that when the volunteers saw the children "that they'd grab these little children by the leg like a jackrabbit and then they'd hit their heads on the ground."[77] Another eyewitness, James Martineau, a Cache Valley settler, reported that much of the infanticide was done under the guise of mercy killing, since many of the babies were half frozen and would not have survived another 24 hours. Martineau told of one instance where a soldier found a dead women clutching her live baby in which the volunteer "in mercy to the babe, killed it."[78]

Perhaps one of the more controversial aspects of the massacre was the act of raping and molesting the Indian women. Even today in the Shoshone community many of the descendents of the survivors deny that rape took place. Yet, in spite of these disavows, many of which come from Shoshone Mormons, the case for rape at Bear River is fairly overwhelming.[79] It not unusual in cases of sexual violence that the victim (in this instance the descendants of victims), afraid of the consequences of cooperation and fearful that admission is tantamount to guilt, denies that rape occurred. In the case of the Bear River Massacre it is difficult to know with any certainty, given the narrow documentary base, how many Indian women survivors were impregnated by rapists—an uncertainty that might explain the reluctance of survival descendants to acknowledge any rapes.

Some eyewitness accounts are available. Again, James Martineau recorded that "Several squaws were killed because they would not submit quietly to be ravished, and other squaws were ravished in the agony of death." A native account was given by the crippled Shoshone Indian Mattigan (sometimes spelled Matigan or Matigund) who delivered his testimony immediately after the event in which he said "that the way the soldiers used the squaws after the battle was shameful." L.D.S. church documents contain testimonies that speak of killing the wounded with axes and ravishing the squaws. The aforementioned leader of the Saints in Cache Valley, Peter Maughan, reported to Brigham Young that 20 Indians had arrived in Franklin and that "all are familiar with the conduct of the troops towards the Squaws" (see Figure 8.3).[80]

David Bigler, in his book *Forgotten Kingdom*, published in 1998, disagreed with the Madsen assessment concerning rape that is outlined above. He notes that it is difficult to verify the charges of rape, and is "even harder to square with his [Connor's] character." But Bigler misses the point. Connor, either willingly or unwillingly, had no control over his army of volunteers.[81] Rape was probably not a conscious military tactic, but the result of a general culture of sexual violence in the west of the nineteenth century.

The California Volunteers shared in the cult of masculinity. Just as Spain in Mexico had its Cortés and Malinche—the conqueror and the violated mistress—so too did the volunteers have their own "squaws" and their own version of "squawter's rights." As Newell Hart said, the California Volunteers "... were gung-ho men—disgruntled miners who didn't make it big—brave men whose patriotism, though real, was perhaps secondary to their desire for adventure."[82] They, and their *compadres* in California and Nevada, had already shown that young Indian girls were always subject to rape and molestation.

As is known today, rape is a highly effective military tool. As one recent study indicates, "the victim is raped in an effort to dehumanize and defeat the enemy, leaving an entire society with long-term suffering as victims cascade across generational divides."[83] It is no coincidence that during and immediately after World War II over 970 American soldiers were convicted by a US Army courts martial of rape, or that the My Lai Massacre that took place in March, 1968, in South Vietnam killed 407 Vietnamese men, women, children, and infants, while many of the women were gang-raped and their bodies mutilated. Another 97 were killed at My Khe. Perhaps the California Volunteers were ahead of their time and were aware of the military value of acts of rape.

Finally, it can be stated, as Cache Valley rancher William Hull did when he visited the massacre scene soon after the fighting ceased, that "... dead bodies were everywhere. I counted eight deep in one place and in several places they were three to five deep; all in all we counted nearly 400; two-thirds of this number being women and children."[84] Although his estimate may be inflated (his count would list over 366 dead women and children, while conservative estimates place the mortality figure for all victims at 250 to 280 deaths), his impression of an overwhelming tragedy was all too correct. A conflict in which murder of noncombatants takes place on a massive scale accompanied by mutilation, infanticide, and rape is not only a massacre, but very likely a form of genocide.[85] The Mormon settlers of Cache Valley, while initially suspicious of Connor's army of "Gentiles" and outsiders, eventually expressed their gratitude for Connor's action "as an intervention of the Almighty."[86]

The battle and massacre were over. The soldiers thought they were in Utah territory, but in actuality they were in Washington territory (soon to become Idaho). What the Shoshone traditionally knew as Bear Creek, the soldiers called Battle Creek—the name it goes by today. If the US Army was confused about its whereabouts, the Shoshone knew where they were. *So-so-goi*, "those that travel on foot," knew that they were at the junction of Bear Creek and *Bia Ogoi*, the Bear River in *Seuhubeogoi* or "willow river" valley—the name they gave to Cache Valley. Those that survived were home in *Ea-da-how*! The closest translation suggests "sunrise ... its morning." Unfortunately, for many of their fallen brethren and sisters there would be no sunrise, *gāi mē na vū ēē gŭn dō āi*, "there will be no moonlight."[87]

Aftermath: Battles, Massacres, and the Collective Memory

Colonel Conner was initially hailed as a hero by the political and military establishment of the United States, with both the Commissioner of Indian Affairs and the Adjutant General's office praising him for the leadership and bravery. Military propaganda insisted the Indians were about to destroy the city of Franklin and had to be stopped. Two months after the Bear River Massacre Connor was rewarded with a commission to brigadier general. In the spring of 1863 he established Fort Connor near Soda Springs, Idaho, near the northeastern edge of Cache Valley. Shortly thereafter he was on the road again fighting those Shoshones, Bannocks, and Utes who had been outraged over the Bear River campaign and the slaughter of their friends and relatives. Included in his fox hunt was Pocatello's band that Connor referred to as "bad Indians" that need to be brought to justice. For six months after the massacre, fighting raged along the Overland Mail route and in Cache Valley.

While contemporaries may have been delighted with Connor, the military critique 100 years after the event was not so favorable. Lt. Colonel Edward J. Barta submitted an M.A. Thesis in 1962 on "Battle Creek: The Battle of Bear River" in which Connor's tactics and strategy were critically examined. Using military jargon such as unity of command, the principles of mass and maneuver, the economy of force, and the elements of surprise and security, Barta came to the following conclusion. Connor, whatever his shortcomings, did achieve his objective of destroying the enemy. In so doing, however, he did tend to use his forces piecemeal. He initiated a frontal assault with only a third of his troops present, did not have the howitzers his troops brought along, and lost troops to the cold and freezing weather by not insuring that they were properly clothed (while his soldiers burned down several Indian lodges that could have been used to protect them from the cold after the fighting). He never created a reserve force that, if conditions had been different, he might have needed. The element of surprise was compromised, both on the march to Idaho and later at the battle site. And, finally, by not hiring professional scouts (available in the form of unemployed beaver trappers) he lost valuable time and did not have a thorough understanding of the terrain.[88] As Lucy Petty Turner, the daughter of the man who at Bear River had aided in preparing a thawed body for burial, said: "Captain Connor had used bad military tactics. He had lost more men than was necessary and he had brought about the death of women and children."[89]

By the end of July, Indian Affairs Superintendent James Doty met with nine bands of the Northwestern Shoshone at Brigham City and together they signed the Treaty of Box Elder. Seven survivors of Bear Hunter's band were there too. The treaty promised the Indians an annual annuity of $5,000, while another article defined Pocatello's country as the land lying between the Portneuf Mountains on the east and Raft River on the west. In October, Doty came to terms with the Western Shoshone at Ruby Valley, the Goshutes at Tuilla Valley, and the Shoshone–Bannock Indians at Soda Springs. When the federal government established a reservation at Fort Hall in 1869, several Cache Valley Shoshone were induced to move there.[90] The remaining beleaguered survivors traveled to their traditional summer camp on the Bear River near the city of Corinne, Utah.

The white residents of Corinne, a "Gentile" group of railway workers and other laborers, did not want the Shoshone in their neighborhood. When many Shoshones converted to Mormonism, the Corinne residents were horrified, believing that the Mormon temple garments were just another form of "Ghost Shirts" that Ghost Dancers wore as they prepared for war against the white man. The citizens of Corinne called in the military who ordered the Indians out of the area. Fearing another massacre the Indians did as they were told. The Mormon Indians, without a place to live, thankfully accepted an invitation of the Mormon Church to settle on a 500-acre tract of land in Box Elder County. This settlement, named Washakie (after the famous chief of the Eastern Shoshone), was located in a "barren, stony wilderness" near present day Tremonton in the Malad Valley. Somehow, by toiling on the land and digging the Samaria Canal, they were able to build a colony of 300 to 500 Shoshone who due to their toil succeeded in raising wheat, barley, oats, and alfalfa. After 1938, the Indians were told that they were renters, not owners, and that the church was their landlord. The town of Washakie then started to lose people to the wartime boom economies of Ogden or to enlistments in the army. By the late 1960s and early 1970s the church seized the final Indian-owned houses and burned them while selling their lands to local farmers and ranchers. Those Indians who refused to turn over their leases to the church were threatened with ex- communication (or in the jargon of Mormonism, "disfellowship").[91]

Throughout the first 100 years after the tragedy of 1863, individuals were uncertain as to whether or not that event should be described as a battle or a massacre. Basically, as explained elsewhere, a battle is a conflict between com- batants, while a massacre involves large numbers of noncombatants, especially women and children. The differences in usage are mostly a matter of tribalism. If your tribe attacks my tribe you very likely engaged in a massacre, but if my tribe attacks your tribe it is a battle. The Mormon pioneers of the late nineteenth century knew that the Bear River fight was a "battle" in which the armed vol- unteers, and the Mormons who assisted them, were to be recognized for their bravery. And when it came to Indian hostilities, most conflicts in which the natives killed several whites were "massacres."

In this context the so-called Almo massacre is of interest. If the tourist, camper, or rock climber traveled south of I-84 to the City of Rocks during the summer of 2014, he or she would likely go through the rural town of Almo adja- cent to the east entry to the City of Rocks. This national reserve in southern Idaho was a landmark for emigrants on the California Trail after 1843. Once buffalo roamed through the park, but today the largest mammals are deer, mountain lions, and coyotes. On August 13, 1849, James F. Wilkins wrote that "we encamped at the city of rocks, a noted place from the granite rocks rising abruptly out of the ground. They are in a romantic valley clustered together which gives them the appearance of a city. I took several sketches of them. 5 miles from this comes in the new Mormon road which goes by the city of salt lake."[92] This was an area where Pocatello's band historically roamed, and where the Shoshone confronted many emigrants headed for Nevada and California.

If our hypothetical traveler had any curiosity, he would stop at the General Store in Almo before going to the national park. Almo itself is a small farming town, mostly made up of Mormon families. It reached its peak in 1920 when it had a population of 260, a number that has declined since then. Across the road from the post office in the General Store, and next to the public school, is a monument to the Almo Massacre. There, on a slab of stone 6 feet in height and carved in the form of the state of Idaho is a marker:

> Almo Idaho
>
> Dedicated to the memory of those who lost their lives in a most horrible Indian massacre 1861 Three hundred migrants west bound. Only five escaped.
>
> Erected by S. & D. [Sons & Daughters] of Idaho pioneers, 1938[93]

Although memories of the Almo massacre might soothe the feelings of the current descendants of Almo's hard working Mormon pioneers of the past, many scholars, and even some residents of Almo, have doubts about whether or not a massacre of white emigrants actually occurred at the Almo Creek on the California Trail.

The first mention in the literature of the so-called "Almo Massacre" appears to be that of Charles S. Walgamott's *Reminiscences of Early Days*. This rendering of the massacre was repeated later in 1936 when he published *Six Decades Past*. According to Walgamott, in the spring of 1861 an emigrant train of some 300 souls and 60 wagons left Missouri headed for California. When they left the Oregon Trail, they crossed the Raft River heading south over the California Road. After three days they arrived at Almo Creek, about seven miles northeast of the Twin Sister Rocks in what became known as the City of Rocks. The next day Pocatello and his followers allowed the emigrants to advance from the area of the creek and then proceeded to attack the wagon train. The Missourians underwent a four day siege in which most of the 300 were either killed by arrows and guns, or died from thirst. Only five of the original number survived the massacre at Almo.[94]

Three years later, in 1864, Captain Samuel P. Smith was ordered by Colonel Patrick Connor to retaliate against Pocatello at Connor Creek between the towns of Malta and Elba immediately north of Almo. As Walgamott told it, "It was this revolting massacre [at Almo] that induced General Connar [sic.], who was quartered at Fort Douglas, to make war against and almost annihilate the entire branch of the Bannack [sic.] tribe governed by Pocatello."[95] The veracity of the Connor Creek massacre has been established. A military detachment did massacre several Indian men, women, and children in 1864 at a site 25 miles northeast of what became Almo, and Pocatello was certainly one of Connor's targets.[96] But it was not in retaliation for the alleged Almo incident, but rather an extension of the Bear River Massacre of 1863.

There are several things wrong with the story of the Almo Massacre, and the message on the town plaque. First, the frontier newspapers were fairly dutiful in reporting on the killings by Native Americans of whites along the western roads. For example, when 50 Indians attacked a company of 14 packers killing 8 men near Steeple Rocks on the Fort Hall road in August of 1851, the *Desert News* gave the story full coverage. So too did several newspapers in articles that appeared between August 19 and October 21, 1851 in Illinois, Iowa, Wisconsin, and Indiana.[97] Yet, the Salt Lake *Desert News* makes no mention throughout its reporting for the year 1861 of a massacre of the magnitude of 300 emigrants and 60 wagons.[98] Nor do any other newspapers—a strange omission for such an auspicious event.

Other reliable sources are also silent about the alleged Almo Massacre. Agents of the Indian Service were usually very prompt in recording Native American attacks. These reports went to state and national officials, including military commanders who were urged to engage in retribution. The National Archives and the Bureau of Native American Affairs have no records. Similarly, the records of the Department of War, including correspondence between the national agency and various field commanders and local militias, are silent. By summer of 1863 the California Volunteers had killed at least 375 Indians in the Great Basin, but the massacre at Almo Creek was not mentioned as a reason for their pursuit of the Shoshone people. Even the five survivors were mute about such a horrific event, an event quite strange and unlikely if the alleged massacre had actually occurred.[99] The Idaho State Historical Society eventually declared the Almo Massacre to be a non-event.[100]

So the story that is commemorated on the plaque about an Almo Massacre is fabricated. Making the memorial was one of several activities taking place in 1938 that was designed to put Almo on the map for tourism. This involved the hope of creating a National Park Service for the City of Rocks, promoting homesteads and the extension of an irrigation system, and providing the community with a sense of historic pride and purpose with the erection of a marker for the fabled "Almo Massacre." As a legend it was an expression by the local community of the values and hardships of pioneer families who faced great dangers, including the threat of a hostile Indian population.[101] And the legend has some historic content, since the Snake and Humboldt River areas, including the City of Rocks region, were scenes of Indian–white conflict throughout the decade of the 1850s. Yet, in the final analysis, it must be understood that the legend is a fable that reflects a century long process of non-Indian thinking that paints the colonizer as the victim, and reverses the actual tendencies of western US history.

In 1932, six years before the Almo Massacre monument was erected, the citizens of Franklin County and Preston, Idaho erected a four-sided obelisk stone monument near the Bear River that commemorated "The Battle of Bear River." The towns of Franklin and Preston, with their wide streets, remind the spectator of the quiet avenues of other rural towns in Idaho, including Almo. This plaque was erected by the Daughters of Utah Pioneers (DUP), the Utah Pioneer Trails and Landmarks Association, and the Cache Valley Council of the Boy Scouts of America. The inscription describes the women and children who were killed as "combatants" and the Bannock and Shoshone Indians as "guilty of hostile attacks on emigrants."

In 1953, the DUP added another plaque to the stone monument. This one honored the Mormon pioneer women who assisted the wounded soldiers after the fight. As historian John Barnes observed, "These two plaques tell a story of marauding Indians getting what they deserved."[102] In between the installation of the two plaques the Preston Post Office had placed a mural in the lobby over the postmaster's door. The "Battle of Bear River," a Roosevelt era F.W.A. project, was painted by Edmond J. Fitzgerald in 1941, and depicts the cavalry raiding the Shoshone camp and setting tepees ablaze.

For nearly 100 years the slaughter of nearly 300 Indian men, women, and children was an accepted fact for the people of Franklin County. Just like the Cache Valley residents of 1863, the later generations of Franklin County accepted the slaughter because a life without Shoshones meant a much easier life for the farmers and ranchers of Preston and its environs. This was the traditional way of viewing the massacre.

In the mid-1970s a shift in scholarly thinking started to take place in which a series of historians and scholars called the tragedy at Bear River a massacre, and not a battle. Newell Hart initiated the new trend in 1982 with his work on *The Bear River Massacre*, while Brigham Madsen's *The Shoshoni Frontier and the Bear River Massacre*, published in 1985, became a major turning point in the interpretation of that event. Since then several scholars, including Harold Schindler, Thom Hatch, and Kass Fleisher have all revised the traditional historiography. These scholarly efforts were paralleled by a switch in popular opinion. By 1990 the state of Idaho had replaced the "Bear River Battle" sign with a "Bear River Massacre" one, and the National Park Service established a new plaque that places the Bear River "Massacre" in a national context with a greater sensitivity toward the American Indian.[103] In 1995 the National Park Service engaged in a special resource study and environmental assessment of the site, arguing that the massacre field should become a federal historic landscape protected by law.[104]

By 2006, the Shoshones, in conjunction with the Idaho Transportation Department, placed on the northern bluff overlooking the massacre site seven interpretive signs that described the tragedy as "the largest Indian massacre in the West" (see again Figures 8.1 and 8.3).[105] Finally, in 2014, Kenneth C. Reid of the Idaho State Historical Society, was leading an archaeological investigation team at the Bear River Massacre National Historic Landmark site outside of Preston, Idaho.[106] The collective memory had come full cycle.

In driving through the area in the summer of 2014, it is apparent to the observer that the local community has changed its traditional views as well. When one drives north from Logan the first town one sees is Franklin, Idaho. There at the entry is a welcoming sign that refers to the event, not as a battle, but as the "Bear River Massacre." Road signs outside of Preston point the way to the "Bear River Massacre." Now is, perhaps, the time to work the local sugar beets and let history take care of itself.

So the Bear River Massacre, so often forgotten in the annals of history, has become an established fact. Its importance is simply that the tactics and strategy of Colonel Conner were quickly mimicked by his contemporaries. Soon after the Bear River event Connor arrived in Denver to consult with Colonel John Chivington. Chivington, after exchanging opinions about Indian fighting with General Connor and evidently being riled by Connor's braggadocio,[107] followed Conner's example and attacked a sleepy village of Cheyenne and Arapaho Indians. And like the California Volunteers, his army raped, mutilated, and murdered 130 men, women, and children at Sand Creek, Colorado on a cold, wintry day in November of 1864.

In November of 1868, George Armstrong Custer destroyed a Cheyenne village on the Washita River in Oklahoma, leaving over 100 dead Indians in the snow. In the dead of winter, Major Eugene Baker attacked and killed 173 Blackfoot Indians at the Marias River in Montana in 1870. And John W. Forsyth's soldiers destroyed a Lakota Sioux camp on December 29, 1890, killing over 150 defenseless Indians at Wounded Knee Creek in South Dakota.[108] Colonel Connor's tactics at Bear River seemed to serve them all very well.[109] If it is not historically accurate to consider these as acts of genocide, they were at least what we would call today "war crimes," and were in the genocidal traditions of California Indian–white (federal troops, volunteers, vigilantes) relations.[110]

9

Slaying the Deer Slayers in Mexico: The Yaqui Experience

itom Juaa Ania, itom ju'upa te jin'neune, bhueituk apo itom kokou, kus ya'atakai, kovapo, itou weeka itom Su'a Achai'wai' tavenasia. "*Defend our forests, and our mesquite, for when one dies, forming a cross, as if it were our father, who cares for and protects us ...*"

José López, Pueblo Yo'owe, Vicam Pueblo, 1880[1]

What we want is that all whites and troops get out. If they go for good, then there will be peace; if not we declare war.

"The Eight Yaqui Towns," Cocorit Pueblo, Sonora, *to General Luís E. Torres*, Governor of Sonora, 1899[2]

Porfirio Díaz itom bwa'avaen. Yoemrata tehalvaen. "*Porfirio Díaz wanted to eat us. He wanted to finish off the Yoeme Nation.*"

Anselma Tonopuame'a Castillo, Yaqui Elder, 1960s[3]

Los Yaquis son un obstáculo constante ...[comparándolos con] un siniestro Renacimiento del ave fénix de las cenizas de las montañas. "The Yaquis are a constant obstacle." They can be compared to "*the sinister resurrection of the [fabled] Phoenix bird [of antiquity] that arose [after burning itself] from the ashes of the mountains.*" [the Bacatete Mountains of Sonora?]

Ravings of an official government publication for Sonora, 1905–1907[4]

Lost Worlds of 1863: Relocation and Removal of American Indians in the Central Rockies and the Greater Southwest, First Edition. W. Dirk Raat.

The Yaqui (or *Yoeme;* pl. *Yoemen*) experience stands alone having few equals in the indigenous history of the Americas. First, the Yaqui resistance to *Yorim* (Spanish and Mexican outsiders) intrusions lasted from 1533 to the second quarter of the twentieth century. Whites who encroached on Yaqui lands in the late nineteenth and the twentieth century were known as *Riingom*. This was the longest opposition movement in American Indian history. Yaqui guerrilla warfare developed in the mountainous environment of the Bacatete in Sonora. The Bacatete Mountains (also known as the "Sierra del Yaqui") are about 60 miles north of the Yaqui River with passes into the mountains that are few in number and easily defended from above.[5] The nearness of the United States border created both an avenue for escape and a source of supplies and munitions. In addition, during the late eighteenth century and throughout most of the nineteenth century, exposure to Apache military maneuvers and strategy reinforced Yaqui military tactics. Both the lengthy duration of the resistance, and the lateness of the discord (lasting until the early twentieth century in comparison to most North American Indian conflicts that were over by 1890), made the Yaqui situation distinctive.

Another distinction of the Yaqui path was the diaspora. A scattering of Yaqui peoples throughout Mexico and the southwestern United States began in the early 1880s and lasted until the mid-twentieth century. The Yaqui people fled from the twin evils of extermination and deportation and sought refuge in Arizona Territory (from Nogales to Yuma and Tucson and Sells, and from Tucson and Sells to the greater Phoenix area), as well as southern California, the Baja peninsula, the Zuñi pueblos of New Mexico, and the mining camps, rural towns, haciendas, and *ranchos* of Sonora, Chihuahua and other Mexican locales.

Those who did not flee from the Río Yaqui area of Sonora were usually executed, imprisoned, or forcibly deported as slave laborers to the coffee plantations of Oaxaca and the henequen fields of the Yucatán. This dispersal was greater than that the Cherokees experienced in 1835 when they were removed from Georgia to Oklahoma, or that of the Chiricahua Apaches who were transported from southeast Arizona to Florida prisons after 1886. As the late anthropologist Edward H. Spicer noted, the Yaquis "had become the most widely scattered native people of North America."[6]

A final factor that distinguishes the Yaquis from other native groups was the trinational and global nature of Yaqui labor and the henequen-wheat complex. Sonoran politics took on an international hue when agave fibers of sisal and henequen in the Yucatán were cut, gathered, packed and loaded by Yaqui slaves and then exported via Progreso and New Orleans to twine factories in the United States and Canada. This twine, often manufactured with penitentiary labor, was then sent to Midwestern farmers on the American and Canadian plains to be used in binders and other harvesting implements that would cut the grain and bind the stalks in bundles for threshing. From 1880 to 1930, Yucatecan fibers, supplied by Yaqui and other indigenous labor, were critical for the North American agricultural revolution (see map, Figure 9.1).[7]

Although 1863 was not a particularly distinctive year in Yaqui history, it was the decade of the 1860s that witnessed the first serious intrusions by outsiders into the Yaqui River country. During that time federal restrictions on foreign investment were loosened. By 1863 mining received a new impetus when the government provided concessions for ore seekers to pursue mineral wealth in Sonora. Of the 20 mines that were initiated in the Guaymas district that year, 15 were owned by either Frenchmen or North Americans. Some of these mines were in or near Yaqui territory. By the end of 1863 the wealthy mining district of Los Alamos, southeast of the Río Yaqui, registered close to 100 mines.

As will be explained later, the victory of the Liberals after the bloody War of La Reforma (1858–1861), and the US Civil War of 1861, followed by the French Intervention in Mexico in 1862, led to the first stages of modernization and the entry of foreign capital into Mexico, especially the Mexican North. Matamoros became a major entrepot for the transshipment of munitions from the European market and cotton from the Confederacy. Economic development in Tamaulipas and Nuevo León y Coahuila spelled over to neighboring Sonora. The beginnings of colonization and encroachment of Yaqui soil was initiated by "yoris and gringos" during the decade of the 1860s. The vicious cycle was started again with encroachments leading to resistance that then brought warfare, massacres, extermination, and deportation. Between 1887, when federal troops began the occupation of Yaqui tribal lands, and the end of the Mexican Revolution in 1910, the Yaqui population dropped from 20,000 to less than 3,000.[8] Only the indigenous nature of Yaqui rituals could retain a Yoemen identity throughout the diaspora.

Hiakam: the Pre-dawn Flower World of Deer and Dancers

The Yaqui word *Hiakim* translates into "Yoeme country," *Yoemen* meaning "the people." The Río Yaqui has it headwaters at 9,000 feet in the Sierra Occidental of northern Mexico, flows north and west as the Río Papigóchic in Chihuahua entering Sonora near Sahuaripa, a distance of about 180 miles. Here the river flows from north to south about 165 miles, then veers west through Yoeme country some 90 miles to empty into the Gulf of California west of Ciudad Obregón. It is known as *Hiak Vatwe* to the Yaquis.[9] Spaniards called the river *Yaquimi*, perhaps the origin of the word "Yaqui."[10]

Figure 9.1 *Map of the henequen-wheat complex in North America.* Reproduced from Sterling Evans' *Bound in Twine* (College Station, Tx.: Texas A&M, 2007), following p. xxiii. Credit: (Ms.) Wenonah van Heyst, Department of Geography and Environment, Brandon University.

The early Yaquis established small settlements along the banks of the river, its flood waters nourishing plant growth and animal shelters. They employed simple ditch or irrigation techniques to grow corn, beans, and squash. Mostly farmers and hunters, the Yaqui did engage in some degree of fishing and shell collection in coastal bays.[11] As traders they scattered as far north as the Gila River to exchange foods, furs, and shells with other indigenous groups such as Comanches and Shoshones.[12]

In precontact times 20,000 to 35,000 Yaquis laid claim to over 6,000 square miles surrounding the Hiak Vatwe of Sonora, including what would become the metropolitan areas of Guaymas and Ciudad Obregón. The boundaries of this area were considered sacred by the Yaquis, a region the mythical *batnaataka* or angels traversed while singing the holy songs. Like other indigenous peoples, the homeland was part of their identity.[13]

The Yaquis had a precontact settlement pattern that preadapted them to the *reduccion* or the concentration policy of the Jesuits, whereby the dispersed population was brought together in eight adobe-walled church-centered towns. Prior to the Spaniards the Yaquis lived in around 80 rancherías (or extended family communities) along the lower section of the Río Yaqui. Like other ranchería groups of the Greater Southwest, they were a Uto-Aztecan-speaking people. Their particular language was Cahitan.

Unlike other ranchería communities, their settlements and houses were less scattered than the dry-farming Tarahumaras southeast of them or the two-village desert dwellers of southern Arizona and northern Mexico. This compactness resulted from living next to a river that provided a regular water supply that created favorable agricultural conditions. Compact settlements translated into political cohesion under a political council of senior authorities, integration of communities for military purposes, a rudimentary form of priesthood in lieu of shamanism, and an organized ceremonial system. All of this, in turn, meant that the Jesuits would have little difficulty in reassembling them into the infamous "Eight Holy Pueblos" of Yaqui mythology or the "Eight Jesuit Villages" of the colonial period.[14]

One Yaqui story that is central to an understanding of the people is known as the "Talking Tree." In the days before the Spanish Conquest, Mexico was called Suré, a land populated by the Surem—the children of Yomumuli or First Woman. Reaching to the sky was a huge stick or tree "that kept talking, making a humming noise like bees." The wise men did not understand what the stick was saying. Only Yomumuli could understand and she interpreted the strange humming sounds for her people. It was telling the Indians how to live, and which animals were to live by hunting and which lived by eating grass. Wars, droughts, floods, and the coming of Christians were foretold. Many of the Surem did not like what they heard. Yomumuli, who was angry, said "I am going north" and she picked up the river and went "on the clouds toward the north." She was followed by the discontented ones known as the Surem. Those who did not flee were known as the "baptized ones" and they stayed in their homeland. They grew taller than the Surem, and they are the people of Hiakim today. To many Yoemen, the Surem are magical people who live in the *huya ania*, the spiritual wilderness world where animals, rocks, and all beings live in harmony.[15]

As some commentators have noted, the Tree Story historicizing Yoeme experiences explains in indigenous terms the coming of the Europeans, and by describing the rift between Surem and Yaqui offers a model of indigenism that allows for both continuity and adaptation. In any case, the Tree Story reflects a kind of Yaqui agency that explains in part their lengthy traditions of resistance as well as accommodation to outsiders.[16]

The oldest of Yaqui songs are the *maso bwikam*, or deer songs. In the Deer Ceremony, the deer dancer embodies the spirit of the deer. Like the Surem, the deer spirit is a magical being that inhabits the *sea ania*, the pre-dawn flower world. Flowers are a metaphor for beauty and goodness, and the harmony of all beings that inhabit the magic pre-Christian world. The killing-of-the-deer ceremony takes place a year after a relative's death and is designed to release the spirit of the dead from the world of the living.

The ceremony (or *pahko*) involves a dear dancer, and several *pahkolam* (*pahko'ola* or "old men of the pahko"; from which *pascola* may be derived) who serve as a clownish counterpoint to the stately manner of the deer dancer. The deer dancer's regalia involve the wearing of a deer head on his head with red ribbons wrapped around the antlers to represent the flowers (*sewa*) of the flower world (*sea ania*). Over the head is a white cloth, and in back of the cloth is a small ironwood stick that supports the deer head and symbolizes the plant world that feeds the deer. Around the dancer's neck is a necklace with the Yaqui cross—a quincunx symbol that represents harmony and the four cardinal points and is pre-Christian in origin. Large gourd rattles are held in both hands, representing the agricultural cycle. On the lower torso is a reboso secured with a leather belt from which are hanging leather strips and deer hooves representing the deer who has voluntarily given his life so that mankind can continue to exist. Finally, on the dancer's ankles are moth cocoons that rattle and remind the living with its sounds of the listener's connection to the homeland and their ancient culture.[17]

After the pahkolam stalk the deer, the deer (dancer) is (symbolically) killed. The deer dancer is then laid out on a stand covered with branches. The pahkolam strip and "butcher" the body of the deer. But then, miracle of miracles, as Thomas Skidmore says, "the deer is transmuted into a 'flower' and reborn in the wilderness world ... . The ritual of the killing of the deer therefore sets the grim reality of the hunt against the transcendent spirituality of the flower world and the huya ania. The wilderness world, immanent and ethereal, survives and triumphs in the face of blood, death, and the absurd antics of the pahkolam."[18] The deer dance ceremony is not just another kind of folk-Christianity. The Maso deer dancer and the pascolas or pahkolam are symbols that are distinctive to the Yoemen and pre-Christian Sonora. Take them away and the Yaquis would lose an important part of their identity (see Figure 9.2).[19]

Figure 9.2 *Fear of a Red Planet: Relocation and Removal, 2000.* Mural at Heard Museum (Phoenix, Az) by Steven Jon Yazzie, Navajo (b. 1970). Oil/acrylic on canvas. Panel: Deer Dancer, traditional dancer of the Yoeme (Yaqui). Behind is Christ on cross. Dear dancer and Christ figure, two sacrificial images and representative of syncretic spiritualism.

Black Robes and Cartridge Belts: From Colony to Imperium, 1617–1863

In 1533 Spanish slave raiders confronted the Yoemen for the first time. A brief battle took place on the banks of the Yaqui River in which the Yaquis were temporarily dispersed. Their Spanish opponents, however, were well impressed with the bravery the Yaquis displayed on the field of battle. Between 1608 and 1610 two other battles took place, the second one involving seven thousand tenacious Yaqui warriors against 50 mounted Spaniards and their 4,000 Indian foot soldier allies. The bloody conflict resulted in the total dispersal of the Spanish army with the Spaniards unable to renew the fighting. The Yaquis had successfully defended their homeland, but, much to the surprise of the defeated *españoles*, asked for peace and petitioned the Jesuit missionaries to come to Hiakim.[20]

After 1623 between 16,000 and 32,000 Yaqui Indians were relocated from their 80 rancherías to the mission towns in settlements that were on the average 10 times larger than before. Instead of the traditional dome-shaped, cane mat-covered dwellings, they lived in rectangular wattle-and-daub residences surrounded by cane fences that defined the family compound. These were located in the vicinity of the church. Not until the 1880s, when the Mexican military occupied the Yaqui towns, was the rectangular grid pattern of city planning introduced to the villages. After 1887 Mexican troops, yoris, and assimilated Yaquis lived in Mexican style houses along the grid, while the traditional fenced compounds were irregularly located around the Mexican dwellings.[21]

Living under the tutelage of a few Jesuit black robes, and allowing the Spanish authorities to appoint Indian officials for the towns, the Yaqui villages became thriving agricultural communities. The Jesuits added wheat and peaches, as well as cattle, sheep, horses and goats, to the traditional Yaqui milieu of corn, beans, squash, and cotton. They also introduced the new technology of the plow. Although European illnesses hit the Mayo River villages south of them, the Yaqui towns appeared to be relatively free of yori diseases.[22]

The Jesuit era had instituted a well organized mission system that left the Yaquis with a sense of territoriality, a new type of cultural cohesion, and feelings of economic security that could be used to resist the outsider culture of the yoris.[23] It was, in effect, a continuation of those ancient folkways that were leading to a path of indigenous nationalism and independence from foreign influence.

The 60 year period of relative tranquility came to an end in 1684 when the silver mines of northern Mexico were discovered at Los Alamos. By the 1730s, as the yori mining and ranching population started to resent the control of Yaqui labor by Jesuit missionaries, and looked with envy on the rich farm and pasture lands of the Río Yaqui, discontent arose among the miners and ranchers. Government officials, missionaries, and Yoemen had their own grievances. It culminated in the 1740 Yaqui-Mayo revolt.[24]

By February acts of banditry led to a widespread but mostly uncoordinated revolt. In a brief time an army of 6,000 Indians had taken possession of all towns of the Mayo and Yaqui rivers, and most Spaniards fled southward, some to the mining community of Alamos. Miners and missionaries fled the Yaqui area. Cattle and horses were killed or scattered. While most yoris were secure in their persons, their property was not. The homes, storehouses, mines and chapels of the Spanish *vecinos* or residents were burned and pillaged. In spite of this, over 1,000 Spaniards were killed, while perhaps as many as 5,000 Indians died. Within the year the revolt was over, but it had been costly for all sides—and the atmosphere of distrust continued for the next two centuries of Indian and non-Indian contact.[25]

Several causes have been suggested for the revolt of 1740. Overlying more basic factors may have been the ongoing political struggle between secular and religious authorities of the Spanish state, a conflict that would eventually lead to the expulsion of all Jesuits from the New World in 1767. Local military and civil authorities asserted their legal authority to control temporal matters in the missions. The use or misuse of food surpluses by the Jesuits became a critical issue in the context of floods and famines that plagued the Río Yaqui valley at that time. Many Yaquis were angry at the missionaries for monopolizing both the labor and foods that created a surplus that went to the California missions rather than the Yaquis. Primarily, the Yoemen wanted the missionaries to reduce their demands on their labor and move away from their paternalistic and authoritarian ways of ruling over them. Instead of reacting to the Yaqui grievances, the Jesuits viewed the revolt as a Spanish conspiracy. With the revolt came the erosion of Jesuit control, erosion that finally resulted in the expulsion of 1767.[26]

By 1760 it was obvious that the old level of prosperity had declined in the mission towns. Of the 32,000 Yaquis reportedly living in Hiakim in 1617, there were only 23,000 inhabitants in 1760. The figure may be distorted though since after the rebellion thousands of Yaquis headed to the mines of Sonora and the pearl fisheries of the Baja, as well as the pit camps, ranches, farms and towns of Sinaloa, Durango, and Chihuahua. The Bourbon Reforms instituted by José de Gálvez (1776–1787), the secretary of state for the Indies, provided many job opportunities, especially in mining. After the expulsion the Yaquis worked directly with the Spanish authorities to provide labor to a thriving mining sector.

Until Mexico's independence from Spain in 1821 the Yaquis were an indispensable part of the mining economy. The mobility of the Yaqui was tolerated by a Spanish state, hacendados, and mining proprietors in the labor-scarce northern frontier, and while working the mines the Yaqui could protect the sovereignty of their pueblos. When Spain was expelled from Mexico the old ways were revived and an unceasing war with the white man continued throughout the nineteenth and early twentieth centuries.[27]

As *gachupines* (Spaniards) fought *criollos* (Americanized Spaniards) in the wars of independence, the river pueblos stood to one side, the struggle of very little interest to them. This situation changed with the Plan of Iguala in 1821 and independence for Mexico. Sonora and Sinaloa set up an independent state of Occidente and drafted a constitution in 1824 that was soon promulgated. As the spirit of the colonial Law of the Indies suggested, and as the Plan of Iguala stated, all citizens of the monarchy were "inhabitants of New Spain, without any distinction between Europeans, Africans, or Indians." This implied that all citizens, including the Yaquis, were taxable. In that same year the government attempted to survey Yaqui land for taxation, and, surprise, the surveyors and tax collectors were met with resistance. This was the beginning of an almost continuous struggle that lasted for over 100 years. Once again the Yaquis had to remind the yoris that the people of Hiakam were a separate political entity with no obligation or allegiance to the new Mexican state.[28]

Juan de la Cruz Banderas was thrown in jail for resisting the land surveyors of 1824. The next year when it was obvious that the Yaquis would refuse to pay taxes, soldiers were sent to the Río Yaqui to enforce the law. Banderas, now released from prison, experienced several visions that instructed him to establish a confederation of Indian tribes from northern Mexico in order to confront the yori threat to their independence. An army of over 2,000 fighting men, armed with bows and arrows and fighting under the banner of Guadalupe (the Indian Virgin), confronted the Mexicans. Although Banderas' messianic fever soon spread throughout the indigenous North with the rebels controlling central Sonora by 1826, in 1832 his army of 1,000 Yaquis, Opatas, and Pimas were defeated. That next year Banderas and 11 other Indian leaders were executed and his followers were left to deal with land surveys, taxation, and political intrusions.[29]

After the death of Banderas, the Yaquis from 1833 to 1863 formed alliances with any person or group that would guarantee Yaqui autonomy. Ideology was not important. Conservative or Liberal, centralist or federalist, foreign or native—those *caudillos* (strong men) who supported them would receive Yaqui support. The one individual who was prominent in Yaqui affairs from the 1830s to 1859 was Manuel Gándara, a wealthy landowner in the Ures district in central Sonora—a conservative and centralist stronghold outside the range of Yaqui conflicts. If he could not get elected to public office, he would simply usurp it. He used the military power of the Yaquis to support his own drive for political power.

He was eliminated from the political scene in 1859 when General Ignacio Pesqueira, a Liberal caudillo and supporter of Benito Juárez, suppressed his revolt. Supporting Gándara's ambitions, the Yaquis were almost in a constant state of rebellion between 1857 and 1863. Pesqueira's attempt to promote colonization of the Yaqui River was delayed when the French army, taking advantage of the American involvement in the Civil War, invaded Mexico.[30]

The Environment of Investment, 1863–1880s

The French arrived in Mexico City in 1863, after a brief delay after their initial defeat at the Battle of Puebla on May 5, 1862 (ergo the Cinco de Mayo holiday). Two years later, four French warships landed in Guaymas, accompanied by none other than Pesqueira's rival, Gándara. He recommended that the local Yaqui leaders obey the instructions of the "jefe francés" in all matters. Marshal Francisco Bazaine, chief of the entire French army, approved the nomination of José María Marquín as leader and "general" of a Yaqui army of 100. Once again the Yaquis were promised by their ally the autonomy and sovereignty of their homeland. Support for the "Imperialists" was found on both sides of the Sierra, with the Papigochic villages of western Chihuahua forming a pro-French Coalition of the Pueblos. In spite of the bravery of their Indian allies, the French were finally driven out of Sonora in 1866. Pasqueira was now able to restore his plans for the pacification and colonization of the Yaqui River country.[31]

While initiating his plans for the economic development of Sonora, Pesqueira continued his hard line tactics against the Yaqui rebels. Throughout 1866 and 1867 Pesqueira's troops established garrisons in Hiakam, sent troops throughout the area shooting Yaqui men on sight, executing "rebel leaders," imprisoning others, rounding up cattle and horses, and driving families into the interior. The march on Medano in 1867 by Pesqueira's army was the first large scale invasion of Yaqui territory in the torrid history of the tribe. The Yaquis responded with guerrilla tactics that had been refined by both their association with the French army and the Apaches, using decoys and ambushes to deter the caudillo's forces. It all came to a head in 1868 with the Bácum Massacre.[32]

Several months before Bácum, in June of 1867, the prefects of Alamos and Guaymas were ordered to direct punitive expeditions against the Yaqui people. Close to 1,180 National Guardsmen were mobilized for the effort. They were also aided by 300 "loyal" Yaqui fighters. In February of 1868, nearly 650 infantrymen, cavalrymen, and Yaqui auxiliaries, plus two pieces of artillery, moved in on the Yaqui community of Cócorit. Over 600 residents of Cócorit were rounded up, including men, women, and children. When these "rebels" refused to surrender their guns, the irate commander took 450 Yaquis prisoners and marched them to nearby Bácum where they were imprisoned in the local church. At least 10 prisoners were held as hostages who would be shot if the others tried to escape.[33]

During the night there was a disturbance in the church. The artillery was trained on the door. With the disturbance the hostages were ordered shot. Then some of the prisoners broke down a wall of the church. Mass confusion broke out. The hostages were shot. The artillery was fired. The church was set aflame. In the morning light one could count at least 120 Indians among the ashes. Only 59 badly burned Yaquis were alive. The others had evidently escaped. The weapons they had refused to surrender had been mostly bows and arrows. The massacre had finally bought Pesqueira a short-lived peace for the yori community.[34]

This incident was what was happening on a smaller scale throughout the Río Yaqui area whenever Yaquis and Mexicans confronted one another. For the Yaqui, their claims to the land preceded the coming of the Mexicans, and they were simply defending their homes, fields, and sacred territory. For the Mexicans it was a holy war against barbarians who were refusing to join the forces of progress and civilization.[35]

The Bácum Massacre was a low point in Yaqui history. No longer would the Yoemen make alliances with the enemies of Pesqueira.[36] The Pesqueira family's demise came in 1877 when the Porfiristas (followers of President Porfirio Díaz) in Sonora opposed José Pesqueira, the son of Ignacio. The Yaquis did not participate in that major power change. The Pesqueira lineage was eventually replaced in June 1879 by General Luís E. Torres from Sinaloa, a strong supporter of the president and the man who became the elected governor of Sonora. The Pesqueira 20 year reign, when Ignacio and his son José were Sonora's caudillo-governors, came to an end. The Porfiristas, especially Luís Torres, Ramón Corral, and Rafael Izábal, would shape Sonora's destinies the next thirty years. With his underlings in place, Porfirio Díaz was coming to Sonora and ushering in a new age for that Northern Province. Now the Yaquis would be forced to face the vengeance of a stable and unified Mexico.[37]

Meanwhile the Pesqueira era had initiated much of the modernization that would eventually characterize the later Porfirian period of Mexican history (1876–1910). During the era of La Reforma (1855–1861) and the French Intervention (1862–1867), the latter witnessing the imposition of the Archduke Ferdinand Maxmilian to the Mexican throne, an environment conducive to foreign investment took hold. Foreigners, including Americans, began to invest and speculate in Mexican properties in a serious way. Benito Juárez, the liberal leader of La Reforma, sought US public and private assistance against the French interventionists. Emperor Maxmilian, for his part, brought infusions of capital to Mexico, especially the textile industry of Puebla, while British capital gave new life to the banking and railroad industries. The imperial government created laws that encouraged European immigration, promoted foreign investments, and guaranteed individual property rights. Both the liberals of the Reform Constitution of 1857, and the conservative supporters of the emperor, wanted to unleash indigenous communal lands for private exploitation.[38] Therefore, the national atmosphere supported the investment and anti-Yaqui colonization schemes of the Pesqueira father-and-son team.

The relationship of Sonora to Mexico City was the first priority for the elder Pesqueira. Since independence the capital city had either been unable or unwilling to promote the security and economic growth of Sonora. The federalist doctrines of Benito Juárez divided authority between the national government and the states, but the balance of power had to be defined. The chaos of a the wars of La Reforma and the Intervention, along with the security needs of a frontier state like Sonora with its many Apache problems, meant that Pesqueira often had to at least have the autonomy necessary to achieve the economic and social improvement of the state. Pesqueira achieved his goals by creating a sphere of freedom from federal restrictions and appropriating any federal powers the Juárez government would allow him to make.[39]

In 1860 Pesqueira resurrected the colonial presidial system by installing a series of forts along the northern frontier and ordering his National Guard troops to pursue the ever present threatening Apaches. Then, with the Yaquis occupying what he thought were the most fertile lands of Sonora but only cultivating a small proportion of them, he sought to colonize the Río Yaqui terrain. The region was garrisoned and a colony of Sonoran émigrés from California was invited to work the Yaqui lands, beginning with the building of a canal to irrigate the farmlands. He then promoted the development of a railroad from El Paso to Guaymas. The legislature granted a concession to General Angel Trías and the Companía Americana y Mexicana.[40]

The concession, obviously written under the influence of the Americans, ceded, as was the custom in the United States, alternate square leagues of public lands along the railroad, to the company. Trías and his colleagues were to be solely under Mexican jurisdiction. It took 21 years of intermittent effort, but a line from Guaymas to Nogales was completed on October 25, 1882. Building the line had been delayed by opposition from Sonoran nationalists in the legislature, and by Yaqui resistance.[41] Shortly thereafter, the Richardson Construction Company of Los Angeles completed a trunk line that followed the banks of the Yaqui River to the coast, linking the Yaqui valley to Guaymas and the American market.[42] By 1910 Sonora would become the world's richest mining area, and the Yaquis were fast becoming a rare species of humanity.

The Pesqueira administration also strove to improve the state's transportation network, stimulate commerce, and promote public education. Several wagon roads were constructed, including one that connected the political headquarters of Ures to the port city of Guaymas. A new port (La Libertad) was built on the Gulf north of Guaymas. By 1862 a steamship line was conducting a round trip every 40 days between Guaymas and San Francisco. New tariff laws stimulated trade between Arizona and Guaymas. Mints were established at Alamos and Hermosillo. Public schools were expanded with the costs being met by a state tax on alcoholic beverages. With these developments the commercial cities of Hermosillo and Guaymas grew in population, attracting many American capitalists to Sonora. Cantinas flourished. Needless to say, during the Pesqueira years, in spite of the spirit of progress embraced by the state's *politicos*, the Yaqui valley remained unpacified.[43]

Bound to and in Twine: the Yaqui Diaspora, 1880 to 1940[44]

By 1880, with the porfiristas in power in Sonora, Mexico City officials decided to survey, subdivide, and colonize the Yaqui valley. Some small parcels of Yaqui land were given to the Yoemen. The federal commissioners set up seven

Mexican towns, most of them the earlier missions of the sixteenth century. Land in each town was to be given to whites and yoris, who, along with the soldiers stationed in the valley, would be an example of civilized life for what they hoped would become Yaqui dirt farmers. Other capitalists quickly established the Sonora and Sinaloa Irrigation Company. The aforementioned Richardson Construction Company bought thousands of hectares of land and developed irrigation systems including storage dams, reservoirs, gates, and feeder canals. They subdivided the land into lots and sold the Yaqui land to enthusiastic buyers in the United States. So began the influx of settlers from the United States and the start of commercial farming in the Yaqui valley.[45]

Entering the historical stage at this time was a young man who had been born in Hermosillo in 1837 and was baptized José María Levya, known to his followers as Cajeme (*Ka He'eme*), "he who does not drink." Unlike most Yaquis at that time, he grew up among the yoris and learned the yori ways at the school in Guaymas where he spoke Spanish and studied the western ways of reading, writing, and arithmetic. He served in the federal army until 1875, initially as a defender of Guaymas in 1854 and later fighting with the troops that captured Maxmilian in 1867.[46] In 1874 he had been appointed by Governor Pesqueira *alcalde mayor* of the Yoeme towns "for the purpose of maintaining the [Yaqui] tribe in peace through the influence of a chieftain of the same race."[47] But the Mexicanized Yaqui listened to his people's concerns and decided to use his military prowess and experience to organize the Yaqui resistance movement. After an unprovoked attack in 1882 at Capetamaya, Cajeme led the Yaqui insurgency until his death in 1887. He was buried in the old Yaqui village of Cócorit.[48]

The Yaqui wars, beginning in 1885, would cost the Porfirian government over 50 million pesos. The Cajeme uprising between 1885 and 1886, in which it was reported that over 200 Yaqui fighters were killed and hundreds of women and children taken prisoner at the battle of Buatachive, cost the Sonoran government 150,000 pesos and depleted the state treasury. Federal troops with Mauser rifles faced off against Yaqui warriors armed with bows and arrows. After Cajeme's death the Yaquis were not fought as much as they were, in the words of muckraking journalist John Kenneth Turner, "merely hunted." Many Yaquis that were not hunted down fled across the international border to become the first political refugees to settle in the Tucson area. Those that chose to continue the fight were led by Tetabiate ("Rolling Stone"), the last of the Yaqui chieftains. They sustained themselves by making raids on haciendas near Guaymas. The rebels also harassed government surveyors who came into the valley.[49]

Dominga Tava, a Yaqui woman born in Hermosillo in 1901 who moved to Barrio Libre Pueblo in Tucson in 1916, would agree that the Yoemen were constantly being hunted throughout the box canyons and crevices of the Sierra Becatete. Her grandfather and his brothers had fought under Cajeme, and in the late 1890s were forced to flee to the Sierra from Vícam. Her father Vicente was a *cabo* or corporal in the rebel army and his main job was leading raiding parties against Mexican ranches to obtain provisions for his fighters. As a cabo he was also expected to buy guns and ammunition in Arizona. A massive military sweep of the Becatetes involving thousands of troops took place in 1900. In 1905, while residing at the Hacienda Gandara (a place that Dominga and her sisters loved to visit) soldiers arrived and arrested her grandfather. Acting on information from a Yaqui traitor that he had aided the Sierra Yaquis (which was true), a rope was placed around his neck and he was hung from a mesquite tree. For her grandfather and others it would be too late to seek shelter in the Arizona territory. The hardships of constantly moving and hiding in the Sierra, suffering from hunger, thirst, and illness were not forgotten by Dominga well into her 70s as she related her experiences to Jane Holden Kelley, the anthropologist and interviewer.[50]

Before and after the death of Tetabiate in 1900, the Yaquis fought on as guerrillas. Their hit-and-run tactics were instituted by the *broncos*, that is, the warriors. They blended in with the *mansos*, the peaceful Yaquis who provided materiel and support for the Yaquis in the mountains. In earlier times the Pesqueira government had reacted to Yaqui resistance by deporting them to haciendas in order to provide the *hacendados* with a form of forced labor. Later many Yaquis were sent to central and southern Mexico as draftees to serve in the military, or to the pearl diving areas of the Sea of Cortez where they spent their nights in chains and fetters. Even women and children were deported. Now, since extermination and colonization were failed policies, deportation appeared to be the only way to deal with the Yaquis. Don Porfirio and his Hermosillo allies reacted to the guerrilla warfare by calling for the deportation of *all* Yaquis, manso and bronco alike.[51]

Immediate enforcement of the deportation policy was difficult to realize, so in the meantime the state authorities moved to restrain the Yaqui guerrillas. Mansos now had to stay in restricted towns in designated *barrios* or neighborhoods. They had to carry proper credentials that could identify the holder of the passport. Those without proper identification papers or found outside the restricted areas were arrested.[52] It was also at this time that the battle of Mazocoba indicated to the Yaquis that life was likely to get more difficult than easier under the Porfirian state.

In mid-January of 1900 the Yaquis suffered a major defeat in the heart of the Becatete Mountains at a place the Mexicans called Mazocoba. Known as the Battle of Mazocoba in Mexican history books, the Yoeme refer to it as the Massacre of Maso Kova (Deer Head). It was at this site, sacred to the Yoemen, located northeast of the Yaqui village of Pótam and 25 miles east of Guaymas, that those Yaquis who were fleeing from the soldiers sought refuge. At least 700 men, women, and children had barricaded themselves inside a box canyon at Maso Kova (although General Lorenzo Torres, the military commander in charge, estimated over 3,000 Yaquis were at the battle site).[53] Over 1,000 soldiers (including 82 Yaquis) were under the command of Torres, who divided his men into three columns that scaled the walls of the natural fort and engaged in hand-to-hand combat. Some of the artillery men positioned themselves at the base of the mountain and aimed their cannons at their human prey. The Yaquis only had 40 rifles to defend themselves. The skirmish lasted all day. When it was over the soldiers found 395 bodies strewn on the battlefield (that is, massacre site). It is alleged by some Yoeme sources that "many others, in an act of self-sacrifice, jumped off the cliffs to escape pending slavery and other abuses." Yaqui sources also state that "Many Yoemen heroically used their bodies to shield the young from bullets and shrapnel," and that "babies were killed by hitting their heads against trees." At least 1,000 persons, mostly women and children were taken prisoner (of which 166 died on the forced march back to Las Guásimas southwest of Mazocoba). According to Pascua Yaqui tribal member Rosario Bacaneri Castillo, some of the wounded were brought down the mountain and taken south "in wagonloads to Tórim and put into big corrals." The Mexican losses were 54 dead and 124 wounded.[54]

In the following months several expeditions were carried out. By the end of the year there were probably no more than 300 Yaquis in the Becatete Mountains. A mopping up expedition eventually killed Tetabiate.[55] One of the most disastrous, yet valorous, efforts in Yaqui history was over. After the Maso Kova Massacre many Yaquis fled north seeking refuge—the second major influx of Yaquis to the Phoenix and Tucson areas of Arizona (the first was in the late 1880s after Cajeme's execution).

After 1900 the pace of deportation increased, slowed at first by opposition from mining interests and old hacendado families like the Maytorenas of Guaymas who believed that forcibly removing the Yaquis meant the loss of a cheap labor source. By 1906–1907 total deportation was being enforced by the combined efforts of the federal army and the Sonoran police.[56] To escape deportation and slavery in Oaxaca and the Yucatán, as well as the army, secret police, and Yaqui informers (*torocoyoris* or *to'o coyeris;* traitors) in the Yaqui valley, many Yaqui families sought shelter in other Sonoran haciendas and mining communities, as well as mining camps and railroad towns in Arizona. To curtail this activity, Díaz effectively expanded the rural constabulary that his predecessor had founded known as the *Rurales* (as one writer has suggested a sort of combination of the Texas Rangers and Spain's *Guardia Civil*).[57]

Colonel Emilio Kosterlitzky, commander of the rurales in Izábel's area of northern Sonora, was given explicit instructions to prevent the flight of Yaquis to Arizona. He was notorious for his activity that included catching fugitives, breaking up their families, and sending their children to be adopted by Mexican families in Hermosillo. Until 1907 the escaping Indians were considered political refugees. When the depression of 1907 resulted in layoffs in the railroad and mining industries, the policy changed. In 1907 Kosterlitzky teamed up with Arizona Rangers across the border to prevent the Yoeme from arriving in Arizona.[58] Although the rurales were not as effective in the rest of the Republic, and as southerners they were not popular in northern Mexico, they were ruthlessly efficient in Sonora.[59]

Between 1900 and 1908 probably as many as 6,000 Yaquis were deported from Sonora. Most were sent to be slave laborers, house servants, or debt peons on the henequen plantations of Yucatán, over 2,500 miles from their Río Yaqui homes. Some were also exported to work on the sugar plantations in the Valle Nacional in Oaxaca. Others went to the territory of Quintana Roo (east of Yucatán), Campeche (south of Yucatán), or were incarcerated in Hermosillo.[60] As Yaqui informants tell it, "Yoeme men and women were captured and tied together with a neck noose and forced to walk to Guaymas. Most Yoeme children were sold to wealthy Mexican families, or killed."[61] As the authorities viewed it, one way to dispose of the Yaquis was to destabilize them by breaking up families, the basic unit of Yoeme society.

Many contemporary critics of Porfirio Díaz's government have asserted that the Sonoran triumvirate of Torres–Izábel–Corral prospered financially from the deportation. According to historian Carleton Beals, the triumvirate, also known to their critics as the Torres clan, "netted so much per head on each Yaqui sold into Yucatán, stole Yaqui lands, trafficked in government military supplies, cleaned up on campaign expenses." Another scholar-critic, Ernest Gruening, noted that "General Luis Torres of Sonora, who speculated in Yaquis, selling them [sic] arms at high prices through intermediaries ... and netting so much per head for each of them sold into slavery in Yucatán, likewise emerged four times a peso millionaire." As for Governor Izábel, again according to Beals, he "once floutingly had his picture taken with eleven Yaqui heads, three of them stuck on bayonets."[62]

Ramón Corral, the Sonoran who was Vice President in the latter years of the Díaz administration, and Olegario Molina, Minister of Development, a henequen planter himself in Yucatán, insisted that Yaqui labor was superior to that of Maya Indians and had to be the main source of workers in the henequen industry. Molina had earlier given a huge grant of land in the Yaqui valley to American interests. All of these men rationalized their behavior by arguing that the Yaquis were a vanishing people and only by forcing them to work would they be able to survive as "civilized" peoples. As the Díaz-friendly US correspondent James Creelmen said in 1911, "President Díaz was confronted with but two alternatives: either the Yaqui must be exterminated or they must be deported ... . This stern, but comparatively merciful, policy has practically settled the fearful Yaqui question, and to-day a thousand new forces of production are at work in Sonora."[63] So the czars of progress were killing two birds with one stone, bringing modernization and development to both Sonora and the Yucatán.

The removal process of the Díaz era was accomplished through the use of government personnel known as *enganchadores*. These individuals, basically bounty hunters working for the triumvirate, would round up Yaquis (sometimes, according to the American muckraker John Kenneth Turner, including anyone who looked like a Yaqui such as Opata or Pima Indians) and encarcerate them at Hermosillo. From there the unlucky ones (not to mention the really unlucky ones who were executed) who were not released were herded on to boxcars bound for the Sonoran port of Guaymas.[64]

A few were ordered to hike to the port city, a distance of 84 miles. As the Yaquis tell it, "Yoeme men and women were captured and tied together and forced to walk to Guaymas." Prior to the forced walk, families were separated, and children were put up for adoption. Romana Sanchez said, *"Tu'isi bwanne ume hamuchim vem kunawam into vem asoawaim nuk saka'awao"* ("The women cried much when their husbands and young sons were being taken away").[65]

The Guaymas captives would then be shipped by boat in a month long trip to Oaxaca and/or the Yucatán peninsula. The entire trip amounted to 2,500 to 3,000 miles depending on the route. From Guaymas the boat would go first to San Blas, near Tepic in Nayarit, or Manzanillo (today a popular tourist town off the coast of Colima). Today, the Pascua Yaquis relate that "During the forced trip to Mansanillo, many Yoeme men and women were thrown overboard when they died or got sick."[66]

From here the "large ships," as the Yaqui described them, continued along the coast to Salina Cruz in Oaxaca. At Salina Cruz the group was split up, with a minority going to the Valle Nacional in Oaxaca while the others went to the Yucatán plantations, either by way of cattle car to Veracruz and then by boat to the Yucatecan port of Progreso, or by a forced march 653 miles across the isthmus of Tehuantepec to Mérida. Newspaper reports from 1900 indicated that 250 widows and their children walked from Salina Cruz to the henequen fields. Old Pascua Yaqui resident Anselma Anguis Tonopuame'a said that her aunt Joaquina and others "walked to Yucatan and were placed in big houses to work as slaves." Joaquina cried every day and her tears fell into the tortilla dough she was making. She would say "They [the Mexicans] ate my tears."[67]

In southeastern Mexico, henequen (and sisal) and sugar cultivation required a lot of semi-skilled labor to plant and harvest the agave and sugar. While some machinery was available, it was still possible in a labor scarce area to use workers whose aggregate cost was less than machinery. At first the labor supply came from the defenseless Maya communities whose men and women were pressed into service either as field hands or domestic workers. But there were not enough Mayas to meet the demands of an expanding industry.[68]

The southern planters turned to outside sources. Indentured servants from China and Korea were introduced to the henequen fields. There was even an attempt to buy workers from Italy. As it turned out, the Asians could not stand the humidity and heat, while the Europeans were too expensive. Given these conditions the planters turned to deported Yaquis (two-thirds of whom died in their first year of service on the plantations usually due to the high humidity), convict laborers, political dissenters, the unemployed, and vagabonds who had been kidnapped from the streets, to meet their labor demands. Needless to say, all of these groups were considered "criminal" by the standards of Porfirio Díaz's Mexico.[69]

Some of the heartbreak of deportation can be seen in the testimony of Rosalio Valencia. Rosalio, born in Mineral Colorada in 1896, was forced, after the Mazocoba massacre, to move along with his grandparents from the Colorada Mine in 1900 to the state capital of Hermosillo. Eventually, as described below, his grandfather was deported. In 1905 his family migrated to Arizona, following Rosalio's father who had entered the Arizona territory a year earlier. In 1934 he met and worked as an interpreter for anthropologist W. C. Holden. For the next 20 years Rosalio travelled back and forth between Texas in the summer and Tucson and the Yaqui villages in the winter. Influenced by Holden, Rosario began his personal chronicle, that is, his life story, in the spring of 1954. Although he was less fluent in English than in either Spanish or Yaqui, he preferred to write in English. The unedited manuscript, filled with grammatical errors and colloquialisms, is what follows. The edited version, in which Rosalio Valencia is known as Rosalio Moisés, was published under the title *The Tall Candle*[70]:

The Life Story of Rosalio Valencia

I born in September the 4–4 oclock dawn 1896. My grand father was a Shoes maker. His name is Nicolas Cochemea Valencia ... . When I get at Hermosillo, Daily I saw the Mexican authority bring the yaquis family from every place of Sonora where they living. The poor Yaquis is only worker peoples. But when the Mexican authority bring them at Hermosillo, They said They caught them in the mount. and every time, they bring the poor Yaquis at Hermosillo, they hang up about 15 or 20 yaquis ... . Well then after 5 years we living at Hermosillo, one early morning about 6: A.M. The Mexicans Soldiers and few of the Yaquis soldiers surrounding our house. and one of the officer. whos name is lieutenant colonel Luis Medinas Baron. He ask my grand father. He said. your name is Nicolas Zapatero he said. and my grand father answer him yes sir I am he said. and then the lieutenant colonel look him up and down and then he said where is your son Martin and my grand father answer him I don't know nothing about my son he said. Oh yes said the' lieutenant .... your son is ride up and down in the mount with a whole bunch of Yaquis and I know too he is captain of the indians he said. and my grand father didn't answer any more. Well then, the lieutenant said alright sergeant and one soldier begin to tie his both arms and then they take him to Hermosillo .... well then after they carry along my grand father.? my grandmother and my aunt and all of the children start to weep ... .the next day we wake up early morning ... and then we go out see the next rich men ... [when the grandmother returns] she said the richer mens told us They can't save him. that all we heard from them. She said. and then all the children start to weeping again. well then. after 7 days my grand father was in the jail. I guess the load of the Yaquis was already complete to pull out to Guaymas and about 6:P.M. The train leave at Hermosillo to Guaymas with 8 Box Cars. all the box cars was full of the yaquis prisoners. And there is the last time we saw the train. Where my grand father was shipment with many Yaquis. and forever. we never heard from him any more.? and he was the last shoes maker. among all the yaquis tribes.[71]

And so, as Rosario testifies, the Yaquis lost their shoemaker to the hidden dangers of the ocean waters and henequen fields.

Another Yaqui testimony comes from Josefa (Chepa) Moreno, who was born sometime around 1890 at La Colorada Mine, Sonora. Chepa had bitter memories about the deportation, the hardships she endured, including her life as a "slave" in Yucatán, and the deaths of her seven babies. When she was freed from service in the henequen fields by the Mexican revolutionaries who overthrew Díaz in 1910, she joined the Mexican Revolution (1910–1920) as a *soldadera* (female soldier and revolutionary) who fought with the Carrancistas (followers of Venustiano Carranza who was an enemy of Francisco "Pancho" Villa) at the battles of Aguascalientes, Zacatecas, and Celaya in Guanajuato. After the Revolution she returned to a neighborhood outside of Hermosillo where she spent the rest of her life.[72]

The relative comfort of her early life in La Colorada came to an end with the already mentioned Mazocoba Massacre of 1900. That event splintered her nuclear family as Chepa moved to Hermosillo with her father's half-brother Abelardo Cochemea and his wife. At the young age of 14 Chepa was married to Pedro Alvarez in an arranged wedding. Pedro, never faithful, went out with women that Chepa described as "bad" but not prostitutes because they were Yaqui and not Mexican. Within a year of her marriage Chepa was pregnant, and when the baby was only a few months old soldiers arrested first, Abelardo, and later Pedro and Chepa. Not long after Abelardo was deported, Pedro and Chepa, pregnant again, and with her infant son Carlos, were deported. With

300 Yaquis rounded up, the group was herded into railroad cars, "just stuffed in like goats" according to Chepa. At Guaymas they were crammed into a boat for San Blas. Both the pregnant Chepa and her baby boy were sick, but they were restricted below deck in crowded rooms and were not allowed on the upper level.[73]

From San Blas, the Yaquis were forced to march to Tepic, where men and women were separated. Again they were crowded into the army post. It was here where the infant Carlos died of hunger and thirst. She begged to be allowed to bury her son, but she was forced back into the barracks. She was certain that they "threw the baby to the dogs since they would not let her bury him." Unlike other Yaqui prisoners, they did not continue down the coast. Instead, after being escorted to the railhead at San Marcos, Jalisco, they entrained for Guadalajara and Mexico City. With little clothing she felt the cold of Mexico City. Sleeping on the frigid dirt floor, she never forgot the pain of her pregnancy and her hunger and thirst. Eventually, now reunited with her husband, she went to Veracruz by train and on to Progreso by boat, passing through Mérida and finally arriving at the Hacienda Nokak. At the hacienda the men were assigned to work in the henequen fields, while women like Chepa cooked and prepared meals in a communal kitchen. Even while pregnant she was beaten and whipped several times. Chepa's second baby, named Nicolás, because he was born on the saint's day, soon sickened and died. All together she bore seven children and lost all of them in exile. When the Yaqui interment was over in 1910 she returned to Mexico City and joined the Revolution.[74]

Sadly, akin to situations elsewhere in the Greater Southwest, sexual abuse of Indian women was very common. In the vicinity of Hermosillo many *dueños* or property owners exploited Yaqui girls and women. For example, Arturo León (a Spaniard with a heavy black beard), the dueño of a large farm called Ranchito, had sex with any of his worker's women that caught his fancy. He fathered an unlimited number of children by Yaqui women.[75] In Yucatán hacienda foremen, not only forced pregnant women to work and tore their children from them, but also forced sexual unions between Yaqui women and Mayan or Chinese laborers in hopes of selling the babies for financial gain.[76]

In early 1910, Don Enrique Segura of Jalapa, Veracruz, an engineering student, spent a short vacation from school at one of the infamous haciendas of the Valle Nacional. There he witnessed that "the peons were locked up at night in a sort of barracks or barn-like structure so they couldn't run away. Armed Spanish guards were the 'foremen' and hacienda police." A day or two before he was to leave to return to his studies, an Indian, who was a house servant or *mozo de confianza* of the master, killed one of the Spanish guards. When the man was questioned about the incident, "He told the *patron* that the Spaniard entered his *choza* [hovel or shanty] and was attempting to violate the girl. The father killed him there, in his own home, defending his [teen-aged] daughter."[77]

Between 1882 (at the beginning of the Porfiriato) and 1935 (after the Mexican Revolution was concluded and Lázaro Cárdenas was president), Yaqui families and individuals made their way to Arizona. Guerrilla warfare in Hiakam continued throughout the decade of the 1920s, with Yaquis constantly on the move seeking refuge and security. In the early 1880s Yaquis were hired by the New Mexico and Arizona Railroad with workers being attracted to Benson, Patagonia, Sahuarita, Nogales, and Tucson. Most laborers lived with their families in rail cars equipped with sleeping space and stoves and were accompanied by a commissary and water tank car.[78]

Other Yaquis ventured as far north as Phoenix seeking employment on farms, ranches, and mining towns. The Yaqui community of Guadalupe, immediately south of Tempe, Arizona, was founded between 1900 and 1910. Today over 5,000 people inhabit Guadalupe, perhaps a third of them Yaqui (the town is 72% Hispanic). A branch of Guadalupe is the diminishing neighborhood of the Penjamo Yaqui tribe of Scottsdale. While outsiders may not distinguish between Yaquis and Mexicans, the Yoemen know the difference. The other major Yaqui communities in Arizona are Barrio Libre (south Tucson), Yoem Pueblo in Marana, Arizona (Yaqui population no more than 40 individuals as of 2010), New Pascua, and Old Pascua.[79]

The history of Old Pascua, the first formally established Yaqui neighborhood in Tucson, makes for a most interesting study. Shortly after 1900 Yaqui refugees squatted on unoccupied land between the Southern Pacific Railroad tracks to the east and the Santa Cruz River to the west. The neighborhood, several miles northwest of Tucson (which had been incorporated in 1877), was called Bwia Bwalko. In 1921 several local businessmen came to Juan Pistola, a self-proclaimed Yaqui leader, and proposed the relocation of the Bwia Bwalko community to a 40 acre area a few miles south and east of Bwia Bwalko and northwest of Tucson. The area had been sub-divided into lots and was available for purchase by the Yoemen. Initially many of the Yaquis were suspicious of the offer. This was due to both a traditional distrust of outsiders, and also, because many of them were aiding the guerrilla effort in Sonora by supplying materiel and shelter to Yoemen warriors, they preferred to keep a low profile. In any case, on Easter Sunday 1921, the squatters moved to the new community named Pascua, the Spanish word for Easter.[80]

At Pascua they once again "squatted" on the land, building their humble shelters out of scrap metal and lumber. The nearness of the railroad tracks provided them with transportation, as well as railroad ties that could be used to support door and window spaces throughout the one or two-room dwellings. Usually these houses had a branched structure attached to the main dwelling. This served as an open-sided ramada for cooking and outdoor living. Most had dirt floors, and perhaps a surrounding fence. The yard was decorated with a simple wooden cross. The promoters eventually sold their interest in the properties to the city of Tucson, since collecting from the "squatters" was a continual problem. With Tucson now inheriting the problem community, the city fathers toiled in vain to collect public taxes. By 1950 the city had expanded beyond Pascua, and yori infiltration, teen-age crimes, and a culture of illegal drugs led many Yoemen to move southwest of the city to what eventually became New Pascua Pueblo. In 1978 the community of New Pascua won federal recognition as a US Indian Tribe, and as such, access to the resources of the Bureau of Indian Affairs.[81]

In the 1930s it appeared that the years of fighting would pay off for the Yaquis. Cárdenas became president in 1934, and by late 1937 he created the Yaqui Zona Indigena. The land on the north bank of the Río Yaqui was reserved for the Yoemen. This area included the traditional pueblos as well as the Bacatete range. Although other Indian groups were granted the use of *ejidos* or communal lands, only the Yaquis had their own special reserve. However, the land reforms came too late to preserve Yaqui culture.

By the 1940s and the economic boom of World War II the new agriculture came to Sonora. This was technology and capital intensive, not labor intensive. New hydraulic projects, such as the Obregón Dam completed in 1952, meant that the Mexican state could control the Yaqui life blood of water. About the same time collectives in the Yaqui Valley were broken up. The state's ejido banks could control credit, and credit would only go for the new agriculture that would create fruits, grain, and crops for export such as oranges, grapes, wheat, chickpeas, and cotton—not corn, beans, and squashes. Machinery took the place of labor, and when it did the Yaquis lost their best weapon. Unskilled labor and subsistence agriculture were relegated to the past.[82]

With over 5,000 Yaquis scattered across the United States, and another 20,000 spread throughout Mexico, pascolas, Maso deer dancers, and the *sea ania* or "flower world" are the pre-Christian symbols that will allow the Yaqui to retain their identity. Yaqui self-awareness can be ignited by the poems that sing the songs of the past:

> For Indians of my native race
> All were persecuted, young and old.
> The wolf was on every trace.
> To away with every Indian household.
> From the great haciendas all over,
> The innocent workers were taken,
> Peons who were all peace lovers,
> But were Indians, thus forsaken.
> Those who were caught were cast in jail.
> "Las embarcaciones ya se van"
> Was then made a song and tale,
> Yaquis taken to Yucatán.

Excerpt from "The Yaquis in Sonora in 1904," an autobiographical poem by Refugio Savala.[83] He was called "Refugio" by his mother who took him as a refugee to Arizona.

Afterthoughts: a Yaqui Way of Knowledge

In 1973 a Peruvian named Carlos Castaneda received a PhD in anthropology at the University of California, Los Angeles. The field reports that were the substance of his dissertation reportedly documented his interviews with and apprenticeship under a mystical old Yaqui Indian named Don Juan Matos that lasted from the summer of 1961 through September 1965. Don Juan was supposedly a Yaqui shaman who lived in Sonora and Arizona. Through the use of peyote, magic mushrooms, and other hallucinogenic drugs, Castaneda the apprentice learned the mysteries of ancient Yaqui mystics. In 1968 the first of Castaneda's writings, *The Teaching of Don Juan: A Yaqui Way of Knowledge* was published.

Very quickly the "new age" advocates of the 1970s—hippies, self-transcenders, pundits, readers, sorcerers, the "Fellow Travelers of Awareness," Timothy Leary psychics, and even a few anthropology professors—jumped on the "energy field" bandwagon that revealed a "nonordinary" reality unknown to everyday science. As the public became aware of *A Yaqui Way of Knowledge*, Castaneda's popularity soared, and he eventually produced an additional 11 books.

On one of his early trips to the border area Castaneda allegedly spent an entire night rolling around on Don Juan's porch searching for the *assemblage point* or spot where a zillion number of energy fields converged. At one point in the early morning hours he became aware of a point in the middle of the floor where he noticed a brilliant color in the periphery of his vision in which a greenish light became purple. He eventually found another spot that had colors associated with it. One spot would create energy, the other would deplete it. This was the beginning of a voyage that would lead to a new vision of a new "inner" reality.[84]

Unfortunately, as early as 1976 Castaneda's epoch was grinding to a halt as critics and disbelievers fell off the energy wagon. The suffering visionary was losing his friends and his vision. One of his earliest distracters was Richard de Mille who called Castenada "one of the world's great hoaxers." He pointed out that the so-called field reports contradicted one another and that somehow in translating Don Juan's Spanish he resurrected the English phrases of hack writers whose major works were still available in occult bookstores. *The Yaqui Way of Knowledge* was nothing other than a hodgepodge of American Indian folklore, European philosophy, and oriental mysticism. De Mille asked "How many stylistic echoes would be needed to prove that Don Juan's teachings and

Carlos's adventures originated not in the Sonoran desert but in the library at UCLA?" Eventually anthropologists like W. C. Holden, Jane Holden Kelley, and Edward Spicer came to question the accuracy of Castaneda's work. He became known as the "Shaman of Academe," the Coyote Trickster and magician that most Indian "witchdoctors" were.[85]

Castaneda died in 1998 at the age of 72. Although he still has his defenders, the brilliance of his reputation has surely dimmed. Perhaps Castaneda, instead of using Don Juan's porch, should have rolled on his stomach through the ravines and canyons of the Bacatete Mountains. He could have practiced a kind of historical anthropology that would have revealed the Maso deer dancers, pascolas, and the *sea ania* flower world of the Yaqui people. That would have been a genuine spiritual voyage.

10

Epilogue: After Relocation, from Geronimo to Houser

North America was already inhabited when Europeans arrived, and from their first days on this continent, Europeans relied on Native peoples for guidance, hospitality, and survival. American historians since the days of the Puritans have tried to rationalize Europeans' taking of Indian lands and lives, and all Indian peoples have endured the many traumas of contact and colonization.

Ned Blackhawk, *Violence over the Land*[1]

Many of us, me particularly, are from the units that have hurt you over the many years. We came. We fought you. We took your land. We signed treaties that we broke. We stole minerals from your sacred hills. We blasted the faces of our presidents onto your sacred mountain. Then we took more land and then we took your children and then we tried ... to eliminate your language that God gave you, and the Creator gave you. We didn't respect you, we polluted your Earth, we've hurt you in so many ways but we have come to say that we are sorry.

Wesley Clark Jr., *Standing Rock, North Dakota, December, 2016*[2]

In looking at Indian–white relations in a world history context, it is obvious that the demographic disaster that the American Indian experienced from 1492 through the early twentieth century, with lingering effects today, was one of the more disastrous events of modern history. Without demeaning the seriousness of the Nazi atrocities toward Jews, gypsies, Slavs, and homosexuals, genocidal activity and holocausts have occurred throughout modern history. The events that took place in the Greater Southwest between 1830 and 1890 were simply the last phase of an ongoing history of genocide that started with

Lost Worlds of 1863: Relocation and Removal of American Indians in the Central Rockies and the Greater Southwest, First Edition. W. Dirk Raat.

Columbus and was pursued by Spaniards, Portuguese, Dutchmen, Englishmen, and the French throughout the colonial and early modern period.

While scholarly opinion varies, the pre-contact population of the Americas may have been somewhere between 75 and 100 million. If these numbers are correct, then after three generations of *conquistadores* and Spanish settlers the population declined to nearly 90% of that number or around 12.5 million. Although the first generation of Spaniards may have been unaware that they were carrying microbes that would destroy the Indian communities, later generations were certainly aware of the impact of European diseases like smallpox on the indigenous populations.

Indian deaths, either by disease and/or genocide, were rationalized by Christian colonists as the "judgment of God." For example, in the late sixteenth century Catholic friars in Guatemala said that it was "the secret judgment of God" that was "responsible for demolishing the Mayan population of the area." The next century witnessed the Puritan minister Cotton Mather rejoicing that "God ended the controversy [with the Pequots] by sending the smallpox amongst the Indians." In 1863 the Mormons of Cache Valley celebrated the genocidal victory over the Northwestern Shoshone at Bear River as "an intervention of the Almighty."

The King of Spain may have been concerned about preserving a diminishing supply of labor, but the colonists were well aware that depopulation meant more land for them to settle while the Catholic missionaries knew that epidemics in which Indian priests were rendered helpless could not but help their own Christian conversion efforts. Enslavement and malnutrition inflicted on the Indians by Europeans eventually led to weaker immune systems for the Native population resulting in the spread of smallpox, measles, flu, and other diseases. By the 1830s the US Army was pursuing genocide through microbes by deliberately dispensing "trade blankets" containing smallpox to the Indians. Many of the pandemics that occurred from northern California to the Kiowas and Comanches of west Texas were facilitated by the microscopic organism that was the invisible invader.

As for relocating the Indians, as early as the 1850s California settlers and militia volunteers were forcibly moving the Indians from their homelands. After 1860 forced marches of Paiute, Navajo, Apache, and Yavapai peoples were organized and carried out by the US Army. Internment followed the marches, with the Paiute herded into corrals near Fort Tejon while the Navajo were prisoners at Bosque Redondo. While the Yavapai were interned along with their Apache cousins in the desolate San Carlos Reservation, the Chiricahua Apaches passed through San Carlos on their way to imprisonment in Florida.

These coercive "walks" not only resulted in a loss of territory and a sense of identity for the Native peoples, but were usually accompanied by enslavement, sexual harassment, and direct and indirect killing of individuals. Rendered destitute and homeless, dislocation also produced famine conditions and increased infertility rates. Finally, dislocation was associated with economic ruin for the Indians who had to give up their traditions of hunting and gathering. Kit Carson implemented the "scorched earth" policy of his military superiors, poisoning the wells, burning hogans, destroying peach orchards and Navajo corn fields. By 1868 Custer's regiments were slaughtering Indian ponies so that the natives could not subsist by hunting. And by the 1870s General Phil Sheridan was exterminating bison so as to destroy the "Indian commissary."[3]

The most extreme form of direct killing was the massacre of innocent women and children, and one of the earlier examples was the Bear River Massacre of 1863 when Shoshone Indians were killed, raped, and mutilated. This massacre, although not the first to occur in the West, did become a precedent for others that followed, especially the Sand Creek Massacre in Colorado that next year. Both of these massacres were examples of the militarization of the American Indian policy, a policy that started with removal and ended with extermination. Both were characterized by mass rapes, sexual violence, and mutilation with sexual overtones. At Sand Creek the troops, led by the officer corps, not only scalped the dead, but manufactured tobacco pouches out of male genitalia. After the massacre the citizenry of Denver celebrated their victory by waving Indian scalps and other war trophies, including female genitals stretched over saddle pommels.[4] Although not intrinsically a white man's custom, this kind of mutilation had a long history in the United States, going back to colonial days and the early nineteenth century era of Indian fighter Andy Jackson and his friends.[5]

As for decapitation and scalping, while some Indian groups engaged in the practice,[6] it became a common Anglo-American practice at the end of the eighteenth century and the beginning of the nineteenth. Most Indians were fearful of the bodies of dead people, especially their enemies. Most had to undergo purification ceremonies after having made contact with their dead opponents. Scalping undoubtedly was increased after the British brought their version to the Americas, a method of dealing with their Scottish and Irish enemies in the British Empire. Initially it was a way to terrorize the enemy and a method for counting the dead.[7] Eventually, instead of placing a bounty on heads, non-Indians encouraged the taking of scalps.

After Spain was expelled from Mexico in 1821, the Mexicans, lacking the resources to administer the northern frontier, used a bounty system to encourage bounty hunters to assist in pacifying the frontier and in so doing profit by taking scalps. These bounty hunters included Americans as well as

Mexicans, and while the prized scalp might be that of an Apache, it often included the dark haired scalps of Mexicans and persons of mixed ancestry.

Particular exceptions to the genocidal practices of the American government and western settlers should be noted. Akin to conditions in Nazi Europe when Polish farmers secretly provided provisions for their Jewish neighbors, or the Dutch family that protected Anne Frank in Holland, so too American Indians had their defenders.

For example, there was the abolitionist William Lloyd Garrison, who as early as 1829 fought for the Indians, like Africans, to be free of the institution of slavery, and abolitionist Wendell Phillips who spoke against Indian slavery. There was also Captain Silas S. Soule who attempted to intervene with Colonel John M. Chivington on behalf of the Indians of Colorado, or the US Senator who was shouted down in an opera house in Denver suggesting that the Colorado Indians should be educated rather than killed. Captain John Cremony tried without success to befriend the Mescalero Indians. Senator Charles Sumner strived to abolish slavery in New Mexico and was instrumental in getting the Peonage Act of 1867 passed.[8] In 1853 a young Captain Ulysses S. Grant sympathized with the Native Americans near the Columbia Barracks (Fort Vancouver) who were being abused by corrupt whites.[9] After 1886 General George Crook advocated for the humane treatment of Chiricahua Apaches in the Florida prisons.

There was, of course, Sarah Winnemucca who, as an acculturated Paiute, never forgot her own people and attempted to protect them from the more extreme actions of her white friends, even going so far as to attempt to create an Indian version of the boarding school idea. There was Mormon missionary Daniel Jones, the founder of Camp Utah in Arizona, who enlisted the assistance of O'odham and Pee Posh Indians in several building and construction projects. Many of the Saints were offended by Jones' "dirty Indians" and so they left Camp Utah for the San Pedro River to establish the town of St. David. Unfortunately, the exceptions were few and far between.

The story of relocation and removal of the American Indian in the Greater Southwest during the nineteenth century is one in which a variety of tales need to be told to present a complete picture.[10] It starts with the relocation of the Santee Dakotas and Winnebagos from Minnesota to Dakota Territory and the Missouri River area in 1863. Relocation and removal covered a wide spectrum, with extermination of the Northwestern Shoshone at Bear River on one end of the scale, and the gradual removal of the O'odham peoples who lost their lands to encroaching settlers at the other.

As can be seen, the friends of the Americans, such as the O'odham who provided foodstuffs and shelter to American emigrants as well as military service against the Apache and Yavapai for the US Army, or the Colorado Utes who were strong allies of the Union forces against their Confederate foes, did not fare well in the long run. Although both received reservation areas after the Civil War, both were eventually forced to either lose land and water and/or remove themselves out of the white man's way. Many O'odham were forced to trade their traditional ways for low status jobs in the white man's world. As for the Colorado Utes, although originally given a huge area in western Colorado as a reward for their service to the Union Army, it was not long before the northern Utes were squeezed out of Colorado to a small reservation in the Uintah Basin of northeastern Utah (leaving today the small Mountain Ute Indian reservation in far southwestern Colorado and the Southern Ute Indians near Ignacio, Colorado).

Mid-way along our theoretical spectrum were the Yaquis who became political refugees in southern Arizona in order to flee from Mexican government extermination and deportation policies and practices. Also near this part of the spectrum were the "force march" peoples such as the Owens Valley Paiutes, Yavapai, Apache, and Navajo. After relocation, when the Paiute and Yavapai returned to their homeland, they discovered that white interlopers had taken the best land and waterworks. The Chiricahua Apache never returned to their southeastern Arizona homeland, resettling in Oklahoma or among the Mescaleros of New Mexico. The Navajos worked out a treaty arrangement in which they were allowed to return to a part of their original homeland, an area most whites did not want at the time. Unfortunately, the Navajo Treaty of 1868 did not mention their neighbors, the Hopi. Thus the Hopis have been involved for over 150 years in a land dispute with their Navajo neighbors.

In addition to the Colorado Utes, another Great Basin group was the Western Shoshone, an indigenous people who had treaty rights to most of eastern Nevada. Because the land was so desolate they were mostly ignored by the federal government for over 80 years until World War II and the atomic age created a need for land that could be used for experimental bomb blasts and atomic wastes. Then they were no longer ignored, and in the process they lost many of their land rights to the federal government and shyster lawyers. A 1962 hearing of the Indian Claims Commission determined that the Shoshone title to land "was extinguished by the gradual encroachment by whites."[11]

The Greater Southwest and Other Sub-themes

The Greater Southwest, including the Great Basin (what would be called the Greater Northwest from the Mexico City point of view) can be defined as that area of the United States and Mexico that runs from the Pacific Ocean in the west to mid-Kansas in the east, and from the 42nd parallel (the northern boundaries of California, Nevada, and Utah, including the Great Basin which extends into southern Idaho) in the north and southward to the Tropic of Cancer in north central Mexico. Through this region an international line was drawn between 1848 and 1853 that divided the country of Mexico from the United States. This area, sometimes called MexAmerica today, shares similar social, economic, and cultural themes.

Historically MexAmerica is a unified region with cultural and social influences moving back and forth across today's invisible international boundary. In pre-contact times Mesoamerica overlapped with the northern frontier sending foodstuffs (like chocolate), parrot feathers, copper bells, ceramics, jade, irrigation technology, and religious ideas (like the Katsina cult or the Quetzalcoatl legend) north, while returning with products from the American Southwest and mid-lands like bison skins, turquoise, pine nuts, or even Indian slaves.

After 1500 the region was known as the Spanish borderlands and witnessed activity by conquerors, Franciscan and Jesuit friars, Spanish governors, ranchers, *hacendados*, small farmers, and miners. It was here where the infamous 1680 Pueblo Revolt took place, and the area where Franciscans established 21 religious outposts between 1769 and 1833. From 1821 to 1845 the region known as the Mexican frontier was called El Norte and was a time when the "barbarous" Indians, especially the Apaches, made constant forays into northern Mexico and along the Old Spanish Trail.

After the Mexican–American War of 1845 the northern part of this region was incorporated into the United States. The Gadsden Treaty of 1853 defined the international boundary between the two states. But that boundary was more an illusion than a reality, as Mexicans, Americans, and American Indians continued to travel without restriction back and forth.

After 1857 as the Mormon empire extended beyond the Salt Lake Valley, missionaries and Saints established contacts and communities throughout the Greater Southwest. They went beyond Fort Hall in Idaho, as well as throughout the fertile Cache Valley of Utah and Idaho. They settled southwest Utah and the Kaibab plateau of northern Arizona, relocating and converting many southern Paiutes in the process. Mormon migrants pushed across the Colorado River at the Hole-in-the-Rock to settle southeastern Utah, and they crossed Lee's Ferry to establish communities along the Little Colorado River in today's Arizona, and later went south to the Salt River Valley, the Gila River country, and the San Pedro River area. Hopis were initially converted, while the settlements in Mesa and Tempe saw the conversion of many O'odham people. While some of the Saints went west through Nevada and southern California, others ventured as far south as Chihuahua, Mexico. During the nineteenth century the predominant religious order throughout the Greater Southwest was not the Catholics or the Presbyterians, but the Mormons. If Catholicism defined the colonial era, and Methodism and "frontier revivalism" the early national period, then Mormonism was synonymous with the nineteenth century Greater Southwest, especially the intermountain west.

After 1870 Apaches and Yaquis were active on both sides of the border. While the southern Chiricahuas lived near the Bavispe River in Sonora and north-western Chihuahua, Cochise's band of Central Chiricahuas roamed between the San Pedro Valley of Arizona through the mountains of southwestern New Mexico and northern Chihuahua. These bands often made raids on ranches in Sonora and then crossed over the boundary to sell their stolen goods to American merchants and traders.

The Yeomen or Yaquis were part of a global economic network that spanned the region of the Greater Southwest. Yaqui slaves were deported from Sonora to henequen plantations in the Yucatán, from whence the henequen was trans-ported to New Orleans to be manufactured into bailing material for use by combines and harvester in the American and Canadian plains. The Yaquis, of course, eventually sought refuge in the United States after 1880 (especially the territory of Arizona) to escape the extermination and deportation policies of the Porfirio Díaz government.

And the O'odham peoples had their homeland divided when the interna-tional boundary was established by two national states that had no interest in maintaining the integrity or identity of O'odham Indians. All of these groups were truly residents, not only of the Southwest, but of the Greater Southwest.

Since the Greater Southwest comprises the four major North American deserts—Sonoran, Mojave, the Great Basin, and Chihuahua—water and conflict among people over its use has been a major historical theme (see map, Figure 10.1). Disputes occurred between settlers and Indians over water rights, just as there were conflicts between and among white settlers, or Americans and Mexicans over grazing rights and water use. The Owens Valley Paiutes learned early on that outsiders would encroach upon their hunting and fishing grounds, and by the early twentieth century the thirst and appetite of Los Angelinos for water would lead to the construction of the Los Angeles Aqueduct and the drying up of Owens Lake. The 2015 drought in contemporary California has led to too many straws sipping up Central Valley waters. With limited sur-face water the farmers of the Central Valley have increased their drilling for underground water, which in turn has dried up many aquifers leading to "sub-sidence" in some areas of the Central Valley. For example, Sack Dam, south of Merced, was (as of 2015) sinking as much as a foot a year.

The Yaqui resistance movement was squelched after 1940 by moderniza-tion and an aggressive state bureaucracy. The Obregón dam completed in

GREAT NORTH AMERICAN DESERT

Ⓝ Great Basin

Ⓜ Mojave

Ⓐ Sonoran

Ⓒ Chihuahuan

Figure 10.1 *Great North American Desert*. Reconfigured by Geraldine Raat from Information Found in Alice Jablonsky, *Desert Life* (Western National Parks Assoc., 1994), P. 3.

1952 meant that the Mexican government would control the Yaqui life blood of water. State *ejido* banks were initiated that manipulated the credit system of the Yoemen people. Technology and machinery eliminated the need for unskilled labor, and by so doing accomplished what the Spanish and Mexican armies had not been able to do—overcome Yaqui opposition and end the traditional ways of the Yoemen. The Mexican state sought to promote an end to Indian folkways and belief systems. Its goal was Mexicanization, not *indigenismo*.

In Arizona, where the O'odham experience (akin to that of the Colorado River Indians) meant that irrigation ditches, canals, pipelines, and reservoirs constructed by the white man only led to the deaths of the Gila and Santa Cruz Rivers. Hydraulic technology changed the natural environment. Today, in the twenty-first century, the Wilcox area of southeastern Arizona (Cochise country) is dry and the farmers, like their California compatriots, are responding by drilling deeper wells. Without the rain and snow that traditionally feed the Wilcox aquifer, combined with increased pumping of underground water by farmers and ranchers, a deficit has been created and the groundwater line is sinking.[12] When the aquifers have finally been depleted the wine grapes will no longer grow, not to mention lettuce, broccoli, and citrus, and the farming industry will come to a halt. Meanwhile, not only is the future of farming in the desert in question, but community members are pitted against one another. As indicated before, with the Indian people finally having their fair share of water, a war between reservation Indians and non-reservation residents over water rights is very likely in the near future.

Warfare between whites and Indians is another sub-theme of this era. The Civil War years, 1861–1865, witnessed more Indian tribes destroyed by whites with more land seizures than in any other comparable period in American history. One explanation for this phenomenon, perhaps, was the magnitude of the disaster of Civil War. The nation had to confront death and destruction in a way that had not been equaled before or since. The casualty figure was close to 1.5 million individuals, with as many as 620,000 Union and Confederate combatants killed. This was more military deaths than the total figure for both World War I and World War II. In the context of this kind of group psychology, a few deaths in Indian wars in the West could be ignored.

In addition, Union hysteria that assumed Confederate plots were behind Indian hostility led to more group violence. Southern secessionists were blamed by Minnesota settlers for the plunder and slaughter of their white neighbors, an ignorance that soon became an expression of a growing national anxiety concerning most of the "agitation" of Indian tribes in the West. One might also note that between the 1830s and the Civil War era political violence surged in the United States, with much of the violence directed at Blacks, abolitionists, immigrants, and Native Americans (at least 35 major riots in the Northeast at this time).[13]

As for those western troops, the militia "volunteers" were more ruthless and threatening to the Indian people than the pre-Civil War Regulars had been. After 1861 most of the professional military went east to join either the Union or Confederate cause. Many of the volunteers were unemployed miners or failed ranchers who took out their frustrations on the Indian peoples of the region. Their activity during the Bear River Massacre is an excellent case of the volunteers' lack of military discipline. That incident, in addition, is a good example of the creeping militarization of Indian policy that was evolving throughout the mid-nineteenth century.

One aspect of the military campaign against the indigenous peoples was the practice of employing Indian allies to serve the white man's cause. From the beginning of the conquest of America Native Americans were used to defeat the indigenous enemy. Hernando Cortés utilized his 20,000 Tlaxcalan allies to defeat the Aztecs of Tenochtitlán. Tlaxcalan troops were later used to pacify the northern frontier, and aided the Spaniards during the Pueblo Revolt of 1680. In the late seventeenth century the Opata Indians were Spanish and Jesuit "allies of convenience" against both the Apache and the O'odham. Around 1763, east of the Mississippi, the French invaders were forming alliances with Hurons to defeat the Iroquois Confederacy and the British army.

In the nineteenth century the O'odham teamed up with Tucson citizens, Mexicans and Americans, to attack the Apache women and children at Camp Grant, while southern Paiutes happily joined the Mormons in attacking their traditional Ute enemies. Mojave Indians aided the US Army in attacking their enemy, the Hualapai. Black "buffalo soldiers" and their Cherokee scout allies fought the Plains Indians.[14] Meanwhile the Utes joined Kit Carson in relocating the Navajos, while the US Army utilized Yavapais and White Mountain Apaches to locate and defeat the remnants of the Chiricahua nation.

As for military tactics, the Apache brought to the theater of war a 44 year experience of guerrilla warfare. Until the mid-1880s the Apaches were militarily superior to American forces. The knowledge of the local environment, including mountainous as well as flat desert terrain, as well as their youth training programs, gave the Apache a major advantage over any interlopers or strangers to their homeland. The physical stamina and knowledge that was necessary for hunting and gathering in rugged terrain was an excellent prelude to ambush and guerrilla tactics. When the technology became available they were flexible enough to change from bow-and-arrow, to Sharps carbines, to, by the 1880s, utilizing Winchester repeating rifles and Springfield single-shot rifles for long-range efficiency. Many of the tactics used by the Apache were shared with their cousins in the field, including the Yaqui guerrilla fighters in the Becatete Mountains of Sonora.

Immediately after the Civil War ex-slaves and other blacks were enlisted in the US Army in segregated units. Known as "buffalo soldiers," many were recruited out of New Orleans and Baton Rouge, home of a large number of black Civil War veterans. By 1867 cavalry regiments had been assigned to Texas, Kansas, and the Indian Territory of Oklahoma. Between 1875 and 1886 many African American units were chasing and fighting Apaches in the District of New Mexico and Arizona, and were involved in the pursuit of Victorio in 1880 and the final chase of Mangas (youngest son of Magnas Coloradas) after Geronimo's surrender of 1886.[15]

Apaches and Utes taunted the "black-whitemen," with the Utes shouting and singing "You ride into battle behind the white soldiers; but you can't take off your black faces, and the white-face soldiers make you ride behind them."[16] For their part, in the context of time and place, it is likely that many of the buffalo soldiers shared the prejudices of some of their white commanders when evaluating the "lesser worth" and "inferior nature" of their indigenous enemies.

The Indian slave trade and Indian slavery is another sub-theme of this work. In pre-contact times many Native American groups practiced a kind of "de facto" slavery or peonage that was kin-ordered and resulted mostly from revenge warfare. Kinship overlapped with slavery as captives were integrated into the tribe. A case in point would be the integration of the Oatman sisters into the Mojave tribe. With the arrival of the Spaniards a second system of slavery developed that was an amalgam of Indian and Spanish practices which mixed the indigenous kin system with Spanish traditions of *compadrazgo* and intermarriage. Finally the northern Europeans introduced chattel slavery in which the slave was simply a movable piece of property. Unlike the earlier forms of Indian slavery, it was usually associated with racism and/or sexism.

From colonial times enslavement of Indians accompanied western expansion, an expansion that was accompanied by violence, rape, and warfare. Between 1670 and 1720 more Indians were exported as slaves to the Caribbean out of Charleston than African slaves were imported, even though Charleston was a major port city for African slaves.

The Indian slave trade flourished in the Greater Southwest during the first three quarters of the nineteenth century. While O'odham were kidnapping Apache children, in the Great Basin Ute Indians captured Paiute women and children and traded them to Mojave merchants or New Mexican traders for horses, blankets, and ceramics from California or Santa Fe. Young female Paiutes brought an especially high price in the Santa Fe market. Because of slave trading by Utes and Mountain Men, the Southern Paiute population was nearly depopulated. By 1863 the Paiute's hate and fear of Ute slave traders was only matched by the Navajo's dislike of the kidnapping of their children by Comanche and New Mexican slave traders. This issue, not the encroachments by American settlers, was the Navajo's major concern.

During the American period many of the western territories passed slave codes not unlike the ones in the South. In New Mexico the 1858 "Otero Slave Code," was supposedly only to apply to African chattel slaves since the Indians were not slaves but "servants," and their obligations to their masters and mistresses were not slavery, but indentured or indebted "servitude." The denial of slavery was rationalized by the fact that this servitude was only imposed on the Indian out of Christian piety and from a desire to civilize the savage beast. In the meantime the Indian had few legal rights, could not take his master to court, could not carry firearms, and had to follow a strict curfew—not unlike the southern codes.

Earlier, when California became a state in 1850 it passed a statute for the "Protection of Indians." In effect, this law extended the Spanish tradition of peonage into post-1850 California. Able bodied Indians who refused to work could be arrested and then bailed out of jail by "any white person" who could then force the Indian to work for that person. Under the apprenticeship clause Indian males under 18 and females under 15 could be legally "apprenticed" to a white person. The law indirectly encouraged a thriving kidnapping trade in women and children, many of whom were used for illicit sex. Indebted and indentured natives were legally bound to perform a variety of services for their owners. It was not called slavery; it was "servitude." At least that is what the law called it. And, as abolitionist John C. Frémont illustrated, his "Free Soil" politics did not extend to the "de facto" Indian slaves at his Mariposa ranch and mines.

The militarization of Indian policy that has been alluded to earlier was realized with the instituting of off-reservation Indian Boarding Schools (beginning in 1879 with the Carlisle school in Pennsylvania). Cultural genocide, as defined by the Convention on Prevention and Punishment of the Crime of Genocide (1997), included destruction of a targeted group of their economy, curtailment of language, suppression of religious practices, forced dislocation, and forced transfer or removal of its children. In the late 1870s, when extermination no longer appeared feasible, the federal government started its Boarding School program. Humanitarians argued that it was better to "kill the Indian in order to save the child." Personnel in the US Army, impressed by the sedentary ways of the Pueblo Indians, argued that a military style of compulsory education would wean Indian children away from their "savage" lives toward the "civilized" state of modern America, or at least the semi-civilized sedentary world of the Pueblo. It was ironic that when the program was implemented Navajo police were used to wrest children away from their Hopi parents.[17]

Children were to be removed, for the most part, from their Native communities and sent to remote boarding schools were they could be deculturated. At the schools they would have their hair cut, not be allowed to speak their indigenous language, learn English, take American names, and be immersed in vocational programs making them suitable as functionaries for the dominant society. They would also be indoctrinated in the values of Christianity and Western society, and denied access to their traditional rituals and ceremonies. The boarding schools, along with the Dawes Act of 1887 and the Indian Citizenship Act of 1924, were intended to assimilate the new generation of indigenous peoples into white American society. The Indian would be imbued with the ideals of private property and capitalism, while the reservations would be eventually dissolved and the Indian population dispersed. This was the policy of assimilation, and had it succeeded it would have been the classic example of cultural genocide.

One experience many girls shared at the boarding school was sexual harassment of students by teachers and supervisors. In the context of Greater Southwestern history this was simply one more instance of sexual violence. Sexism, sexual violence, and rape were constant themes in the entire Greater Southwest in the nineteenth century. In general, women in the Southwest, including white women, were considered inferior by their dominant male counterparts. There were some women, such as Josefa, the Mexican wife of Kit Carson, who held property and was an entrepreneur, or Manualito's Navajo wife Juanita, who reigned over a matrilineal society, but these were the exception—at least in the minds of most western men. The sexist attitudes held by most white males were often accompanied by racist notions concerning the natural inferiority of the Indian people, especially Indian women and girls.

Although all Indians were thought to be uncivilized "savages," little better than animals, the non-equestrians were especially considered to be primitives unworthy of any humanitarian considerations. As has been noted, pioneers on their way westward through the Great Basin thought nothing of using the Indians for target practice.

Racism and rape were everyday occurrences. The California Indians were often the target of kidnappers who then traded the women and girls as sex slaves. The Paiute spokesperson, Sarah Winnemucca, always spoke about her fear of being raped by California settlers (as her sister had been raped) as well as soldiers in and around US Army posts in Nevada. Rape and emasculation were constant concerns for Indians living near mining camps. Kit Carson's troops' recreational activities included playing catch with the female breasts that they had hacked from their Indian victims. Mutilation in the form of scalping and removing genitalia, along with gang rape, was common after 1863. American males in the West, often militia volunteers who were fleeing justice elsewhere, had, like their Mexican male counterparts (who pursued their own version of *machismo*), their own cult of masculinity. Unfortunately, violating the rights of Indian women and girls was an integral part of that cult.[18]

Finally a word about the role of women in the West: Although this work is not a biographical study, several individual women do appear that suggest the varied role that women had in the nineteenth century history of the Greater Southwest. They range from Jessie (Benton) Frémont, the maternalistic wife of John Frémont who supervised the Mariposa household of her husband, making certain that her black and Indian servants learned the values of Christianity, including obedience, laundering, and servitude, to the Chiricahua Apache female warrior Lozen, who had the "Power" to "locate the enemy" no matter how far away. Lozen was with Geronimo when he surrendered to General Nelson Miles at Skeleton Canyon in 1886. Other notables included the already mentioned Josefa, wife of Kit Carson; Juanita, wife of Manualito; Mojave captive Olive Oatman; Cynthia Ann Parker, the mother of Comanche leader Quanah, who was kidnapped by Comanche warriors[19]; and, of course, Sarah Winnemucca. Most of the mothers, pioneers, prostitutes, female warriors, headwomen, and other western women remain unnamed or unknown to history.

Some female writers who have attempted to bridge this historical gap are as follows: Contemporaries who have written about their own people include Mae Timbimbo Parry on the Shoshone, Frances Manuel on Tohono O'odham ways, and Jennifer Denetdale on her Navajo heritage. Other female authors and editors include Carolina C. Butler on the Yavapai, Kass Fleister on the Bear River Shoshone, Eve Ball on the Indeh or Apaches, Deborah Neff for the Tohono O'odham, and Evelyn Hu-Dehart and Jane Kelly Holden on the Yaqui peoples. These authors and their work can be found in the "For Further Reading" section at the end of this book.

From Geronimo to Houser: Survival in Today's World

For a century and a half non-indigenous observers of the Indian world have been predicting the demise and disappearance of the Native American. But in spite of many indigenous cultures losing their native language, American Indians from the Inuit to the Navajo have managed to survive the holocaust of colonization. They have resisted, opposed, adapted, accommodated, changed, protested and in a variety of ways have reacted to the attempts by outsiders to disrupt and destroy their communities. Through it all the indigenous peoples of the Greater Southwest have maintained their customs and traditions. As political scientist Ken S. Coates notes, "Even in highly developed western industrial countries, indigenous societies are not dead—and in most instances are not even dying—despite the efforts of newcomers and analysts to signal their impending doom."[20]

Some scholars, such as the Anishinaabe cultural theorist Gerald Vizenor, would go further to change the word "survival" to "survivance." The latter term suggests an active survival in which Native Americans go beyond merely subsisting in the ruins of tribal culture, repair the consequences of a genocidal past, and actively refashion their societies for the postmodern era. The traditional view of the Indians as victims involves the white destroyer's view of the natives. Vizenor calls upon his indigenous comrades to abandon victimization and become self-reliant.[21] Thus, in fact, the uncommon gains of Native American politicians, artists, and academics since 1970 have been called by Ojibwe historian David Treuer, "The Self-Determination Era."[22]

For example, several groups have been making valiant efforts to revive their linguistic traditions, but none better than the Yurok Tribe of Northern California where Eureka High School and three other high schools are offering immersion programs in the Yurok language. The Yurok program has become a model for other native groups who are redefining what it means to have a living language and bewildering the linguists, who, a generation earlier, had predicted the extinction of the language. Among the Havasupai of the Grand Canyon every tribal member, about 500, speaks the native language.[23]

The Hopi nation and their Pascua Yaqui neighbors have launched low-power FM radio stations where their people can hear about local events in their own language. Navajo, the language that aided in winning World War II through the celebrated "code talkers," is used in daily life by two-thirds of the nation's 300,000 citizens, who call it "Diné bizaad," "the people's language." Two major movies have been dubbed in Navajo, "Star Wars Episode IV" in 2013, and "Finding Nemo" in 2016.[24]

The Navajo and the Pueblo peoples of Arizona and New Mexico have taken the lead in promoting the education of their people. In 2013 16 Navajo students graduated from the ironworker union's apprenticeship program near downtown Phoenix,[25] while academic training of indigenous peoples was taking place at the University of Arizona in Tucson, Northern Arizona University in Flagstaff, and Arizona State University in Tempe.

The Navajo's motto can be found in the words of Chief Manuelito. After returning from a journey to Washington, D.C., a group of Navajos asked him what he had seen. Manuelito replied, "This is how many White People are out there. We cannot fight them, there are very few of us compared to them. We have to fight the injustices of our people with education."[26] As for the Pueblo people, in the spring of 2015 ten newly minted PhD's left Arizona State University's commencement ceremony planning to return to New Mexico to engage in tribal governance, social work, and youth outreach programs.[27] These students and programs are the exception, but it takes exceptional people to realize the Native American dream of survival.

Unlike many indigenous groups, the Navajos had more human and natural resources with which to work. At the same time, because of the magnitude of the numbers they have had larger problems. Many of the troubles faced in the first half of the twentieth century have been resolved, at least in part. These included stock reduction, land depletion, tuberculosis, lack of roads, and chronic unemployment.[28] Yet misuse of lethal drugs, including opioids (akin to other Indian and non-Indian communities), as well as environmental concerns, remain as current worries. As wild man Edward Abbey reminds us, the Navajo are still underemployed, have a high infant mortality rate, a homicide rate higher than Seattle or Boston, with many of their tribe suffering extreme poverty due to a lack of resources and a population ten times the size of a century ago on a reservation, even though larger now than it was then, does not provide an adequate resource base. Until recently most of their solutions have come from the outside, so, as Abbey says, "Red-skinned black men at present, they must learn to become dark-brown white men with credit cards and crew-cut sensibilities."[29]

The environment continues to be a major issue for the Navajo. The post-Cold War era left a heritage of over 500 abandoned uranium mines that now need to be cleaned up. The Kerr–McGee Company, an energy and oil-exploration outfit, mined uranium and left behind several years' worth of pollution across the reservation. Outside of Church Rock, New Mexico two plateaus of radioactive dirt and rock stand as testimony to the madness of the Cold War era. Contamination has had untold medical consequences on sheep (contaminated mutton) and the miners and the Navajo people who live and draw water near the mines. These include cancers and kidney maladies. Pregnant women and small children have been the major victims. A settlement with the Department of Justice will resolve some of the contamination problems, but will not help those who have already died from uranium poisoning.[30]

The coronavirus pandemic of 2020 illustrated another problem for the Navajos. A lack of adequate medical facilities, crowded homes, and with 30% of the population without drinking water and electricity, the Navajo reservation became a hot spot of infectious disease. Those who were seriously ill were flown to Phoenix and elsewhere but the infection and mortality rates remained seriously high. The discipline of the Navajo people and their social consciousness (in which they followed public health advice about social distancing, curfews, and wearing of masks) has aided what would be otherwise a more serious situation (see Figure 10.2).[31] Even so, as of October 2020 the Navajo Nation has recorded at least 560 deaths—a tally larger than the coronavirus related deaths in 13 states and a higher death rate than every other state.[32]

Another environmental concern for the Navajo, Hopi, and their indigenous neighbors is the white man's misuse of their hallowed San Francisco Peaks outside Flagstaff, the "abalone mountain" sacred to the Navajo and a critical part of his and her hózhó. That misuse, from the indigenous point of view, involves the snow-making machines of the Snowbowl ski resort that spews polluted water on a sacrosanct site.[33] This conflict, which will not be resolved by the Justice Department or any governmental bureaucracy, is symbolic of

Figure 10.2 *Navajo and Hopi Families COVID-19 Relief Fund.* Courtesy of Walter Yazzie, Chapter Manager, Chinle Chapter, Navajo Reservation, December 13, 2020.

Indian–white relations in the nineteenth century where the religious rights of the indigenous people were ignored or destroyed.

Not all the Navajo's current problems revolve around the environment. As important are the social issues of the day, including the on-going debate on gay marriage. Although Navajo culture and society, like many indigenous ones, dictates acceptance of all Navajo children and families regardless of gender, a 2005 Navajo law prohibits same-sex marriage.[34] And, of course, the Hopi–Navajo relocation efforts continue, in spite of the fact that the program was to be completed in 1986. In early 2015 at least 120 Navajos were still awaiting homes.[35]

On another front, Navajo woman Amanda Blackhorse and four other Native American advocates are fighting to get the Washington "Redskins," considered a slur in mainstream dictionaries, to change their name. They argue that the word is offensive and therefore not eligible for trademark registration. Meanwhile her only reward has been a suit that the Washington team filed against her, *Profootball Inc. v. Blackhorse et al*, in the US District Court of Virginia. In case she wins there will be no monetary award, but it will bring an unlimited amount of pride to the indigenous peoples. By mid-July of 2020, with corporate pressure from FedEx, Nike, and others, the Washington team owner announced that the "Redskins" were dropping the controversial name.[36]

Meanwhile, in northern Mexico and southern Arizona the Pascua Yaquis and the Tohono O'odham have made great strides in removing their people from the past horrors of the nineteenth century. The twentieth-first century Sonoran Yaquis possess a relatively adequate standard of living. Their local authorities are recognized by higher level Mexican officialdom, the mestizo response to Yaqui cultural expressions is one of toleration, there is very little alcoholism, and the Sonoran Yaquis have a very low propensity for either class or ethnic conflict. All of this contrasts with the impoverished Mayo Indians and poorer Mexican citizens of Sonora.[37]

The Arizona Yaqui have also improved their traditional situation. A reauthorization of the Violence Against Women Act passed in 2013 allows tribes to bring cases against non-Indians in domestic violence crimes. The Pascua Yaqui tribe in Arizona was one of three tribes to receive such authorization (the other two were in Washington and Oregon).[38] As for cultural development, the New Pascua tribe in south Tucson (the only Yaqui entity recognized by the federal government) has created a highly modernistic facility for advancing the education of their people. Instructor Anabel Galindo, a Yaqui tribe member and graduate student at the University of Arizona, taught (as of 2015) a class on the "History and Culture of Yaqui People." On the other side of town, Guillermo "Bill" Quiroga, the director of the Old Pascua Museum, has produced and directed a fictionalized saga video called "Yaqui Journey: 1910–1920." This documentary is based on historical events about the sacrifice and resilience of the Yaqui Nation. It is part entertainment, but mostly created for the education of the Yaqui children. It is a story of survival in the face of overwhelming odds.

A major threat to the survival of the Tohono O'odham community has been the high rate of adult-onset diabetes. Since 1960 obesity has become widespread among the O'odham. Although diabetes was virtually unknown among the Tohono O'odham before 1960, by 2016 more than 60% of the population developed the disease, the highest rate in the world! In 1996, thanks to the work of Terrol Dew Johnson and others, the Tohono O'odham Community Action (TOCA) non-profit corporation was founded. Taking as its motto, "You are What You Eat," TOCA has started a reservation program intended to revitalize the Tohono O'odham traditional food system both to support the local economy and to improve the health of the tribal members.[39]

Traditional farming includes *Ak Chin* (*ciñ*), or flood farming, and harvesting of wild foods, many of which were preserved throughout the year. TOCA promotes farming of traditional desert crops, including mesquite beans, tepary beans, and acorns that reduce blood sugar levels, and other foods like prickly pear fruits and cholla buds that slow the absorption of sugary foods. They also published *From I'itoi's Garden*, a living document designed to instruct the O'odham people on how and why to eat traditional foods.[40]

The O'odham Cultural Center in Topawa has a "Stewardship Project," known as *Himdag Ki*. The purpose of the project is to encourage the preservation of artifacts and archival materials that are part of the O'odham cultural patrimony. The Cultural Center also has a museum that stores, preserves, and displays items of O'odham history. In the area of language preservation, the San Xavier mission school has published *Our Book, T-O'ohana, Nuestro Libro* which tells the tale to first and second graders of San Xavier and Father Kino in English, Papago, and Spanish.[41]

The O'odham people are not the only indigenous group to build cultural centers and resurrect historical sites. Along with casinos,[42] the O'odham are justifiably proud of their cultural center and museum in Topawa. So too are the Hopis of their Hopi Cultural Preservation Center in Kykotsmovi, Arizona; the Diné of their Navajo Cultural Center Museum in Window Rock; the Numu of the Pyramid Lake Museum in Nixon, Nevada; the Indé of the San Carlos Apache Center near Globe, Arizona; the Yavapai of the Yavapai-Apache Cultural Center in Camp Verde, Arizona and the Ft. McDowell Yavapai Nation Cultural Center on the reservation adjacent to Fountain Hills, Arizona; the Northwestern Shoshoni of the Bannock-Shoshone Tribal Museum in Fort Hall, Idaho; and the Yoemen of the Pascua Yaqui Museum and Cultural Center in Tucson, Arizona. In addition the Northwestern Shoshone have been very active in restoring the Bear River Massacre site near Preston, Idaho, while the Navajo gem remains the museum at the Bosque Redondo Memorial at Fort Sumner, New Mexico.

A word about Pueblo relocation ought to be noted, even though a survey of 21 communities is outside the scope of this work. After 1868 the Pueblos had their ancestral lands encroached upon by Hispanic and Anglo squatters. They were forced to use a US court system that favored private over collective land rights. In 1913 the Supreme Court declared the Pueblos wards of the federal government with trust protection. Communal land rights were recognized in the 1924 Pueblo Lands Act and the Indian Reorganization Act of 1934, the latter ending further allotment of indigenous territories, although previously allocated land was not restored. Adjudication continues.[43]

It is fitting that the conclusion of this work should mention the role of fine arts in preserving the traditional cultures of the indigenous peoples. It is an important tool in the survival kit of American Indians in confronting "settler colonialism." Janet Cantley, a curator at the Heard Museum in Phoenix, Arizona, in an essay on "Current Trends in American Indian Art" states that "American Indian art is a testimony to the existence and vibrancy of tribal life in Native communities .... Art is and has been a strategy to respond to assimilationist policies and attempts at cultural genocide. American Indians have adapted and responded to outsider threats with a resilience that is expressed in art—both visual arts and the continuity of age-old ceremony and traditions."[44]

Cantley goes on to give several examples including the "ledger book drawings" of the 1860s and the Fort Marion prisoners of the 1870s who transitioned from painting on hides to pictographic drawing on paper. After 1930 the Santa Fe Indian School promoted indigenous art at Dorothy Dunn's studio. Many artists, like Apache Alan Houser or Ojibway George Morrison went further to bridge the gap between "traditional style" and mainstream art. In fact, as Shawnee Ruthe Blalock Jones has noted, the boarding schools "were started to stamp out the Indian from the Indian ... it didn't work. It made us stronger as Indian people." The political activism of the 1970s revitalized community art, and several female artists started to gain recognition, including Kay Walking Stick (Cherokee/Winnebago) and Helen Hardin (Santa Clara Pueblo). Contemporary artists, like Navajo Steven Yazzie, while continuing the indigenous tradition, have incorporated new materials like photography, film and video (see Figure 10.3).[45]

In fusing fine art with identity no person and family deserves more credit than Allan Houser and the Houser/Haozous family of the Santa Fe area. Houser was born in Oklahoma in 1914, the first member of his Warm Springs clan to be born outside of captivity. Houser's father, Sam Haozous, was Geronimo's nephew, and Sam Haozous' mother was the daughter of Mangas Coloradas. Sam Haozous was a prisoner along with Geronimo in Florida. Allan Houser died at the age of 80 in 1994. His life work was a testament to his courage and the survival of his people.[46]

When Allan was a young man starting his life work, he was influenced more by his father's love of tradition, community and family, than Geronimo's late life commercialization of the Chiricahua past. Unlike Geronimo's preoccupation with military conflict and constant flight, Houser, while recognizing the role of the shaman-warrior in Apache culture, mostly chose for his subject matter the family bond—in particular, like his contemporary the Mexican artist Rodolfo Morales, that special relationship between mother and child.[47]

While his sculpture celebrated Apache traditions, especially the *Ga'an* dancers, he also gave attention to Pueblos, the Native American Church in Oklahoma, and the folkways of the Plains Indians. His paintings and drawings celebrated other tribes, including illustrations for children books that spoke to the O'odham experience. His work embraced diversity in both materials and subject matter, from bronze and marble sculptures to watercolor landscapes

Figure 10.3 *Gazer.* Oil Painting. Courtesy of Artist Steven Jon Yazzie and the Heard Museum (Phoenix, Az.).

and acrylic paintings; from abstract forms to realistic scenes of traditional Indian conflict and survival.

Once in awhile he would contemplate that tradition. As for his father being a prisoner of the US Army, Houser said that "It makes me mad sometimes when I'm reading about it, but I don't carry that with me." He goes on to say that "I often wonder about the fact that we were the only one of all the Apache groups who stood up and said 'this is my land.' We were the only ones who were brave enough to say 'that's enough.' And we are the only ones who ended up with nothing."[48] His work could have dwelled on the victimhood of the Apache, but instead Houser chose to depict more humanistic themes. Outsiders thought of Geronimo and the Apaches as warriors. But, as Houser noted, the Apaches were just as concerned about the safety and health of their families as the white man and woman.

Houser, whose family tradition is being continued by his sons, Phillip and Bob Haozous (and a grandson, Sam), was a modern, indigenous artist. He drew his inspiration from Mexican and European sources, but the predominant influence came from his Warm Springs Apache community. Just as Naiche's actions in creating his hide paintings in the early twentieth century was an act of Chiricahua identity, so too did Houser's work assert the reality of the contemporary Indian, a product of past conflict and of present survival and future spiritual growth. He is, at least in this writer's estimation, the finest exemplar of Southwestern Indian art.

Houser represents what historian Roxanne Dunbar-Ortiz calls the "culture of resistance." He demonstrated that fighting for survival did not require cultural abandonment, but included a partial accommodation to the society of the "colonizer." His father Sam Haozous married an Anglo woman named Blossom Wratten, whose father was an interpreter for the Chiricahua at Fort Sill. Blossom and her sister were educated in English at the Dutch Reform Church Mission School. Intermarrying with Anglo settlers, speaking the English language of the colonizer, and adopting Christianity were all characteristics of the "culture of resistance."[49]

All of these traits were inherited by Alan, who initially abandoned his native name of Haozous for the German-sounding "Houser." As an artist Houser transformed the regionalism of the American West and the traditionalism of indigenous forms into a synthesis of Native and Euro-American artistic paradigms. His inspiration came from indigenous ritual objects like Apache baskets, ceremonies (Gh'an Dancer, see again Figure 5.1) and drums, the muralist traditions from Diego Rivera to Rodolfo Morales, and the vitalism and modernism of Henry Moore. His art was the best kind of cultural resistance, a resistance that avoided total assimilation. It was the art of survival.

If the indigenous cultures of yesteryear are with us today in modified form, then perhaps the Tarahumara and Numu of today will be with us in four centuries from now—but of course in a changed way. Survival for all of us—western and non-western—is not assured, especially from pandemics. One curmudgeon friend of mine once asserted that if the contemporary transportation network were to break down that modern man and woman would only be two weeks away from destruction. Indigenous people, especially those few that are removed from the modern transportation nets, are surely more than two weeks away.

In an era when climate change is threatening to shrink land from all peoples on mother earth, it might be time to acknowledge the tremendous loss of land and identity that the colonizer brought to the indigenous community. Maybe Usen and the other indigenous gods are doing to the terrain of mother earth what the colonizers did to the American Indians.

Looking back at the planet from the perspective of outer space one can see the earth as a pale blue dot floating in space. As Carl Sagan once suggested, "Every saint and sinner in the history of our species lived there—on a mote of dust suspended in a sunbeam."[50] Perhaps the human species should extend its collective consciousness from the tribal level to move beyond egocentric and ethnocentric concerns and achieve a universal view. At the least this improved species would be able to extend the notion of humanity to others. We might eventually learn to live together on this mote of dust. We might learn that there is a little sinner in every saint, and a bit of saint in every sinner.

Notes

Preface

1 As quoted by Isabel Wilkerson, "America's Enduring Caste System," *The New York Times Magazine* (July 5, 2020): 53.
2 Menand, *The New Yorker* (March 30, 2015).
3 Weston, "Defining American Indian Identity," *Heard Museum Journal* (July–December 2006): 6–9.
4 Gerald Vizenor, *Native American Literature* (Berkley, CA: University of California, HarperCollins College Publishers, 1955), pp. 1–2.
5 James W. Loewen, *Lies My Teacher Told Me* (N.Y.: Touchtone, 2007): 124–125.
6 See Alex Ross, "The Hitler Vortex: How American Racism Influenced Nazi Thought," *The New Yorker* (April 30, 2018): 66–73.
7 As quoted by Benjamin Madley, *An American Genocide: The United States and the California Indian Catastrope* (New Haven, CT: Yale University Press, 2016), p. 7.
8 Gerald Vizenor, *The Heirs of Columbus* (Hanover & London: Wesleyan University, University Press of New England, 1991), p. 184.
9 Brendan C. Lindsay, *Murder State* (Lincoln, NE: University of Nebraska, 2012), p. 31.
10 Larissa Behrendt, "The Semantics of Genocide," *Critical Indigenous Studies* (Tucson, AZ: University of Arizona, 2016), pp. 138–156.
11 David Stannard, *American Holocaust* (N.Y.: Oxford University Press, 1992).
12 Financial data from Terry Anderson, "Biden's Chance to Renew Reservation Economies," *The Hill* (1/2/2021).

Prologue

1 Patricia Nelson Limerick, *The Legacy of Conquest: The Unbroken Past of the American West* (New York: W. W. Norton & Company, 1987), pp. 322–323. For another description of the American "Myth of the Pristine Wilderness" see Roxanne Dunbar-Ortiz, *An Indigenous Peoples' History of the United States* (Boston: Beacon Press, 2014), pp. 45–55.

2 Eve Ball, *Indeh: An Apache Odyssey* (Norman: University of Oklahoma Press, 1988), p. 19.

3 Roger Naylor, "Injustice in the Desert," *Arizona Republic* (April 25, 2015): 1D & 6D. Arizona hosted another prisoner camp about ten miles from Tucson known as the Catalina Federal Honor Camp. This "camp" housed various individuals including Japanese such as Gordon Hirabayashi. These Japanese-Americans, and other prisoners, built the highway that accessed the Santa Catalina Mountains and Mt. Lemon. Also see the unpublished manuscript by Myla Vicinti Carpio and Karen Leong, "American Movements: Understanding the Ideological and Institutional Reasoning for Japanese American and American Indian Relocations, 1940–1970" (ASU, 2020).

4 Karen Comeau, a Standing Rock Sioux, described this type of relocation of individuals in her speech entitled "A Reflection of Indian/Alaskan Education—Past and Present" at a Heard Museum Guild meeting in Phoenix, Arizona on March 21, 2018. Her presentation included her testimony about her brother's relocation from North Dakota to Los Angeles in the late 1950s. For the 1950s "reawakening" of urban Indians see Margaret Connell Szasz, *Education and the American Indian: The Road to Self-Determination since 1928* (University of New Mexico Press, 3rd ed., 1999), p. 165. Forcible removal still remains today as the Trump administration recently tried to terminate the Wampanoag. See "Indian Affairs" by L. A, Urrea in The New York Times *Book Review* (March 29, 2020), p. 15.

5 This does not mean that Wounded Knee represented the failure of Indian culture or came to embody the abyss between primitive and modern as many writers have argued. Indian spiritualist and educational movements thrived in the past and the present. See Louis S. Warren, *God's Red Son: The Ghost Dance and the Making of Modern America* (N.Y.: Basic Books, 2017), pp. 3–6.

6 Inter-tribal warfare existed long before Custer's march on the Black Hills. Custer's enemies, the Lakotas, had wrested them from the Cheyennes who had seized them from the Comanches. The latter had ejected the Crows a century earlier. See James Donovan, *A Terrible Glory: Custer and the Little Bighorn* (N.Y., Boston and London: Black Bay Books, 2008), p. 82.

7 Walter Johnson, "King Cotton's Long Shadow," *New York Times* (March 31, 2013). This is not to say that forced removal of Indians did not have a longer

history. In colonial times the European colonists justified their acquisition of native lands, and eventually control over the natives on the lands, through the Doctrine of Discovery. This combined need, law and the Bible in which European Royalty, and the "divine grace" that royalty represented, justified land grabbing and slavery. See Simon Winchester, *Land: How the Hunger for Ownership Shaped the Modern World* (NY: HarperCollins Publishers, 2021), pp. 131–138.

As early as 1776, Jefferson's list of abuses by the English monarch recited at the end of the Declaration of Independence included the charge that the King endeavored "to bring on the inhabitants of our frontiers, the merciless Indian Savages." Jefferson's audience, white men eager for westward expansion, spoke of removal of Indians so their land could be appropriated. Jefferson even proposed an "Indian Amendment" to the Constitution calling for "removal" and transfer of eastern tribes from their lands to the West.

Again, as John P. Bowes has shown for the Old Northwest, Delaware Indians were forced out of the east coast to Ohio and Indiana in the eighteenth century, and later were relocated to Canada, Kansas, and Texas. Similar removals occurred for other tribal groups, including the Seneca and Cayuga. All of this happened before the Indian Removal Act of 1830. See both Annette Gordon-Reed, "The Captive Aliens Who Remain Our Shame," (a review of *The Common Cause* by Robert Parkinson [Univ. of North Carolina Press]) in *The New York Review* (January 19, 2017): 54–56, and Scott W. Berg, *38 Nooses: Lincoln, Little Crow, and the Beginning of the Frontier's End* (N.Y.: Vintage Books, 2012), p. 67. Also see Bowes, *Land Too Good for Indians: Northern Indian Removal* (Norman: University of Oklahoma Press, 2016). Beyond the scope of the present study a major relocation took place in 1856 when the US government forced 30 Indian groups scattered between Washington and California to settle on a reservation in Oregon known as Grand Ronde. See Gillian Flaccus, "Tribe welcomes artifacts from British Museum," *Arizona Republic* (June 6, 2018): 4A.

8 Gary Clayton Anderson, *Ethnic Cleansing and the Indian: The Crime That Should Haunt America* (Norman: University of Oklahoma, 2014), p. 369, note 2.

9 Malise Ruthven, "Will Geography Decide Our Destiny?" *New York Review of Books* (February 21, 2013): 43–45. At times, as a result of the Mexican War, settlers came before the surveyors and treaty makers. Treaty-making lasted in US history from 1778 to the Indian Appropriations Act of 1871. This act terminated the treaty-making process. See also Duane Champagne, "In Search of Theory and Method in American Indian Studies" in *The American Indian Quarterly*, 31 (Summer 2007): 368.

10 As quoted by Trudy Griffin-Pierce, *The Columbia Guide to American Indians of the Southwest* (New York: Columbia University Press, 2010), p. 50.

11 Ken S. Coates, *A Global History of Indigenous Peoples: Struggle and Survival* (New York: Palgrave MacMillan, 2004), pp. 51–63; "Brazil Tribes Fear 'Ethnocide'," N.Y. *Times* (April 19, 2020), pp. 20–21.

12 Judith Thurman, "A Loss for Words: Can a dying language be saved?" *The New Yorker* (March 30, 2015), pp. 32–39.

13 Coates, *A Global History*, pp. 51–63.

14 Ibid., pp. 18–24.

15 Michelle Rindels, "Tribes turn to apps to save endangered languages," *Arizona Republic* (April 18, 2013): D1 & D4.

16 Betty Reid, "Navajo Speech Comes to Life ...," *Arizona Republic* (June 30, 2013): A1 & A12.

17 W. Jackson Rushing III, *Allan Houser: An American Master* (New York: Harry N. Abrams, Inc., 2004).

Chapter One

1 Clifford Canku and Michael Simon, *The Dakota Prisoners of War Letters: Dakota Kaśkapi Okicize Wowapi* (St. Paul, MN: Minnesota Historical Society Press, 2013), p. 11.

2 As quoted by David A. Nichols, *Lincoln and the Indians* (St. Paul, MN: Minnesota Historical Society Press, 2012), p. 187.

3 www.archives.gov/exhibits/featured_documents/emancipation_ (US National Archives & Records Administration). As David Nichols noted, "The significant date was 25 August (1862). That is the day that Secretary (Edwin) Stanton authorized Gen. Rufus Saxton to organize black soldiers." See Nichols, *Lincoln and the Indians*, pp. 82–83.

4 David Brion Davis, "How They Stopped Slavery: A New Perspective," in *The New York Review of Books* (June 6, 2013): 59.

5 "John C. Frémont," in *Wikipedia: the Free Encyclopedia*, http://en.wikipedia.org/wiki/John_C._Fr%C3%A9mont, p. 5 of 9.

6 "Slavery among Native Americans in the United States," *Wikipedia: The Free Encyclopedia*, http://en.wikipedia.org/wiki/Slavery_among_Native_Americans_in_the_United_States.

7 "Historical Society Learns about Paiute Indians," *Emery County Progress* (May 22, 2012): 1–2. In the late eighteenth and early nineteenth century the Comanche became a part of this slave trade network, using firearms obtained from French trappers, explorers and merchants to capture Indian slaves

(Navajos, Paiutes, Apaches, et al.) that were then traded in Mexico for horses, mules and furs.

8   Allan Gallay, "Indian Slavery in the Americas," *The Gilder Lehrman Institute of American History*, p. 3: http://www.gilderlehrman.org/history-by-era/origins-slavery/essays/indian-slavery/americas.

9   James F. Brooks gives several examples of chattel slavery in the Southwest Borderlands and adjacent areas, including the black slaves who comprised 25 percent of the non-Mexican population of pre-Independence Texas, as well as Africans among Delaware Indian hunters in Arkansas known by the Cheyennes as "Black Shawnees." See Brooks, *Captives and Cousins: Slavery, Kinship, and Community in the Southwest Borderlands* (Chapel Hill and London: University of North Carolina Press, 2002), pp. 307–308.

10 "Slavery among Native Americans in the United States," *Wikipedia*, pp. 2–3. See also Brooks, *Captives and Cousins*, p. 307.

11 Brooks, *Captives and Cousins*, pp. 34–35, fn.54. Brooks notes the disagreements in the literature treating the topic of kinship in African captivity and slavery, but still believes the borderland slave system can be compared to the kin-based slave societies of Africa. For pawnage and chattel bondage in Africa see Ira Berlin, *Many Thousands Gone: The First Two Centuries of Slavery in North Africa* (Cambridge: Harvard University Press, 1998), pp. 22–28.

12 Gallay, "Indian Slavery in the Americas," p. 2.

13 The reconquest or *reconquista* was the seventh century attempt at reconquering Christian Spain from its Muslim conquerors that ended in 1492. Sometimes the Spanish *conquista* of the New World is considered the final or eighth chapter of the *reconquista* of Spain in the Old World.

14 James Lockhart and Stuart B. Schwartz, *Early Latin America: A history of colonial Spanish America and Brazil* (Cambridge: Cambridge University Press, 1984), pp. 71 & 78.

15 Ibid., 94–95 & 293.

16 Several studies exist on the Pueblo Revolt. One recommended work would be *The Pueblo Revolt: The Secret Rebellion that Drove the Spaniards out of the Southwest* by David Roberts (N.Y.: Simon & Shuster, 2004).

17 Lockhart and Schwartz, *Early Latin America*, p. 140.

18 Scott K. Williams, "Slavery in St. Louis," http://www.usgennet.org/usa/mo/county/stlouis/slavery.htm, p. 2 of 23.

19 David J. Weber, *The Mexican Frontier, 1821-1846: The American Southwest Under Mexico* (Albuquerque, N.M.: University of New Mexico Press, 1982), pp. 170 & 176.

20 Aurora Hunt, *Kirby Benedict: Frontier Federal Judge* (Glendale, CA.: The Arthur H. Clark Company, 1961), pp. 112–114.

21 Ibid., pp. 117–118.

22 Brooks, *Captives and Cousins*, pp. 345–346.

23 As quoted by Brooks in Ibid., pp. 346–347.

24 Andrés Reséndez, *The Other Slavery: The Uncovered Story of Indian Enslavement in America* (N.Y. & Boston: Houghton Mifflin Harcourt, 2016), pp. 308–314.

25 Ibid., pp. 347–349.

26 Weber, *The Mexican Frontier*, pp. 4 & 212.

27 Quoted by Weber, Ibid., p. 212.

28 R. Bailey, *Indian Slave Trade in the Southwest* (Los Angeles: Westernlore Press, 1966), p. 126. On the other hand, it must be remembered that the Navajos held several slaves seized in raids on Pueblos, Utes, Apaches, Americans and Hispanics. See Andrés Reséndez, *The Other Slavery*, p. 244.

29 Bailey, *Indian Slave Trade in the Southwest*, pp. 190 & 270.

30 William B. Carter, *Indian Alliances and the Spanish in the Southwest, 750-1750* (Norman: University of Oklahoma Press, 2009), pp. 171 & 176.

31 Ibid., pp. 214–216. When Comanches and Utes were able to obtain firearms and horses from Europeans they became prominent traffickers who provided Indian slaves to their Spanish and New Mexican counterparts. See Andrés Reséndez, *The Other Slavery*, pp. 172–195.

32 Quote by Andrea Smith, *Conquest: Sexual Violence and American Indian Genocide* (Cambridge, MA: South End Press, 2005), p. 9.

33 Quoted by Smith, *Conquest*, pp. 9–10.

34 Ibid., p. 10.

35 George Frederick Ruxton, *Life in the Far West*, ed. by Leroy R. Hafen (Norman: University of Oklahoma Press, 1951), pp. 81–85. Ruxton was an English soldier of fortune whose account of western ways was filled with dramatic stories in which his heroes Killbuck and La Bonté engaged in many daring feats and experienced a number of hair-breadth escapes from "Spanish" and Indian enemies. It is not clear how many of his descriptions were fictional, partly fictional, or true accounts of western realities.

36 Ibid., p. 86.

37 The most illustrious incident of cannibalism in the west was the Donner party of 1846. It also occurred in the Pikes Pike gold rush of 1859. One early trapper was even nicknamed "Big Phil, the Cannibal." See again Ruxton, *Life in the Far West*, pp. 86-87, fn. 13.

38 "John C. Frémont," *Wikipedia*, p. 2 of 9, and A.D. Hopkins, "John C. Fremont," Las Vegas *Review-Journal* (February 7, 1999).

39 "Frémont," *Wikipedia*, p. 2.

40 Ibid. Scott Lankford, in his *Tahoe Beneath the Surface* (Berkeley & Rocklin, CA.: Heyday and Sierra College Press, 2010), pp. 41–42, does note that

Frémont's California map places Lake Tahoe further west than it actually was and erroneously showed an outlet river flowing from Lake Tahoe to the ocean near San Francisco Bay. Lake Tahoe's outlet mostly travels northeast to Pyramid Lake in the Nevada sink.

41 "Frémont," *Wikipedia*, p. 3, and Lankford, *Tahoe Beneath the Surface*, pp. 43–44.

42 "Frémont," *Wikipedia*, p. 3.

43 "California Republic," *Wikipedia: The Free Encyclopedia*, pp. 1 & 2 of 5. The proclamation of June 15, 1846 is reproduced on pp. 3–4. Frémont's role as a mythmaker is documented in "Untrue West: The very American adventures of Jessie and John Frémont," *The New Yorker* (Jan. 27, 2020): 66–69.

44 "Frémont," *Wikipedia*, p. 3.

45 Ibid., pp. 3–4.

46 "Free Soil Party," *Wikipedia, The Free Encyclopedia*, pp. 1–2 of 4, http://en.wikipedia.org/wiki/Free_Soil_Party.

47 "Frémont," *Wikipedia*, p. 4.

48 "United States Presidential Election, 1856," *Wikipedia, The Free Encyclopedia*, pp. 1, 11–12, & 14 of 16, http://en.wikipedia.org/w/index.php?title= United_States_presidential_election,_1856.

49 Lankford, *Tahoe Beneath the Surface*, p. 42.

50 Pestilence and genocide in Spanish and American California is the topic of David E. Stannard, *American Holocaust: The Conquest of the New World* (N.Y. & Oxford: Oxford University Press, 1992), pp. 134–146.

51 James J. Rawls, *Indians of California: The Changing Image* (Norman: University of Oklahoma Press, 1984), pp. 81–85.

52 Ibid., pp. 86–87. See also Edward D. Castillo, *Short Overview of California Indian History* (California Native American Heritage Commission, 1998), p. 6. According to Castillo, "… this legislation takes away basic citizenship rights for Native Americans, and allows for their enslavement. By the end of the 1850s, over 10,000 California Indians had been sold as slaves. The law will not be repealed until 1937." An in-depth analysis of "An Act for the Government and Protection of Indians," especially the infamous Chapter 33 that legalized genocidal crimes of Native peoples, can be found in Brendan C. Lindsay's *Murder State: California's Native American Genocide, 1846-1873* (Lincoln: University of Nebraska Press, 2012), pp. 245–270. For background to the 1850 Act, see Andrés Reséndez, *The Other Slavery*, pp. 263–266.

53 Rawls, *Indians of California*, pp. 86–87.

54 Ibid., pp. 95–96. See also Roxanne Dunbar-Ortiz, *An Indigenous Peoples' History of the United States* (Boston: Beacon Press, 2014), p. 41. Dunbar-Ortiz also notes that US armed forces killed 4,000 California Indians in the last half of the nineteenth century, while disease took another 6,000. Benjamin

Madley, in his *An American Genocide: The United States and the California Indian Catastrophe* (New Haven: Yale University Press, 2014) argues that California's Indian population plunged from 150,000 to 30,000 between 1846 and 1873. This decline was mostly due to extermination campaigns. Concerning genocide, Alex Alvarez concluded that "The case of the Natives of California illustrates one of the clearest examples of genocide in North America." See Alvarez, *Native America and the Question of Genocide* (N.Y.: Rowman & Littlefield, 2014), p. 113.

55 Ibid., pp. 99–101.

56 Ibid., pp. 107–108.

57 Ibid., pp. 109–115.

58 Ibid., pp. 115–121.

59 Ibid., pp. 126–133. One of Sutter's managers, Pierson Reading, said in 1844 that "The Indians of California make as obedient and humble slaves as the Negro in the south." See quote by James W. Loewen, *Lies My Teacher Told Me* (N.Y.: Touchstone, 2007), pp. 104–105. Loewen also notes that "the Native population of California sank from three hundred thousand in 1769 ... to thirty thousand a century later, owing mainly to the gold rush, which brought 'disease, starvation, homicide, and a declining birthrate'." See p. 79. As indicated in endnote 53, these depopulation figures are reinforced by the recent study by Benjamin Madley who in his *An American Genocide* argues that between 1846 and 1873 the California Indian population plunged from 150,000 to 30,000. This decline, according to Madley, was the result of a slaughter of Indians that was caused by a state-sanctioned killing machine that had broad societal and political support for genocide.

60 Allan Nevins, *Fremont: Pathmarker of the West* (N.Y. & London: Longmans, Green and Co., 1955), pp. 383–386. Ironically, after the Hopi Indians had enjoyed the shade of cottonwood trees for over a thousand years, it was the conqueror Frémont who got a subspecies of southwestern cottonwood named after him—the Frémont cottonwood. For this and other ironies of Frémont see Don Lago, *Where the Sky touched the Earth: The Cosmological Landscapes of the Southwest* (Reno & Las Vegas: University of Nevada Press, 2017), p. 37.

61 Rawls, *Indians of California*, p. 115.

62 David A. Nichols, *Lincoln and the Indians*, p. 130.

63 Scott K. Williams, "Slavery in St. Louis," p. 15.

64 Castillo, *Short Overview of California Indian History*, p. 130.

65 Dale Mason, "The Indian Policy of Abraham Lincoln," *Indigenous Policy Journal* 20:3 (2009): pp. 1 & 2 of 6, http://www.indigenouspolicy,org/index.php/ipj/article/view/71. Lincoln's Interior Secretary, John P. Usher, went even further than Lincoln saying that Indians who resisted white advances were furthering the Confederate cause and "should be pursued by the military and punished." See Alvin M. Josephy, Jr., *The Civil War in the American West* (N.Y.: Vintage Books, 1991), pp. 231–232.

66 Nichols, *Lincoln and the Indians*, pp. 5–15. Quote from pp. 6–7.

67 Ibid., pp. 76–93 & Mason, "The Indian Policy of Abraham Lincoln," p. 3 of 6. For a thorough examination of the Minnesota uprising and Lincoln's reaction to it see Josephy, Jr., *The Civil War in the American West*, pp. 95–121.

68 "Wabasha (Dakota) Explains How Nefarious Trading Practices Caused the 1862 Minnesota War, 1868," in *Major Problems in American Indian History*, ed. by Albert L. Hurtado and Peter Iverson (Boston & New York: Houghton Mifflin Company, 2001), pp. 277–278.

69 Gary Clayton Anderson, in his essay entitled "Dakota Sioux Uprising, 1862," argues that of the 500 whites who lost their lives many were of German descent and had little history, knowledge, or intimate contact with the Sioux people. As for the Indians, a large number of "farmer Indians" and mixed-bloods who had kinship ties (even fictive kinship ties) attempted to save the lives of whites from death at the hands of their fellow tribesmen. He also indicates that Minnesota newspaper charges exaggerated their accounts of rape, noting that most Sioux war parties held strong taboos against rape believing that it would anger the native spirits. See Ibid., pp. 299–311.

70 Nichols, *Lincoln and the Indians*, pp. 81–83 & 98–99. See also Scott W. Berg, *38 Nooses: Lincoln, Little Crow, and the Beginning of the Frontier's End* (New York: Vintage Books, Random House, 2012). Berg places the execution of 38 Dakota men in the larger context of the Civil War and the US-Indian wars.

71 Ibid., pp. 111–112 & 117. See also Mason, "The Indian Policy of Abraham Lincoln," p. 3 of 6.

72 Canku and Simon, *The Dakota Prisoner of War Letters* and Nichols, *Lincoln and the Indians*, pp. 120 & 126.

73 Ibid., pp. 113 & 121–122.

74 For William P. Dole's activity see *The Commissioners of Indian Affairs, 1824-1977*, ed. by Robert M. Kvasnicka and Herman J. Viola (Lincoln and London: University of Nebraska Press, 1979), pp. 89–98. The information about Catalina Island can be found on p. 95. During the 1860s the War Department attempted to regain control of the Bureau of Indian Affairs. As noted in the text, the Bureau had been created in 1824 by Secretary of War John C. Calhoun. It remained there until 1849 at which time it was transferred to the Department of Interior.In 1870 the Marias River Massacre brought about the death of 173 Blackfeet Indians in Montana. This event set back the so-called Grant Peace Policy (began in 1869 as a substitute for war) in which Grant planned to extend citizenship to Indians through a gradual process of Christianization on indigenous peoples resettled as farmers on reservations. In the long run, the Grant Peace Policy was ultimately a quixotic idea that never gained traction among the Indian population. Grant, although well-meaning, was naïve in thinking the indigenes would copy the white man's way while repudiating their own past. See Ron Chernow, *Grant* (N.Y.: Penguin Press, 2017), pp. 657–660.

75 Nichols, *Lincoln and the Indians*, p. 207. "Militarization" was not a totally bad thing since many of the causes of the Dakota War were the results of corruption associated with the Bureau of Indian Affairs, especially the roles of local agents and traders. A military action in lieu of civilian behavior was often the better of two evils. In 1867 General John Pope argued for placing Indian reservations under the administration of the Department of War and the United States Army, rather than the "corrupt and lazy administrators" in the Bureau of Indian Affairs. See Berg, *38 Nooses: Lincoln, Little Crow ...*, p. 296.

76 Stephen Douglas in the first of the Lincoln-Douglas debates, Ottawa, Illinois, August 21, 1858, from Wikipeida, The Free Encyclopedia (https:// en.wikipedia.org/wiki./Lincoln-Douglas_debate).

77 As quoted by Berg, *38 Nooses: Lincoln, Little Crow ...*, p. 275.

78 For a general view of Lincoln's worldview see Chapter 13 of Nichols, *Lincoln and the Indians* entitled "Lincolnian Attitudes toward Indians," pp. 175–201.

79 Aurora Hunt, *Kirby Benedict: Frontier Federal Judge* (Glendale, CA.: The Arthur H. Clark Company, 1961), p. 172.

80 Michael Hogan, *Abraham Lincoln and Mexico: A History of Courage, Intrigue and Unlikely Friendships* (Guadalajara, Jalisco [Mexico]: Fondo Editorial Universitario, 2016), pp. 173–178.

Commentary: Lincoln and the Pueblos

1 See W. Dale Mason, "The Indian Policy of Abraham Lincoln," *Indigenous Policy Journal*, 20:3 (2009–2012), http://indigenouspolicy.org/Articles/ ArticleArchive/Vol.XX,No.3.

Chapter Two

1 Reproduced by the author from a wall poster, Fort Tejon Historical Park, California, August 11, 2014.

2 Quote from Myron Angel, ed., *History of Nevada* (Oakland: Thompson and West, 1881), p. 151 by Sally Zanjani in *Sarah Winnemucca* (Lincoln: University of Nebraska Press, 2001), pp. 58–59.

3 Solberg, *Tales of Wovoka* (Reno: Nevada Historical Society, 2012), p. 21.

4 Stella Riesbeck, "Nevada Indian 'War' of 1863 Recalled," Las Vegas *Sun* (July 17, 1966).

5 "Keyesville Massacre," *Wikipedia, The Free Encyclopedia* (en.wikipedia.org/wiki/Keyesville_massacre). The massacre site was near the community of Keyesville located in the lower elevations of the Greenhorn Mountains on the south branch of the Kern River in southern California.

6 Zanjani, *Sarah Winnemucca*, p. 79.

7 Pyramid Lake Elder Ralph Burns, co-director of the Pyramid Lake Museum, insists that the word for his people is *Numu*, not *Numa*. Conversation with the author, Pyramid Lake Reservation, Nixon, Nevada, July 22, 2014. See his language lesson booklet, *Kooyooee Panunadu Numu Yadooana (Pyramid Lake Paiute Tribe's Language CD Project)*, created by Ralph Burns and compiled by Lesley Hawley (available at the Pyramid Lake Reservation Museum). For the Owens Valley "Numu" see Bertram L. Roberts, "Descendants of the Numu," *The Masterkey* (January-March 1965): 13–22.

8 Sven Liljeblad and Catherine S. Fowler, "Owens Valley Paiute," *Handbook of North American Indians: Great Basin*, vol. 11, ed. by Warren L. D'Azevedo (Washington: Smithsonian Institution, 1986): 415, and Catherine S. Fowler and Sven Liljeblad, "Northern Paiute," *Handbook of North American Indians: Great Basin*, vol. 11, ed. by Warren L. D'Azevedo (Washington: Smithsonian Institution, 1986): 457 & 461.

9 Liljeblad and Fowler, "Owens Valley Paiute," p. 412.

10 Map 1, Northern Paiute Bands, Clippings, Vertical File, Nevada Historical Society, Reno, Nevada.

11 "Paiute," *Wikipedia, The Free Encyclopedia* (en.wikipedia.org/wiki/Paiute), pp. 2–11.

12 Liljeblad & Fowler, "Owens Valley Paiute," pp. 412 & 416. See also Fowler and Liljeblad, "Northern Paiute," p. 436. An excellent cultural survey of the Pyramid Lake Paiutes can be found in Nellie Shaw Harnar, *Indians of Coo-yu-ee Pah (Pyramid Lake): The History of the Pyramid Lake Indians in Nevada* (Sparks, Nev.: Dave's Printing and Publishing, 1974), pp. 21–28.

13 Liljebald & Fowler, "Owens Valley Paiute," pp. 422–425, & Julian H. Steward, "Ethnography of the Owens Valley Paiute," *University of California Publications in American Archaeology and Ethnology* 33:3 (September 6, 1933): 263–266.

14 Liljeblad & Fowler, "Owens Valley Paiute," p. 3. See also Bernard Mergen, *At Pyramid Lake* (Reno & Las Vegas: University of Nevada Press, 2014), p. 1.

15 Harry W. Lawton et al., "Agriculture Among the Paiute of Owens Valley," *The Journal of California Anthropology* 3:1 (Summer 1976): 13. Also see Robert A. Sauder, "The Agricultural Colonization of a Great Basin Frontier: Economic Organization and Environmental Alteration in Owens Valley, California, 1860-1925," *Agricultural History* 64:4 (Autumn, 1990): 80.

16 Liljebald & Fowler, "Owens Valley Paiute," p. 417.

17 Lawton, et al., "Agriculture Among the Paiute of Owens Valley," p. 43.

18 Zanjani, *Sarah Winnemuca*, pp. 16–19, 65–67, 99–100 & 233–235. Also see Gae Whitney Canfield, *Sarah Winnemucca of the Northern Paiutes* (Norman: University of Oklahoma Press, 1983), pp. 4–5.

19 Steward, "Ethnography of the Owens Valley Paiute," p. 293. & Richard C. Hanes and Laurie Collier Hillstrom, "Paiutes," *Countries and Their Cultures-Le Pa-Paiutes*, p. 5 of 28 pp., www.everyculture.com/multi/Le-Pa/ Paiutes.html. See also L. Daniel Myers, "Myth as Ritual: Reflections from a Symbolic Analysis of Numic Origin Myths," *Journal of California and Great Basin Anthropology* 23 (2001): 41.

20 Julian Steward, *Myths of the Owens Valley Paiute* (Berkeley: University of California Publications in American Archaeology and Ethnology, 1936), p. 364.

21 Ibid., pp. 365–368.

22 Mergen, *At Pyramid Lake*, pp. 27–30.

23 Steward, *Myths*, p. 369.

24 Roberts, "Descendants of the Numu," p. 21.

25 Zanjani, *Sarah Winnemuca*, p. 219.

26 Hanes & Hillstrom, "Paiutes," pp. 6–7.

27 Gregory E. Smoak, *Ghost Dances and Identity* (Berkeley: University of California Press, 2006), pp. 16–17 & 20–23.

28 Fowler & Liljeblad, "Northern Paiute," p. 455.

29 Ibid., p, 456.

30 Henry DeGroot, *The Comstock Papers* (Reno: The Grace Dangberg Foundation, Inc., 1985), p. i.

31 W. A. Chalfant, *The Story of Inyo* (Bishop, Ca.: Piñon Book Store,1933 [reprinted 1964]; photocopy, University of Nevada, Reno), pp. 119–120.

32 Sauder, "The Agricultural Colonization of a Great Basin Frontier," p. 82.

33 Francis P. Farquhar, *History of the Sierra Nevada* (Berkeley & L.A.: University of California Press, 1965), p. 71.

34 Ibid., pp. 71–77. For a more detailed description of the destruction of the Ahwahnee (or Ahwahneechee) people of Yosemite by the Mariposa Battalion see Daniel Duane, "Goodbye, Yosemite. Hello, What?" in the Sunday Review section of the *New York Times* (Sept. 3, 2017): 1 & 4–5.

35 Ibid., pp. 78–79.

36 "Sebastian Indian Reservation," 3 pp. & "Fort Tejon," 6 pp., *Wikipedia, The Free Encyclopedia* (en.wikipedia.org/wiki/Sebastian_Indian_Reservation, and en.wikipedia,org/wiki/FortL_Tejon). The small Spanish village of *El Pueblo de Nuestra Señora la Reina de Los Ángeles del Río de Porciúncula* was founded in 1781. By April 1850 it was incorporated into the municipality of Los Angeles five months before statehood. Fort Tejon was also the terminus in 1858 of the experimental US Camel Corps in which the US army used imported camels to carry supplies across the arid regions of the Southwest. For the Camel Corps see George Stammerjohan, "History of Fort Tejon," 2 pp. & "The Mythical Fort Tejon 'Camel Corps'," 10 pp., published by the Fort Tejon Historical Association (www.forttejonj.org/camel.thml).

37 Chalfant, *The Story of Inyo*, p. 123.

38 Philip J. Wilke and Harry W. Lawton, eds., *The Expedition of Capt. J. W. Davidson From Fort Tejon to the Owens Valley in 1859* (Socorro, N.M.: Ballena Press, 1976), pp. 6 & 12. Also see Benjamin Madley, *An American Genocide: The United States and the California Indian Catastrophe* (New Haven: Yale University Press, 2016), p. 310. According to historian Brendan Lindsay, by the early 1850s the Owens Valley Paiutes pursued the well-established practice of horse stealing in the Central Valley, and then followed up by trading their contraband for food with whites waiting east of the Sierra Nevada. See Lindsay, *Murder State* (Lincoln: University of Nebraska Press, 2012), pp. 163–164.

39 Quotation from Dorothy Clora Cragen, *The Boys in the Sky-Blue Pants: The Men and Events at Camp Independence and Forts of Eastern California, Nevada and Utah, 1862-1877* (Independence, California: 1975; photocopy, University of Nevada, Reno), p. 4.

40 Wilke & Lawton, *The Expedition of Capt. J. W. Davidson*, p. 7. See also *The Story of Inyo*, pp. 125–126. The site of Camp Independence was immediately north of the present town of Independence and is the Fort Independence Indian Reservation today.

41 Chalfant, *The Story of Inyo*, pp. 126–127.

42 "Aurora, Nevada," *Wikipedia, The Free Encyclopedia*, (en.wikipedia.org/wiki/Aurora_Nevada), pp. 2–3.

43 Chalfant, *The Story of Inyo*, pp. 127–128.

44 "The American West: An Eclectic History: The Owens Valley Indian War," pp. 1–2 (theamericanwestaneclectihistory.blogspot.com/2012/12/the-owens-valley-indian-war).

45 Ibid., pp. 3–4.

46 Cragen, *The Boys in the Sky-Blue Pants*, pp. 4–11. Quotation from p. 5. In that same month Colonel Warren Wassen, the Walker Reservation Indian Agent, left with troops from Fort Churchill near Carson City and joined up with Lt. Colonel George Evans on the Owens River. Unlike Evans, Wassen's mission was more diplomatic than military. See Myron T. Angel, ed., *History of Nevada* (Oakland, Ca.: Thompson & West, 1881), pp. 166–168.

47 Ibid., p. 55.

48 Ibid., pp. 56–59 & Wilke & Lawton, *The Expedition of Capt. J. W. Davidson*, pp. 7–8. See also Chalfant, *The Story of Inyo*, pp. 192–193, and "Owens Valley

Indian War," *Wikipedia, The Free Encyclopedia*, p. 5 of 10 (en.wikipedia.org/wiki/Owens_Valley_Indian_War). While Colonel Evans had not tolerated rape by his men, McLaughlin, who intended to kill uncooperative Indians, had no such reservations. The estimate of Owens Valley and Kern River California Indian dead is from Madley, *An American Genocide*, p. 315.

49 Cragen, *The Boys in the Sky-Blue Pants*, pp. 59–61.

50 Ibid., p. 60.

51 Ibid., p. 61 & Chalfant, *The Story of Inyo*, p. 194.

52 Cragan, *The Boys in the Sky-Blue Pants*, pp. 69–70.

53 *Annual Report of the Commissioner of Indian Affairs, for the year 1864* (United States, Office of Indian Affairs, California Superintendency, September 1, 1864), p. 118.

54 A detailed account of the "Owens Valley War" can be found in Madley, *An American Genocide*, pp. 309–316.

55 Madley, *An American Genocide*, pp. 328–330. According to Lindsay the war of 1865 was brought to a close with at least 100 Paiutes (men, women, and children) killed in retaliation for the murder of a white woman and child. The two culprits who murdered the victims were later found to be non-Native Americans. Lindsay called this event "one of the most disturbing episodes in the history of the OwensValley." See Lindsay, *Murder State*, p. 174.

56 Alex Schmidt, "Paiute Indians Help Make the History of the L.A. Aqueduct," *The California Report* (Feb. 15–17, 2013), 3 pp., (www.californiareport.org/archive/R201302151630/e).

57 Description of Plains Indians by the writers of the Virginia (City) *Evening Bulletin*, July 18, 1863.

58 Mergen, *At Pyramid Lake*, p. 9.

59 Ibid., pp. 1 & 9–10. Quotation from p. 10.

60 Fowler & Liljeblad, "Northern Paiute," p. 457.

61 Mergen, *At Pyramid Lake*, p. 12. The population estimate for 1860 probably included areas adjacent to Pyramid Lake including the Truckee River region, Mud Lake, and Honey Lake. For the population estimate of Northern Paiute bands in western Nevada in 1859 see Fowler & Liljeblad, "Northern Paiute," p. 457.

62 Canfield, *Sarah Winnemuca of the Northern Paiutes*, pp. 18–19 & Zanjani, *Sarah Winnemuca*, pp. 55–56. The Governor of Nevada Territory eventually sought federal support in the form of arms and ammunition to go after the Paiutes that he knew killed Lassen and others. See Carson City, Nevada, *Territorial Enterprise*, March 3, 1860, Clippings/Vertical File, Nevada Historical Society, Reno, Nevada.

63 Canfield, *Sarah Winnemuca of the Northern Paiutes*, pp. 11–14, & Zanjani, *Sarah Winnemuca*, p. 49. See also Ferol Egan, "Victims of Justice Tragedy," *The American West* 9:5 (September 1972): 42–47 & 60–61.

64 Sarah Winnemuca Hopkins, *Life Among the Piutes [sic]* (Reno & Las Vegas: University of Nevada Press, 1994; originally published in 1883), p. 64.

65 Zanjani, *Sarah Winnemucca*, pp. 59–60 & Canfield, *Sarah Winnemucca of the Northern Paiutes*, p. 24.

66 For a somewhat dated but complete treatment of the Pyramid Lake War see Angel, *History of Nevada*, pp. 159–164.

67 Zanjani, *Sarah Winnemucca*, p. 60.

68 Sarah Winnemucca, *Life Among the Piutes*, pp. 71–72.

69 Henry DeGroot, *The Comstock Papers* (Reno: Grace Dangberg Foundation, Dangberg Historical Series, ed. by Donald Dickerson, 1985; reprint of 1876 edition), pp. 26–27.

70 Mergen, *At Pyramid Lake*, p. 11, & "Paiute War," *Wikipedia, The Free Encyclopedia* (en.wikipedia.org/wiki/Pyramid_Lake_War), pp. 1–4. See also the popular history, now dated, by Ferol Egan called *Sand in a Whirlwind: The Paiute Indian War of 1860* (Reno & Las Vegas: University of Nevada, reprint 1972; 1985).

71 Mergen, *At Pyramid Lake*, pp. 11–12 & "Paiute War," *Wikipedia*, p. 4. See also Gregory Michno, *The Deadliest Indian War in the West: The Snake Conflict, 1864-1868* (Caldwell, Idaho: Caxton Press, 2007), p. 63.

72 Angel, *History of Nevada*, p. 165.

73 "Fort Churchill State Historic Park," *Nevada State Parks* (Department of Conservation and Natural Resources), 8 pp. (parks.nv.gov/parks/fort-churchill-state-historic-park/). Fort Churchill was abandoned in 1869 and the buildings were auctioned off.

74 Angel, *History of Mexico*, p. 165.

75 Ibid., pp. 169–170.

76 Zanjani, *Sarah Winnemucca*, pp. 77–79. For a different estimate of Indian dead see Angel, *History of Nevada*, p. 170.

77 Philip Dodd Smith, Jr., "Nevada Volunteers in the Civil War," (M.A. Thesis, University of Nevada, July 31, 1959), p. 94.

78 Zanjani, *Sarah Winnemucca*, pp. 79–81. See also Canfield, *Sarah Winnemucca of the Northern Paiutes*, pp. 44–45. For the irreconcilable differences between the US Army version of the Mud Lake event and that of Sarah Winnemucca, see Gregory Michno, *The Deadliest Indian War in the West*, pp. 81–82.

79 Smith, "Nevada Volunteers in the Civil War," pp. 70–72.

80 Zanjani, *Sarah Winnemucca*, p. 87.

81 Ibid., pp. 82–84, 90–91, 97 & 103. See also Canfield, *Sarah Winnemucca of the Northern Paiutes*, pp. 56 & 58–59.

82 Zanjani, *Sarah Winnemucca*, pp. 5 & 22.

83 Hopkins, *Life Among the Piutes*, p. 11.

84 Canfield, *Sarah Winnemucca of the Northern Paiutes*, p. 5.

85 Julian H. Steward, "Panatűbiji': An Owens Valley Paiute,"*Bulletin 119, Bureau of American Ethnology, Anthropological Papers, No. 6* (Washington: US Govt. Printing Office, Smithsonian Institution, 1938), p. 190.

86 Zanjani, *Sarah Winnemucca*, pp. 106–107.

87 Hopkins, *Life Among the Piutes*, p. 34.

88 Canfield, *Sarah Winnemucca of the Northern Paiutes*, p. 8.

89 Zanjani, *Sarah Winnemucca*, p. 147.

90 Ibid., pp. 129–135.

91 Ibid., pp. 133–139.

92 "Bannock War," *Wikipedia, The Free Encyclopedia*, 7pp. (en.wikipedia.org/wiki/Bannock_War).

93 Canfield, *Sarah Winnemucca of the Northern Paiutes*, 151–152.

94 Ibid., pp. 154–155 & Zanjani, *Sarah Winnemucca*, p. 192.

95 Canfield, *Sarah Winnemucca of the Northern Paiutes*, pp. 155–156.

96 Fowler & Liljeblad, "Northern Paiute," p. 458.

97 Ibid., p. 459.

98 Canfield, *Sarah Winnemuca of the Northern Paiutes*, p. 159 & 161.

99 Smoak, *Ghost Dances and Identity*, pp. 199–205. Similarly to the Round Dance that paved the way for the Ghost Dance, so too did the Sun Dance of the Lakota, when suppressed by the authorities, lead the way to the acceptance of the Ghost Dance ceremony by the Lakotas. See Louis S. Warren, *God's Red Son: The Ghost Dance Religion and the Making of Modern America* (N.Y.: Basic Books, 2017), p. 250.

100 Ibid., p. 198 & Gunard Solbert, *Tales of Wovoka*, p. 73.

101 Solbert, *Tales of Wovoka*, pp. 72–74.

102 Angel, *History of Nevada*, p. 165.

103 Zanjani, *Sarah Winnemucca*, p. 133.

104 Solbert, *Tales of Wovoka*, p. 73.

105 R. F. Heizer and M. A. Whipple, comps. & eds., *The California Indians: A Source Book* (Berkeley: University of California Press, 2nd ed., 1971), pp. 54–59.

106 Zanjani, *Sarah Winnemucca*, 284.

107 Solbert, *Tales of Wovoka*, p. 175.

108 Louis S. Warren, the historian who wrote one of the better studies on the Ghost Dance Religion, argues that "Mormons probably influenced Paiute cosmology, but evidence for their influence on Wodziwob or Wovoka is slight at best." See Warren, *God's Red Son: The Ghost Dance Religion and the Making of Modern America*, p. 97.

109 Ibid., pp. 170–171 & 174.

110 Mergen, *At Pyramid Lake*, pp. 13–14 & Smoak, *Ghost Dances and Identity*, p. 171.

111 Solbert, *Tales of Wovoka*, pp. 170–171.
112 Warren, *God's Red Son*, pp. 374–378 & 388–395.

Commentary: The Military and the Boarding School

1 Carleton (Santa Fe, N.M.) to Thomas (Washington, D.C.), September 6, 1863, reprinted in Lawrence C. Kelly, *Navajo Roundup: Selected Correspondence of Kit Carson's Expedition Against the Navajo, 1863-1865* (Boulder, Colorado: The Pruett Publishing Company, 1970), p. 57.
2 *Wikipedia: The Free Encyclopedia*, "American Indian boarding schools," (en. wikipedia.org/wiki/American_Indian_boarding_schools). K. Tsianina Lomawaima and Jeffery Ostler published a "revisionist" view of Pratt in which the latter is considered to be more than simply a "victimizer." According to these authors he was a multidimensional person who made friends as well as enemies, a rebellious employee of the Office of Indian Affairs, and a persistent gadfly. The slogan of "kill the Indian, save the man," while a formidable slogan that was conceptually powerful, is much too simplistic to embrace the several dimensions of Pratt's being. See their article "Reconsidering Richard Henry Pratt: Cultural Genocide and Native Liberation in an Era of Racial Oppression," *Journal of American Indian Education*, 57, 1 (Spring 2018): 79–100.
3 Heard Museum, Phoenix, Arizona, December 3, 2014: Exhibit entitled "Remembering our Indian School Days: The Boarding School Experience, 1879–Present."
4 Ibid.
5 Ibid.
6 *Wikipedia*, "American Indian boarding schools."
7 David Wallace Adams, *Education for Extinction: American Indians and the Boarding School Experience, 1875-1928* (Lawrence, Kansas: University Press of Kansas, 1995), p. 57.
8 Carol A. Barrett, "'Into the Light of Christian Civilization': St. Elizabeth's Boarding School for Indian Children (1886-1967)," PhD Dissertation, University of North Dakota (Grand Forks, N.D., May 2005): 5.
9 Adams, *Education for Extinction*, pp. 21–24.
10 Adams, *Education for Extinction*.
11 Ibid., p. 38.
12 Sally Jenkins, *The Real All Americans* (N.Y.: Broadway Books, 2007), pp. 28 & 39–41.
13 Ibid., pp. 46–47. A description of the use of art at Fort Marion is the article by Arthur Silberman, "The Art of Fort Marion," *Native Peoples* 6:4 (Summer 1993): 32–39.

14 Ibid, pp. 47, 53–55 & 57–61.

15 The idea of "marketing" the students was first suggested to me in a presentation delivered by curator Janet Cantley at the Heard Museum on January 8, 2019. Her comments were entitled "Away from Home: An Overview of American Indian Boarding School Stories." Also see K. Tsianina Lomawaima, "Indian Boarding Schools, Before and After: A Personal Introduction," in K. Tsianina Lomawaima, Bryan McKinley, et al. eds., Special issue of the *Journal of American Indian Education*, 57, 1 (Spring 2018): 11–21.

16 Margaret L. Archuleta, Brenda J. Child, and K. Tsianina Lomawaima, *Away from Home: American Indian Boarding School Experiences, 1979-2000* (Phoenix, Az.: Heard Museum, 2000), pp. 26–27, 63, & 75–77.

17 Heard Museum, Exhibit entitled "Remembering our Indian School Days," Dec. 3, 2014.

18 Archuleta, et al., *Away from Home*, pp. 31–32.

19 Sarah Shillinger, *A Case Study of the American Boarding School Movement: An Oral History of Saint Joseph's Indian Industrial School* (Lewiston, N.Y., Queenston, Ontario & Lampater, Wales, UK: The Edwin Muellen Press, 2008), p. 85.

20 Archuelta, et al., *Away from Home*, pp. 26, 42 & 48.

21 Ibid., pp. 42–42.

22 Although the extent of sexual abuse is open to discussion since the historical record is limited, there are several instances in the contemporary world. For example, the policies of the Church of Jesus Christ of Latter-day Saints (Mormons) established a volunteer foster program in the 1940s that was called the Indian Student Placement Program. The program ended around 2000. Several foster children were sexually abused during the reign of the program, including a Navajo foster child who was allegedly molested by a church bishop in the 1980s. See Felicia Fonseca, "More sex abuse alleged in Mormon program," *Arizona Republic* (Jan. 11, 2019): 4A.

23 Barrett, "'Into the Light of Christian Civilization'," pp. 10 & 203–204.

24 Quoted by Adams, *Education for Extinction*, pp. 124–135.

25 Heard Museum, Exhibit entitled "Remembering our Indian School Days," Dec. 3, 2014. See also Archuelta, pp. 38–41.

26 Shillinger, *A Case Study of the Boarding School Movement*, pp. 91 & 114–115.

27 The phrase "turned the power" was originally used by historians like Clifford E. Trafzer and others. See Matthew Sakiestewa Gilbert, *Education beyond the Mesas: Hopi Students at Sherman Institute, 1902-1929* (Lincoln & London: University of Nebraska Press, 2010), p. xxx; and Kevin Patrick Whalen, "Beyond School Walls: Race, Labor, and Indian Education in Southern California, 1902-1940" (PhD dissertation, University of California, Riverside, June 2014).

28 Sally Zanjani, *Sarah Winnemucca* (Lincoln: University of Nebraska Press, 2001), pp. 256–257 & 263–265.

29 Ibid., pp. 266–267.

30 Ibid., pp. 276–283.

31 Ibid., p. 286.

32 Sarah evidently suffered severe stomach pains following a meal of chokecherry wine. The suspicion is that she may have been poisoned by her sister Elma. Chokeberry poisoning had caused the death of Elma's husband two years earlier. Although Winnemucca's biographer argues that Sarah was not buried in Targhee Cemetery because it had not been created in 1891, other sources indicate that the old private cemetery was built and donated by the Salisbury Ranch in the early 1800s. She may have been buried below the old Richards Ranch east of the lake, or she may be in an unmarked grave in the Targhee Cemetery, near the dear sister who may have cost Sarah her own life. See Dean H. Green, *History of Island Park* (Ashton, Idaho: Gateway Publishing, 1990), pp. 105–107; Zanjani, *Winnemucca*, pp. 295–298.

Chapter Three

1 Quoted by Ward Churchill, *Struggle for the Land: Native North American Resistance to Genocide, Ecocide and Colonization* (San Francisco: City Lights, 2002), p. 181.

2 Quoted by Ronald L. Holt, *Beneath These Red Cliffs: An Ethnohistory of the Utah Paiutes* (Logan, Utah: Utah State University Press, 2006), p. 33.

3 Dale L. Morgan, *Shoshonean Peoples and the Overland Trails* (Logan, Utah: Utah State University Press, 2007), pp. 303–305 & 315–319.

4 Churchill, *Struggle for the Land*, pp. 173–174.

5 From Thompson & West's *History of Nevada* (1881) as reprinted by *The Nevada Observer: Nevada's Online State News Journal* (December 9, 2005), p. 22 of 37 pp.; http://nevadaobserver.com/Owen%20River%20War%20(1881).htm.

6 Churchill, *Struggle for the Land*, p. 184.

7 Ibid., pp. 174–178.

8 Ibid., pp. 181–185.

9 Ned Blackhawk, *Violence over the Land: Indians and Empires in the Early American West* (Cambridge: Harvard University Press, 2006), p. 268.

10 Holt, *Beneath These Red Cliffs*, pp. 29–30.

11 Ibid., pp. 27 & 34–35.

12 Andrés Resénez, *The Other Slavery: The Uncovered Story of Indian Enslavement in America* (Boston & New York: Houghton Mifflin Harcourt, 2016), p. 277. In spite of the early history, the Chemehuevi or Nǖwǖ are a

Southern Paiute group in southern California who have maintained their cultural traditions through songs, prayers, and stories that connect them with their sacred landscape. See Clifford E. Trafzer, *A Chemehuevi Song: The Resilience of a Southern Paiute Tribe* (Seattle and London: University of Washington Press, 2015), p. xvi.

13 Blackhawk, *Violence over the Land*, pp. 200–203.

14 Ibid., pp. 205–206 & 213–214.

15 Ibid., pp. 216–224.

16 William H. Leckie with Shirley A. Leckie, *The Buffalo Soldiers: A Narrative of the Black Cavalry in the West* (Norman: University of Oklahoma press, 2012), p. 208.

17 Ibid., pp. 208–210.

18 Blackhawk, *Violence over the Land*, pp. 224–225. A more in-depth treatment of the Colorado Ute's "cleansing" and removal can be found in Gary Clayton Anderson, *Ethnic Cleansing and the Indian: The Crime That Should Haunt America* (Norman: University of Oklahoma, 2003), pp. 320–324.

19 Holt, *Beneath These Red Cliffs*, p. 32.

Chapter Four

1 Manuelito to Gus Bighorse, Diné Warrior. Wall inscription at Navajo Cultural Center Museum, Window Rock, Arizona (August 23, 2013). Also quoted by Jennifer Nez Denetdale in *Reclaiming Diné History: The Legacies of Navajo Chief Manuelito and Juanita* (Tucson: University of Arizona Press, 2007), p. 73.

2 Wall inscription at Navajo Culture Center Museum, Window Rock, Arizona (August 23, 2013).

3 Denetdale, *Reclaiming Diné History*, p. 13. See also the brochure *"The Meek Shall Inherit the Earth unless they are Hopi Indians,"*: *A Brief History of the 1882 Hopi-Navajo Land Problem* (Kykotsmovi, Az.: The Hopi Tribe, n.d.). The recent population figures can be found in *The Story of Bosque Redondo: Strength, Survival, and New Beginnings* (Santa Fe, N.M.: New Mexico Dept. of Cultural Affairs, New Mexico State Monuments, Fort Sumner, N.M., n.d.), p. 15.

4 Emily Benedek, *The Wind Won't Know Me: A History of the Navajo-Hopi Land Dispute* (N.Y.: Vintage Books, 1993), p. 61, and David M. Brugge, "Navajo Prehistory and History to 1850," in *Handbook of North American Indians: Southwest*, vol. 10, ed. by Alfonso Ortiz (Wash. D.C.: Smithsonian Press, 1983), pp. 490–491 & 497. While Benedek speaks of "Tavusahs," author Raymond Friday Locke spells the word "Tasavuh." Both agree in translating it as "head pounders." See Locke, *The Book of the Navajo* (N.Y.: Kensington Publishing Corp., Holloway House Classics, 2010), p. 7.

5   Ibid. See also Jennifer Denetdale, *The Long Walk: The Forced Navajo Exile* (N.Y.: Chelsea House, 2008), p. 17. Today's 21 Pueblos speak languages from four distinct linguistic families. The Hopi are Uto-Aztecan speakers, a family that includes Shoshones in the north and Nahua speaking Aztecs in central Mexico. The Zuni family of languages is Zunian, an isolate that is only remotely related to other North American indigenous languages. The western Pueblos from Acoma and Laguna to Cochiti speak Keresan, while the Rio Grande Pueblos belong to the Tanoan family, a grouping that includes the three dialects of Tiwa, Tewa, and Towa.

6   Brugge, "Navajo Prehistory," p. 497, and Denetdale, *Reclaiming Diné History*, pp. 10 & 190.

7   Denetdale, *Reclaiming Diné History*, p. 10. The word "Dinétah" is also used by scholars to refer to the area of the San Juan Valley in northwestern New Mexico where Pueblo and Diné culture intermixed from 1692 to the third quarter of the eighteenth century.

8   Ibid., p. 43.

9   Irvin Morris, *From the Glittering World: A Navajo Story* (Norman: University of Oklahoma Press, 1997),pp. 3–15. See also Denetdale, *Reclaiming Diné History*, p. 10, and Sam D. Gill, "Navajo Views of Their Origin," in *Handbook of North American Indians: Southwest*, vol. 10, ed. by Alfonso Ortiz (Wash. D.C.: Smithsonian Press, 1983), 502–504.

10 The Navajo spellings of the sacred mountains can be found in Denetdale, *Reclaiming Diné History*, p. 10. The association of colors with the cardinal directions is typical of indigenous peoples, even though the colors change between groups. For Mesoamericans, red, the fiery color of the sun, is usually east. All Pueblos, like their cousins the Navajo, couple white with east, while only the Tiwa speakers of Picuris have color associations identical to the Navajo. For color associations see Edward P. Dozier, *The Pueblo Indians of North America* (Long Grove, Ill.: Waveland Press, 1970), p. 205.

11 Although most versions of the Navajo creation story indicate that Changing Woman and White Shell Woman are the same entity, some accounts state that they two women are sisters. See Paul G. Zolbrod, *Diné bahane: The Navajo Creation Story* (Albuquerque, N.M.: University of New Mexico Press, 1984), pp. 179–180.

12 Denetdale, *Reclaiming Diné History*, p. 137. The Blessingway Ceremony is distinct from northern Athapaskan usage in that it celebrates the young girl's menses, while northerners avoided menstruating women and isolated them.

13 Quoted from Zolbrod, p. 181.

14 Ernie Bulow, *Navajo Taboos* (Gallup, N.M.: Simon & Shuster, 1985), pp. 14–15.

15 As quoted by Ann Lane Hedlund, "A Turning Point: Viewing Modern Navajo Weaving as Art," in *American Indian Art Magazine* (Spring 2011): 75. The exact origin of the Storm Pattern design is difficult to determine. Most observers agree that it originated in the western reservation, anywhere between Tuba City and Kayenta, with Red Lake, Piñon and Black Mesa being mentioned most often. On Storm Patterns see Don Lago, *Where the Sky touched the Earth: The Cosmological Landscapes of the Southwest* (Reno & Las Vegas: University of Nevada Press, 2017), p. 85.

16 Robert Yazzie, Chief Justice of the Navajo Nation, speaks about *restorative* justice as a process of renewing community relationships and *reparative* justice as making things right for the victim. He calls it *Hozhooji Naat'aanii*, "talking things out in a good way." See Richard Rohr's "Daily Meditation: A Healing Process," (Sept. 10, 2020, Meditations@cac.org).

17 Zolbrod, *Diné bahane'*, p. 408.

18 Brian M. Fagan, *Ancient North America: The Archaeology of a Continent* (N.Y.: Thames and Hudson, 1995), pp. 70 & 176–177. For a more sophisticated view of the genetic evidence for four prehistoric migrations to America see David Reich, *Who We Are and How We Got Here: Ancient DNA and the New Science of the Human Past* (N.Y.: Pantheon Books, 2018), pp. 154–185.

19 William B. Carter, *Indian Alliances and the Spanish in the Southwest, 750-1750* (Norman: University of Oklahoma Press, 2009), pp. 21–23.

20 Brugge, "Navajo Prehistory," p. 489.

21 Benedek, *The Wind Won't Know Me*, p. 61.

22 Ibid., p. 58.

23 For Promontory Point see "Apachean Origins," Department of Anthropology, University of Alberta (http:/www.anthropology, ualberta.ca/en/The-Institute-of-Prarie-Archaeology/ResearchInterests/Apachean%20Origins. aspx), and John W. Ives, et.al., "A High Resolution Chronology for Steward's Promontory Culture Collections, Promontory Point, Utah" (unpublished manuscript). Also see Locke, *The Book of the Navajo*, p. 12.

24 Klara Kelly & Harris Francis, "Abalone Shell Buffalo People: Navajo Narrated Routes & Pre-Columbian Archaeological Sites," *New Mexico Historical Review* 78, no. 1 (Winter 2003): 29. The word *Anasazi* (Navajo *Anaasází*) can be translated many ways to mean "enemies," "enemy ancestors," "forebears," or "ancestors." Because of the confusion and complexity of Navajo ancestry, many anthropologists, some influenced by their Pueblo informants, do not want to use a Navajo word to describe what they think to be the ancestors of the current Pueblo Indians. Therefore they prefer the term "Ancestral Pueblo" to Anasazi. My preference is to use the traditional Navajo usage of "Anasazi," a word that is found in the popular and traditional literature.

25 Robert M. Begay, "Exploring Navajo-Anaasází Relationships Using Traditional (Oral) Histories," (M.A. Thesis, Northern Arizona University, 2003), pp. 36, 48 & 56.

26 Denetdale, *The Long Walk*, p. 19. Peter Iverson, in *Diné: A History of the Navajos* (Albuquerque: University of New Mexico Press, 2002, 2003), pp. 18–19, makes a persuasive case regarding the Navajo connection to the Anasazi.

27 Locke, *The Book of the Navajo*, p. 12.

28 Brugge, "Navajo Prehistory," p. 491 & Benedek, *The Wind Won't Know Me*, p. 60.

29 Benedek, *The Wind Won't Know Me*, p. 60.

30 Denetdale, *The Long Walk*, pp. 18–19 & Brugge, "Navajo Prehistory," pp. 493 & 495.

31 David M. Brugge, "A Military History of Canyon de Chelly," in *Houses Beneath the Rock: The Anasazi of Canyon de Chelly and Navajo National Monument*, ed. by David Grant Noble (Santa Fe, N.M.: Ancient City Press, 1986), p. 45.

32 Benedek, *The Wind Won't Know Me*, p. 65.

33 Brugge, "Navajo Prehistory," pp. 491–493 & Benedek, *The Wind Won't Know Me*, p. 63. For an interpretation that considers coercive labor as a major cause of the Pueblo Revolt see Andrés Reséndez, *The Other Slavery* (Boston & New York: Houghton Mifflin Harcourt, 2016), pp. 149–171.

34 Brugge, "Navajo Prehistory," pp. 493–494. It is interesting to note that the Navajos neither abandoned the hogan for Puebloan-style construction nor acquired the Pueblo kiva. Like many issues in New World archaeology, "regionalism" affects the arguments for and against the "Puebloization" of the Navajo in the Dinétah. While experts in Albuquerque and Santa Fe argue that escaping Puebloan refugees brought crops, rock art, and "pueblitos" to the Navajo, BLM archaeologists in Farmington contend that all of these traits were indigenous Diné inventions. See David Roberts, *The Lost World of the Old Ones: Discoveries in the Ancient Southwest* (N.Y.: W. W. Norton & Co., 2015), pp. 216–226.

35 Benedek, *The Wind Won't Know Me*, p. 63. Since the Hopi language has no "ch" sound, the popular usage of "kachina" is rendered "katsina" here.

36 Ibid., pp. 63–64.

37 Brugge, "Navajo Prehistory," pp. 495–496.

38 Denetdale, *The Long Walk*, pp. 22–25 (Kearny quote from p. 25) & Robert A. Roessel, Jr., "Navajo History, 1850-1923," in *Handbook of North American Indians: Southwest*, vol. 10, ed. by Alfonso Ortiz (Washington, D.C.: Smithsonian Press, 1983), p. 507. Andrés Reséndez, citing data from the classic *Navajos in the Catholic Church Records of New Mexico, 1694-1875* (1968) by David Brugge, notes an upsurge in trafficking of Navajo children and women in the 1820s that

continued until the 1870s. During this period Navajos replaced Apaches and Paiutes as the most heavily enslaved Indian nation of New Mexico. See Reséndez, *The Other Slavery: The Uncovered Story of Indian Enslavement in America* (N.Y. & Boston: Houghton Mifflin Harcourt, 2016), p. 279.

39 Roessel, "Navajo History," pp. 506–510.
40 Denetdale, *Reclaiming Diné History*, pp. 65–66 & Roessel, "Navajo History," p. 506.
41 Andrea Smith, *Conquest: Sexual Violence and American Indian Genocide* (Cambridge, MA: South End Press, 2005), pp. 10–11 (quote from p. 10).
42 Denetdale, *Reclaiming Diné History*, p. 66.
43 Dee Brown, *Bury My Heart at Wounded Knee* (N.Y.: Sterling Innovation, 2009), p. 34.
44 As quoted in *The Story of Bosque Redondo*, p. 3.
45 Roessel, "Navajo History," p. 511. From statistics exhibited at the Bosque Redondo Memorial, Fort Sumner (August 28, 2013), there were 248 Mescalero prisoners in January of 1863. By June of 1865 the prison population reached a high of 498 individuals, then slowed descended to 372 Mescaleros in October. On November 3, 1865, 350 people crept away at night, many on horseback. Only 17 people were recorded as being at Bosque Redondo for the month of March, mostly the sick and the weak. For Cremony see Paul Andrew Hutton, *The Apache Wars* (N.Y.: Crown, 2016), pp. 108–110.
46 Joseph Bruchac, *Navajo Long Walk: The Tragic Story of a Proud People's Forced March from their Homeland*, illus. by Shonto Begay (Washington, D.C.: National Geographic Society, 2002), pp. 18–19.
47 Carleton (Santa Fe, N.M.) to Thomas (Wash. D.D.), September 6, 1863, reprinted in Lawrence C. Kelly, *Navajo Roundup: Selected Correspondence of Kit Carson's Expedition Against the Navajo, 1863–1865* (Boulder, Colorado: The Pruett Publishing Company, 1970), p. 57.
48 There is evidence of wholesale murder and cannibalism at Sleeping Ute Mountain, with fire destroying much of the area. This occurred during the later period of Anasazi migrations in the Four Corners area. Later, in 1680, there was the Pueblo Revolt in which the Spaniards were expelled from New Mexico. And in 1700, the Hopi murdered their Christianized Hopi brothers and sisters and destroyed the village of Awatovi (Aguatubi). For cannibalism see Craig Childs, *House of Rain* (N.Y.: Little, Brown and Company, 2006), pp. 147–148, 160, & 281. The Pueblo Revolt is narrated by David Roberts in *The Pueblo Revolt* (N.Y.: Simon & Shuster, 2004). The Awatovi incident can be found in Harry C. James, *Pages from Hopi History* (Tucson, Az.: University of Arizona Press, 1974), pp. 61–64.
49 For the Boarding School experience see David Wallace Adams, *Education for Extinction* (Lawrence, Kansas: University Press of Kansas, 1995).

50 Quote from *The Story of Bosque Redondo*, p. 5. For a brief overview of the Navajo Long Walk see Andrés Reséndez, *The Other Slavery*, pp. 277–294.

51 As quoted by Bruchac, *Navajo Long Walk*, 19 & Roessel, "Navajo History," p. 511.

52 Roessel, "Navajo History," pp. 511–512.

53 Exhibit, Bosque Redondo Memorial (August 28, 2013).

54 Hampton Sides, *Blood and Thunder* (New York: Doubleday, 2006), p. 350.

55 *The Story of Bosque Redondo*, p. 6. When Kit Carson removed the Navajos many of his Ute allies moved to the land that was forcibly abandoned. For example, the Ute Indian Chee Poots and his two wives went to the Kava Karus Mountain area (Navajo Mountain). His first wife's son, born in 1864, was named Paniav (Water Warrior). Paniav later changed his name to Posey, after the blacksmith William "Posey" Porter. Posey was the Ute warrior who led the final battle against the US in 1923. This took place near Blanding, Utah, the site of Posey's death in that same year. This information comes from the "Posey Display" at the Blanding Visitor Center, and was created by Gary and Sharon Guyman (Raat, August 22, 2015). See also Steve Lacy and Pearl Baker, *Posey: The Last Indian War* (Layton, Utah: Gibbs Smith, 2007). For the role of Mexican and Indian volunteers, and in particular Ute war parties, in the relocation of the Navajo, see Andrés Reséndez, *The Other Slavery: The Uncovered Story of Indian Enslavement in America* (Boston & New York: Houghton Mifflin Harcourt, 2016), pp. 281–294.

56 Sides, *Blood and Thunder*, pp. 347 & 353–354.

57 Irene Silentman, Interview of Mrs. Mae Thompson, "Canyon de Chelly: A Navajo View," in *Houses Beneath the Rock*, pp. 54–55.

58 Ibid., p. 54.

59 Quoted by Sides, *Blood and Thunder*, p. 355. See also Crawford R. Buell, "The Navajo 'Long Walk': Recollections by Navajos," in *The Changing Ways of Southwestern Indians: A Historic Perspective*, ed. by Albert H. Schroeder (Glorieta, New Mexico: The Rio Grande Press, Inc., 1973), p. 179.

60 Estimate by Rod and Winona Passmore, "The Long Walk: The History of Navajo Captivity," Ketoh Lecture (Unpublished ms, Heard Museum, Phoenix, Az., April 15, 2009, 15 pp.), p. 9.

61 The best study of the various routes traveled during the Long Walk is by Frank McNitt and is entitled "The Long March, 1863–1867," in *The Changing Ways of Southwestern Indians: A Historic Perspective*, ed. by Albert H. Schroeder, pp. 145–146, 149 & 153.

62 McNitt, "The Long March," pp. 155–156.

63 Ibid., p. 145.

64 Because Navajo phonetics is very complicated, one can find the same Navajo word spelled many ways. "Hwéeldi (Bosque Redondo) is the preference of author Jennifer Nez Denetdale, a Diné with her PhD in history from Northern Arizona University. Many Navajo informants prefer "Huelte" or "Hwelte." Hwelte is supposedly derived from the Spanish *fuerte*, meaning fort, but pronounced colloquially as *juerte*. See Crawford R. Buell, "The Navajo 'Long Walk': Recollections by Navajos," in *The Changing Ways of Southwestern Indians*, ed. by Albert H. Schroeder, p. 172.

65 Peshlakai Etsedi, as told to Sallie Pierce Brewer, "The 'Long Walk' to Bosque Redondo," *Museum Notes: Museum of Northern Arizona* 9, no. 11 (May 1937): 55–62. The interview was later published by *Navajo Times*, Oct. 17, 1963, pp. 12, 14–15.

66 Crawford R. Buell, "The Navajo 'Long Walk': Recollections by Navajos," pp. 175–177.

67 Ibid., p. 177.

68 Andrea Smith, *Conquest: Sexual Violence and American Indian Genocide*, pp. 7 & 15.

69 Passmore, "The Long Walk," p. 8.

70 Roessel, "Navajo History," pp. 514–515.

71 For the impact of fry bread on the diet of contemporary Native Americans see Patty Talahongva (Hopi), "No More 'Die Bread': How Boarding Schools Impacted Native Diet and the Resurgence of Indigenous Food Sovereignty," *Journal of American Indian Education*, 57, 1 (Spring 2018): 145–153.

72 Denetdale, *The Long Walk*, p. 82.

73 Ibid., pp. 81–82.

74 Roessel, "Navajo History," p. 515.

75 Denetdale, *The Long Walk*, p. 75.

76 Ibid., p. 65.

77 The issue of Kit Carson's role in the Navajo Wars and Bosque Redondo is treated by Lawrence C. Kelly in "The Historiography of the Navajo Roundup," R. C. Gordon-McCutchan, ed., *Kit Carson: Indian Fighter or Indian Killer?* (Niwot: University Press of Colorado, 1996), pp. 49–71.

78 Hampton Sides, *Blood and Thunder* (N.Y.: Doubleday, 2006), pp. 5, 7 & 265.

79 Ibid., 7 & 269.

80 Ibid., 6 & 268. See also "Kit Carson," *Wikipedia, the Free Encyclopedia*, http://en.wikipedia.org/wiki/Kit_Carson.

81 For an overview of Kit Carson's female companions see Marc Simmons, *Kit Carson & His Three Wives: A Family History* (Albuquerque: University of New Mexico Press, 2003).

82 Denetdale, *Reclaiming Diné History*, p. 58.

83 Simmons, *Kit Carson & His Three Wives*, vii-viii. See also Dunlay, *Kit Carson & the Indians*, xii-xvii.

84 Dunlay, *Kit Carson & the Indians*, pp. 120–121. See also "John C. Frémont," *Wikipedia, the Free Encyclopedia*, p. 3 of 9, http://en.wikipedia.org/wiki/John_C._Fremont.

85 Simmons, *Kit Carson & His Three Wives*, p. 26 & 145.

86 The "Spot Resolution" requested from President James K. Polk that he provide congress with the exact location (spot) upon where blood was spilled on American soil. Polk had justified the entry of the United States in to war against Mexico on the grounds that American blood had been spilled on American soil, even though the area in question actually belonged to Mexico.

87 As quoted by Clifford E. Trafzer, *The Kit Carson Campaign: The Last Great Navajo War* (Norman: University of Oklahoma Press, 1982), p. 237.

88 Denetdale, *Reclaiming Diné History*, pp. 57–86.

89 Quote from Ibid., p. 60.

90 Simmons, *Kit Carson & His Three Wives*, pp. 58–59.

91 Ibid., pp. 63–64.

92 Ibid., pp. 100 & 103.

93 David J. Weber, *The Mexican Frontier, 1821-1846: The American Southwest Under Mexico* (Albuquerque: University of New Mexico, 1982), pp. 215–216.

94 Simmons, *Kit Carson & His Three Wives*, pp. 109–110.

95 Ibid., pp. 141–144.

96 Denetdale, *Reclaiming Diné History*, pp. 100–101.

97 Ibid., pp. 88–89.

98 Ibid., pp. 97–98 & 100.

99 Ibid., p. 105.

100 *The Story of Bosque Redondo*, p. 11. The Sherman quote is from Andrés Reséndez, *The Other Slavery: The Uncovered Story of Indian Enslavement in America* (Boston & New York: Houghton Mifflin Harcourt, 2016), p. 310. See also Trafzer, *The Kit Carson Campaign*, p. 240.

101 Martin A. Link, intro., *Treaty Between the United States of America & the Navajo Tribe of Indians/With a record of the discussions that led to it's signing* (Las Vegas, Nev.: K.C. Publications, 1968), p. 1.

102 Quote by Link, Ibid., pp. 5–6.

103 *The Story of Bosque Redondo*, p. 11. For the return of a copy of the treaty to the homeland see Shondlin Silversmith, "1868 treaty returns to Navajo Nation," *Arizona Republic* (May 31, 2019), pp. 1A & 8A.

104 Link, *Treaty Between the USA & the Navajo Tribe*, p. 19.

105 Ibid., pp. 21–24.

106 *The Story of Bosque Redondo*, p. 12.

107 Martin Link, *Signers of the Treaty of Peace, June 1, 1868* (Gallup, N.M.: The Indian Trader, Inc., 2001), p. 25.

Commentary: The Hopi-Navajo Land Controversy

1 Harry C. James, *Pages from Hopi History* (Tucson: University of Arizona Press, 1974), p. 81.

2 Ibid.

3 Frank Waters, *Book of the Hopi* (N.Y.: Penguin Books, 1963), p. 283.

4 As quoted by Lawrence C. Kelly in *Navajo Roundup: Selected Correspondence of Kit Carson's Expedition Against the Navajo, 1863-1865* (Boulder, Col.: Pruett Publishing Co., 1970), pp. 75-77.

5 Emily Benedek, *The Wind Won't Know Me* (N.Y.: Random House, Inc., 1993), p. 55.

6 Waters, *Book of the Hopi*, p. 266.

7 Ibid., pp. 283–284.

8 Jerry Kammer, *The Second Long Walk: The Navajo-Hopi Land Dispute* (Albuquerque, N.M.: University of New Mexico Press, 1980), pp. 26–27.

9 Ibid. See also Benedek, *The Wind Won't Know Me*, p. 33, and Malcolm D. Benally, ed., *Bitter Water: Diné Oral Histories of the Navajo-Hopi Land Dispute*, foreword by Jennifer Nez Denetdale (Tucson: University of Arizona Press, 2011), p. xii.

10 *The Meek Shall Inherit the Earth, Unless they are Hopi Indians* (Kykotsmovi, Arizona: The Hopi Tribe, n.d.).

11 Benally, *Bitter Water*, xiii, & Kammer, *The Second Long Walk*, "A Chronology of Important Events in the Land Dispute." See also Benedek, *The Wind Won't Know Me*, p. 36.

12 Krammer, *The Second Long Walk*, pp. 66–90, & Ward Churchill, *Struggle for the Land: Native North American Resistance to Genocide, Ecocide and Colonization* (San Francisco, Ca.: City Lights, 2002), pp. 135–162. The Navajo Generating Station coal-fired power plant near Page, Arizona faces impending closure as early as December 2019. If the utility plant closes it is likely the Peabody Energy's Kayenta Mine would also close; the two closures resulting in the loss of hundreds of plant workers and coal miners.

13 Kammer, pp. 69–70.

14 Benally, *Bitter Water*, pp. 80 & 83.

15 *The Meek Shall Inherit the Earth, Unless they are Hopi Indians*, p. 3 and Benedek, *The Wind Won't Know Me*, p. 395.

16 Benedek, *The Wind Won't Know Me*, pp. 398–400. McCain quote on pp. 399–400.

17 Ibid., p. 44. See also Chapter 5 on "Sheep Is Life" in Benally, *Bitter Water*, pp. 62–83.

18 The origins of the contemporary Hopi peoples is undoubtedly more complicated then the traditional theory that they are derived from the Anasazi of the Four Corners area. In addition to having Anasazi ancestors, the Hopi very likely derived from both the southern Paiutes north of the Grand Canyon and the Hohokam-O'odham tribes from the Verde Valley and the Phoenix Basin. Linguistic evidence, archaeological remains, and oral history traditions all bear witness to the similarities and contacts between the Hohokam and the Hopi. Hopi traditions speak of the migration of the *Patki ngum* (Water Clan) from a homeland that could either be Montezuma's Castle in the Verde Valley or near the Gila, Verde and Salt River sites of the Hohokam (or both). O'odham traditions suggest that O'odham warriors who attacked the Hohokam spoke the language of their enemies, and linguists tell us that the Hopi, like the O'odham, speak Uto-Aztecan (unlike other Pueblos). In addition, historians have documented an ancient trial that runs from Jerome and Camp Verde to Winslow (historically the "Chavez" trail), and from there north to Walpi and first mesa. This trail (and later road) was used from CE 1200 to the 1880s, and has been named the Palatkwapi Trail. See both Lynn S. Teague, "Prehistory and the Traditions of the O'odham and Hopi," *Kiva* 58:4 (1993): 435–454, and James W. Byrkit, *The Palatkwapi Trail* (Flagstaff, Az.: Museum of Northern Arizona, 1988).

19 Benedek, *The Wind Won't Know Me*, p. 45. Eric Polingyouma (Hopi) and his son Lance have traced some of the migration trails detailed in the oral traditions. Mesoamerica, in particular Guatemala, is the source of many of these tales. This information comes from a presentation delivered by Eric and Lance Polingyouma at a Heard Museum Guild meeting in Phoenix, Arizona, April 16, 2014.

20 See the testimony by Hopi-Tewa Albert Yava cited in Kammer, *The Second Long Walk*, p. 68.

21 Jake Page, "Inside the Sacred Hopi Homeland," *National Geographic* 162 (November 1982): 606–629.

22 An indication of that humor was experienced personally by me upon leaving the Director of the Hopi Cultural Preservation office in Kykotsmovi, Arizona on August 23, 2013. On the way out the door I told the Hopi Director that I was headed for Window Rock to interview the Head of the Navajo Museum there. He cautioned me not to tell them (the Navajos) that I had talked with him or "they might take me on a long walk." This event made me chuckle. When I retold it to Manuelito Wheeler, Director at the Navajo Museum in Window Rock, he got a chuckle out of it too.

Chapter Five

1 These instructions were allegedly overheard by Clark Stocking, a private in Company A, Fifth California Infantry, and one of West's men. It is quoted by Edwin R. Sweeney, *Mangas Coloradas: Chief of the Chiricahua Apaches* (Norman: University of Oklahoma Press, 1998), p. 455. A similar quotation can be found in "Mangas Coloradas," *Wikipeida, the Free Encyclopedia*, http://en.wikipedia.org/wiki/Mangas_Coloradas, p. 2 of 4.

2 *Geronimo, His Own Story: The Autobiography of a Great Patriot Warrior*, as told to S. M. Barrett (New York: Meridian, 1996), pp. 21 & 118.

3 Eve Ball, *Indeh: An Apache Odyssey* (Norman: University of Oklahoma Press, 1988), p. xvii.

4 David Roberts, *Once They Moved Like the Wind: Cochise, Geronimo, and the Apache* (New York: Touchstone, 1993), front matter.

5 Although relocation as a practice has a long history in the United States, it first became Indian Policy when George Washington advanced his 1782 plan that outlined a federal proposal to move the entire indigenous population east of the Mississippi to the "regions of the West" to which the US government was not pressing any claims. This "plan" reflected the arrogance and superiority of Anglo thinking that was later known as "Manifest Destiny." See Ward Churchill, *A Little Matter of Genocide: Holocaust and Denial in the Americas, 1492 to the Present* (San Francisco, CA: City Lights, 1997), pp. 211–218. For the discussion on nature and removal see *Geronimo, His Own Story*, pp. 6–11. Quote from p.11. In Geronimo's words, "Thus it was in the beginning: the Apaches and their homes each created for the other by Usen himself. When they are taken from these homes they sicken and die. How long will it be until it is said, there are no Apaches?" See again *Geronimo, His Own Story* (N.Y.: Ballantine Books, 1971 ed.), p. 68.

6 While most scholars translate the word *apachu* enemy, there is some disagreement among linguists as to whether the word is derived from Tewa or Zuni. H. Henrietta Stockel suggests that the word comes from *e-patch*, the Yuman word for enemy. See Karl Jacoby, *Shadows at Dawn: An Apache Massacre and the Violence of History* (New York: Penguin Books, 2008), p. 285, and Stockel, *Survival of the Spirit: Chiricahua Apaches in Captivity* (Reno & Las Vegas: University of Nevada Press, 1993), p. 2.

7 Ibid., p. 288. For "Indeh" see Ball, *Indeh*, pp. 64 & 76–77.

8 Life Giver or the Creator of Life and Usen refer to the same supernatural entity. Usen is at times spelled with two "s" as Ussen. It is also spelled Yusn or Yus and is simply an Apache adaptation of the Spanish word *Dios*. See Morris Edward Opler, *Myths and Tales of the Chiricahua Apache Indians* (n.p.: 1942), p. 3.

9 Sweeney, *Mangas Coloradas*, p. 7.

10 Stephen Trimble, *The People: Indians of the American Southwest* (Santa Fe: School of American Research, 1993), p. 251.

11 Charles Collins, *Apache Nightmare: The Battle at Cibecue Creek* (Norman: University of Oklahoma Press, 1999), front matter map.

12 Sweeney, *Mangas Coloradas*, pp. 5–8. See also *"Chiricahua," Wikipedia, the Free Encyclopedia*, http://en.wikipedia.org/wiki/Chiricahua. The lack of unanimity among scholars concerning the social and political organization of the Apaches is due in part to the constant fission and fusion of families and groups in which individuals would join related bands and sub-groups for reasons related to marriage, social events, or other circumstances.

13 Jacoby, *Shadows at Dawn*, pp. 144–145.

14 Trimble, *The People*, pp. 249 & 251.

15 Ball, *Indeh*, pp. 56–57.

16 This example comes from Anna Early Goseyun, "Carla's Sunrise," *Native People* (Summer, 1991): 8–16.

17 Opler, *Myths and Tales of the Chiricahua Apache Indians*, pp. 2–3. Other versions say that White-Painted Woman lay in the rocks where water dripped into her vagina, and that Lightning was the father of Child-of-the-Water. Another account, related by H. Henrietta Stockel, is that there were no human beings in the beginning. Child-of-the-water was a supernatural being, who disappeared then reappeared in human form along with Changing Woman. See Stockel, *Survival of the Spirit: Chiricahua Apaches in Captivity* (Reno: University of Nevada Press, 1993), pp. 6–7.

18 Ibid., pp. 3–28. While Child-of-the-Water is the principal culture hero for the Chiricahua and Mescalero Apaches, Killer-of-Enemies is the more important of the twin sons for the Western Apache, Lipan, and Jicarilla.

19 H. Henrietta Stockel, *Survival of the Spirit*, p. 29.

20 Ibid., p. 25.

21 W. Jackson Rushing III, *Alan Houser: An American Master [Chiricahua Apache, 1914-1994]* (N.Y.: Harry N. Abrams, Inc., 2004), pp. 45–46.

22 As quoted by Rushing in Ibid., p. 4.

23 Eve Ball, *Indeh*, p. 58.

24 Peter Aleshire, *The Fox and the Whirlwind: General George Crook and Geronimo, A Paired Biography* (N.Y.: John Wiley and Sons, Inc., 2000), pp. 20–24, and Robert M. Utley, *Geronimo* (New Haven: Yale University Press, 2012), p. 10. Quotation from Stockel, *Survival of the Spirit*, p. 248. Stockel goes further to say that "since hogs ate snakes and entered the water, pork was not eaten." See again Ibid., p. 11.

25 Eve Ball, *Indeh*, pp. 61–62. Lozen, who was an excellent horsewoman and skilled at stealing horses, not only engaged in warfare with the male warriors but also took on the female role of caring for the safety of the women and children. Her supernatural powers, starting at puberty, allowed her to tell the direction from which the enemy was coming. She would stand at the top of a mesa and move in a clockwise direction until her palms began to tingle and get warm. When that happened the enemy was near. She was unmarried and stayed that way, only longing for her handsome "Gray Ghost" of her youth. She got her Power from Usen, for "This power he grants me for locating the enemy. I search for that enemy which only Ussen [sic], Creator of Life can reveal to me." See H. Henrietta Stockel, *Chiricahua Apache Women and Children: Safekeepers of the Heritage* (College Station: Texas A & M University Press, 2000), pp. 70–75.

26 Utley, *Geronimo*, p. 11.
27 As quoted by Aleshire, *The Fox and the Whirlwind*, p. 34.
28 Jacoby, *Shadows at Dawn*, pp. 148–149 & 154–155.
29 Ibid., pp. 149–151.
30 Trimble, *The People*, pp. 256–257.
31 W. Dirk Raat and Michael M. Brescia, *Mexico and the United States: Ambivalent Vistas* (Athens: University of Georgia Press, 2010, 4th ed.), pp. 190–191. See also Andrés Resénez, *The Other Slavery* (Boston & New York: Houghton Mifflin Harcourt, 2016), p. 147.
32 Ibid., p. 61.
33 Trimble, *The People*, p. 257. In addition, the government of Chihuahua, according to Daklugie, not only offered $100 for adult male scalps, but $50 for women and $25 for children. See Ball, *Indeh*, p. 22.
34 "Mangas Coloradas," *Wikipedia, the Free Encyclopedia*, http://en.wikipedia.org/wiki/Mangas_Coloradas, p. 1 of 4, and Sweeney, *Mangas Coloradas*, pp. xix–xxii.
35 Sweeney, *Mangas Coloradas*, p. xvii.
36 Ibid., pp. 70–71.
37 Ibid., pp. 71–72.
38 Ibid., pp. 133–136 & 474.
39 Quoted by Sweeney, ibid., p. 135.
40 Ibid., p. 136.
41 Ibid., pp. 140–143.
42 Nathaniel Philbrick, *The Last Stand: Custer, Sitting Bull, and the Battle of the Little Bighorn* (N.Y.: Penguin Books, 2010), pp. 3–4.
43 Sweeney, *Mangas Coloradas*, pp. 385–387.
44 Ball, *Indeh*, p. 61.
45 "Jack Swilling," *Wikipedia, the Free Encyclopedia*, http://en.wikipedia.org/wiki/Jack_Swilling, p. 2 of 5.
46 Ibid., p. 25 & Sweeney, *Mangas Coloradas*, pp. 398–399. A more detailed account of the kidnapping of Mickey Free, the Bascom Affair, and the

resulting conflict at Apache Pass can be found in *The Apache Wars* by Paul Andrew Hutton (N.Y.: Crown, 2016), pp. 34–70. For the kidnapping and aftermath also see Paul Andrew Hutton and Bob Boze Bell, "Mickey Free: The True Story behind Our Graphic Novel," *True West Magazine* (August 2016): 30–39.

47 The two authors differ in the sequence of events with Sweeny arguing that Cochise tortured and killed his captives before Bascom, while the Apache account as recounted by Daklugie says that Cochise "dragged one captive to death and had the others hanged in *retaliation* [italics mine]." Compare Sweeney, *Mangas Coloradas*, p. 399 with Daklugie's account found in Ball, *Indeh*, p. 25. Quotes from Daklugie in Ball, p. 25 and Sweeney, p. 399. Another incident or "misunderstanding" might have been an event that allegedly occurred sometime between 1850 and 1860 in which Mangas Coloradas was attacked by a group of white miners near Pinos Altos who tied him to a tree and severely flogged him. The story has been discredited by Sweeney who believes that it originated with John C. Cremony's 1872 article in *Overland Monthly* and that Cremony's writings lack veracity. The story is probably apocryphal. See again Sweeney, pp. 400–405. See also "Mangas Coloradas," *Wikipedia, the Free Encyclopedia*, http://en.wikipedia.org/wiki/ Mangas_Coloradas, p. 2 of 4.

48 Sweeney, *Mangas Coloradas*, pp. 410–412.

49 Ibid., pp. 430–435.

50 Ibid., pp. 438–440.

51 Ibid., pp. 445–446.

52 Ibid., pp. 448–455. See also Albert R. Bates, *Jack Swilling: Arizona's Most Lied About Pioneer* (Tucson: Wheatmark Pub. Company, 2008).

53 Ibid., pp. 455–456. See also Geronimo's account in S. M. Barrett, *Geronimo: His Own Story*, pp. 118–121. For Fowler see "Orson Squire Fowler," *Wikipedia, the Free Encyclopedia*, http://en.wikipedia.org/wiki/Orson_Squire_Fowler, 3pp.

54 Trimble, *The People*, pp. 259–260.

55 "Apache Wars," *Wikipedia, the Free Encyclopedia*, http://en.wikipedia.org/ wiki/Apache_Wars, p. 4 of 10.

56 Trimble, *The People*, p. 260 & "Apache Wars," *Wikipedia, the Free Encyclopedia*, p. 5 of 10. The best study of the "Camp Grant Massacre" is Karl Jacoby, *Shadows at Dawn*. Grant's Peace Policy, beginning in 1869, would substitute reservation building and "feeding stations" for warfare and extermination. The old treaty system would be abandoned and Indian agents were nominated by church groups, including Quakers. As time went on it was apparent that the reservations created were drastically diminished and forced a change in lifestyle from hunting to farming. For the Peace Policy see Gary

Clayton Anderson, *Ethnic Cleansing and the Indian: The Crime That Should Haunt America* (Norman: University of Oklahoma Press, 2014), pp. 258–274. Also see Paul Andrew Hutton, *The Apache Wars* (N.Y.: Crown, 2016), pp. 124–125.

57 Jacoby, *Shadows at Dawn*, pp. 225–229.

58 O. O. Howard, *Famous Indian Chiefs I Have Known*, intro. By Bruce J. Dinges (Lincoln: University of Nebraska Press, 1989), pp. xiii–xix.

59 Ibid., pp. 112—127. See also Ball, *Indeh*, pp. 23 & 28–29.

60 Quoted by Howard in *Famous Indian Chiefs*, p. 131.

61 Quoted by Ball, *Indeh*, p. 28.

62 Edwin R. Sweeney, *From Cochise to Geronimo: The Chiricahua Apaches 1874-1886* (Norman: University of Oklahoma Press, 2012), pp. 15–16. The issue became more complicated in 1878 when the Mexican government of Porfirio Díaz, as the price of US recognition agreed to grant generous concessions to those Texan bankers, railroad men, and ranchers who had given financial support to Díaz during the Tuxtepec uprising that brought him to power. The agreement of 1878 also provided for reciprocal border crossings by troops in pursuit of hostile Indians. For an excellent discussion of the Tuxtepec uprising see John Mason Hart, *Revolutionary Mexico: The Coming and Process of the Mexican Revolution* (Berkeley: University of California press, 1987), pp. 105–31. See also Raat & Brescia, *Mexico and the United States*, p. 96.

63 Trimble, *The People*, p. 261. Sweeney cites different numbers for the populations of the Chiricahua and Tularosa Reservations. By late 1872, according to Sweeney, the two reservations had a total of 1,244 individuals, with 700 at Chiricahua and 544 at Tularosa. See Sweeney, *From Cochise to Geronimo*, p. 16.

64 Sweeney, *From Cochise to Geronimo*, p. 30.

65 Eve Ball quotes Daklugie on San Carlos in *Indeh*, p. 37.

66 Trimble, *The People*, p. 262.

67 Geronimo's hatred of Mexicans began in 1851 when Mexican troops attacked an Apache camp outside of Janos killing and capturing most of the women and children. Most of the male warriors were in town trading and socializing with the *mexicanos* while this occurred. The next day Geronimo discovered that his mother, wife, and three children had been killed by the Mexicans. In mourning he had a visitation from Usen and received the Power. That Power was demonstrated later in 1858 while fighting the Mexicans. The bullets seemingly bounced off his body. The apocryphal story relates that the Mexicans were so fearful and overwhelmed by Goyathlay's courage that they prayed to their patron, Saint Jerome, yelling out loud several times his name, "Jerónimo." Thus Goyathlay was then afterwards called "Geronimo." Whether or not tough and rough Mexican fighters would take St. Jerome, the scholar who promoted monasticism and translated Greek and Hebrew texts into the Latin Vulgate Bible, as their patron saint I leave up to the reader. The event in which Geronimo's mother, wife, and children were killed is called the Kaskiyeh Massacre and was told to S. M. Barrett in *Geronimo: His Own Story*, pp. 75–84.

68 Robert M. Utley, *Geronimo* (New Haven: Yale University Press, 2012), p. 88. Geronimo, like his fellow Chiricahuas, found himself arriving in San Carlos and being forced to settle in those unhealthy and barren parts not already occupied by Western Apaches—whom they regarded with hostility.

69 Ibid., pp. 100 & 131–132. Victorio was trapped and killed by Mexican state troops commanded by Joaquin Terrazas, supported by a large contingency of US troops. The second-in-command of Mexican troops was Juan Mata Ortíz, who himself was later killed on November 13, 1882 at Chocolate Pass near Galeana southeast of Janos. The troops who killed Mata Ortíz and 21 Mexicans were led by Juh and Geronimo. The attack at Chocolate Pass was in retaliation for the battle of Tres Castillos.

70 As quoted by Peter Aleshire, *Warrior Woman: The Story of Lozen, Apache Warrior and Shaman* (N.Y.: St. Martin's Press, 2001), p. 2.

71 Utley, *Geronimo*, p. 100.

72 Charles Collins, *Apache Nightmare: The Battle at Cibecue Creek* (Norman: University of Oklahoma Press, 1999), p. 11.

73 Peter Aleshire, *Warrior Woman*, pp. 177–179. Evidently Nana was converted by the vision and spoke in favor of the Prophet. Juh and Geronimo decided to stop recruiting warriors temporarily in order to see what the Ghost Dances would bring. The presence of Naiche, Juh, and Geronimo at Cibecue is attested to by Daklugie in Eve Ball, *Indeh*, p. 53. They were invited guests of the Cibecue and were still formally residing at San Carlos at the time. Aleshire also describes Lozen's role as an excellent horsewoman who was able to retrieve ammunition from an army mule in the midst of the chaos (Aleshire, p. 181).

74 As quoted by Collins, *Apache Nightmare*, p. 20. This is the view of the military as reported by the Fort Apache commander, Colonel Eugene Asa Carr. Charles Hurrle, the post interpreter, very likely provided this point of view and Hurrle was an incompetent translator and perpetual liar.

75 Utley, *Geronimo*, pp. 108–110; "Battle of Cibecue Creek,"*Wikipedia, the Free Encyclopedia*, http://en.wikipedia.org/wiki/Battle_of_Cibecue_Creek, 12 pp. The *Wikipedia* article is based mostly on official military reports that suggest the army was ambushed by the Cibecue, that the Prophet had refused to turn himself in peacefully, and that the ambush and later attack on Fort

Apache was the prelude to a larger insurrection. Na-Pas (Thomas Friday), the son of "Dead Shot," a White Mountain scout who was executed at Fort Grant in 1882 on charges of mutiny, said that the Prophet was cooperative and that the chaos was ignited after the commanding officer shot the Prophet. See William B. Kessel, "The Battle of Cibecue and Its Aftermath: A White Mountain Apache's Account," *Ethnohistory* 21:2 (Spring 1974): 123–134.

76 Utley, *Geronimo*, 109–110. For the return of Geronimo to San Carlos in 1883–1884, and his last breakout in 1885, see Utley, pp. 143–181.

77 Utley, *Geronimo*, pp. 187–189.

78 Ibid., pp. 217–218.

79 Aleshire, *Warrior Woman*, pp. 265–267. Lozen was also sent into exile in Florida and died later of tuberculosis in Mt. Vernon, Alabama. See also Trimble, *The People*, pp. 263–264 and Eve Ball, *Indeh*, pp. 127–133. The numbers involved vary with the source.

80 Jason Betzinez (with Wilbur Sturtevant Nye), *I Fought with Geronimo* (Lincoln: University of Nebraska Press, 1959), p. 139.

81 Robert N. Watt, *Apache Tactics 1830-1886* (Oxford, UK: Osprey Publishing, 2012), pp. 13–14.

82 Ibid., pp. 14–16.

83 Ibid., pp. 8 & 16–18. Watt defines "strategy" to mean "... maneuvers on the battlefield out of sight of the enemy, and 'tactics' refers to maneuvers on the battlefield within sight of the enemy".

84 Ibid., pp. 16–20, 23–24, 29–31, 36–40 & 44.

85 Ibid., pp. 53–58. The new weaponry also created a new dependency, and the Apaches were seldom adequately supplied with ammunition.

86 Ibid., pp. 59–60. Two of the scouts who served in the 1886 campaign against Geronimo were Navajo women serving with the Army's 20th Infantry Regiment. They may have been the first women to have officially enlisted in the US Army. See essay by Charles Brunt, "Historian: Navajos may have been 1st GI Janes," *The Arizona Republic* (Nov. 13, 2016), p. 15A.

87 This quote was taken from a sign posted in the interior of the Fort Whipple Museum on the grounds of the Veterans Affairs Medical Center in Prescott, Arizona [July 2013].

88 Utley, *Geronimo*, pp. 11 & 262. For the differences between alcoholism and alcohol abuse among American Indians see Roxanne Dunbar-Ortiz and Dina Gilio-Whitaker, *"All the Real Indians Died Off" and 20 Other Myths about Native Americans* (Boston: Beacon Press, 2016), pp. 130–136. Today Native Americans have difficulty with the use of alcohol. Death due to alcohol is about four times more common among Native Americans than the general population.

89 As quoted by H. Henrietta Stockel, *Shame and Endurance: The Untold Story of the Chiricahua Apache Prisoners of War*, p. 9.

90 Eve Ball, *Indeh*, pp. 125–137; Stockel, *Shame and Endurance*, pp. 8–27. Fort Marion had been used earlier to house Native American prisoners of war, including Seminoles in the 1830s and Kiowas, Southern Cheyennes, Comanches, and Arapahos in 1875.

91 Stockel, *Shame and Endurance*, pp. 29–50.

92 Ibid., pp. 21–22.

93 Ibid., pp. 23–27 & 101. Also see Eve Ball, *Indeh*, p. 158 and Trimble, *The People*, p. 266. The official statistics are somewhat suspect as the numbers vary with the report, and people were constantly dying while new babies were being born. As for the fate of the teenagers and youngsters, in late 1886 at least 95 children, half under 12 years of age, were scheduled to be removed from their parents at Fort Marion and sent to the Carlisle Boarding School.

94 Eve Ball, *Indeh*, pp. 138–139 & 152.

95 Ibid., pp. 152–159. Again the numbers vary with the source. H. Henrietta Stockel argues that as of October 1, 1894, there were 261 individuals at Fort Sill. See Stockel, *Shame and Endurance*, p. 104.

96 Quoted by Eve Ball, *Indeh*, p. 160.

97 Stockel, *Survival of the Spirit*, p. 261.

98 Stockel, *Shame and Endurance*, pp. 107–110; Eve Ball, *Indeh*, p. 161.

99 Stockel, *Shame and Endurance*, pp. 123–124 & 131; Eve Ball, *Indeh*, pp. 179–182.

100 Stockel, *Survival of the Spirit*, p. 246.

101 For differing data cf. Trimble, *The People*, p. 266 with Stockel, *Shame and Endurance*, p.144. See also Stockel, *Survival of the Spirit*, p. 257. For the fate of Naiche and other Apaches after the liberation of 1913 see Paul Andrew Hutton, *The Apache Wars* (N.Y.: Crown, 2016), pp. 420–421.

102 Trimble, *The People*, p. 266; Richard Grant, *God's Middle Finger: Into the Lawless Heart of the Sierra Madre* (N.Y.: Free Press, 2008), p. 65; "Apacheria," excerpt from the *Journal of the Southwest* (March 22, 2001), http://apacheria.blogspot.com/2008/02/serra-madre-apache,html.

103 "Apacheria, p. 1/7; Grant, *God's Middle Finger*, p. 66.

104 David J. Weber, "The Apache Indians: In Search of the Missing Tribe," (review) from *The Americas* 62:4 (April 2006): 664–665; Grant. *God's Middle Finger*, p. 67.

Chapter Six

1 Carolina C. Butler, ed., *Oral History of the Yavapai* (Gilbert, Az.: Acacia, 2012), pp. 103–104.

2 Ibid., p. 68.

3 Butler, pp. 35–36.

4 Butler, pp. 15, 35–44 & 53–54. See also Timothy Braatz, *Surviving Conquest: A History of the Yavapai Peoples* (Lincoln: University of Nebraska, 2003), pp. 28–40.

5 "Yavapai" in *Wikipedia: The Free Encyclopedia*, www.mediawiki.org.

6 Connie L. Stone, *People of the Desert, Canyons and Pines: Prehistory of the Patayan Country in West Central Arizona* (Bureau of Land Management, Arizona; Cultural Resource Series No. 5, 1987), p. 31.

7 Braatz, p. 12.

8 Butler, pp. 46–47.

9 *Indian Genealogy Records: Yavapai Indians*, www.FamilyLink.com/Genealogy. See also *All of My People Were Killed: The Memoir of Mike Burns (Hoomothya), A Captive Indian* (Prescott, Az.: The Sharlot Hall Museum, 2010), pp. iii–iv.

10 Butler, pp. 167–168, 174, 176, 181 & 186; Braatz, pp. 25–26.

11 Cf. Irvin Morris, *From the Glittering World: A Navajo Story* (Norman: University of Oklahoma Press, 1997), pp. 3–15 with Linda Schele and David Freidel, *A Forest of Kings: The Untold Story of The Ancient Maya* (N.Y.: William Morrow & Co., 1990), pp. 74–77. For the Chiricahua Apache view see Morris Edward Opler, *An Apache Life-Way* (Lincoln: University of Nebraska Press, 1996), pp. 16–17 & 280–282. For Mayalore see *Popol Vuh*, trans. By Dennis Tedlock (N.Y.: Simon & Shuster, 1985).

12 Stone, *People of the Desert Canyons and Pines*, p. 27.

13 Stephen Hirst, *I Am the Grand Canyon: The Story of the Havasupai People* (Grand Canyon, Az.: Grand Canyon Association, 2006), p. 33.

14 Ibid., p. 34 & Braatz, p. 27.

15 Butler, pp. 49–50.

16 Braatz, p. 47.

17 Stone, pp. 31–32 & Braatz, pp. 36–37 & 68.

18 Stone, p. 32.

19 Ibid., & Braatz, pp. 28–30.

20 Stone, p. 35.

21 For the Kumeyaay see Melicent Lee, *Indians of the Oaks* (San Diego Museum of Man, 1989). They were especially close to the Cocopa and other Yuma Indians (Lee, *Indians of the Oaks*, pp. 138–149).

22 Braatz, pp. 43, 65–66 & Stone, pp. 35–36.

23 Edward H. Spicer, *Cycles of Conquest: The Impact of Spain, Mexico, and the United States on the Indians of the Southwest, 1533-1960* (Tucson: University of Arizona Press, 1962), pp. 265–266.

24 "Yavapai People," in *Wikipedia*, en.wikipedia.org/wiki/Yavapai_people.

25 Stone, p. 35.

26 Noble David Cook, *Born to Die: Disease and New World Conquest, 1492-1650* (Cambridge University Press, 1998), p. 206.

27 Braatz, pp. 67–68.

28 Spicer, *Cycles of Conquest*, pp. 334–342. George Phillips, in his essay on "Indians and the Breakdown of the Spanish Mission System in California," *Ethnohistory* 21:4 (Fall 1974): 291–302, argues that most neophytes were "... not forced to leave [the missions], but withdrew willingly." The Spanish mission system did not collapse solely to the activities of land-hungry officials in the 1830s, but also by Indians as active agents who withdrew in mass from their emasculated rulers."

29 Braatz, pp. 69–73. In typical understatement, Kit Carson (or the collaborator who recorded his words) said that the hills around the Salt River were covered with Indians, and the "... commander allowed them to enter the camp and then ordered us to fire on them, which was done, the Indians having fifteen or twenty warriors killed ... . Were routed, and we continued our march, trapping down Salt River to the [Verde], and up to the head of the latter stream." See *Kit Carson's Autobiography*, ed. by Milo Milton Quaife (Lincoln: University of Nebraska Press, 1966, reprint of a 1935 ed.), pp. 9–10.

30 David V. Alexander, *Arizona Frontier Military Place Names, 1846-1912* (Las Cruces, N.M.: Yuca Tree Press, 1998), pp. 88–89 & 132.

31 For the battle at Maricopa Wells see Clifton B. Kroeber & Bernard L. Fontanta, *Massacre on the Gila* (Tucson: University of Arizona Press, 1986 & 1992). See also Braatz, p. 78.

32 Margot Mifflin, *The Blue Tattoo: The Life of Olive Oatman* (Lincoln: University of Nebraska Press, 2009), pp. 161–122, 44–52, 78–81, 96–99 & 106–110. The issue of the sexual relationship that Olive had with her captors, and the possibility that she had children by a Mojave mate, is dealt with in Bob Boze Bell, "Heart Gone Wild: Did Olive Oatman Want to be Rescued?," *True West* (March 2018): 18–29.

33 Mifflin, pp. 44–52.

34 Quoted by Braatz in *All of My People Were Killed: The Memoir of Mike Burns (Hoomothya), A Captive Indian* (Prescott, Az.: The Sharlot Hall Museum, 2010), x. The deceased, esteemed ethnographer, A. L. Kroeber, argued that the attackers were Yavapai. His information, however, was derived from a 1913 interview with the Mojave guide Tokwaoa. See Foreword by Wilcomb E. Washburn in R. B. Stratton, *Captivity of the Oatman Girls* (Lincoln: University of Nebraska Press, 1983; reprint of 1875 ed.), pp. viii–xi.

35 *All of My People Were Killed*, p. 68.

36 Butler, *Oral History of the Yavapai*, pp. 121–122. Contrary to the implications of Kehedwa's testimony, some ethnologists claim that the Yavapai do tattoo themselves—on the face as well as the chin. See E. W. Gifford, *Northeastern and Western Yavapai* (University of California

Publications in American Archaeology and Ethnology, vol. 14, no. 4), p. 276. On another issue, not to belabor the obvious, but it is curious that the term "massacre" when used in the literature of western US history was usually reserved for instances when Indians murdered whites, not the other way around. Thus, when troops were sent out from Fort Whipple in 1869 and killed 35 "Apaches" and wounded several others, and then captured several bows, knives, rifles, horses, and saddles, and destroyed at least one rancheria and over twenty *uwas* (akin to Apache dwellings or wickiups), the event was called a "mission" or "campaign" by military historians, not a massacre. The 1864 massacre of over 70 Cheyenne and Arapaho men, women, and children at Sand Creek, Colorado by the troops of Colonel John M. Chivington was known in western circles as the "Battle of Sand Creek." Even the partially assimilated Hoomothya described the Skeleton Cave slaughter of 1872 as a "battle." See *All My People Were Killed*, pp. 25–35.

37 Mifflin, p. 150.

38 Gregory McNamee, *Gila: The Life and Death of an American River* (Albuquerque, N.M.: University of New Mexico Press, 2012), pp. 89–91. For samples of Stratton's rhetoric see *Captivity of the Oatman Girls*, pp. 114–115.

39 Arizona *Republic* (August 18, 2013).

40 As quoted by Trudy Griffin-Pierce in *Native Peoples of the Southwest* (Albuquerque, N.M.: University of New Mexico Press, 2000), p. 295.

41 The first trans-Panama train ran in January 1855. Between 1848 and 1869 about 375,000 persons crossed the isthmus from the Atlantic to the Pacific. The "travelers" were not always friendly. In 1856 there was a race riot at Taboga Island known as the "Watermelon War" which resulted in the death of 15 Americans and 2 Panamanians.

42 *Arizona's Gold Adventures: Rich Hill, Arizona History* (arizonagoldadventures.com/id8.html).

43 *Vulture Mine: Wikipedia, the free encyclopedia* (Wikipedia.org/wiki/Vulture_Mine). Jack Swilling, a notorious Indian fighter who was known for reopening the irrigation canals in Phoenix left by the ancient Hohokam, established a grain route between the developing city of Phoenix and Wickenburg (today's Hwy 60 or Grand Avenue).

44 Gregory McNamee, *Gila*, p. 104; Bil Gilbert, *Westering Man: The Life of Joseph Walker, Master of the Frontier* (N.Y.: Atheneum, 1983), pp. 265–271. Also see Sharlot Hall Museum Library & Archives, Prescott, Az., "Walker Party: Places & Things," Vertical File. Pieter Burggraaf has an overview map of the Walker party's route in *The Walker Party: The Revised Story* (Surprise, Az.: Burggraaf, 2015), pp. 16–17 & 203. Burggraaf provides a revised view of the Gilbert account of the Walker party (see pp. 228–233).

45 Phillip D. Yoder, "History of Fort Whipple" (University of Arizona, Tucson: M.A. Thesis, 1951), p. 23.

46 Alexander, *Frontier Military Place Names*, pp. 88–89, and Yoder, "History of Fort Whipple," p. 25.

47 Yoder, "History of Fort Whipple," pp. 11–20.

48 As quoted by Gilbert, *Westering Man*, pp. 274–275.

49 Alexander, *Frontier Military Place Names*, p. 129.

50 Yoder, "History of Fort Whipple," pp. 67–69; Gilbert, *Westering Man*, p. 275.

51 Butler, *Oral History of the Yavapai*, pp. 81 & 112. The current residents of Skull Valley have a very different version of the origin of the name of the Valley. They say that the skulls that were found were remnants of a battle between Apaches and Maricopas, and at least 35 additional skulls were the result of a fight between a few citizens and soldiers and over 100 Indians. See the pamphlet, "The Skull Valley Story," comp. by Mary Kukal (Skull Valley, Arizona: The Skull Valley Historical Society, n.d.), p. 1. A similar account is given by Will C. Barnes in his *Arizona Place Names*, revised by Byrd H. Grander (Tucson: University of Arizona, 1960), pp. 357–358, in which he noted that not only was there a battle between Apaches and Maricopas, but the latter were the victors. There may be a lack of clarity by some witnesses in which the battle of Maricopa Wells of 1857 was confused with the later Skull Valley massacre. Barnes' version, needless to say, was based on reports from the notorious *Arizona Miner*, not always a reliable source. Some of the uncertainty is due to the fact that there were two or more Skull Valley "massacres." Both Hoomothya (Mike Burns) and contemporary historian Timothy Braatz allege that sometime between 1864 and 1866 a slaughter of unarmed Yavapais by American soldiers occurred somewhere in the vicinity of Skull Valley. Then in 1866 the Skull Valley massacre happened. My own historical intuition would be to go with the accounts of John Williams, Mike Burns, and Timothy Braatz. See Burns, *All My People Were Killed*, pp. 67 & 79 and Braatz, pp. 105–106.

52 Butler, *Oral History of the Yavapai*, p. 82. See also Braatz, pp. 2 & 138. For Hoomothya's testimony see *All of My People Were Killed*, pp. 26–35. His account, which tells of his own kidnapping by the US Army, exaggerates the number of dead at "225 souls ... [who] were slaughtered like cattle."

53 Yoder, "History of Fort Whipple," p. 92.

54 Butler, *Oral History of the Yavapai*, p. 124.

55 Braatz, pp. 111–119.

56 Karl Jacoby, *Shadows at Dawn: An Apache Massacre and the Violence of History* (New York: Penguin Books, 2008). See also Braatz, pp. 120–122.

57 Braatz, pp. 132–134. Grant's Peace Plan (1868 to mid-1870s) created drastically diminished reservations with farms and food in place of hunting grounds. See Gary Clayton Anderson, *Ethnic Cleansing and the Indian: The Crime That Should Haunt America* (Norman: University of Oklahoma, 2014), pp. 277–288.

58 Conversations with Judie Piner, Yavapai-Apache Cultural Center, Camp Verde, Arizona, September 6, 2013.

59 Braatz, pp. 145–146 & 156; *A Short History of the Yavapai-Apache Nation* (Yavapai-Apache Nation: Office of Public Relations, 2007), p. 13.

60 Conversations with Judie Piner; Braatz, pp. 147–150 & 158; *A Short History of the Yavapai-Apache Nation*, p. 15.

61 Braatz, p. 163; Nathaniel Philbrick, *The Last Stand: Custer, Sitting Bull, and the Battle of the Little Bighorn* (N.Y.: Penguin Books, 2011), pp. 90–93; Butler, *Oral History of the Yavapai*, p. 135.

62 Braatz, pp. 163–168; Conversations with Judie Piner. September 6, 2013; Conversations with Vicent E. Randall, Yavapai-Apache Cultural Center, Camp Verde, Arizona, August 22, 2013.

63 Braatz, pp. 159–162.

64 *A Short History of the Yavapai-Apache Nation*, pp. 15–16. The entire account of the expulsion of the Yavapai from Camp Verde and the trip from Verde to San Carlos has been narrated by the army doctor who marched with the Yavapai and Tonto Indians—William Henry Corbusier. See the family history compiled by William T. Corbusier, the fourth son of William Henry Corbusier, entitled *Verde to San Carlos: Recollections of a famous Army Surgeon and His Observant family on the Western Frontier 1869-1886* (Tucson, Az.: Six Shooter Gulch, Dale Stuart King, Publisher, 1969), esp. pp. 259–286. A brief overview of the Yavapai-Tonto forced march of 1875 is by Annette McGivney, "The Exodus Trail," *Arizona Highways* (May 2020): 36–41.

65 Braatz, pp. 171–173.

66 Ibid. 175.

67 As quoted in *A Short History of the Yavapai-Apache Nation*, p. 16. See also Corbusier, *Verde to San Carlos*, pp. 265–280.

68 Braatz, pp. 176–177.

69 *A Short History of the Yavapai-Apache Nation*, pp. 17–19.

70 Braatz, pp. 190–193.

71 *A Short History of the Yavapai-Apache Nation*, p. 21.

72 Butler, *Oral History of the Yavapai*, pp. 142–143.

73 *A Short History of the Yavapai-Apache Nation*, p. 22.

74 Braatz, pp. 220–221.

75 Braatz, p. 1; *All of My People Were Killed*, p. 72.

76 Braatz, pp. 5–6.

Chapter Seven

1 Paraphrase of Poston's 1863 report by Bernard L. Fontana in *Of Earth & Little Rain* (Tucson: University of Arizona Press, 1989), pp. 73–74.

2 Zepeda, "Poems of Home," *Home: Native People in the Southwest*, ed. by Ann Marshall (Phoenix, Az.: Heard Museum, 2005), p. 145.

3 Zepeda "Pulling Down the Clouds" in Ann Marshall, *Rain: Native Expressions from the American Southwest* (Phoenix and Santa Fe: Heard Museum and Museum of New Mexico Press, 2000), p. 14.

4 From an O'odham song as paraphrased by Thomas E. Sheridan in his chapter on "The O'odham" in *Paths of Life: American Indians of the Southwest and Northern Mexico*, ed. by Thomas E. Sheridan & Nancy J. Parezo (Tucson: University of Arizona Press, 1996), pp. 115–116.

5 As quoted by Stephen Trimble in *The People: Indians of the American Southwest* (Santa Fe: School of American Research, 1993), p. 355.

6 Ibid., p. 379.

7 Fontana, *Of Earth & Little Rain*, p. 74.

8 Sheridan & Parezo, *Paths of Life*, pp. 126–127.

9 Trimble, *The People*, p. 379.

10 Gregory McNamee, *Gila: The Life and Death of an American River* (Albuquerque, N.M.: University of New Mexico Press, 1998), pp. 155–156. Merton quotation is from McNamee, *Gila*, p. 144.

11 This description of Ed Abbey's burial was taken from Ron Dungan, "The defiant death and secret burial of Ed Abbey," *Arizona Republic* (April 19, 2015): 1A & 9–10A.

12 Edward Abbey, *Desert Solitaire* (N.Y.: Simon & Schuster, 1968), p. 83.

13 Ibid., pp. 117–118.

14 Dean Saxton, Lucille Saxton, & Susie Enos, *Dictionary: Tohono O'odham/Pima to English, English to Tohono O'odham/Pima* (Tucson: University of Arizona Press, 1983, 2nd ed.), p. 122.

15 Jim Griffith, *A Border Runs Through It: Journeys in Regional History and Folklore* (Tucson: Rio Nuevo, 2011), p. 90.

16 Trimble, *The People*, pp. 351–353.

17 For insight on traveling today the 130-mile dirt road known as the Devil's Highway see Michael Benanav, "A Drive With the Devil," *New York Times* (Travel Section; May 5, 2019), TR 1 & 4–5.

18 Roberta J. Stabel, "The Natural Setting," in James E. Officer, Mardith Schuetz-Miller, and Bernard L. Fontana, eds., *The Pimería Alta: Missions and More* (Tucson: The Southwestern Mission Research Center, 1996), pp. 11–13.

19 Ibid., pp. 14–15.

20 Ruth M. Underhill, *The Papago (Tohono O'odham) and Pima Indians of Arizona* (Palmer Lake, Colorado: Filter Press, Llc., 2000 reprint of 1941 BIA publication), p. 8. This interpretation can be questioned. Anthropologist Bernard Fontana argues that the word "Pima" was derived from the O'odham *pimahaitu* meaning "nothing." See Officer, et al., *The Pimería Alta*, p. 19.

21 Sheridan & Parezo, *Paths of Life*, pp. 114–115. See also Winston P. Ericson, *Sharing the Desert: The Tohono O'odham in History* (Tucson: University of Arizona Press, 1994), pp. 9–18, and Officer, et al., *The Pimería Alta*, pp. 19–20.

22 Saxton et al., *Dictionary*, pp. 128–131, and Ericson, *Sharing the Desert*, p. 14.

23 Officer, et al., *The Pimería Alta*, pp. 20–21. For human populations in the Pinacate see Larry G. Marshall and Clark Blake, *Land of Black Volcanoes and White Sands: The Pinacate and Gran Desierto de Altar Biosphere Reserve* (Tucson, Az.: Environmental Education Exchange, 2009), pp. 95–115.

24 Ibid., pp. 22–23, and Robert A. Hackenberg, "Pima and Papago Ecological Adaptations," *Handbook of North American Indians: Southwest*, vol. 10, ed. by Alfonso Ortiz (Washington: Smithsonian Institution, 1983), pp. 163–164.

25 Hackenberg, "Pima and Papago Ecological Adaptations," p. 164.

26 Bernard L. Fontana, "Pima and Papago: Introduction," *Handbook of North American Indians: Southwest*, vol. 10, ed. by Alfonso Ortiz (Washington: Smithsonian Institution, 1983), pp. 133–134.

27 Hackenberg, "Pima and Papago Ecological Adaptations," p. 165.

28 Paul H. Ezell, "History of the Pima,"*Handbook of North American Indians: Southwest*, vol. 10, ed. by Alfonso Ortiz (Washington: Smithsonian Institution, 1983), pp. 151–152.

29 Edward H. Spicer, *Cycles of Conquest* (Tucson: University of Arizona Press, 1970), pp. 12–13, and William H. Kelly, *The Papago Indians of Arizona: A Population and Economic Study: A Report Prepared for the Bureau of Indian Affairs, Sells Agency* (Tucson: University of Arizona, Bureau of Ethnic Research, 1963), pp. 2–3.

30 Ericson, *Sharing the Desert*, pp. 47–48, and Ezell, "History of the Pima," pp. 149 & 151.

31 Presentation by Bernard Siquieros, "Introduction and History & Culture of Tohono O'odham," Heard Museum Guild O'odham Short Course, Phoenix, Az., February 3, 2014, and Presentation by Royce Manuel, "O'odham Himdag—The O'odham Way of Life," Heard Museum Guild O'odham Short Course, Phoenix, Az., February 10, 2014. Also interview of Bernard Siquieros by W. Dirk Raat, Tohono O'odham Cultural Center, Topowa, Az., January 24, 2015, and presentation by Kelly Washington entitled "Four Hundred Years of Authm and Piipaash History Through Their Eyes," Heard Museum Guild Meeting, Heard Museum, Phoenix, Az., April 17, 2019.

32 Deni J. Seymour, *Where the Earth and Sky Are Sewn Together: Sobaipuri-O'odham Contexts of Contact and Colonialism* (Salt Lake City: University of Utah Press, 2011), pp. 7–8 & 222.

33 The "class revolt" theory is espoused by Stephen H. Lekson in *A History of the Ancient Southwest* (Santa Fe, N.M.: School for Advanced Research Press 2008), pp. 206–207.

34 Royce Manuel, "O'odham Himdag," Feb. 10, 2015. See also Griffith, *A Border Runs Through It*, p. 81.

35 Gary Paul Nabhan, *The Desert Smells Like Rain: A Naturalist in O'odham Country* (Tucson: University of Arizona Press, 1982), pp. 13–14 & 21. The contemporary O'odham often refer to themselves as of the Huhugam culture, with the word "Hohokam" referring to "those ancestors who are deceased."

36 Underhill, *The Papago*, pp. 49–51. As the story goes, Mockingbird was sent to find "dustdevil" (wind) and rain to urge them to return to the O'odham after a four year drought. Dustdevil had originally attacked the chief's daughter and was sent away as a punishment. After Coyote and Rabbit were unable to locate wind and rain, the Mockingbird was sent to look for them. Mockingbird found wind and rain and returned to the chief. Mockingbird told the chief that if his people sang songs and prayed for four days the clouds would be pulled down and wind and rain would return (hence the origin of the rainmaking ceremony).

37 Hazel McFeely Fontana, transcriber, *Trails to Tiburón: The 1894 and 1895 Field Diaries of W. J. McGee* (Tucson: University of Arizona Press, 2000), p. 128, en. 131.

38 Underhill, *The Papago*, pp. 51–52. According to native food nutrionist Felicia Cocotzin Ruiz, the first fruit picked is opened up and the red, moist side is laid down facing the sun. The sun then draws the moisture up to make clouds and rain. Ruiz, "Indigenous Food as Storytelling. Reclaiming Our Food and Our Stories," lecture (or story) delivered to the Heard Guild, Heard Museum, Phoenix, Arizona, March 15, 2017.

39 See again Lekson, *A History of the Ancient Southwest*, pp. 206–207.

40 Sheridan & Parezo, *Paths of Life*, pp. 116–117.

41 James W. Byrkit, *The Palatkwapi Trail* (Flagstaff, Az.: Museum of Northern Arizona, 1988).

42 Underhill, *The Papago*, pp. 54–55. Other Mexican traits of O'odham society include the Water Snake lore and the architectural characteristics of the O'odham folk chapel, a version of what is called *santo himdag* to the O'odham and Sonoran Catholicism to outsiders. See James S. Griffith, *Beliefs and Holy Places: A Spiritual Geography of the Pimería Alta* (Tucson: University of Arizona Press, 1992), pp. 9–13 & 75–78.

43 Karl Jacoby, *Shadows at Dawn* (N.Y.: Penguin Books, 2008), pp. 17–18.

44 M. Schuetz-Miller and Bernard Fontana, "Mission Churches of Northern Sonora," in Officer, et al., *The Pimería Alta*, pp. 62–65. The history of Kino and the process of discovering his body in Magdalena is described in a unique journalistic-novelistic way in Ben Clevenger, *The Far Side of the Sea: The Story of Kino and Manje in the Pimería—A Novel* (Tucson: Jesuit Fathers of Southern Arizona, 2003).

45 Ezell, "History of the Pimas," pp. 153–154.

46 Erickson, *Sharing the Desert*, p. 49.

47 Ibid., pp. 27–29.

48 Ibid., pp. 40–45. It is interesting to note that the previous decade witnessed the Yaqui-Mayo Revolt in colonial Sonora against Jesuit control. That revolt took place in 1740 and eventually was one factor that led to the expulsion of the Jesuits in the New World in 1767.

49 Jacoby, *Shadows at Dawn*, p. 20.

50 Herbert Eugene Bolton, *The Rim of Christendom: A Biography of Eusebio Francisco Kino* (Tucson: University of Arizona Press, 1984), p. 245.

51 Ezell, "History of the Pima," pp. 154–155 & Erickson, *Sharing the Desert*, pp. 54–55.

52 Erickson, *Sharing the Desert*, pp. 54–55.

53 Ibid., pp. 63–66.

54 Francisco Suárez and Francisco Suástegui (Secretario) al Excelentisimo Señor Vice-Gobernador del Estado de Sonora, en Arizpe, Octubre 1, 1832, in MS 434, Box no. 17, Folder no. 20, University of Arizona Library Special Collections, Tucson, Arizona. Translator unknown.

55 Erickson, *Sharing the Desert*, pp. 66–67.

56 Ibid., pp. 70–73.

57 Fontana, "History of the Papago," *Handbook of North American Indians: Southwest*, vol. 10, ed by Alfonso Ortiz (Washington: Smithsonian Institution, 1983), p. 140.

58 Jacoby, *Shadows at Dawn,"* pp. 41–42. As Jacoby notes, the People's calendar stick for 1864–1865 read: "In a raid in this year two Apaches were killed and their ears cut off and nailed on a stick."

59 Ezell, "History of the Pima," p. 156.

60 Ibid., pp. 156–157.

61 Erickson, *Sharing the Desert*, pp. 76–77.

62 Ibid., p. 77.

63 Jacoby, *Shadows at Dawn*, p. 2. The number of dead is questionable. Erickson says 125 died in the raid. See Erickson, *Sharing the Power*, p. 81.

64 Ibid.

65 Ibid, pp. 77–78 & Fontana, *Of Earth and Little Rain*, pp. 73–74.

66 Erickson, *Sharing the Desert*, p. 78.

67 Ibid., p. 82.

68 Fontana, *Of Earth and Little Rain*, pp. 74–75.

69 Erickson, *Sharing the Desert*, pp. 94–95.

70 Sheridan & Parezo, *Paths of Life*, p. 126.

71 Ibid., p. 127.

72 Trimble, *The People*, p. 369.

73 Ibid., pp. 373–374.

74 Ibid., pp. 374 & 376.

75 Clifton B. Kroeber & Bernard L. Fontana, *Massacre on the Gila: An Account of the Last Major Battle Between American Indians, with Reflections on the Origin of War* (Tucson: University of Arizona Press, 1986), pp. 4–5.

76 Ibid., pp. 7–8.

77 "Salt River stick," in Frank Russell, *The Pima Indian* (Tucson: University of Arizona Press, 1975), p. 47 [reprint of 1908 ed. published in Washington by the US Government Printing Office], Fontana Collection, MS 434, Folder 20, University of Arizona Library, Special Collections, Tucson, Arizona.

78 Isaiah Woods estimates differ in that he argues that 94 warriors were killed while 11 survived. Other eyewitnesses reported that there were anywhere from one to seven survivors. See Kroeber & Fontana, *Massacre on the Gila*, pp. 7–9. Another interesting aside is that the Tohono O'odham had been friendly with the Quechan enemies of the Akimel O'odham since pre-contact days.

79 Sheridan & Parezo, *Paths of Life*, p. 134. For Pima-Maricopa agricultural production in the Maricopa Wells area in the early 1860s see Pieter Burglar, *The Walker Party: the Revised Story* (Surprise, Az.: Pieter S. Burglar, 2015), p. 161. Quotation from Trimble, *the People*, p. 378.

80 Sheridan & Parezo, *Paths of Life*, pp. 134–135.

81 As quoted by Jacoby in *Shadows at Dawn*, p. 196.

82 Arizona *Daily Star* (January 31, 1879), Tucson, Fontana Collection, MS 434, Pima and Maricopa Clippings, Folder 14, University of Arizona Library, Special Collections, Tucson, Arizona. See also McNamee, *Gila*, p.111.

83 Presentation by Kelly Washington, Heard Museum, Phoenix, Az., April 17, 2019.

84 Sheridan & Parezo, *Paths of Life*, p. 135 & Trimble, *The People*, p. 379.

85 Sheridan & Parezo, *Paths of Life*, pp. 136–139.

86 Fontana, "History of the Papago," p. 141.

87 Andrae M. Marak & Laura Tuennerman, *At the Border of Empires: The Tohono O'odham, Gender, and Assimilation, 1880-1934* (Tucson: University of Arizona Press, 2013), pp. 130–132.

88 Ibid., pp. 138–139 & 142. Marak & Tunnerman suggest that the population is no greater than 1,400.

89 Fontana, "History of the Papago," p. 141.

90 Elmer W. Flaccus, "Arizona's Last Great Indian War: The Saga of Pia Machita," *The Journal of Arizona History* 22:1 (Spring 1981): 1–4.

91 Peter Blaine, Sr., as told to Michael S. Adams, *Papagos and Politics* (Tucson: Arizona Historical Society, 1981), p. 91.

92 Flaccus, "Arizona's Last Great Indian War," pp. 15–19.

93 Ibid., p. 19.

94 Trimble, *The People*, p. 380. See also n. 85 for complete citation of the mentioned book. Today (2019) many O'odham think of themselves as one people who have an international border running through their tribal land. The 2016 proposal of the Trump administration to build a wall though their nation is being met with opposition from many reservation members. As tribal member Alex Soto said, "This is our home, our way of life is here, our stories and songs are here. When people like Trump or any outside government takes actions that affect us, we have to act." See Dianna M. Náñez, "Tohono O'odham wall foes lobby McCain," *The Arizona Republic* (March 25, 2017): 16A. Also see Náñez, "Drawing a Line: Tohono O'odham leader warns of protest if tribe's land on border is divided," *The Arizona Republic* (May 21, 2017): 1E-2E and Náñez, "The Wall: Silent and Sacred," *The Arizona Republic* (Sept. 30, 2017): 1A & 8A. In 2020 the O'odham Nation was not consulted when several Native American burial sites were blown up by construction crews building the US border wall. See "Native burial sites blown up for US border wall," *BBC News* (Feb. 10, 2020); bbc.com/news/world-us-canada-51449739.

95 Gary Paul Nabhan, *The Desert Smells Like Rain: A Naturalist in O'odham Country* (Tucson: University of Arizona Press, 1982), pp. 89–97. Quitovac has declined in the 30-plus years since Nabhan wrote his account. The O'odham elder who tended the garden there died, and with his death much of the orchard returned to it wild state. Jesús García and the staff of the Arizona Sonora Desert Museum in Tucson, working with young people at Quitovac, are currently (as of 2017–18) attempting a restoration.

96 As historian David E. Stannard reminds us, the "Tohono O'odham in Arizona (where more than 60 percent of homes are without adequate plumbing, compared with barely 2 percent for the rest of the country) the poverty rate is nearly five times greater than the nation at large." See Stannard, *American Holocaust: The Conquest of the New World* (N.Y. & Oxford: Oxford University Press, 1992), p. 257.

97 Earl Zarbin, "The coming clash on Indian water rights," Arizona *Republic*, April 19, 2015. Also see "As the River Runs Dry" by Brandon Loomis in the Arizona *Republic*, Nov. 4, 2015, and Kathryn Sorensen, "The ABCs of Water," a presentation delivered at a conference entitled *The Water Scare: What's real?* at the Arizona Historical Society Museum at Papago Park, Tempe, Az.,

November 3, 2015. It should be noted that there are a few optimistic trends as well, including the fact that over the last two decades 13 Arizona tribes have agreed to exchange their rights to surface water of rivers running through their reservations for Colorado River water delivered through the Central Arizona Project. For this topic see Robert Glennon, "Arizona's progressive steps to secure water," Arizona *Republic*, April 11, 2018, 16A.

Commentary: Mormons and Lamanites

1 Quoted from William B. Carter, *Indian Alliances and the Spanish in the Southwest, 750-1750* (Norman: University of Oklahoma Press, 2009), p. 93.
2 Quoted by Brigham D. Madsen in *The Shoshoni Frontier and the Bear River Massacre* (Salt Lake City: University of Utah Press, 1985), p. 29 from Young's "Manuscript History," May 30, 1852, Church of Jesus Christ of Latter-day Saints, Historian's Office, Salt Lake City.
3 "Morrill Anti-Bigamy Act," *Wikipedia, The Free Encyclopedia* (en.wikipedia. org/wiki/Morrill_Anti-Bigamy_Act).
4 As quoted by Andrés Reséndez, *The Other Slavery: The Uncovered Story of Indian Enslavement in America* (Boston & New York: Houghton Mifflin Harcourt, 2016), p. 3.
5 John A. Price, "Mormon Missions to the Indians," in William C. Sturtevant, gen. ed., *Handbook of North American Indians*, vol. 4, *History of Indian-White Relations*, vol. ed. Wilcomb E. Washburn (Washington: Smithsonian Institution, 1988), pp. 461–462.
6 Douglas O. Linder, "The Mountain Meadows Massacre of 1857 and the Trials of John D. Lee: An Account," (law2.umkc.edu/faculty/projects/ftrails/ mountainmeadows/leeaccount.html, 2006). In September 1857, at least 120 members of the Missouri emigrant party were killed near Mountain Meadows north of St. George, Utah. Although the Saints attributed the killings to the Paiute Indians, later investigations proved that John D. Lee and the Mormons were mainly responsible for the Mountain Meadows Massacre. See also Ronald W. Walker, Richard E. Turley Jr., and Glen M. Leonard, *Massacre at Mountain Meadows* (N.Y. & Oxford: Oxford University Press, 2008).
7 This is a conclusion shared by Howard A. Christy, "Open Hand and Mailed Fist: Mormon-Indian Relations in Utah, 1847-52," *Utah Historical Quarterly* 46 (Summer 1978): 216–235, & Sandy Cosgrove, "Mormons and Native Americans: A Historical Overview," (www.onlinenevada.org/articles/ mormons-and-native-americans-historical-overview).
8 Scientific proof today does not support the theory of a Hebrew origin or connection with the American Indian. DNA tests, linguistic evidence, and

dental morphology all point to East and North Asia as the homeland of the American Indian. One interesting if puzzling bit of evidence links the Zuni Indians with the Japanese. See the controversial work by Nancy Yaw Davis, *The Zuni Enigma* (N.Y.: W.W. Norton & Co., 2001).

9 Quotes from Nephi in *Book of Mormon* by John A. Price, "Mormon Missions," p. 459. "Dark and loathsome" quote from Robert Gottlieb & Peter Wiley, *America's Saints: The Rise of Mormon Power* (N.Y.: G. P. Putnam's Sons, 1984), p. 174.

10 Carter, *Indian Alliances*, p. 93.

11 Gottlieb & Wiley, *America's Saints*, p. 160.

12 Ibid., p. 161.

13 Thomas E. Sheridan, *Arizona: A History* (Tucson: University of Arizona Press, 2012), pp. 119–121.

14 Ibid., pp. 201–203.

15 Ibid., pp. 203–204.

16 Ibid, p. 203.

17 Ibid., p. 204.

18 W. Dirk Raat and George R. Janeček, *Mexico's Sierra Tarahumara: A Photohistory of the People of the Edge* (Norman: University of Oklahoma Press, 1996), pp. 82–83.

19 Ibid.

20 Price, "Mormon Missions to the Indians," pp. 462–463.

21 Reséndez, *The Other Slavery*, p. 273.

22 Ibid., p. 463.

Chapter Eight

1 As quoted by Newell Hart, *The Bear River Massacre* (Preston, Idaho: Cache Valley Newsletter Publishing Company, 1982; 2nd printing 1983), pp. 157 & 159.

2 Mae T. Parry, "Massacre at Boa Ogoi," Appendix B in Brigham D. Madsen, *The Shoshoni Frontier and the Bear River Massacre* (Salt Lake City: University of Utah Press, 1985), p. 233.

3 Hart, *Bear River Massacre*, p. 84.

4 United States. Office of Indian Affairs/*Annual report of the commissioner of Indian Affairs, for the year 1863* (Washington, D.C., 1864), p. 38.

5 Madsen's study was published in Salt Lake City by the University of Utah Press. He issued an earlier study as the Dello G. Dayton Memorial Lecture called "Encounter with the Northwestern Shoshoni at Bear River in 1863: Battle or Massacre," May 11, 1983 (Ogden, Utah: Weber State College, 1984,

32pp.). Prior to Madsen's study the best available work was Newell Hart's *The Bear River Massacre* (Preston, Idaho: Newell Hart and the Cache Valley Newsletter Publishing Company, 1982; 2nd printing 1983). Hart's work consists of a collection of primary and secondary sources. Other studies since Madsen include Kass Fleisher, *The Bear River Massacre and the Making of History* (Albany, N.Y.: State University of New York, 2004); Aaron L. Crawford, "The people of bear hunter speak: Oral histories of the Cache Valley Shoshones regarding the Bear River Massacre," M.A. Thesis, Utah State University, Logan Utah, 2007 (Ann Arbor, Mi: UMI Microform, 2008); Rod Miller, *Massacre at Bear River: First, Worst, Forgotten* (Caldwell, Idaho: Caxton Press, 2008). A good summary can be found in Thom Hatch, *The Blue, the Gray, & the Red: Indian Campaigns of the Civil War* (Harrisburg, Pa.: Stackpole Books, 2003), Chapter Two, "Bear River Massacre," pp. 25–46 & 231–233.

6   Robert F. Heizer, *The Destruction of California Indians* (Lincoln and London: University of Nebraska Press, 1974), pp. 253–265.

7   As quoted by Eugene P. Moehring, "The Civil War and Town Founding in the Intermountain West," *The Western Historical Quarterly*, 28:3 (Autumn, 1997): 319. Moehring cites Alvin Josephy, Jr., as the source of his quotation which was taken from Josephy's *The Civil War in the American West* (N.Y.: Vintage, 1991), xiii. The actual number of Indian casualties (dead and wounded) that occurred during the Civil War years, 1861–1865, is difficult to derive. Scholar Henry F. Dobyns estimates that North America had 18 million Indians that declined to 350,000 by 1900. Russell Thorton suggests that the population of the US Indian was several million in pre-Columbian times and had declined by 1800 to 600,000 individuals, and by 1890 the Indian population of North America had declined to 250,000. Gregory Michno in the *Encyclopedia of Indian Wars: western battles and skirmishes, 1850-1890* (Mountain Press, p.353) argues that Indian casualties numbered over 6,000 between 1850 and 1890. Michno's statistics are questionable since they were based on army estimates that usually were incomplete and underestimated the numbers of Indian dead. My own "guesstimate" would range widely from 6,000 to 31,000 dead during the Civil War era resulting from both military actions and acts of civilian violence. See *Wikipedia: The Free Encyclopedia*, https//en.wikipedia. org/wki/American_Indian_Wars.

8   Ned Blackhawk, *Violence over the Land: Indians and Empires in the Early American West* (Cambridge, Mass.: Harvard University Press, 2006), p. 213. See also Madsen, *The Shoshoni Frontier*, pp. 20–21.

9   "Uto-Aztecan languages," *Wikipedia, the Free Encyclopedia*, pp. 1–8, http:// en.wikipedia.org/wiki/Uto-Aztecan languages.

10   Demographic data comes from Donald H. Shannon, *The Boise Massacre on the Oregon Trail* (Caldwell, Idaho: Snake Country Publishing, 2004), p. 19. For

ethnographical information see Robert F. Murphy and Yolanda Murphy, "Northern Shoshone and Bannock," *Handbook of North American Indians*, vol. 11, *Great Basin*, ed. by Warren L. D'Azevedo (Washington: Smithsonian Institution, 1986), pp. 284 & 287. See also Madsen, *The Shoshoni Frontier*, pp. 4–5. The word "Digger" was used by whites as an epithet for Indians who were considered "inferior" and lacked civilization. They were usually hunters of small game and gatherers who dug out seeds from grass and other plants. Many were Paiutes, Goshutes, and Western Shoshones who lived in the Great Basin area, or they were the Indians of northern California. "Digger" rhymes with "red nigger," another derogatory term used by whites. Again, another epithet, "redskins," was usually offensive to Indians and referred to everything and everyone from Indian scalps and flayed human skins to the red paint used for body decoration and the people themselves. For the current debate over the Washington "Redskins" from an American Indian point of view, see Leo Killsback, "Don't use Washington team's name on game day," *The Arizona Republic* (October 9, 2014): A17.

11 Shannon, *The Boise Massacre*, p. 19 & Miller, *Massacre at Bear River*, p. xix. The "willow river" name came from a KUED Video Loop, channel 7, "We Shall Remain" series, American West Heritage Center, Wellsville, Utah (July 11, 2014).

12 Madsen, *The Shoshoni Frontier*, p. 7 & Hatch, *The Blue, the Grey, & the Red*, p. 27. Cache Valley begins around Wellsville in northern Utah and runs north through today's communities of Logan and Smithfield through Franklin and Preston, Idaho to an area near Soda Springs. The Bear River, beginning in Utah, runs into Wyoming and then heads east south of Soda Springs, finally running south and west past Preston to the Great Salt Lake in Utah.

13 Murphy & Murphy, *Northern Shoshone and Bannock*, p. 291. Also see Madsen, *The Shoshoni Frontier*, pp. 7–8. For Pocatello see Brigham D. Madsen, *Chief Pocatello* (Moscow, Idaho: University of Idaho Press, 1999).

14 Murphy & Murphy, *Northern Shoshone and Bannock*, pp. 296 & 300.

15 Ibid., pp. 285, 300 & 302. Also see Lt. Col. Edward J. Barta, "Battle Creek: The Battle of Bear River," M.A. in Ed.Thesis, Idaho State College (currently Idaho State University), 1962, pp. 11–19.

16 William B. Carter, *Indian Alliances and the Spanish in the Southwest, 750-1750* (Norman: University of Oklahoma Press, 2009), pp. 109, 151, 174–175, 193, & 215–216.

17 Murphy & Murphy, *Northern Shoshoni and Bannock*, p. 286.

18 Ibid., p. 302.

19 As quoted by Madsen, *The Shoshoni Frontier*, p. 29. See also Hatch, *The Blue, the Gray, & the Red*, p. 26.

20 Ibid., p. 71 & 96–98.

21 As quoted by Rod Miller, *Massacre at Bear River*, p. 70.

22 Hatch, *The Blue, the Gray, & the Red*, pp. 27–30.

23 As quoted by Miller, *Massacre at Bear River*, p. 63.

24 Madsen, *The Shoshoni Frontier*, p. 30. One of the more notorious examples of "white Indians" was the Mountain Meadows Massacre in southeastern Utah in September 1857. There Mormon vigilantes killed non-Mormon ("Gentile") emigrants with some of the Mormons dressed as Paiutes and with the Mormons blaming the Paiutes for the massacre. In 1859 General James Carleton, famous (or infamous?) for his role in the Navajo Long Walk and the Bosque Redondo experiment, was detailed with his troops to bury the victims of the Mountain Meadows Massacre. Thirty-four individuals were buried in a mass grave. For a general overview see Virginia Cole Trenholm and Maurine Carley, *The Shoshonis: Sentinels of the Rockies* (Norman: University of Oklahoma Press, 1964), p. 182. The classic study remains Juanita Brooks, *The Mountain Meadows Massacre* (Norman: University of Oklahoma Press, 1970).

25 Ibid., pp. 30 & 55.

26 Moehring, "The Civil War and Town Founding," pp. 321 & 326.

27 Ibid., pp. 318–319 & 325–327.

28 Road Sign, Idaho Transportation Department, near Massacre Rocks (outside Pocatello), reproduced by author, July 18, 2014. For the Oregon Trail see Martin Potucek, *Idaho's Historic Trails: From Lewis and Clark to Railroads* (Caldwell, Idaho: Caxton Press, 2003), pp. 37–58. For the early history of the Raft River Valley see Kent and Janis Durfee, *The Raft River Valley: Part One 1780-1848* (Almo, Idaho: 2013).

29 *California Trail*, California National Historic Trail, National Park Service, US Department of the Interior, National Trails System Office, Salt Lake City, Utah.

30 Road Sign, Idaho Transportation Department, near Massacre Rocks (outside Pocatello), reproduced by author, July 18, 2014. See also Madsen, *Chief Pocatello*, pp. 45–49, and John C. Hilman (Snake River) to Mrs. Bronson (St. Louis, Mo.), August 11, 1862 in *Massacre Rocks: Historical Leaflet*, National Park Service, Washington, D.C. (September 5, 2000).

31 Road Sign, Idaho Transportation Department, near Massacre Rocks (outside Pocatello), reproduced by author, July 18, 2014.

32 William H. Rideing, *The Overland Express* (Ashland: Lewis Osborne, 1970), pp. 33–36.

33 Ibid., pp. 37–42; Hatch, *The Blue, the Gray, & the Red*, pp. 27–28; Madsen, *The Shoshoni Frontier*, p. 122. In March 1861, a federal law was enacted that rerouted the semiweekly Pony Express and the daily Mail stages from the southern "Butterfield" route that went from Memphis and St. Louis to southern California to the central "Shoshone" route. The law was designed to secure the mails and place them away from Confederate centers. In that year Wells-Fargo took over the western leg of the Central Overland Pony Express route, and by 1866 controlled all the major stage routes in the West.

34 William E. Unrau, ed., *Tending the Talking Wire: A Buck Soldier's* [Hervey Johnson] *View of Indian Country, 1863-1866* (Salt Lake City: University of Utah Press, 1979), pp. 10–12 & 50.

35 As quoted by Dale L. Morgan, *Shoshonean Peoples and the Overland Trails: Frontiers of the Utah Superintendency of Indian Affairs, 1849-1869*, ed. by Richard L. Saunders (Logan, Utah: Utah State University Press, 2007), p. 92.

36 Ibid., pp. 99 & 108–109.

37 Madsen, *The Shoshoni Frontier*, pp. 57–59 and Shannon, *The Boise Massacre*, pp. 96–97.

38 Hatch, *The Blue, The Gray, & the Red*, pp. 28–32.

39 Ibid., pp. 28–29 & 33.

40 Ibid., p. 34; Madsen, *The Shoshoni Frontier*, p. 143.

41 The best biography of Connor was written by Brigham D. Madsen and is known as *Glory Hunter: A Biography of Patrick Edward Connor* (Salt Lake City: University of Utah Press, 1990). For a review of Madsen's book see Richard N. Ellis, "Glory Hunter: A Biography of Patrick Edward Connor," *Pacific Historical Review* 63:2 (May, 1994): 252–252.

42 Ibid.

43 Perhaps it is no coincidence that the Bear River massacre of 1863, in which many of the volunteers were either Irish immigrants or of Irish ancestry, was also the year in which the Irish of New York City in response to the Union Army draft, engaged in lynch mob activity that resulted in the murder of many African Americans, Chinese, and American Indians. See Louis S. Warren, *God's Red Son: The Ghost Dance Religion and the Making of Modern America* (N.Y.: Basic Books, 2017), p. 337.

44 Alvin Josephy describes the Texas volunteers, who may be typical of most volunteers, as individuals who wore a variety of clothing from day clothes to Confederate gray uniforms or Union Blue outfits, young (under 25), providing their own mounts and guns including "squirrel guns, sportsman's guns, shotguns, both single and double barrels, in fact guns of all sorts." Credit was used by the army to purchase guns on the open market for those volunteers who lacked arms. On the other hand, thousands of soldiers in the California Volunteers were fed, clothed, armed and paid directly by the federal government. See both Alvin M. Josephy, Jr., *The Civil War in the American West* (N.Y.: Vintage Books, 1991), p. 55 and Benjamin Madley, *An American Genocide: The United States and the California Indian Catastrophe* (New Haven: Yale University Press, 2016), pp. 316–317.

45 John E. Wool, Department of the Pacific, Benicia, California (April 4, 1856) to John S. Cunningham, Esq., Reprint by Ed O'Dyer, Shamrock Books (*historybks@juno.com*), brochure, Fort Tejon Historical Park, California (August 11, 2014).

46 Ibid.

47 Quotes by Hatch, *The Blue, The Gray & The Red*, pp. 34–35. Also see Madsen, *The Shoshoni Frontier*, p. 169.

48 As quoted by Hatch, *The Blue, The Gray & The Red*, p. 35.

49 Madsen, *The Shoshoni Frontier*, p. 168.

50 Ibid., p. 169 and Hatch, *The Blue, The Gray & The Red*, p. 36.

51 Hatch, Ibid., p. 37.

52 Ibid., p. 38.

53 Quote from Irma Watson Hance and Irene Warr, comps., *Johnston, Connor, and the Mormons: An Outline of Military History in Northern Utah* (Fort Douglas, Utah: October 22, 1962), p. 70.

54 *Record of California Men in the War of the Rebellion*, Adjutant General's Office, 1890, revised and compiled by Brig. Gen. Richard H. Orton, Adjutant-General of California, pp. 175–177, as compiled by Hance and Warr, Ibid., p. 69.

55 See both Madsen, *The Shoshoni Frontier*, p. 176, and Blackhawk, *Violence over the Land*, p. 263.

56 Robert S. McPherson, *Staff Ride Handbook for the Battle of Bear River—29 January 1863* (Riverton, Utah: Utah National Guard, Camp Williams, 2000), p. 20.

57 Hatch, *The Blue, The Gray & The Red*, p.39; Madsen, *The Shoshoni Frontier*, pp. 178–179 & 182. The number of cavalry officers and volunteers varies with the source, with Hatch saying 225 while Madsen estimates approximately 275 officers and men.

58 Madsen, *The Shoshoni Frontier*, pp. 182–183.

59 Ibid., p. 183.

60 Ibid., p. 182. Porter Rockwell had recently shot and killed Lot Huntington at Faust's Station on January 12, 1862. See Rod Miller, "Utah Bloodbath," *True West* (May 2017): 30–33.

61 Rod Miller, *Massacre at Bear River*, pp. 79–80; Madsen, *The Shoshoni Frontier*, pp. 185–186.

62 These observations are taken from the author's field notes when he visited the massacre site on July 12, 2014. His guide for this field trip was Kenneth P. Cannon of the Utah State University Archeological Services, Inc.

63 Hart, *The Bear River Massacre*, p. 11.

64 Author's field notes, July 12, 2014. Connor's view of the valley was observed from a point on the southern bluffs where Connor, the cavalry, and the infantry first congregated. It was situated on private land on which my guide and I received permission to pass from the landowner.

65 Hart, *The Bear River Massacre*, p. 160.

66 Crawford, "The people of bear hunter speak," p. 24.

67 Mae T. Parry, "Massacre at Boa Ogoi," in Appendix B of Madsen, *The Shoshoni Frontier*, p. 232; see also Madsen, *The Shoshoni Frontier*, p. 186 & Hart, *The Bear River Massacre*, pp. 160–161.

68 There is a difference of opinion between various sectors of the Shoshone community concerning the importance and role of Chief Sagwitch at the Bear River Massacre. The official Indian version is that Sagwitch had a significant role to play. This is the version of the Timbimboo family, especially Mae Parry. Other Shoshones and Bannocks suggest that he was not even of Shoshone stock, but a mixed ancestry of Ute and white parentage. And that his escape from the Massacre Site was not an act of bravery, but a sign of disloyalty. For the controversy see Crawford, "The people of bear hunter speak," pp. 52–66.

69 A brief biography of Mae Parry can be found in Hart, *The Bear River Massacre*, pp. 141–142.

70 *Record of California Men in the War* in Hance and Warr, *Johnston, Connor, and the Mormons*, p. 72.

71 McPherson, *Staff Ride Handbook*, pp. 19–20.

72 As quoted by Miller, *Massacre at Bear River*, p. 103.

73 Appendix in McPherson, *Staff Ride Handbook*, p. 74. See also Harold Schindler, "The Bear River Massacre: New Historical Evidence," *Utah Historical Quarterly* 67:4 (Fall 1999): 300–308.

74 Parry, Appendix B of Madsen, *The Shoshoni Frontier*, pp. 234–235.

75 Ibid., pp. 233–234.

76 Hart, *The Bear River Massacre*, pp. 156–159.

77 Crawford, "The people of bear hunter speak," p. 86.

78 Miller, *Massacre at Bear River*, p. 107. See also Madsen, *The Shoshoni Frontier*, p. 193.

79 Shoshone historian Mae Parry asserted that rape that followed the Bear River massacre did not happen. See Kass Fleisher, *The Bear River Massacre and the Making of History*, p. 246. See also Crawford, "The people of bear hunter speak," p. 38.

80 Most of these examples come from Madsen, *The Shoshoni Indian Frontier*, p. 193. Also see Joshua T. Evans, "The Northwestern Shoshone Indians," M.S. Thesis, Utah State Agricultural College, 1938, p. 57. Evans' account is based on correspondence and accounts found in the Brigham Young manuscript collection and reproduced in the *Journal History of the Church*, entries for February 7 & 8, 1863.

81 The full title of Bigler's work is *Forgotten Kingdom: The Mormon Theocracy in the American West, 1847-1896.* Vol. 2 of *Kingdom of the West: The Mormons and the American Frontier* (Spokane: Clark, 1998). For Kass Fleisher's critique of Bigler see *The Bear River Massacre and the Making of History*, pp. 61–62. Although some writers, like Matthew Carr, argue that military officers like General William Tecumseh Sherman, in keeping with the moral conventions of nineteenth-century society, did not resort to sexual violence, it is fairly obvious that individuals, civilians and military, in the nineteenth-century Southwest generally held that Indian girls and young women were fair game for sexual molestation. See the review of Carr's work, *Sherman's Ghosts*, by James M. McPherson, "Uncivil War," *The New York Times Book Review* (March 29, 2015): 12.

82 Newell Hart, "The Battle of Bear River," Cache Valley *Newsletter* (December 1974): p. 3, Newell Hart Papers, MS Collection 3, Box 28, folder 3, Marie Eccles Caine Archives, Special Collections, Merrill-Cazier Library, Utah State University, Logan, Utah.

83 Cassandra Clifford, "Rape as a Weapon of War and its Long-term Effects on Victims and Society," 7th Global Conference, Violence and the Contexts of Hostility, May 5–7, 2008, Budapest, Hungary, p. 4. Statistics on My Lai and My Khe came from Seymour M. Hersh, "The Scene of the Crime: A reporter's journey to My Lai and the secrets of the Past," *The New Yorker* (March 30, 2015): 57.

84 Newell Hart, "The Battle of Bear River," Cache Valley *Newsletter*, p. 8.

85 See the examples and definitions in "Genocides in history, *Wikipedia, The Free Encyclopedia*, http://org/wiki/Genocides_in_history#United_States, and "Massacre," *Wikipedia, The Free Encyclopedia*, http://www.google.com/?gws_rd=ssl#ql=massacre.

86 Madsen, *The Shoshoni Frontier*, p. 194.

87 Newell Hart, Walnut Creek, Ca., to Woodrow Butterworth, April 4, 1961, Hart Papers, MS 3, Box 28, folder 3, Special Collections, Merrill-Cazier Library, Utah State University, Logan; Video, KUED channel 7, "We Shall Remain" Series, American West Heritage Center, Wellsville, Utah; Lew Martin, *Shoshone Language Dictionary* (Fort Hall, Idaho: Martin Enterprises, 2013), p. 110.

88 Barta, M.S. Thesis, Idaho State College, Pocatello, 1962, pp. 167–176.

89 Lucy Petty Turner, "Interview [by Meriette Robinson] on the Battle of Bear River," Eli M. Oboler Library, Idaho State University, Turner Papers, Box 7, folder 16 (1940–1941?).

90 Madsen, *The Shoshoni Frontier*, pp. 212–213.

91 Crawford, "The people of bear hunter speak," pp. 29–36. See also Lorena Washines, Utah History 457, Oral History Project, December 2, 1979, Hart

Papers, MS 3, Box 31, folder 15, Special Collections, Merrill-Cazier Library, Utah State University, Logan, pp. 8–9.

92 Rest Stop Sign, Idaho Transportation Department, Massacre Rocks, Idaho, July 18, 2014.

93 As transcribed by the author, Almo, Idaho, July 18, 2014.

94 Charles Shirley Walgamott, *Six Decades Back: A Series of Historical Sketches of Early Days in Idaho* (Caldwell, Idaho: The Caxton Printers, LTD, 1936), pp. 121–126.

95 Ibid., p. 43.

96 "Connor Creek, Idaho," *Wikipedia, The Free Encyclopedia* (http://en.wikipedia.org/wiki/Connor_Creek_Idaho).

97 See, for example, the following newspapers: *Desert News*, Salt Lake City, Aug. 19, 1851; Alton *Telegraph*, Illinois, Oct. 10, 1851; Burlington *Hawk Eye*, Iowa, Nov. 20, 1851; *Daily Free Democrat*, Milwaukee, Oct. 13, 20 & 22, 1851; *Daily Tribune*, Madison, Oct. 8, 1851.

98 Brigham D. Madsen, "The 'Almo Massacre' Revisited," *Idaho Yesterdays* (Fall, 1993): 58–59.

99 Ibid., p. 59.

100 Fleisher, *The Bear River Massacre*, p. 140.

101 Jonathan A. Floyd, "The Legend of the Almo Massacre: Ostensive Action and the Commodification of Folklore," M.S. Thesis, Utah State University, Logan, Utah, 2011, p. 72.

102 John Barnes, "The Struggle to Control the Past: Commemoration, Memory, and the Bear River Massacre of 1863," *The Public Historian* 30:1 (February 2008): 83–86.

103 Ibid., pp. 93–100.

104 "Bear River Massacre Site: Draft, Special Resource Study, and Environmental Assessment," Washington: National Park Service, 1995.

105 Author's field notes, July 12, 2014. While most Shoshone informants consider the battle to have become a massacre, some Shoshones who have been either converted to Mormonism or born into a family tradition of Mormonism believe the massacre to have been a divine act. For example, Darren Parry, a sixth generation descendent of Sagwitch and the grandson of Mae Parry, told the author that "I am grateful for the massacre at Bia Ogi ... . By accepting the gospel, Sagwitch allowed his people and all future generations the blessings of having the Gospel of Jesus Christ in their every day life." This perspective is derived from the Mormon doctrine that the Lamanites (the name the Church used to describe the American Indian) should be preserved and "that this remnant of Joseph should again come into their promised inheritance." The preceding comes from e-mail correspondence between Darren Parry and Raat, August 27, 2014, Attachment: D. Parry, Speech, "Church History," docx(35KB).

106 Kenneth C. Reid, "Research Design for Archaeological Investigations at the Bear River Massacre National Historic Landmark, Idaho, Idaho State Historical Society, 2013–2014.

107 Gary Clayton Anderson, *Ethnic Cleansing and the Indian: The Crime That Should Haunt America* (Norman: University of Oklahoma Press, 2014), p. 245.

108 Miller, *Massacre at Bear River*, pp. 129–130. As for the Washita event, Custer reported a total of 103 warriors killed, while the Cheyennes' count was less than half of that figure. Writer James Donovan called Washita a battle and not a massacre. See Donovan's *A Terrible Glory: Custer and the Little Bighorn* (N.Y., Boston, London: Back Bay Books; Little, Brown and Company, 2008), pp. 65, 92 & 120.

109 Parallels do not necessarily imply causation. But the relationship of Connor to Chivington has been fairly well established, and certainly the participants in the massacres after 1864 were undoubtedly aware of the military successes of the earlier winter war tactics of Connor and Chivington. For a discussion of "parallelisms" in American military history see the review of Matthew Carr's *Sherman's Ghosts* in the essay by James M. McPherson, "Uncivil War: A journalist assesses claims about Sherman's March, and considers it later effects," in *The New York Times Book Review* (March 29, 2015): 12.

110 For the California genocide see the well documented study by Benjamin Madley, *An American Genocide: The United States and the California Indian Catastrophe* (New Haven: Yale University Press, 2016).

Chapter Nine

1 From the program "Old Pascua Museum Presents: Yaqui Journey: 1910-1920," Tucson, Az., Old Pascua Museum, May 30, 2014.

2 As quoted by Edward H. Spicer, *Cycles of Conquest* (Tucson: University of Arizona Press, 1962), p. 79.

3 Felipe S. Molina, Avertano Olivas, Rebecca Tapia, Horminia Valenzuela, *Wame Vatnataka im Hohhoasukame* [The Ones who lived here in the beginning] (Tucson, Arizona: Pascua Yaqui Tribal Council, March 2003), p. ii.

4 As quoted from "Yaquis," in Federico Garcia y Alva Editores, *México y sus progresos: album-directorio del estado de Sonora* (Hermosillo: Impresión Oficial, 1905–1907), n.p. by Evelyn Hu-Dehart in "Solución final: la expulsion de los Yaquis de su Sonora natal," *Seis expulsiones y un adios: Despojos y exclusions en Sonora*, coordinated by Aarón Grageda Bustamante

(Hermosillo, Sonora: Universidad de Sonora: Plaza Y Valdes Editores, 2003), p. 156.

5   William Curry Holden, "Introduction" to "Studies of the Yaqui Indians of Sonora, Mexico," in *Texas Technological College Bulletin*, XII: 1 (Lubbock, Tx.: Texas Technological College, Jan. 1936; AMS reprint, 1979), pp. 9–10.

6   Edward H. Spicer, *The Yaquis: A Cultural History* (Tucson: University of Arizona Press, 1980), p. 158.

7   Sterling Evans, *Bound in Twine: The History and Ecology of the Henequen-Wheat Complex for Mexico and the American and Canadian Plains, 1880-1950* (College Station: Texas A&M University Press, 2007), pp. 67–90.

8   Edward H. Spicer, "Yaqui," in *Handbook of North American Indians: Southwest*, vol. 10, ed. by Alfonso Ortiz (Washington: Smithsonian Institution, 1983), p. 251. By the mid-1970s the Yoeme population in the Río Yaqui area had increased to 20,000, with, by the 1980s, another 5,400 individuals in the United States.

9   Felípe S. Molína and David Leedom Shaul, *A Concise Yoeme and English Dictionary* (Tucson: Tucson Unified School District, 1993), pp. 20 & 59. Also see William Kurath and Edward H. Spicer, "A Brief Introduction to Yaqui: A Native Language of Sonora," in *University of Arizona Bulletin: Social Science Bulletin No. 15* (Tucson: University of Arizona Press, 1947), pp. 5–35.

10 Edward H. Spicer, "Yaqui," p. 262.

11 Steven V. Lutes, "Yaqui Indian Enclavement: The Effects of an Experimental Indian Policy in Northwestern Mexico," Chapter 2 of *Ejidos and Regions of Refuge in Northwestern Mexico*, ed. by N. Ross Crumrine and Phil C. Weigand (Tucson: University of Arizona Press, Anthropological Papers Number 46, 1987), p. 12.

12 "Pascua Yaqui Tribe," *Wikipedia: The Free Encyclopedia*, p. 1 of 5 (en. wikipedia.org/wiki/Pascua_Yaqui_Tribe).

13 Edward H. Spicer, "Yaqui," pp. 250–251.

14 Spicer, *Cycles of Conquest*, p. 13. The "Eight Holy Pueblos" were the mission towns, going from east to west of intervals of 6 to 8 miles from 50 miles upstream to the mouth of the Río Yaqui, named Cócorit, Bácum (*Vahkom*), Tórim, Vícam, Pótam, Ráhum, Huírivis (Huíribis), and Belem (the last three towns lying north of the others). See Spicer above, p. 50, and María de los Angeles Orduño García, *En el País de los Yaquis* (Hermosillo, Sonora: Colección Voces del Desierto, 1999), p. 98.

15 Ruth Warner Giddings, *Yaqui Myths and Legends* (Tucson: University of Arizona Press, 1959), pp. 25–27. There are several versions of the "Talking Tree" story. In another account Yomumuli, the First Woman, is replaced by Yomomoli, the Wise Man from Grandmothers' Mountain. It is his twin daughters who translate for the people the hummings of the tree. See Thomas E. Sheridan, "The Yoemen

(Yaquis): An Enduring People," in *Paths of Life: American Indians of the Southwest and Northern Mexico*, ed. by Thomas E. Sheridan & Nancy J. Parezo (Tucson: University of Arizona Press, 1996), pp. 36–39.

16 David Delgado Shorter, *We Will Dance Our Truth: Yaqui History in Yoeme Performances* (Lincoln: University of Nebraska Press, 2009), pp. 15 & 22.

17 Stan Padilla, *Deer Dancer: Yaqui Legends of Life* (Summertown, Tenn.: Book Publishing Company, 1998), pp. 45–49.

18 Sheridan & Parezo, *Paths of Life*, pp. 51 & 53.

19 This is also the conclusion of Edward H. Spicer. See Spicer, *People of Pascua* (Tucson: University of Arizona Press, 1988), p. 29.

20 Spicer, *Cycles of Conquest*, pp. 46–47 & Ernesto Quiroga Sandoval [Historian, Pascua Yaqui Tribe], "Yaqui History" (August 2009), pp. 1 & 2 of 4 (pascuayaqui-nsn.gov/index.php?option=com_content&view=article&id=28 &Itemid=14).

21 Spicer, "Yaqui," pp. 251–252.

22 Spicer, *Cycles of Conquest*, p. 49 & Spicer, "Yaqui," p. 254.

23 Evelyn Hu-DeHart, *Missionaries Miners & Indians: Spanish Contact With the Yaqui Nation of Northwestern New Spain, 1533-1820* (Tucson: University of Arizona Press, 1981), p. 3.

24 Spicer, *Cycles of Conquest*, p. 51.

25 Ibid., pp. 51–53 & Hu-Dehart, *Missionaries*, pp. 68–70.

26 Hu-Dehart, *Missionaries*, p. 5. See also Evelyn Hu-Dehart, "The Yaqui Rebellion of 1740: Prelude to Jesuit Expulsion from New Spain," *Memoria Americana* 12 (2004): 197–219.

27 Hu-Dehart, *Missionaries*, pp. 5–7.

28 Spicer, *Cycles of Conquest*, p. 60 & Linda Zoontjens and Yaomi Glenlivet, "A Brief History of the Yaqui and Their Land," pp. 2 & 3 of 12 (//sustainedaction. org/Explorations/history_of_the_yaqui.htm).

29 Zoontjens, "A Brief History of the Yaqui," p. 3 of 12.

30 Ibid., pp. 3–4 of 12.

31 Ibid., pp. 4–5 of 12 & Evelyn Hu-Dehart, *Yaqui Resistance and Survival: The Struggle for Land and Autonomy, 1821-1910* (Madison: University of Wisconsin Press, 1984), pp. 84–86. Also see Paul Vanderwood, "Betterment for Whom? The Reform Period, 1855–1875," *The Oxford History of Mexico*, ed. by Michael C. Meyer and William H. Beezley (Oxford: Oxford University Press, 2000), p. 383.

32 Hu-Dehart, *Yaqui Resistance and Survival*, p. 88.

33 Ibid., pp. 88 & Spicer, *Cycles of Conquest*, p. 66.

34 Hu-Dehart, *Yaqui Resistance and Survival*, pp. 88–89 & Spicer, *Cycles of Conquest*, pp. 66–67.

35 Spicer, *The Yaquis: A Cultural History*, p. 144.

36 This is not to say that the Yaquis reduced their resistance to Pesqueira. In 1875, the same year that the Yaqui people declared their independence from Mexico, José María Leyva, called Cajeme by Yaquis, led 1,500 Yaqui warriors in a battle against Governor José Pesqueira's 500 troops at Pitahaya. See Edward H. Spicer, "The Military History of the Yaquis," published by the United States Army, Fort Huachuca, Az., 2/2/2015, p. 2 or 12 (//huachuca. army.mil/pages/history/spicer.html).

37 Hu-Dehart, *Yaqui Resistance and Survival*, pp. 91–93.

38 W. Dirk Raat and Michael M. Brescia, *Mexico and the United States: Ambivalent Vistas* (Athens: University of Georgia Press, 4th ed., 2010), pp. 98–99.

39 Stuart F. Voss, *On the Periphery of Nineteenth-Century Mexico: Sonora and Sinaloa, 1810-1877* (Tucson: University of Arizona Press, 1982), pp. 148–149.

40 Voss, *On the Periphery*, pp. 151–152.

41 Consuelo Boyd, "Twenty Years to Nogales: The Building of the Guaymas-Nogales Railroad," *The Journal of Arizona History* 22:3 (Autumn 1981): 295. Also see John Mason Hart, *Empire and Revolution: The Americans in Mexico since the Civil War* (Berkeley & Los Angeles: The University of California Press, 2002), pp. 36–39 & 119–122.

42 Ramón Eduardo Ruiz, *The People of Sonora and Yankee Capitalists* (Tucson: University of Arizona Press, 1988), pp. 148–149.

43 Voss, *On the Periphery*, pp. 152–160.

44 The subheading is borrowed from Sterling Evans' book *Bound in Twine*.

45 Ruiz, *The People of Sonora*, pp. 147–150.

46 Ibid., p. 182. The Cajeme years are well narrated in Bruce Vandervort's *Indian Wars of Mexico, Canada and the United States, 1812-1900* (New York & London: Routledge, 2006), pp. 230–236.

47 As quoted by Spicer, "The Military History of the Yaquis," p. 3 of 12.

48 Not all Yaquis supported Cajeme. Dominga Tava, who was born in Hermosillo in 1901 and moved to Arizona in 1916, said that her father and his brothers thought Cajeme was a traitor who betrayed the Yaqui tribe. See Jane Holden Kelly, *Yaqui Women: Contemporary Life Histories* [interview of Tava by Holden Kelly] (Lincoln: University of Nebraska Press, 1991), pp. 82–83.

49 Ruiz, *The People of Sonora*, pp. 178–179.

50 As related by Dominga Tava to Jane Holden Kelley in *Yaqui Women: Contemporary Life Histories* (Lincoln & London: University of Nebraska Press, 1991), pp. 78–85 & 88–89. See also Evans, *Bound in Twine*, p. 78.

51 Ibid., p. 179. See also Tonya Yirka, "The History of Pearl Diving in Mexico," p. 3 of 7 (www.ehow.com/about_6690169_history-pearl-diving-mexico.html).

52 Ibid., p. 180.

53 Molina, et al., *Wame Vatnataka*, p. iii. See also Hu-Dehart, *Yaqui Resistance and Survival*, p. 89.

54 Quotations from Molina, et al, *Wame Vatnataka*, p. iii, and Rosalio Moisés, Jane Holden Kelley, and William Curry Holden, *The Tall Candle: The Personal Chronicle of a Yaqui Indian* (Lincoln: University of Nebraska Press, 1971), p. 15. Also see Hu-Dehart, *Yaqui Resistance and Survival*, pp. 88–89, & Spicer, "The Military History of the Yaquis," p. 5 of 12.

55 Spicer, "The Military History of the Yaquis," p. 5 of 12.

56 Ruiz, *The People of Sonora*, p. 181.

57 Vandervort, *Indian Wars*, pp. 229–230.

58 Evans, *Bound in Twine*, pp. 71–72.

59 One attitude that Yaquis shared with yoris was their disgust and fear of the rurales. Mexican informants in Hermosillo, La Colorada, and Minas Prietas, like their Yaqui neighbors, "hated these southern outsiders." See Celia E. Duarte, "Mexican-Yaqui Relations during the Revolution," Student Paper, Anthropology 212, "Peoples of Mexico," May 22, 1961, on file at the Arizona State Museum, Library and Archives, University of Arizona, Tucson.

60 Evans, *Bound in Twine*, pp. 76–77.

61 Quotations from Molina, et al., *Wame Vatnataka*, p. iv.

62 Quotations from Beals, *Porfirio Diaz: Dictator of Mexico* (Philadelphia & London: J. B. Lippincott Company, 1932), pp. 373–374, and Gruening, *Mexico and its Heritage* (New York & London: The Century Co., 1928), p. 59. For the most notorious and thorough criticism by one of Díaz's contemporaries, see the work by the "muckraking" socialist newspaperman, John Kenneth Turner, *Barbarous Mexico* (Austin: University of Texas Press, 1969, reprint of an earlier edition).

63 Hu-Dehart, "Solución final," pp. 156–157, and James Creelman, *Diaz: Master of Mexico* (New York & London: D. Appleton & Co., 1911), p. 27.

64 Evans, *Bound in Twine*, pp. 75–76.

65 Quoted in Molina, et al., *Wame Vatnataka*, p. iv.

66 Ibid.

67 Evans, *Bound in Twine*, p. 76. Quotation from Molina, et al., *Wame Vatnataka*, p. iv.

68 Leslie Bethell, ed., "The Periphery" in *The Cambridge History of Latin America*, vol. IV, c. 1870 to 1930 (Cambridge: University Press, 1986), p. 184.

69 Ibid. Also see Evans, *Bound in Twine*, p. 80.

70 Rosalio Moisés, Jane Holden Kelley, and William Curry Holden, *The Tall Candle: The Personal Chronicle of a Yaqui Indian* (Lincoln: University of Nebraska Press, 1971), esp. pp. ix-lviii.

71 "The Life Story of Rosalio Valencia," pp. 1–7 of autobiographical notebooks, A-0472a, volume 1, Arizona State Museum, Library and Archives, University of Arizona, Tucson.

72 As related by Josefa (Chepa) Moreno to Jane Holden Kelley in *Yaqui Women*, pp. 126 & 140–142. See also Evans, *Bound in Twine*, p. 79.

73 Kelley, *Yaqui Women*, pp. 130–134.

74 Ibid., pp. 134–139.

75 Kelley, *The Tall Candle*, pp. 17 & 46.

76 Evans, *Bound in Twine*, p. 80.

77 "Memories of Valle Nacional as told by Don Enrique Segura of Xalapa, Ver. in 1962," Tucson, Feb. 7, 1976, MS 5, Edward H. & Rosamond B. Spicer Papers, Arizona State Museum, University of Arizona, Tucson.

78 Refugio Savala, *The Autobiography of a Yaqui Poet*, ed. by Kathleen M. Sands (Tucson: University of Arizona Press, 1980), pp. 147–149.

79 In the early 1900s there were many Yaqui communities in and around Tucson which either no longer exist or have lost their traditional identity, including Mesquital, Mesquitalito, Barrio Anita, Siki Puentes, Chukui Tanki, Huukim, Fuerte, Pooteo, and Bwe'u Hu'upa. See maps in Savala, *Autobiography*, p. 10 & Molina, et al., *Wame Vatnataka*, p. vii.

80 Molina, et al., *Wame Vatnataka*, pp. v-vi.

81 Interview of Guillermo Quiroga, Director of Pascua Yaqui Museum and Cultural Center, by W. Dirk Raat, January 28, 2015, Old Pascua Pueblo, Tucson, Arizona. Quiroga mentioned to me that he never knew his grandfather's name since he used many aliases for fear that Mexican and Yaqui spies (*to'o coyoris* or *torocoyoris*) would come to Tucson and assassinate him for having been a Yaqui warrior.

82 Hu-Dehart, *Yaqui Resistance and Survival*, pp. 212–219. For a critique that compares Hu-Dehart's narrative and historical approach to that of Spicer's ethnohistorical one, see Thomas E. Sheridan, "How to Tell the Story of a 'People Without History': Narrative versus Ethnohistorical Approaches to the Study of the Yaqui Indians Through Time," *Journal of the Southwest* 30:2 (Summer 1988): 168–189.

83 Savala, *The Autobiography of a Yaqui Poet*, pp. 147–149.

84 Carlos Castaneda, *The Teachings of Don Juan: A Yaqui Way of Knowledge* (Berkeley & Los Angeles: University of California Press, 1998), pp. 15–22.

85 Richard de Mille, "The Art of Stalking Castaneda" and "The Shaman of Academe" in *The Don Juan Papers: Further Castaneda Controversies*, ed. by Richard de Mille (Lincoln, Nebraska: An Authors Guild Backinprint.com Edition, 2001), pp. 10 & 17–23. Quotation from p. 20.

Epilogue

1 Blackhawk, *Violence over the Land: Indians and Empires in the Early Ameican West* (Cambridge, Mass.: Harvard University Press, 1997), p. 3.

2 As quoted by Naomi Klein in *No Is Not Enough* (Chicago: Haymarket Books, 2017), p. 227.

3 The buffalo slaughter affected today's Indian in that bison-reliant tribal nations have per capita incomes 20 to 40 percent below the average of all American Indian nations. So, in spite of the fact that many indigenous communities survived "settler colonialism," the effects of colonialism are still with many contemporary Indian nations. See the article in the Minneapolis *Star Tribune* by Evan Ramstad at www.startribune.com/nearly-150yearslater-the-buffalo-slaughter-hangs-over-american-indian-wealth-study-finds/5059 (February 17, 2019). As an aside, it should be noted that Indian men pursuing the bison robe trade were also somewhat responsible for the near-extinction of the buffalo. The latter is described by Louis S. Warren in his article entitled "The Nature of Conquest: Indians, Americans, and Environmental History," in *A Companion to American Indian History*, ed. by Philip J. Deloria and Neal Salisbury (Malden, MA; Oxford, UK; and Victoria, Australia: Blackwell Publishing Ltd, 2004), pp. 295–296.

4 Sexual mutilation was also practiced by Native Americans. Reports about Plains Indians indicate that indigenous women when taking a victory lap around their camps would wear severed penises around their necks as a form of ornamentation, or that a man's genitalia would be stuffed into the mouth of a dead victim as both a practical joke and a spiritual ceremony designed to humiliate the deceased in the next world (allegedly this was done to several corpses after the Battle of the Little Big Horn). See both George Black, *Empire of Shadows: The Epic Story of Yellowstone* (N.Y.: St. Martin's Griffin, 2012), pp. 169 & 460, note 10 and James Donovan, *A Terrible Glory* (N.Y.: Black Bay Books, 2008), pp. 243–244. For a brief description of the Sand Creek Massacre see David E. Stannard, *American Holocaust: The Conquest of the New World* (N.Y. & Oxford: Oxford University Press, 1992), pp. 129–134.

5 For the "Trail of Tears" and Andy Jackson, see Stannard, pp. 121–125.

6 The Iroquois (comprising the Cayuga, Mohawk, Oneida, Onondaga, Seneca, and Tuscarora) instilled fear into the Huron and their neighbors by skinning their enemies alive. So too were the Sioux known for their killing by flaying their victims. Scalp wars were practiced by California and Colorado River tribes in seeking revenge against rival clans. Scalping was also engaged in by the Natchez people of the Mississippi Valley on their enemy warriors while the Comanche killed Apaches by scalping the latter. Lakota scalping also took place in the Custer fight at Little Big Horn. See Jonathan J. Moore, *Hung, Drawn, and Quartered: The Story of Execution Through the Ages* (N.Y.: Metro Books, 2017), pp. 168–69 & 172–74. According to author George Black, torture

and mutilation, including scalping, had been a universal constant since pre-*Homo sapiens* times through the Parthians of ancient Greece to the indigenous populations of the Caribbean and the Spanish conquistadores of America. See Black, *Empire of Shadows*, pp. 168–169. Indian warfare, including scalping and taking captives, is the topic of Tom Holm's "American Indian Warfare" in *A Companion to American Indian History*, ed. by Philip J. Deloria and Neal Salisbury (Malden, MA; Oxford, UK; Victoria Australia: Blackwell Publishing, Ltd, 2002, 2004), pp. 152–157 (esp. p. 157).

7 One English soldier in the Irish wars was Humphrey Gilbert, half-brother of Sir Walter Raleigh. To bring the Irish to heel he ordered "the heddes of all those ... which were killed in the daie, should be cutte off from their bodies and brought to the place where he incamped at night." As quoted by David E. Stannard, *American Holocaust: The Conquest of the New World* (N.Y. & Oxford: Oxford University, 1992), p. 99.

8 Andrés Reséndez, *The Other Slavery* (Boston & N.Y.: Houghton Mifflin Harcourt, 2016), pp. 309–310. The record is mixed concerning black abolitionist Frederick Douglas who, although declaring the equality of all peoples, including Native Americans, allegedly argued that Native Americans, unlike black Americans, were opposed to the civilizing work of the white majority culture. This was an argument that white supremacists had used against him. See the magazine *Teen Vogue* (teenvogue.com/story/five-things-didnt-know-frederick-douglas).

9 Ron Chernow, *Grant* (New York: Penguin Press, 2017), p. 78. For Grant's own words about his Fort Vancouver experiences see *Ulysses S. Grant: Memoirs and Selected Letters—Personal Memoirs of US Grant, Selected Letters 1839-1865*, ed. by Mary Drake McFeely & William S. McFeely (N.Y.: The Library of America, Literary Classics of the United States, 1990), pp. 136–139. See also James Donovan, *A Terrible Glory*, p.29.

10 The statistics of death and violence need to be remembered when talking about relocation, removal, and deportation. The Yaquis probably faced the worst deportation situation with the forced removal of over 6,000 individuals between 1900 and 1907 from the Yaqui River area to the Yucatán. The Mazocoba massacre cost them around 395 dead while over a thousand women and children became prisoners. While 1,476 Yavapai were sent to San Carlos in 1875, only 1,000 arrived. The largest number of Navajos removed to Bosque Redondo was 11,468. The Owens Valley Paiutes had 998 individuals at Camp Independence with 850 finally arriving at Fort Tejon. The number for the Chiricahua Apache removal came to 519. Between 250 and 366 Shoshones were killed at the Bear River Massacre.

11 Blackhawk, *Violence over the Land*, p. 268.

12 Joanna Allhands, "Willcox's wells are running dry," *Arizona Republic* (August 6, 2018), p. 12A.

13 Evan Osnos, "The Violent Style," *The New Yorker* (Nov. 16, 2020): 30–37.

14 Roxanne Dunbar-Ortiz quotes native historian Jace Weaver to the effect that "The Indian Wars were not fought by the blindingly white American cavalry of John Ford westerns but by African Americans and Irish and German immigrants." One might also add, "and their Indian allies." See Dunbar-Ortiz, *An Indigenous Peoples' History of the United States* (Boston: Beacon Press, 2014), pp. 146–149.

15 William H. Leckie with Shirley A. Leckie, *The Buffalo Soldiers: A Narrative of the Black Cavalry in the West* (Norman: University of Oklahoma Press, 2003), pp. 172–189, 211–233 & 251–252.

16 Ibid., p. 210.

17 In 1894 19 traditional Hopis from Oraibi were arrested and shipped to military prison at Alcatraz Island for refusing to cooperate with the government in sending their children to an off-reservation boarding school. See Peter M. Whiteley, *Deliberate Acts: Changing Hopi Culture Through the Oraibi Split* (Tucson: University of Arizona Press, 1988), pp. 86–88.

18 In March of 2015 the United Nations issued a report asserting that one in three women worldwide experience sexual violence in their lifetimes, and that in the United States 83% of girls between the ages of 12 and 16 are subjected to sexual harassment in school. See "Comment: Today's Woman" in "The Talk of the Town," *The New Yorker* (March 23, 2015): 35.

19 For Quanah Parker and the Comanches see S. C. Gwynne, *Empire of the Summer Moon* (N.Y.: Scribner, 2010).

20 Ken S. Coates, *A Global History of Indigenous Peoples: Struggle and Survival* (N.Y.: Palgrave Macmillan, 2004), p. 22.

21 Gerald Vizenor, *Manifest Manners: Postindian Warriors of Survivance* (Hanover & London: Wesleyan University Press, University Press of New England, 1994), pp. 4 & 167.

22 See Ned Blackhawk, "Standing Tall" in the N.Y. *Times Book Review* (January 27, 2019): 1 & 16.

23 Norimitsu Onishi, "In California, Saving a Language That Predates Spanish and English," N.Y. *Times* (April 13, 2014). Also Raquel Cepeda, "The Lure of Havasu Falls," N.Y. *Times* (Sept. 6, 2015), TR 1, 6–7.This is not to say that the Havasupai do not have their troubles, especially when it comes to educating their children. For their recent problems (as of 2018) see Alden Woods, "Amid suit, more woes for Canyon tribe school" in *Arizona Republic* (May 26, 2018), pp. 1A, 6A & 8A.

24 Spencer Higgins, "Low-power FM radio stations will triple in the state," *Arizona Republic* (April 11, 2015), p. 16A; Judith Thurman, "A Loss for Words: Can a dying language be saved," *The New Yorker* (March 30, 2015): 32–39; Betty Reid, "Disney to dub 'Finding Nemo' in Navajo," *Arizona Republic* (December 5, 2014), p. A7.

25 Justin McDuffie, "16 Navajos graduate program targeting ironworking careers," *Arizona Republic* (September 9, 2013).

26 Carlyle Begay, "'Go and tell the Navajo People that Education is the Ladder," *Arizona Republic* (December 6, 2014), pp. F6-F7.

27 Kaila White, "Oh, the places these grads will go (home)," *Arizona Republic* (May 12, 2015), pp. 3A & 6A. The school outside of Arizona with the largest number of Indian students is BYU in Provo, Utah.

28 Martin A. Link, *Navajo: A Century of Progress, 1868-1968* (Window Rock, Az.: Navajo Tribe, 1968), p. 55. Recently the Navajo nation has extended the electric grid under "The Light Up Navajo" project. See Shondlin Silversmith, "Navajo families get onto the grid," *Arizona Republic* (May 26, 2019), pp. 1D & 5D.

29 Edward Abbey, *Desert Solitude*, pp. 102–109, quote on p. 109. For the homicide rates see Felicia Fonseca, "Navajo Reservations homicide total higher than some big cities," *Arizona Republic* (April 30, 2014).

30 Brandon Loomis, "It's going to take 100 years," *Arizona Republic* (August 15, 2014), pp. A1, A-10 & A-11. Also see article by Loomis, "Navajos will get $1 bil to clean up uranium," *Arizona Republic* (April 4, 2014), pp. A1 & A9. The data on the number of abandoned mines comes from a presentation by Bill Pierce, candidate for Arizona state mine inspector, Sun City Grand, Surprise, Az. (Sept. 29, 2018).

31 "New Map gives detailed picture of coronavirus outbreak on Navajo Nation," by Justin Price, et al., *Arizona Republic* (May 22, 2020).

32 "A Devastating Blow: Virus Kills 81 Members of Native American Tribe," New *York Times* (Oct. 8, 2020).

33 Dennis Wagner, "Tribe asks human-rights panel to fight Snowbowl," *Arizona Republic* (March 5, 2015), pp. A3 & A10. See also Megan Finnerty, "On the slopes, spirituality and commerce collide," *Arizona Republic* (March 15, 2015), pp. F1-F3 and Alden Woods, "Court rejects Hopi snowmaking claims," *Arizona Republic* (December 1, 2018), pp. 3A & 14A. Another environmental problem is declining snowfall and climate warming. Water shortages continue to be a problem for the people on the Navajo reservation. See Brandon Loomis, "As the River Runs Dry" in *Arizona Republic* (August 29, 2015), 1 F & 2 F. In addition, a coal burning utility near Page, Arizona, known as the Navajo Generating Station, has been shut down after 2021 throwing many

Navajo out of their coal mining jobs. Consult Ryan Randazzo, "Navajo Nation signs lease to extend use of coal plant," *Arizona Republic* (June 28, 2017), p. 18A.

34 Julie Turkewitz, "Among the Navajos, A Renewed Debate about Gay Marriage," *Arizona Republic* (February 22, 2015), p. 14.

35 Felicia Fonseca, "Navajo-Hopi relocation efforts drag on," *Arizona Republic* (Feb. 10, 2015), p. A5; Felicia Fonseca, "Navajo woman is family's last link to land," *Arizona Republic* (March 22, 2014), A6; Krystle Henderson, "Navajo family's land rights might die with matriarch," *Arizona Republic* (April 26, 2014), A27. One area of agreement between Navajo and Hopi is the mutual attempt to prevent Paris auction houses from auctioning off sacred Navajo masks and Hopi katsina dolls. See Thomas Adamson, "Navajo buy back artifacts at Paris auction," *Arizona Republic* (Dec. 16, 2014), A11.

36 Megan Finnerty, "Defending Native Honor: Navajo Woman Being Sued by Washington Team Remains Defiant," *Arizona Republic* (Sept. 28, 2014), pp. F1-F3. On July 8, 2015 a federal judge ordered the Patent and Trademark Office to cancel registration of the Washington Redskins' trademark, a ruling that meant that Blackhorse is no longer a defendant in the case. The Supreme Court on June 19, 2017 ruled that even trademarks considered to be derogatory deserve First Amendment protection, a decision that favored the position of the Washington Redskins. See Richard Wolf, "Justices: Offensive trademarks are protected speech," *Arizona Republic* (June 20, 2017), p. 3B. As of 2020 the brain trust at the NFL and the Washington team reconsidered the issue and changed the name to the Washington Football Team.

37 Steven V. Lutes, "Yaqui Indian Enclavement: The Effects of an Experimental Indian Policy in Northwestern Mexico," in *Ejidos and Regions of Refuge in Northwestern Mexico*, ed. by N. Ross Crumrine and Phil C. Weigand (Tucson: University of Arizona Press, 1987), p. 19.

38 Felicia Fonseca, "Anti-violence measure will allow tribes to prosecute non-Indians," *Arizona Republic* (Feb. 7, 2014).

39 Tohono O'odham Community Action (TOCA) is not the only indigenous group that is concerned with Indian diseases and the need to create indigenous food programs. Patty Talahongva, a Hopi from First Mesa who is currently (2019) the curator for the Phoenix Indian School Visitor Center, describes the emergence and resurgence of indigenous foods in "No More 'Die Bread': How Boarding Schools Impacted Native Diet and the Resurgence of Indigenous Food Sovereignty," *Journal of American Indian Education*, 57, 1 (Spring 2018): 145–153. In addition to TOCA, she mentions Roxanne Swentzell and *The Pueblo Food Experiment*, the Ojibwe Honor the Earth organization, the role of Nephi Craig (Apache and Navajo) and the Native

American Culinary Association, and Sean Sherman (Oglala Lakota) or as he is better known, the Sioux Chef.

40 Mary Paganelli Votto and Frances Manuel, *From I'itoi's Garden: Tohono O'odham Food Traditions* (Topawa, Az.: TOCA, 2010). Traditional foods not only provide nutrition for O'odham bodies, but are also a source of spiritual energy that is a part of the sacred landscape and indigenous identity. Storytelling is often centered on food and is an integral part of O'odham (and indigenous in general) distinctiveness. Stories equal heritage equals culture equals the values of "wellness." For example, the Mexica story derived from the Quetzalcoatl legend of Tamal being ground into people, with the descendants of the Aztecs consuming tamales or "ancestor bones." Or the "Three Sisters Story" who supported each other and grew together (corn, bean, and squash); or the Coyote who took a basket of tepary beans and ran through the sky scattering them across the horizon and thereby creating the Milky Way. These ideas come from a speech chef Felicia Cocotzin Ruiz delivered to the Guild members of the Heard Museum entitled "Indigenous Food as Storytelling: Reclaiming Our Food and Our Stories," March 15, 2017. Other tribes affected by high rates of diabetes include the Navajo with one in three Navajos suffering from diabetes and obesity rates three times the national average. The reservation is a food desert of junk foods, contaminated mutton, and greasy fry bread—this last item a symbol of oppression as well as perseverance. Consult Laurel Morales, "Finding a Healthy Balance," *Arizona Republic* (July 2, 2017), pp. 1E & 2E.

41 Sister M. Antoninus Hubatch, O.S.F, *Our Book, T-O'ohana, Nuestro Libro*, Papago trans. by Dean Saxton, D.V.M, and Spanish trans. by Brother Lawrence Hogan, O.F.M. (Tucson, Az.: San Xavier Mission School, 1971, 6th printing).

42 The O'odham in 2015 began the construction of a $400 million tribal casino in the West Valley of the Greater Phoenix area. They were being opposed by other tribal casinos in the East Valley, including the Pima owned Gila River Casinos, as well as some officials of the city of Glendale and state and national Arizona politicians. The casino was completed in 2018. See Peter Corbett, "Casino begins to rise in West Valley," *Surprise Republic* (Feb. 28, 2015), p. 3.

43 Roxanne Dunbar-Ortiz, *An Indigenous Peoples' History of the United States* (Boston: Beacon Press, 2014), pp. 159–161, 170–171 & 179–180. The Taos Pueblo's sixty-four year struggle to reclaim their sacred Blue Lake was resolved in December of 1970 when legislation was passed and approved by President Richard Nixon that restored 48,000 acres that had previously been taken from the Taos Indians. This was the first land restitution to any indigenous nation.

44 Janet Cantley, "Current Trends in American Indian Art," unpublished essay, Heard Museum, Phoenix, Arizona, 2015, p. 1 of 5 pages.

45 Ibid., pp. 1–5. The Ruthe Blalock Jones quote is from page 2 of Cantley's essay. Her source was M. Archuleta, B. Child & K. T. Tsianina, *Away From Home: American Indian Boarding School Experiences* (Phoenix, Az.: Heard Museum, 2000), inside cover.

46 To speculate a bit, it would appear that Alan changed his last name from Haozous to Houser at a time when he was attempting to identify not with his Indian background but with the larger world of cosmopolitan artists in Latin America and Europe. Toward the end of his life he often took the name of Allan Houser Haozous. It is interesting to note that the surname of his father was reintroduced to the family by that third generation of Houser's sons, Philip and Bob Haozous. For a brief biographical outline see "Allan Houser Haozous: Warm Springs Chiricahua Apache, June 30, 1914-August 22, 1994" (Santa Fe, N.M.: Allan Houser Inc., 2008).

47 This focus on family and community relationships can be found in this generation of Navajo artists, especially Steven J. Yazzie. His exhibit during the summer of 2013 entitled "The Mountain" at the Museum of Contemporary Native Arts in Santa Fe takes the idea of "place" and Navajo identity associated with the four sacred mountains and combines that idea with three generations of Navajos—child, father, and grandfather or medicine man. The multidimensional interpretation includes sculpture, painting, digital photographic prints, and a three-channel video. His family history is one point of departure that places the physical world with the metaphysical, and is a tribute to both Yazzie, his family, and the Navajo people. See "The Mountain" in the bulletin of MoCNA (Santa Fe, N.M.: Museum of Contemporary Native Arts, Summer/Fall 2013).

48 Quotations from H. Henriatta Stockel, *Survival of the Spirit: Chiricahua Apaches in Captivity* (Reno: University of Nevada Press, 1993), p. 249.

49 Dunbar-Ortiz, *An Indigenous Peoples' History*, p. 79.

50 Priyamvada Natarajan, "Revelations from Outer Space," *The New York Review* (May 21, 2015): 34.

For Further Reading

Recent developments in indigenous studies have moved the history profession away from traditional views of Indian culture and society that were consciously or unconsciously biased in favor of colonialism and the western, non-Indian point of view. Indigenous studies scholarship has improved my own work by providing several recent studies that I have used to increase my understanding of the indigenous past. Works by Ned Blackhawk, Jennifer Nez Denetdale, and Gerald Vizenor (see below) were especially important for my studies.

For those seeking an introduction to the field I would recommend *Critical Indigenous Studies* edited by Aileen Moreton-Robinson (Tucson: University of Arizona Press, 2016). Chickasaw Jodi A. Byrd contends that the colonialization of the American Indian needs to be reimagined with indigenous peoples having the agency to transform life and land on their own terms. See Byrd, *The Transit of Empire: Indigenous Critiques of Colonialism* (Minneapolis/London: University of Minnesota Press, 2011). Also see the essay on "Historiography" by Philip Deloria (in *A Companion to American Indian History*, ed. by Philip J. Deloria and Neal Salisbury; Malden, MA: Blackwell Publishing, 2002, 2004, pp. 6-24) that surveys the history of indigenous history writing from the frontier period to today's postmodern era.

As for journals, the *Native American and Indigenous Studies Journal*, while US-based, is globally focused. It is a product of the Native American and Indigenous Studies Association (NAISA). A journal article to see is "In Search of Theory and Method in American Indian Studies" by Duane Champagne in *The American Indian Quarterly* 31:3 (Summer 2007): 353–372. For the topics of survival and survivance see Gerald Vizenor, *Manifest Manners: Postindian*

Lost Worlds of 1863: Relocation and Removal of American Indians in the Central Rockies and the Greater Southwest, First Edition. W. Dirk Raat.
© 2022 John Wiley & Sons, Inc. Published 2022 by John Wiley & Sons, Inc.

Warriors of Survivance (Hanover & London: Wesleyan University Press, University Press of New England, 1994).

Opposite yet similar to my non-Indian critics for being too sympathetic to indigenous peoples, some Native American readers are wont to criticize me for being a non-Indian writing about indigenous cultures. As for not being an Indian I cannot change my cultural and genetic heritage. I can, however, try to use several indigenous sources so as to give my work an Indian voice. History writing for me is ultimately an act of faith—a belief that while no scholar can be totally objective, a partial truth is simply that, partial, but not false. Some works are less partial than others. The best any historian (whatever their ethnicity, gender, or nationality) can do is to attempt to be objective and to have empathy for his or her subject.

Some critics complain that a non-Indian historian should not treat "creation stories" from a non-Indian point of view which is simply another form of "intellectual imperialism." Yet as Kiowa storyteller and Pulitzer Prize winner Scott Momaday notes, stories are told in three voices: the ancestral voice (oral tradition); historical commentary; and personal reminiscence. As he says, "There is a turning and returning of myth, history, and memoir throughout ..." (N. Scott Momaday, *The Way to Rainy Mountain* [Albuquerque: University of New Mexico Press, 1969], p. ix). The precepts of historical inquiry that include veracity, authorship, external criticism, etc. should be an integral part of indigenous history, whether the historian is Indian or non-Indian. Finally, one should be able to recognize the historical and non-historical content of popular myths.

In any case, this work is the product of library research and fieldwork, what my mentor the late C. Gregory Crampton at the University of Utah called "historical archaeology." Because of the scope of this study, and with limited financial resources, very little archival research was done. Instead the work is more a synthesis of secondary sources, with archival work limited to research on the Shoshone at Utah State University in Logan, Utah and Idaho State University in Pocatello, Idaho; the Northern and Owens Valley Paiutes at the University of Nevada at Reno; and the Tohono O'odham and Yaqui peoples at the University of Arizona in Tucson.

Travel and research at the Heard Museum in Phoenix, Arizona plus interviews with several indigenous informants at a variety of reservations, shapes the basis of this work. Most of the historical sites, from Fort Tejon in the West to Bosque Redondo in the East, or from the Bear River Massacre site in southern Idaho in the North, to O'odham and Yaqui places in southern Arizona and northern Sonora in the South, were visited during the course of my research. Refer to the acknowledgements section for a complete listing of research sources. A more complete bibliography can be found by examining the notes at the end of the book which contain again, in the language of my Utah mentor, "chatty footnotes" concerning content and conflicting interpretations not suitable for the main text.

For the individual interested in the worldwide history of the conflict between indigenous peoples and their industrialized counterparts, see Ken S. Coates, *A Global History of Indigenous Peoples: Struggle and Survival* (N.Y.: Palgrave MacMillan, 2004). If one is interested in breaking down the stereotypes that often surface when an Anglo American looks across the border at Mexicans, or peers into an Indian reservation, then reading Patricia Nelson Limerick's *The Legacy of Conquest* (N.Y.: W.W. Norton, 1987) is recommended. A book that compliments the present study by concentrating on the removal of Indians from the Old Northwest is *Land Too Good for Indians: Northern Indian Removal* (Norman: University of Oklahoma Press, 2016) by John P. Bowes. Bowes takes an expansive view of the removal of the Delaware before 1830, as well as the Seneca and others in Northwestern Ohio, the Potawatomi communities of Illinois and Indiana, and the Ojibwas in Michigan Territory . For the "Trail of Tears" of the Jackson Administration see Claudio Saunt, *Unworthy Republic* (NY: Norton & Co., 2020).

For the dark chapter on holocaust and genocide there is no better read than the comprehensive and intelligent study by David E. Stannard entitled *American Holocaust: The Conquest of the New World* (N.Y. & Oxford: Oxford University Press, 1992). See also Ward Churchill's *A Little Matter of Genocide: Holocaust and Denial in the Americas, 1492 to the Present* (San Francisco: City Lights, 1997). Likewise see Andrea Smith, *Conquest: Sexual Violence and American Indian Genocide* (Cambridge, Mass.: South End Press, 2005), and Roxanne Dunbar-Ortiz, *An Indigenous Peoples' History of the United States* (Boston: Beacon Press, 2014). This latter work summarizes the general history of the indigenous peoples of North America. Her study spans more than 400 years of North American history and outlines a general practice and policy of colonialism and genocide.

Brandon C. Lindsay made a major contribution to genocide studies when he published his *Murder State: California's Native American Genocide, 1846-1873* (Lincoln: University of Nebraska, 2012; paperback 2015). This work narrates the grassroots movement to exterminate and dispossess Native peoples of their ancestral homelands. A recent study by Benjamin Madley brings to light the state-sanctioned killing machine in nineteenth century California that had broad societal support in *An American Genocide: The United States and the California Indian Catastrophe* (New Haven: Yale University Press, 2016). Gary Clayton Anderson focuses on "ethnic cleansing" in *Ethnic Cleansing and the Indian: The Crime That Should Haunt America* (Norman: University of Oklahoma Press, 2014). Unlike Madley, Anderson argues that diseases like malaria were more important than genocide for reducing the large number of nineteenth century California Indians, and that most Indian disasters were the result of forced removals or "ethnic cleansing" rather than genocide.

Similarly, for those interested in theoretical matters and "indigenous studies theories," see Patrick Wolfe, "Settler Colonialism and the Elimination of the Nation" in *Journal of Genocide Research*, 8 (4K) (online Dec. 21, 2006, pp. 387–401). Wolfe notes that elimination of indigenous societies is a continuous feature of settler societies and not equivalent to genocide since settlers are only concerned with the destruction of indigenous societies to the extent that it is required for possession of the land.

The difficulties of defining "genocide" are discussed in Alex Alvarez, *Native America and the Question of Genocide* (N.Y.: Rowman & Littlefield, 2014). Also see Chapter "Myth 8" entitled "The United States Did Not Have a Policy of Genocide" in Roxanne Dunbar-Ortiz and Dina Gilio-Whitaker, *"All the Real Indians Died Off" and 20 Other Myths about Native Americans* (Boston: Beacon Press, 2016), pp. 58–66. Chapter four of James W. Loewen, *Lies My Teacher Told Me* (N.Y.: Touchstone, 2007) contains a first-rate survey of American indigenous history and the conflict between Native Americans and whites.

An excellent general history of Southwestern and Northern Mexican Indians is Thomas E. Sheridan & Nancy J. Parezo, eds., *Paths of Life* (Tucson: University of Arizona Press, 1996). Anthropologist Trudy Griffin-Pierce provides a comprehensive look at Native American cultures in the Southwest in *Native Peoples of the Southwest* (Albuquerque: University of New Mexico Press, 2000). She is also the author of *The Columbia Guide to American Indians of the Southwest* (New York: Columbia University Press, 2010). For the Indian viewpoint see Peter Nabokov, *Native American Testimony: A Chronicle of Indian–White Relations from Prophecy to the Present, 1492-2000* (N.Y.: Penguin Compass, 1999). This collection includes several testimonials from Southwestern Indian groups, especially Zuñi, Hopi, Apache, and Navajo. The best general study of the life and work of artist Allan Houser remains W. Jackson Rushing III, *Allan Houser* (N.Y.: Harry N. Abrams, 2004).

For the idea of the "Greater Southwest," called the *Gran Chichimeca* by the early scholars, the pioneering work was done by Charles C. Di Peso, *Casas Grandes: A Fallen Trading Center of the Gran Chichimeca*, vols. 1–3 (Dragoon, Az.: Amerind Foundation, 1974). If the non-Hispanic reader wants to practice his/her Spanish they can try to find a copy of De Peso's *Las sociedades no nucleares de Norteamérica: La Gran Chichimeca* (Caracas: 1983). Also see Carroll L. Riley, *Becoming Aztlan: Mesoamerican Influences in the Greater Southwest, AD 1200-1500* (Salt Lake City: University of Utah Press, 2005). Stephen H. Lekson's book, *A History of the Ancient Southwest* (Santa Fe, N.M.: School for Advanced

Research, 2009) surveys Hohokam–Salado–Anasazi cultures by reference to Mexico and the Mississippi Basin.

An excellent history of the indigenous peoples in the early pre-colonial and colonial days would be William B. Carter, *Indian Alliances and the Spanish in the Southwest, 750–1750* (Norman: University of Oklahoma Press, 2009). For the Mexican period there is no better survey than David J. Weber, *The Mexican Frontier, 1821–1846: The American Southwest Under Mexico* (Albuquerque, N.M.: University of New Mexico Press, 1982).

Slavery and the slave trade can be found in L. R. Bailey, *Indian Slave Trade in the Southwest* (Los Angeles: Westernlore Press, 1966). For the untold tale of Indian enslavement in the Americas see Andrés Reséndez, *The Other Slavery: The Uncovered Story of Indian Enslavement in America* (Boston & N.Y.: Houghton Mifflin Harcourt, 2016). A good study on Lincoln's attitudes toward the Indians can be found in David A. Nichols" work, *Lincoln and the Indians* (St. Paul, MN: Minnesota Historical Society Press, 2012). A work that places the execution of 38 Dakota Indians in the larger context of the Civil War is Scott W. Berg, *38 Nooses: Lincoln, Little Crow, and the Beginning of the Frontier's End* (N.Y.: Random House, 2012). The classic biography of John C. Frémont remains Allen Nevins, *Fremont: Pathmarker of the West* (N.Y. & London: Longmans, Green and Co., 1955).

For the Civil War in the American West the traditional work was written by Ray C. Colton and is entitled *The Civil War in the Western Territories: Arizona, Colorado, New Mexico, and Utah* (Norman: University of Oklahoma, 1959). Colton has largely been supplemented by the more recent study by Alvin M Josephy, Jr., *The Civil War in the American West* (N.Y.: Vintage Books, 1991). Josephy's work is a detailed military history of the Southwest from Arkansas and the Indian Territory to New Mexico Territory and southern California. His is one of the better accounts of the Minnesota insurrection of 1862 and the impact on western history of the post-insurrectional removal of the Sioux to Dakota Territory.

There exists no in-depth study of the Owens Valley Paiute relocation and removal. George H. Phillips, *Bringing Them Under Subjection* (Lincoln: University of Nebraska, 2004) is recommended. For the Northern Paiutes see *As Long as the River Shall Run* by Martha C. Knack and Omar C. Stewart (1984) and Bernard Mergen's At *Pyramid Lake* (2014; both published at Reno and Las Vegas, University of Nevada Press). A popular history of the Paiute War of 1860 by Ferol Egan has been reprinted after three decades by the University of Nevada Press (Reno & Las Vegas: 1972; 1985) and is entitled *Sand in the Whirlwind: The Paiute Indian War of 1860*. Most of the existing works are auto-biographical or biographical. The essential work is by Sarah Winnemucca Hopkins and is called *Life Among the Piutes* (Reno & Las Vegas: University of

Nevada Press, 1994). Gae Whitney Canfield has written a biography entitled *Sarah Winnemucca of the Northern Paiutes* (Norman: University of Oklahoma Press, 1983), as has Sally Zanjani who authored *Sarah Winnemucca* (Lincoln: University of Nebraska Press, 2001).

The Ghost Dance religion is described by Gunard Solberg in *Tales of Wovoka* (Reno: Nevada Historical Society, 2012), and Gregory E. Smoak, *Ghost Dances and Identity* (Berkeley: University of California Press, 2006). An earlier work by Michael Hittman based on interviews of Wovoka's family is called *Wovoka and the Ghost Dance* (Expanded Edition; Lincoln: University of Nebraska, 1997).

The classic study remains James Mooney's 1896 study entitled *The Ghost Dance Religion and Sioux Outbreak of 1890: Fourteenth Annual Report of the US Bureau of Ethnology, 1892-1893, pt.2* (Washington, DC: US Government Printing Office).

Ethnographer James Mooney's "Ghost Dance Recordings" can be heard at the Library of Congress in Washington, D.C. Library of Congress notes alert the listener that the performances were probably performed by Mooney himself and not Native Americans. The most recent and complete study of the Ghost Dance religion is Louis S. Warren, *God's Red Son: The Ghost Dance Religion and the Making of Modern America* (N.Y.: Basic Books, 2017). Warren's study includes a critique of James Mooney as both student of and participant in the Ghost Dance movement.

For the Great Basin indigenous peoples in general see Ned Blackhawk, *Violence over the Land: Indians and Empires in the Early American West* (Cambridge: Harvard University Press, 2006). Blackhawk's study is a necessary introduction to the painful history of the Northern Paiute, Shoshone, Southern Paiute, and Ute peoples.

As for the Boarding School experience, in addition to Sarah Winnemucca's attempt to develop an indigenous Boarding School run by and for Indians (see literature on Sarah Winnemucca above), three works should be consulted. The first is David Wallace Adams, *Education for Extinction: American Indians and the Boarding School Experience, 1875-1928* (Lawrence, Kansas: University Press of Kansas, 1995). Next would be Sally Jenkins, *The Real All Americans* (N.Y.: Broadway Books, 2007). And finally, Margaret L. Archuleta et al., *Away from Home: American Indian Boarding School Experiences, 1979-2000* (Phoenix, Az.: The Heard Museum, 2000).

The literature on the Navajo "Long Walk" is fairly extensive. An excellent beginning would be Jennifer Denetdale, *The Long Walk: The Forced Navajo Exile* (N.Y.: Chelsea House, 2008), as well as Denetdale's *Reclaiming Diné History: The Legacies of Navajo Chief Manuelito and Juanita* (Tucson: University of Arizona Press, 2007). A short overview of the "Long Walk" can be found in

Dee Brown, *Bury My Heart at Wounded Knee* (N.Y.: Sterling Innovation, 2009), pp. 22-51, and Hampton Sides, *Blood and Thunder* (N.Y.: Doubleday, 2006), pp. 359–369. Also see Tom Dunlay *Kit Carson & the Indians* (Lincoln: University of Nebraska Press, 2000). For Native California see *We are the Land* by Damon Akins And William Bauer, Jr. (University of California, 2021).

On the land controversy between Navajo and Hopi see Emily Benedek, *The Wind Won't Know Me: A History of the Navajo–Hopi Land Dispute* (N.Y.: Vintage Books, 1993). For a naturalist's account of Hopi and Navajo ceremonial and religious beliefs along with the geological wonders of northern Arizona see Don Lago's *Where the Sky touched the Earth: The Cosmological Landscapes of the Southwest* (Reno & Las Vegas: University of Nevada Press, 2017).

The reader of Apache history and folkways has a long list from which to choose. A masterpiece of oral history is Eve Ball's *Indeh* (Norman: University of Oklahoma Press, 1988). Interviews with Asa (Ace) Daklugie, the surviving son of Juh, the most militant of Apaches after Victorio, provides the content for this volume. A most interesting kind of "New History" in which an event is covered from four distinct cultural views is the study of the Camp Grant Massacre of over 150 men, women, and children by Karl Jacoby in *Shadows At Dawn: An Apache Massacre and the Violence of History* (N.Y.: Penguin Books, 2008). A narration which focuses on Geronimo, Mickey Free, the Apache Kid and the longest war in American history is Paul Andrew Hutton, *The Apache Wars* (N.Y.: Crown, 2016).

Biographical studies include Edwin R. Sweeney's *Mangas Coloradas* (Norman: University of Oklahoma Press, 1998) and *From Cochise to Geronimo* (Norman: University of Oklahoma Press, 2010). Also see Robert Utley, *Geronimo* (New Haven: Yale University Press, 2012) and Peter Aleshire's paired biography of Geronimo and General George Cook, *The Fox and the Whirlwind* (N.Y.: John Wiley & Sons, 2000). Aleshire has also written the biography of Lozen in *Warrior Women: The Story of Lozen, Apache Warrior and Shaman* (N.Y.: St. Martin's Press, 2001). Also see Janet Cantley, *Beyond Geronimo: The Apache Experience* (Phoenix, Az.: The Heard Museum, 2012).

Four works that are must reading on the Yavapai experience are: Carolina C. Butler, ed., *Oral History of the Yavapai* (Gilbert, Az.: Acacia Publishing, 2012). Butler has edited the manuscript and documents that anthropologist Sigrid Khera created from oral interviews conducted in the 1970s of two Yavapai elders from the Fort McDowell reservation in Arizona. These indigenous informants were John Williams (1904–1983) and Mike Harrison (1886–1983). These materials are now part of the Labriola National American Indian Data Center at Arizona State University in Tempe.

Another printed primary source is the memoir by Mike Burns (Hoomothya), a captive Indian. It is called *All My People Were Killed* (Prescott, Az.: The Sharlot Hall Museum, 2010). It is a story of the conquest of Arizona from a Yavapai perspective. The account of the Yavapai relocation is narrated by the army surgeon participant William Henry Corbusier by his son William T. Corbusier in *Verde to San Carlos* (Tucson, Az.: Dale Stuart King, Publisher, 1969). Finally, the best secondary work remains Timothy Braatz, *Surviving Conquest: A History of the Yavapai Peoples* (Lincoln: University of Nebraska Press, 2003).

The classic yet somewhat dated account of the Tohono O'odham people would be Ruth M. Underhill, *The Papago (Tohono O'odham) and Pima Indians of Arizona* (Palmer Lake, Colorado: Filter Press, Llc., 2000 reprint of 1941 BIA publication). For an ethnological overview of the Tohono O'odham see Bernard L. Fontana, *Of Earth & Little Rain* (Tucson: University of Arizona Press, 1989). A historical treatment can be found in Winston P. Erickson's *Sharing the Desert* (Tucson: University of Arizona Press, 1994), while colonial religious history is the topic of *The Pimeria Alta: Missions & More*, edited by James E. Officer, Mardith Schuetz-Miller and Bernard L. Fontana (Tucson, Az.: The Southwestern Mission Research Center, Arizona State Museum, 1996).

Regional history and folklore are examined in Jim Griffith's *A Border Runs Through It* (Tucson: Rio Nuevo Publishers, 2011). This work complements an earlier book by Griffith entitled *Beliefs and Holy Places: A Spiritual Geography of the Pimeria Alta* (Tucson: University of Arizona Press, 1992). Deborah Neff presents an oral history of Frances Manuel in her *Desert Indian Woman: Stories and Dreams* (Tucson: University of Arizona Press, 2001). A humane essay on nature can be found in Gary Paul Nabhan's *The Desert Smells Like Rain: A Naturalist in O'odham Country* (Tucson: University of Arizona Press, 1982).

The pioneering study on the Bear River Massacre is Newell Hart, *The Bear River Massacre* (Preston, Idaho: Cache Valley Newsletter Publishing Company, 1982; 2nd printing 1983). The best scholarly examination remains Brigham Madsen's *The Shoshoni Frontier and the Bear River Massacre* (Salt Lake City: University of Utah Press, 1985). Other studies since Madsen include Kass Fleisher, *The Bear River Massacre and the Making of History* (Albany, N.Y.: State University of New York, 2004), and Rod Miller, *Massacre at Bear River: First, Worst, Forgotten* (Caldwell, Idaho: Caxton Press, 2008).

The best general work, for Southwestern Indians in general and the Yaqui people in particular, remains the classic *Cycles of Conquest* (Tucson: University of Arizona Press, 1962) by Edward H. Spicer. Evelyn Hu-Dehart has written two books on the Yaqui, the earlier one on the colonial period known as *Missionaries, Miners & Indians: Spanish Contact With the Yaqui Nation of Northwestern New Spain, 1533–1820* (Tucson: University of Arizona Press, 1981), and the second one on the modern era entitled *Yaqui Resistance and Survival: The Struggle for Land and Autonomy, 1821–1910* (Madison: University of Wisconsin Press, 1984). The anthropologist Jane Holden Kelly has produced oral interviews in *Yaqui Women: Contemporary Life Histories*

(Lincoln: University of Nebraska Press, 1991). It is complemented by an earlier work by her father William Curry Holden, his colleague Rosalio Moisés, and herself, entitled *The Tall Candle: The Personal Chronicle of a Yaqui Indian* (Lincoln: University of Nebraska Press, 1971). Finally, for an example of global history in which Yaqui labor plays a major role see Sterling Evans, *Bound in Twine: The History and Ecology of the Henequen-Wheat Complex for Mexico and the American and Canadian Plains, 1880-1950* (College Station: Texas A&M University Press 2007).

One disclaimer should be made before concluding this bibliographical section. The astute reader might notice that the 21 Pueblo communities (19 in New Mexico, one in Texas, and one, if the Hopi are a Pueblo, in Arizona) have, for the most part, been overlooked in this survey of the Greater Southwest. Fleeting references have been made to the Pueblos in general and the Hopi in particular. Generally speaking, to include all of the Pueblo nations would have been outside the scope of this study.

I would recommend for the "Pueblophiles" among us, however, the following: Craig Childs *House of Rain* (N.Y.: Little, Brown and Company, 2006) which tracks the vanished civilizations of the ancient American Southwest. In addition, David Roberts has three books worth reading, the first called *In Search of the Old Ones: Exploring the Anasazi World of the Southwest* (N.Y.: Simon & Schuster, 1996), and the second *The Pueblo Revolt: The Secret Rebellion That Drove the Spaniards Out of the Southwest* (N.Y.: Simon & Shuster, 2004). Roberts, who has written at least 28 books (mostly on either hiking deserts or climbing mountains, although others on the Apache wars and the American West), has supplemented his earlier study with a new book entitled *The Lost Worlds of the Old Ones: Discoveries in the Ancient Southwest* (N.Y.: Norton, 2015). And for those of you, who want a textbook survey, see Edward P. Dozier, *The Pueblo Indians of North America* (Long Grove, Illinois: Waveland Press, Inc., 1983).

For illustrative history it would be difficult to beat *The Native Americans: An Illustrated History* with an introduction by Alvin M. Josephy, Jr. with contributions by David Hurst Thomas, Jay Miller, Richard White, Peter Nabokov, and Philip J. Deloria. This work was published in 1993 by Turner Publishing, Inc., a subsidiary of the Turner Broadcasting System based in Atlanta, Georgia.

Acknowledgments

This project would not have been possible without the assistance and encouragement provided to me by the staff and employees of the Heard Museum in downtown Phoenix, Arizona. First on my priority list of acknowledgments is Mario Nick Klimiades, Director of Library and Archives at the Billie Jane Baguley Library at the Heard Museum. Without Mario in my corner this fight never would have been initiated or completed. His assistant, Betty Murphy, was also most helpful. About fifty percent of the research effort for this project took place at the Heard Library which permitted this researcher total photoduplicating privileges. Ann Marshall, Director of Research, was most supportive, aiding the project in the beginning and assisting in the permissions process. Andrew Minton, Associate Managing Editor at Wiley, was most helpful as my contact with Wiley publishers.

Other people at the Heard include Janet Cantley, a curator who proofread some of the copy, made "gentle" suggestions concerning the Apache content, and provided general support. Janet was also helpful in selecting visuals for the project. Her husband Gary, an archaeologist, aided me in making contacts at the Pyramid Lake Museum in Nevada. Lance Polingyouma, a former Hopi employee at the Heard, shared information with me on Hopi lifestyles and customs. Affiliated with the Heard is Steven Jon Yazzie, the Navajo artist who has not only contributed several works as Heard Museum exhibits, but agreed as well to write the foreword to this work. My fellow docents have also been helpful, especially Diane Leonte, Linda Hefter, Rex Nelson, Jerry Cowdrey, and Jack Brock. My "Las Guias" instructor, Barbara Johnson, and her trusty aid, Rusty Hale, provided me with the background information I needed to summon the courage to take on this topic.

Many people aided in the permissions process, none more helpful than Durwood Ball, editor of *The New Mexico Historical Review*. Also, the Chief Curator at the Heard, Diana Pardue, acquired images and guided me through permissions procedures. Again the aid provided me by Mario Klimiades and Janet Cantley should be noted. Andrew Minton, Associate Managing Editor at Wiley, was most helpful as my contact with Wiley publishers, especially when it came to illustrations, captions, and permissions. Also helpful were Jennifer Manias, Acquisitions Editor, Sophie Bradwell, Editorial Coordinator, Pallavi Gosavi, Content Specialist and Jacky Mucklow, Copyeditor.

The staff at several indigenous institutions assisted me in this project. Many of them preferred to remain anonymous. Following in order of their appearance in the book the institutions are: Pyramid Lake Museum, Nixon, Nevada; The Navajo Nation Museum, Window Rock, Arizona; Hopi Cultural Preservation Office, Kykotsmovi, Arizona; San Carlos Apache Tribal Cultural Center, Globe, Arizona; Yavapai-Apache Cultural Center, Camp Verde, Arizona; Fort McDowell Yavapai Nation Cultural Center, Fort McDowell, Arizona; Tohono O'odham Nation Cultural Center and Museum, Topawa, Arizona; Bannock-Shoshone Tribal Museum, Fort Hall, Idaho; and the Pascua Yaqui Museum and Cultural Center, Tucson, Arizona.

Individuals associated with these institutions include Shannon Mandell, Museum Director and Ralph Burns, Paiute Elder, Pyramid Lake Museum; Manuelito Wheeler, Director, Navajo Nation Museum; Herb Stevens, Manager, San Carlos Cultural Center; Vicent E. Randall, Apache Cultural Manager, Yavapai-Apache Nation, Clarkdale, Arizona; Judie Piner, Preservation and Technology Administrator, Yavapai-Apache Nation, Camp Verde, Arizona; Gertie Smith, Yavapai-Apache Center, Camp Verde; Albert Nelson, Director, Fort McDowell Yavapai Nation Cultural Center; Bernard Siquieros, Director, and Jeannette García, Librarian, Tohono O'odham Cultural Center, Topawa, Arizona; the late Royce Manual, Salt River Pima-Maricopa Community; Guillermo Quiroga, Director, Pascua Yaqui Museum and Cultural Center, Tucson, Arizona. Additional indigenous informants include Darren Parry, Shoshone; Jeff Begay, Navajo, Native American ASU Alumni; Daniel R. Vega, Director, Department of Languages and Culture, New Pascua Pueblo, and Anabel Galindo, Instructor, Pascua Yaqui Tribe, Tucson, Arizona.

Individuals at state parks, memorials, and sculpture parks, most of whom remain unnamed, were helpful. Among those who gave me critical information include Shella Stubler, an employee at the Fort Verde State Historic Park in Camp Verde, Arizona, who assisted me in getting the army point-of-view on the Yavapai. Grace Roybal, a Ranger at the Bosque Redondo Monument in New Mexico was a wealth of information on the Navajo "Long Walk." Kristen Bastis, Chief of Cultural Resources, City of Rocks National Reserve, Castle

Rocks State Park in Almo, Idaho shared with me sources and ideas relating to the Almo Massacre. Barbara Harber, a docent at Fort Whipple (in Prescott, Arizona) directed me to information about the US Army and the Yavapai people. Santanna Ortiz of Allan Houser, Inc. provided ideas on Allan Houser and his art. A trip to the Fort Tejon Historical Park in California, although unmanned, was fruitful.

In Prescott, Arizona the staff at the Sharlot Hall Museum and Library was supportive. I especially want to note the assistance of John Langellier, Director; Brenda Taylor, Archivist-Librarian; and Judy Simpson, Volunteer. They gave me information about the Yavapai and reoriented me as to the headwaters of the Hassayampa River. Martin A. Link, an instructor at the University of New Mexico at Gallup, was a one man resource for the Diné. Scott Lankford, a professor of English at Foothill College, California provided me with ideas and bibliography on the Owens Valley Paiutes and the Northern Paiutes, as did Susan McKenna of the Island Park Ranger Station in Idaho. Jesús M. García, education specialist at the Arizona-Sonora Desert Museum in Tucson, was a fountain of information concerning the Sonoran Desert peoples.

Much of my research took place at academic institutions and libraries in Utah, Idaho, and Nevada, as well as field work at the Bear River site outside of Preston, Idaho. At my hometown college in Ogden, Utah, Trudy Le Goede, reference librarian at the Stewart Library at Weber State University, assisted me. Melissa Johnson, Special Collection Coordinator at the Stewart Library was also of help. At Utah State University in Logan, Utah, I wish to thank Robert Parson, University Archivist at the Merrill-Frazier Library, for his aid. For revealing to me their fieldwork on the Bear River Massacre I am indebted to the efforts of Ken Reid, State Archaeologist for the State Historical Preservation Office in Boise, Idaho, and Robert Parson, University Archivist, Utah State University. The work of Kenneth P. Cannon, President, Utah State University Archaeological Series, Inc. should also be acknowledged.

Ellen Ryan, Special Collections Librarian at Idaho State University in Pocatello, Idaho enhanced my knowledge of Shoshone history. While working on Paiute history I was aided by Jacquelyn Sundstrand, Manuscript and Archives Librarian, at the University of Nevada at Reno. Donnelyn Curtis is the Head of Special Collections at the University of Nevada at Reno. Michael Maher, Librarian, Nevada Historical Society in Reno should be recognized, as well as student Linda Fine Conaboy. Both gave me information about the Numu. Although I did not travel to Carson City, I did have correspondence with Jeff Kintop, State Archivist at the Nevada State Archives in Carson City, Nevada. Lynne Shumway of the Blanding Visitor Center provided information on Ute–Navajo relations.

Most of my research on the Yaqui people of Sonora and the O'odham of Sonora and southern Arizona was done at the libraries and museums at the University of Arizona, Tucson. Two people who were especially helpful to my research were Amy Rule, Archivist, and Mary E. Grahm, Head Librarian, at the Arizona State Museum Library and Archives, University of Arizona, Tucson. I also worked in the general library as well as the special collections section. Thanks also to Roger Myers, Special Collections, University of Arizona, Tucson.

As a retired history professor I no longer have the institutional support that would usually finance projects such as this one. I am grateful, therefore, for the monetary assistance in the form of a travel grant that I received from the Arizona State University (in Tempe) Emeritus College Grants and Awards Committee for 2014. William Glaunsinger was the chair of that committee. Thanks also to Quentin Bogart, former Dean, ASU Emeritus College, and Dana Aguilar, administrative assistant.

I also wish to note the special contributions of old friends and colleagues. Charles S. Peterson, an old graduate student friend from the University of Utah and currently a Professor Emeritus at Utah State University, opened the door for me to his "cronies" and friends at Utah State. The multi-talented and highly professional scholar from Brown University, Evelyn Hu-Dehart, shared with me her sources and ideas on Yaqui history. My friend, co-author, and colleague Michael Brescia paved the way for my work at the Arizona State Museum in Tucson. He is affiliated Professor of History and Law at the University of Arizona and Curator of Ethnohistory at the Arizona State Museum. Markus Vink of the State University of New York at Fredonia suggested the title.

Melvin Aikens, an old school friend from Ogden High days who is Professor Emeritus from the University of Oregon in Eugene, not only loaned me his expertise on Great Basin archaeology, but he, along with his lovely wife Alice, provided my wife and me with a fantastic Asiatic lunch at their home in Eugene. My son-in-law's parents, Michael and Irma Kelly, schooled me on Navajo healing. And my old pal John Hart from the University of Houston always leaves me with a smile on my face. Need I say more?

While on the road several friends and acquaintances provided me, and sometimes my wife, with hospitality. Rick and Louise Merring gave me shelter and food in Prescott, Arizona, while my niece Renae and her husband Kevin Oswold of Rigby, Idaho let me use their house as a sanctuary. Brian and Patty Parkes did the same in Ogden, Utah, while Jay and Marlene Boylan provided me with a safe haven in Orange, California. The pinnacle of hospitality must go to Alan Ferg and Tobi López Taylor who rented me their casita at their horse ranch in Tucson for $10.00 a day. It is likely that I learned more about Arabian horses than I did Yaqui Indians while there, but it was a special experience.

At home my neighbors in Sun City Grand gave me computer advice, especially Bob Towe, Nancy Collins, and Janice Oeswein and her brother Dennis Gebele. Towe, in particular, was most helpful in translating into usable English the technical language relating to photograph requirements (including distinguishing jpeg files from tif and other electronic formats). Another neighbor and friend, Jack Ballentine, provided me with several ideas concerning the Indian situation generally and this relocation project in particular. Most of these conversations took place over a cup of Starbucks coffee, with the topics of discussion usually hotter than the coffee. So too did I share a cup of java with amateur historian and neighbor Pieter Burggraaf who schooled me on the subtleties of the Walker party expedition.

Like many writers I had the support of my immediate family. Thanks to my son David for exposing me to the nuances of the iPad. I must also acknowledge the support and backing of my wife Gerry Raat, and, of course, our dog Nacho. These two travelled with me through Yavapai country, on to the Hopi mesas, over the Navajo Reservation, on to Santa Fe, and to Bosque Redondo. They were with me on my trip to Tahoe where, like Paul on the road to Damascus, I first had my initial inspiration for this book. Gerry even assisted me in interviewing Paiute Elder Ralph Burns at Pyramid Lake, Nevada. She also assisted the project by creating some of the maps that appear in the text. Thanks to all my family and friends for making this project possible. All errors of fact and erroneous opinions belong solely to the author.

W. Dirk Raat
Surprise, Arizona

Index

Lost Worlds of 1863: Relocation and Removal of American Indians in the Central Rockies and the Greater Southwest, First Edition. W. Dirk Raat.
© 2022 John Wiley & Sons, Inc. Published 2022 by John Wiley & Sons, Inc.